HEARING THE MOVIES

HEARING THE MOVIES
Music and Sound in Film History

James Buhler
The University of Texas at Austin

David Neumeyer
The University of Texas at Austin

Rob Deemer
The State University of New York at Fredonia

New York   Oxford
OXFORD UNIVERSITY PRESS
2010

Oxford University Press, Inc., publishes works that further Oxford University's
objective of excellence in research, scholarship, and education.

Oxford New York
Auckland   Cape Town   Dar es Salaam   Hong Kong   Karachi
Kuala Lumpur   Madrid   Melbourne   Mexico City   Nairobi
New Delhi   Shanghai   Taipei   Toronto

With offices in
Argentina   Austria   Brazil   Chile   Czech Republic   France   Greece
Guatemala   Hungary   Italy   Japan   Poland   Portugal   Singapore
South Korea   Switzerland   Thailand   Turkey   Ukraine   Vietnam

Published by Oxford University Press, Inc.
198 Madison Avenue, New York, New York 10016
http://www.oup.com

Oxford is a registered trademark of Oxford University Press

Library of Congress Cataloging-in-Publication Data
Buhler, James, 1964–
    Hearing the movies : music and sound in film history / James Buhler, David Neumeyer, Rob Deemer.
       p. cm.
    ISBN 978-0-19-532779-3 (pbk.)
   1. Motion picture music—History and criticism. 2. Motion picture music—Analysis, appreciation.
3. Motion Picture soundtracks—Production and direction—History.   I. Neumeyer, David. II. Deemer,
Rob. III. Title.
    ML2075.B84 2010
    781.5'42—dc22
                                                                                    2008051021

9 8 7 6 5 4 3 2 1

Printed in the United States of America
on acid-free paper

Contents

Chapter 3: Music, Sound, and the Space of Narrative: Concepts and Terminology 65

Chapter 4: Music, Sound, and Time 92

Interlude: Writing About Film Sound: Analysis and Description 114

Preface

This book is about music in cinema, and it proceeds from the view that "hearing the movies" involves skills that are different from listening to music for its own sake. Film is a technology-dependent medium that relies on reproduced sound, and the aesthetics of film sound have changed over time with changes in technology. In the cinema, music is positioned in the sound track. Accordingly, we focus on music in the context of the film sound track and on the sound track in the context of a history of film technology.

Approach

Our goal is to facilitate critical viewing and listening within the context of an appreciation of the impact of the history of film technology. The book is designed to teach a general method for analyzing and interpreting the sound track and its music and a general framework of technological history in which to position individual films and practices. The skill set involved is applicable to almost any film experience. We do not aim to promote a particular historical narrative that valorizes certain repertories. Instead, the overarching viewpoint is that the sound cinema as a medium and the narrative feature film as a broad genre can be understood to constrain practice in ways that allow analysis, despite cultural and historical differences, but that also permit taking account of those differences.

At the same time, it is true that film studies pedagogy has steadily—though not deliberately—worked toward a canon, that is, a list of "core" films that need to be taught and discussed in all introductory-level or survey-style film courses. The teaching of film music and film sound courses has, to date, not produced any comparable list of works (especially if one wants to include repertoires outside classical Hollywood), but certain titles do come up again and again, among them

The Jazz Singer, *King Kong*, *Citizen Kane*, *Casablanca*, *Laura*, *Psycho*, and *Apocalypse Now*. *Hearing the Movies* is not intended primarily as a chronological film music or sound track "masterworks" history, but we have worked at achieving a reasonably open level of coverage of repertoires and decades, in addition to making ample use of films that are commonly taught. If a very few familiar films and their musics are given short shrift (*Citizen Kane* may be the most obvious example), that is in part because they are covered well elsewhere in the scholarly and textbook literature, and in part because we preferred to assist pedagogical convenience by citing a few titles and scenes in several chapters rather than continually naming and discussing new films for the sake of broad coverage (titles that do have multiple citations include, among a few others, *Casablanca*, *The Big Sleep*, *Psycho*, *The Apartment*, *Sleepless in Seattle*, *Good Will Hunting*, *Catch Me If You Can*, and *De-Lovely*).

The recurrent commentary on these titles should not be taken as advocacy for some particular film music canon. As in most contemporary film textbooks, we have tried to give at least some minimal attention to repertoires outside the United States, but we also readily acknowledge that there is much more work to be done in that respect: the tension between the traditional, Hollywood-based canon and a contemporary culture of world cinema is very much in play now, and it will be some time before the outcome can be codified in pedagogy, all the more so as it pertains to sound or music. The repertoire of feature film is very large and growing—steadily in the older traditions of the United States, Europe, Russia, and Japan, rapidly if one factors in trans-national cinemas, and the design and priorities of *Hearing the Movies* should make it quite feasible to augment the list of films discussed—or to make substitutions—with titles reflecting the instructor's or students' preferences.

Organization

Hearing the Movies is laid out in three parts and fifteen chapters, a design intended to facilitate use on its own as the textbook for a semester course on film music and film sound. The book may also serve effectively as a substantial supplementary or reference text in introductory film courses, courses on sound design and aesthetics, courses on film music composition, courses on twentieth-century and contemporary music, courses on music and media, or even seminar courses on specific repertoires—for example, science fiction films after 1970, composers (such as Bernard Herrmann or John Williams), or periods (Hollywood in the 1930s, film and rock and roll in the 1950s and 1960s, etc.). We have mapped out basic syllabi for many of these options in files on this text's companion website, where we have also made suggestions for adapting the book to ten-week term formats. The URL is http://www.hearingthemovies.net.

The four chapters of Part I encourage development of basic listening and viewing skills. Chapter 1 introduces the sound track elements and the concept of an integrated sound track, the aesthetic standard for sound film since the 1930s. The emphasis here is on general relations of sound and image, in particular, the narrative functions of sound. In chapter 2, we stress the musicality of the sound track by introducing musical terms (such as tempo and timbre) that can also be used to describe speech or sound effects or the sound track as a whole. Chapter 3 turns to sound and music in relation to narrative space, with special attention to the diegetic/nondiegetic pair. In chapter 4, then, we concentrate on terms associated with sound and time—including, among others, the pair synchronization/counterpoint—but also some related terms for the analysis of affect (empathetic/anempathetic). The overall goal of Part I is to position music within the sound track as one of its elements, as a peer (and partner) of speech and effects, and to introduce terms that are essential to the analysis of spatial and temporal aspects of sound and music.

The Interlude following chapter 4 covers methods and motivations for writing about films in terms of their sound tracks, particularly their musics, and then details the construction of an analysis report or response paper for *Catch Me If You Can*. (The Interlude following chapter 9 continues and expands the work to essays of analytic appreciation and interpretation, including essays of critical and ideological analysis.)

The five chapters of Part II turn attention more narrowly to music and its characteristic treatment in the sound feature film. Chapter 5 discusses general questions of music in relation to film form; chapters 6 and 7 provide a set of scene analyses that illustrate the function of music as a sound track element in common sequence types, including opening and end credit sequences, as well as montage/fantasy scenes. Film style in broader and narrower senses (genre in the first case, themes and topics in the second) is addressed in chapter 8, and chapter 9 provides illustrations through analyses of dialogue scenes, love scenes, and action scenes.

Part III lays out a concise history of music and film sound organized around technological innovations and their role in film production and exhibition. The stages of that history include the remarkably varied practices of the early cinema (ch. 10), the rapid series of technological and aesthetic changes in the first few years of sound film (ch. 11), the settling in and standardization of practices for sound film in the studio era (ch. 12), the shifts in aesthetics (especially with respect to musical styles) but relative conservatism in sound technology in the two subsequent decades (ch. 13), the revolution in sound technology (and birth of modern sound design) with the introduction of Dolby stereo (ch. 14), and the characteristics of digital sound production and post-production (including music) in the decades since then (ch. 15). An afterword comments on the current—and prospective—situation for music and sound in film production and in other venues, particularly those that are Internet-based.

Features

- As the focus of this book is on critical listening and analysis skills, we include detailed sample analyses with timings, tying the image track to the sound track.
- Copious examples and screen stills help bring film music into the context of sound, and sound into the context of the whole film.
- Extended exercises in Part I encourage skill development and suggest tools for basic analysis of a sound track.
- Students can get full benefit from the book without the ability to read music notation (the authors have taught courses based on this material to general undergraduate audiences successfully for more than ten years), but some musical examples have been included to enhance understanding for those who can read them.
- We have made every effort to bring together the broadest range of scholarship on film music currently available, spanning both music scholarship and film/media studies.
- Sidebars feature behind-the-scenes commentary from historical and contemporary industry professionals.
- Key terms are included in a glossary at the back for easy reference.
- At the ends of Parts I and II, chapter-sized Interludes provide guidelines for writing about films in terms of their sound and music.
- A companion website at http://sites.google.com/site/hearingthemovies/ offers basic syllabi for ten- and fifteen-week courses in which *Hearing the Movies* is the principal textbook, along with suggestions for using the book in other courses. The site also contains electronic copies of many of the screen stills (but not other graphics) from the book, a list of the DVD editions we used, additional timings for scenes with music in the films discussed here, annotated film music bibliographies, commentary on articles we particularly recommend for class readings, links to relevant film and film music websites, supplementary scene analyses, and suggestions for assignments and projects.

A Note on the Films

As a practical matter, films were chosen on the basis of availability in DVD format with region coding for North America. Timings for specific scenes are given in the usual DVD player format: 00:00:00 (= hours:minutes:seconds). Many films have multiple DVD editions, some of which feature quite different versions of the film (for example, the theatrical release versus the director's cut). Wherever possible, we have used editions readily available in video stores and through major distributors at the time this book was written. On the course website, we have provided a reference list of those DVD editions.

Acknowledgments

We thank a number of individuals who gave support, encouragement, and help (including information or materials): first of all, Jan Beatty, our music editor at Oxford; Lauren Mine, her assistant; Brian Black, production manager; indexer June Sawyers; and the following reviewers, who provided a wealth of ideas and advice: Anthony Bushard, University of Nebraska-Lincoln; James Deaville, Carleton University; Richard Freedman, Haverford College; Daniel Goldmark, Case Western Reserve University; Julie Hubbert, University of South Carolina; Neil Lerner, Davidson College; Michael Pisani, Vassar College; Gayle Sherwood Magee, University of Illinois at Urbana-Champaign; Scott Murphy, University of Kansas; and Frank Ryan, University of Tulsa. For graphics materials and help with permissions, we also thank Dan Goldwasser, who supplied the series of Hollywood session photographs; and John Waxman, for images of his father.

James Buhler would like to thank John Belton, Bruce Calvert, Jeff Cohen, Lynn E. Eaton, and Antoinette Follett for their assistance in obtaining images. He is also very appreciative of the early support and encouragement shown by Neil Lerner, who offered timely advice and provided images and other documentation.

David Neumeyer is grateful to Martin Marks, Paul Riseman, John Waxman, and James Wierzbicki for documents and permission to use materials; Tim Lynch for information relevant to *Good Will Hunting*; to Michael Pisani for steadfast support, advice, and critical input, including a detailed list of films from the 1950s to the 1970s; and to Laura Neumeyer for her assistance with the scene analyses from *The Sound of Music*, *Grease*, *Shadowlands*, *Good Night and Good Luck*, and *Pride & Prejudice*. Some of the text for the latter is revised from David and Laura Neumeyer, "On Motion and Stasis: Photography, 'Moving Pictures,' Music," in *Music, Meaning and Media*, ed. by Richard Littlefield, Erkki Pekkilä, and David Neumeyer (Imatra/Helsinki: International Semiotics Institute, 2007).

Rob Deemer thanks Jason Poss for his unique recollections of the *Lord of the Rings* scoring sessions; Lee Sanders for his invaluable knowledge and insight into the film music industry; Graham Reynolds for his interview on the scoring process for *A Scanner Darkly*; Lukas Kendall, Justin Baron, and Jill Streater for their assistance in acquiring graphics materials; Catherine Saucier and Gordon Root for their critical input; and Lori Deemer for her love and support.

Introduction

In the opening minutes of *Citizen Kane* (1941), low orchestral instruments and percussion create an eerie atmosphere for a series of exterior images of Xanadu, Kane's ruined mansion—music more appropriate to a horror film than a drama. Out of this eventually emerges, during an extreme close-up of Kane's mouth, the famously enigmatic word, "Rosebud." In Akira Kurosawa's *Rashômon* (1950), four witnesses tell markedly different versions of an event involving (perhaps) a rape and a murder. It was a samurai who died, and throughout his wife's account, as she justifies her own actions, a repetitive music strongly resembling Ravel's *Bolero* pushes the scene toward a trance-like or even hallucinatory state, seeming to undermine her veracity. During the main title sequence in the recent film *Atonement* (2007), we hear the quiet chirping of birds as we see one of the studio logos, then the sound of a manual typewriter, which types out the film's title. Both the rather loud typing and the quiet bird sounds continue into the first scene, during which the camera pans slowly from an interior wall to the outside wall of a child's room. At the end of this, we see an adolescent girl at the machine; we never see the birds, but the windows are open and, thanks to their chirping, it is easy to understand those birds as existing in an outdoors that extends the film's physical space beyond what the camera has framed for us.

Films achieve their effects with sound as well as images. Although people usually speak of "watching a movie," in fact speech, music, and noise fundamentally and routinely influence our understanding of what we see. (Speech is often called *dialogue*; the term used for noise is *sound effects* or just *effects*.) To achieve that influence, the sound track is as carefully constructed as the image track. Since the 1930s, production personnel have referred to this work as *sound editing*, by which they mean the process of creating and blending the sound track elements. Since about 1970, the commonly used term for the same process is *sound design*. In recent years, some scholars have begun using the term *soundscape*—the aural complement to the image's "landscape"—to refer to this aspect of film.

Thus, it would be better to say that we "watch and listen to a movie"— unfortunately, this expression is clumsy, as are terms such as *audioviewing* or *viewing-hearing*. In short, we do not (yet) have an easy way to point in language to this complex interplay of hearing and seeing in the experience of a film (or a television show, or commercials, or Internet content with an auditory component).

In some types of films, the importance—and foregrounding—of sound is obvious, but sound design is important to all movies. As film music scholar Robynn Stilwell wrote, "In the film industry, sound seems to be of greatest concern to those who produce big movies; we have come to expect teeth-rattling explosions and bombastic scores in modern blockbusters. However, sound can be even more intensely felt in intimate, quiet films, where the slightest whisper or silence can have a marked effect."[1]* Similarly, director David Lynch said that "[Although] half the film is picture, the other half is sound . . . [and] they've got to work together."[2]

In some respects, music stands in a special place within sound design: We tend to take speech and effects sounds, such as footfalls or airplane noises, for granted because they are understood as natural, or what we would expect to hear if we found ourselves in the environment depicted on the screen (on a city street, in a forest or jungle, in the middle of a sports event, in a house with persons in conversation, etc.), but music is only "natural" when someone is performing or when a radio—or other mechanical sound source—is shown onscreen. Yet "background music," or music that has no apparent natural placement, has been a part of film exhibition from its beginnings in the 1890s, long before the sound film replaced the "silent" film in most countries by the early 1930s. Surprisingly perhaps, this practice of accompanimental music has continued in the sound tracks of almost all films down to the present day, and it does mean that music poses a special problem for film viewing—or as another film music scholar, Claudia Gorbman, put it, "an issue central to film music aesthetics is the question of music's place in the hierarchy of the spectator's attention."[4]

Our goal in this book is to bring music into the context of sound, and sound into the context of the whole film. Broadly speaking, we try to avoid isolating music from the whole of the film experience. Instead, we concentrate on show-

Although the feature film is perceived as a visual medium, 50 percent of the motion picture experience is aural. As the sound track reaches the audience via the theater sound system, it creates the illusion that the sound for a film has been captured by a single, magical microphone which records dialogue, sound effects, and music on-set in perfect balance. The fact is, just as every visual component in a film is designed and executed by the writer, director, cinematographer, and design team, each single sound in a film is carefully conceived, chosen, recorded, edited, and mixed by an array of sound artists and technicians.

—Vincent LoBrutto (sound designer)[3]

---

* Source citations for all quotes, including those in the sidebars, can be found in the endnotes for each chapter.

ing how film viewers integrate music and sound, sound track and image track. Thus, most of the book's chapters are designed to help you learn to hear the musicality of the sound track as a whole, to grasp the structuring principles of the sound track, to recognize that the sound track is rendered (designed), to understand contemporary production methods and priorities, and to appreciate the interdependence of technology and aesthetics throughout the course of film history. In the chapters of Part I, terminology, concepts, and examples are introduced to enable you to analyze and describe a film's sound track, including its music, in relation to narrative, both broadly (in terms of the film as a whole) and down to detail (the sound within a scene, or even the sound within a shot). An Interlude, an unnumbered intermediate chapter between Parts I and II, describes how to construct and write-up reports and analyses of films in terms of their sound tracks. The five chapters in Part II do focus on music to introduce aspects of film style and form in which music is often highlighted (as in main title sequences, performances, love scenes, and action scenes). A second Interlude then takes up the skill of writing essays that go beyond analyses or descriptions to interpret films in terms of their sound or, more specifically, their music. Part III, then, offers an historical account of sound within film production and exhibition—an account that necessarily pays attention to technological change and the way it has affected sound and music throughout film history. Finally, an afterword makes some comments about sound in contemporary film and some projections about sound and music aesthetics in the Internet age.

Knowing more of what goes into the scoring of a picture may help the movie listener to get more out of it.

—Aaron Copland (composer)[5]

A decade ago, in the wake of the invention of computer literacy, some authors began to refer to an analogous visual literacy, which builds on our everyday visual capacities, or how we handle understanding what we see. Because basic visual literacy is a skill learned in the everyday, not through specialized training, we all have the ability needed to understand films. Increasing visual literacy starts by making us aware of those skills and employing them self-consciously. In that way, we become (and remain) aware of how images and editing methods construct meaning; that is, how they are rhetorical (they try to make us believe or accept an idea, a point of view, a particular way of understanding a story or a character). It is not difficult to extend the range of this sort of critical viewing to include the constructedness of sound. In studying film sound tracks or writing about them, then, it can be helpful, but is by no means necessary, to have a specialized knowledge of music history, music theory, or film history or theory. This book is designed for students with any background—musical, film studies, film production, or simply avid filmgoer—and it can be readily and productively used by readers with a wide range of backgrounds. The main requirement is a willingness to listen carefully and to articulate what you hear.

When I write music for a film I try to imagine what the sound of that music will be in a theater, what it will sound like in relation to the dialogue and the action.

—Franz Waxman (composer)[6]

By the end of the book, then, you should have reached the stage where you can not only watch but also listen to historical and contemporary films and write productively about them in terms of sound and music.

PART ONE

The Sound Track and Film Narrative

BASIC TERMS AND CONCEPTS

Catch Me If You Can (2002) tells the **story** of Frank Abagnale, Jr. (played by Leonardo DiCaprio), who runs away from home rather than face the trauma of his parents' divorce and his father's slow financial ruin. Frank is a risk taker, who discovers that he has innate talent for imitating professionals (airline pilots, doctors, and lawyers), and he develops great skill in forging checks. The story, told mostly in flashback, is about FBI agent Carl Hanratty's (Tom Hanks) campaign to capture Frank, who spends several years in prison but eventually, thanks to Hanratty's advocacy, works for the FBI cracking check forgery cases. In one **scene**, midway through the film, Carl is working alone on Christmas Eve (DVD timing 01:03:38); a radio sits on his desk and resonates weakly in the large empty room of desks and metal fixtures (see Figure I-1: Carl is turning the volume knob). From the radio, we hear Bing Crosby singing "Mele Kalikimaka" (Hawaiian for "Merry Christmas") as Carl examines some evidence. The phone rings; Frank is calling from his hotel room. Very near the end of their conversation, Carl tells Frank that he will be caught eventually, and **orchestral music** enters with a melancholy theme that was associated earlier in the movie with Frank's feelings about his father.

In this book's general introduction, we asserted that "Films achieve their effects with sound as well as images." The image track of a sound film in fact is not complete and autonomous in itself—if that were true, any added sound could do no better than to mimic or duplicate emotions, **rhythms**, and other information already apparent in the image. Although all of those uses of sound do happen in films, it is even more common that sound "adds value"[1] to the image (according to sound designer, composer, and film theorist, Michel Chion). In other words, the three components of the **sound track—speech**, music, and **sound effects**—transform the image.

Figure I-1. *Catch Me If You Can.* Carl works on Christmas Eve.

In the phone conversation from *Catch Me If You Can*, the radio transforms what is visually a stark, even forbidding, environment into something like an everyday workplace—Carl keeps the radio on as background while he does his repetitive work tasks. The music on the radio tells us something about Carl's character as well—because he chose this station, we can reasonably assume that his tastes are middlebrow and a bit out of date for the mid-1960s. Similarly, when the orchestral music enters while we see a **close-up** of Frank's face, by convention we understand that the music is representing Frank's emotions, which are not immediately obvious in his face (Figure I-2).

It works the other way around, too: A sound track is changed—transformed—by the image, a point that can be easily demonstrated by listening to a popular song, then watching a music video with that song as the sound track, and perhaps then a film scene that uses the same song as part of the orchestral **under-score**. According to Chion, sound and image achieve what he calls an "audio-visual contract,"[2] according to which film viewers intuitively accept the notion that image and sound mutually influence one another (that, of course, is what allows sound and image to add value to each other). Imagine the difference between listening to "Mele Kalikimaka" on the radio yourself and listening to it while watching this scene. What has happened to that music because it was included here? We cannot say that it suddenly acquired meaning where it had none before: Any music will have a collection of cultural meanings gathered around it (here, at the very least, Bing Crosby as a radio performer, Bing Crosby as a star, and "Hawaiian" style popular music in the 1930s and early 1940s). "Mele Kalikimaka," however, has also acquired some specific meanings in relation to Carl Hanratty's character—and, as it happens, Christmas music be-

Figure I-2. *Catch Me If You Can*. Frank listens as Carl talks.

comes an aural **motif** in *Catch Me If You Can*, a motif that has substantial dramatic significance later in the film as Nat King Cole sings the "Christmas Song" while Frank stands outside his mother's house in the snow and the police and FBI appear to arrest him for the final time.

    Although the three sound track elements usually work together to transform the image track, each also has unique capacities for "adding value." The ability to supply voluminous and specific information is an obvious property of speech ("dialogue"), and the naturalizing or realistic effect of speech and sound effects is equally evident. (Note that the privileged role of speech is so strongly assumed that we did not even comment on it in our discussion. As it happens, sound effects are minimal.) Music's role is more complicated, or perhaps we should say more flexible. Music is sometimes very much involved with speech, as in a song performance or, less obviously, in **dialogue underscoring** (music that accompanies speech, playing "under" it). At other times, music interacts with sound effects, as in many science fiction and action-thrillers, where music and effects dovetail to create what often seems like a single continuous strand of sound. Music can also mimic sound effects (for example, percussion instruments were routinely used to generate sound effects during silent-film performances). Finally, music can float in its own sphere, in effect outside the story and the physical world of the images: "Background music" (like the orchestral music that reflects Frank's suddenly dejected mood) can affect a film in a manner very much like that of the voice-over narrator, an unseen person who comments on characters and action.

    It is important to understand, however, that film music is not just the **symphonic underscore** that has been a part of cinema practice since the late 1920s (and has its roots in music played for silent films before that), nor is film music restricted to this accompanimental role (no matter what musical style it may be). *Film music is any music used in a film.* In this respect, film music follows the changing social and cultural patterns of music over the past century. In the present day, it can be difficult to recognize that, before the sudden rise of commercial radio and the mass-market phonograph in the early 1920s, access to a variety of musical styles was difficult for almost anyone to achieve. From that time forward, music making of all kinds has drawn to a wholly unprecedented degree on a variety of historical and cultural sources. Every sort of music can find its way into a film score, from the latest song by Radiohead to medieval Gregorian chant, from modernist concert composer Gyorgy Ligeti's *Atmospheres* to a Balinese gamelan. A music's functions are not restricted stylistically: Any of the four radically different kinds of music named in the previous sentence could be part of the underscore, heard on a radio, or be part of an onscreen performance. In Figures I-3 to I-7, we have gathered five other examples from the enormous range of possibilities: Figure I-3 shows a traditional Texas dancehall scene in *Hope Floats* (1998); Figure I-4 is a contemporary photo of a Hollywood studio **orchestra** recording a musical cue; Figure I-5 is an 18th-century orchestra from a country dance scene in *Pride & Prejudice* (2005); in Figure I-6, Robert Redford's character, Denys Finch Hatton, adjusts the gramophone he is presenting as a gift to Karen Blixen (Meryl Streep)

Figure I-3. *Hope Floats.* Dancehall scene: in the background (right center) Jack Ingram sings "Coming Back for More" (the scene begins at 01:00:50 or DVD chap. 12).

Figure I-4. Studio orchestra in recording session (photo: Dan Goldwasser).

in *Out of Africa* (1983); and in Figure I-7, Chico Hamilton's jazz quintet is just finishing a number in *Sweet Smell of Success* (1957; Hamilton is the drummer).

A description of a film in terms of its sound and music must inevitably deal with the way the sound track is organized and the effects its makes, how it adds to (or detracts from) the film, and how it helps to tell the story. The chapters of Part I cover this ground by first introducing terms and concepts associated with the narrative functions of sound and general sound–image relations (ch. 1), then

Figure I-5. *Pride & Prejudice.* An 18th-century orchestra plays for a country dance (the dance begins at 00:05:00).

Figure I-6. *Out of Africa.* Denys presents Karen with a gramophone (the scene begins at 01:19:20 or DVD ch. 11).

Figure I-7. *Sweet Smell of Success.* The Chico Hamilton Quintet plays at a nightclub (the scene begins at 00:07:15 or DVD ch. 2).

emphasizing the sound track as an entity by invoking musical terms that can also be used to analyze sound (ch. 2). Chapter 3 turns attention to the physical world of the narrative (because sound always presupposes space), and chapter 4 to aspects of film sound and time.

The Sound Track and Narrative

Introduction

Even in the digital age, a sound film consists of two separate components: image track and sound track (or "audio track"). This is a technological division: The image track appears on the screen, the sound track comes through the speakers. Consequently, this division also requires a technology to synchronize image and sound track. Today, just as in the earliest days of commercial film exhibition, almost all films are narrative films; that is, they tell stories. In this chapter, we discuss in general terms the ways the three sound track components interact to inflect and influence the image track and, with it, to form and enrich narrative. In addition to many short examples, scenes from *Sleepless in Seattle* (1993) and *Good Will Hunting* (1997) provide detailed case studies. Suggested exercises at the end of the chapter include "masking"—watching the image track without audio or listening to the sound track without images—and analysis using a checklist format for sound, image, and narrative.

Basics: Image Track, Sound Track, Narrative

The film we discussed in the introduction to Part I, *Catch Me If You Can* (2002), tells the story of Frank Abagnale, Jr.—a "true story," as the image track informs us during the opening credits. Stories are essentially reports that involve time, persons, and events. It is important, however, to distinguish between time of the events and time in the telling—that is, we need to make a basic distinction between the terms story and **plot**. *Story* is the chronological series of events; *plot* is the order in which those events are presented to us in the film. Thus, the story of *Catch Me If You Can* begins when Frank's father meets and marries his mother in France during World War II (this is the earliest event mentioned in the film) and continues into the present (the final **intertitle** informs us that Frank and his FBI captor and mentor, Carl Hanratty, remain close friends). All these events happen in "linear time" (clock time or calendar time).

Note, first, that this story is selective; it does not include *all* events between WWII and the present, only those that are relevant to the life and career of Frank Abagnale, Jr., and even then only a small selection of those. Second, note that the story is independent of the film *Catch Me If You Can*—it is the story of Frank Abagnale, Jr., whether that story was ever made into a film. (This is just as true of fictional stories as it is of Frank's true story.) Plot, however, belongs to *this* film because the term plot means the order in which the events of the story are presented to us. The first event we see in the film is Frank's release from a French prison—an event that occurs much later in his life than most of the events shown after that in the film. Although much of the film is in linear time thereafter, occasional short scenes in the airplane as Carl and Frank return to the United States suggest that the plot of the film is an elaborate flashback, a recollection of past events from the vantage point of the present. In this case, the "present," or present time, is a particular moment late in the story because the film's plot continues in a linear fashion past the plane flight, as Frank escapes through the airplane's toilet, is later apprehended, goes to prison, and finally begins to consult for the FBI on bank fraud cases.

Narrative feature films inevitably are concerned with the actions and interactions of persons, but the aesthetic product of the sound film is very complex—it throws a great deal of visual and aural information at the viewer-listener. As psychologist Annabel Cohen put it, "In the language of cognitive psychology, cinema is a multisensory stimulus that, millisecond by millisecond, impinges on sensory receptors and excites networks of neuronal activity in the mind of every film spectator. [This is] the daunting perceptual-cognitive challenge that cinema presents to each member of the audience."[1] Therefore, much of the work in film postproduction is ordered toward adjusting all the film's elements to make its points or tell its story as clearly as possible. The sound track's three components, which are normally recorded as separate tracks and then mixed, are heavily implicated in this process.

Most of us, of course, do not think much about technique or technology when we watch a movie. Filmmakers can be more or less adept at using them, but for the viewer it is the narrative that counts: Technique and technology are a means to an end. Indeed, they seem most effective when we are not aware of their presence, when we are absorbed by a convincing narrative. Such a narrative resonates—it clarifies our experience of the world: What we endure as more or less random or contingent events becomes suddenly coherent and significant when woven into a narrative. Thus, the "realism" of a successful narrative film is not a product of its fidelity (the actual contingency of our world) but of its clarity (its construction of a world that makes sense to us).

This substitution of clarity for fidelity extends down to basic elements of cinematic technology and technique. With respect to sound, this might seem counterintuitive. We tend to think of recording as "reproducing" sound; we also tend to think that we evaluate the quality of a recording by how faithfully it has reproduced the sound, but fidelity has not historically been a value in and of itself in the cinema; rather, fidelity is pursued only to the extent that it enhances the clarity of the narrative.

Microphones, for example, are designed and positioned to record the voice clearly, without **distortion**, and to minimize noises other than the voice. To accomplish this, microphone technology has developed along two lines, neither of which is related primarily to fidelity. First, manufacturers worked to increase the range so that the microphone could be placed outside of the view of the camera. Second, the sensitivity was focused so that the microphone could isolate the voice from its surroundings; that is, from the extraneous noises of the camera and soundstage. Sound **mixing** works on the same principle: Dialogue is almost always rendered clearly, whatever the actual acoustical setting. The isolation of the voice when the microphone records it ensures that the dialogue can remain intelligible in postproduction because mixing can elevate its level no matter what else may be contained on the sound track.

The historical privileging of the voice also suggests that a primary way in which the principle of narrative clarity is realized on the sound track is through hierarchy: Dialogue occupies the sonic foreground and music and effects the background. The image track is set up similarly, of course, in the familiar foreground/background distinction of visual staging (although it is important to understand that the levels of the sound track do not have to match those of the image track.) The foreground/background structure ensures that narratively important figures are placed in the foreground, less important ones in the background. In other words, image and sound tracks are arranged in such a way that we know what to pay attention to, what is important for us to understand the narrative. Foreground clarity thus gives us a sense of omniscience: We know what is important in a way that those inhabiting the world of the film do not.

If the foreground shows us where to direct attention, the background provides a sense of presence, of a continuous, uniform space that joins the sound and image edits into the appearance of a unified physical place, a "world." A background sound common to a series of **shots** helps convince us that each piece of dialogue comes from the same space—although, in fact, dialogue is typically edited along with the images and is often rerecorded after the fact.

The background obscures the production space (sound stage) and transforms it into the fictional world represented on film; this constructed background is therefore precisely what allows the fictional world to appear to us as something "real." Establishing such continuity is one of the main functions of both music and ambient sound.

Sound can also serve narrative clarity through redundancy. Visual and aural motifs (recurring figures, including musical themes) are obvious devices for this function, but music also routinely serves in this capacity by reinforcing narrative associations and references. For example, the waltzes played in the opening scenes of Alfred Hitchcock's *Rebecca* (1940) are historically accurate and appropriate for a fancy European resort hotel in the early 20th century, but they are not necessary to identify the hotel or its elegance. By confirming these things, the music suggests that the environment is important, as it turns out to be, because the very elegance of the place is upsetting to Joan Fontaine's "I," whose social uncertainties are central to the plot.

Thus, in the usual experience of audio-viewing a film, the sound track shapes or interprets the image track for us: It encourages us to look at the images in a certain way, to notice particular things, and to remember them. As Figure 1-1a suggests, the distinctions between the sound track components are clear enough: We know the difference between human speech and the sound of footfalls, or between a saxophone playing and an airplane flying overhead. On the other hand, that clarity of definition is not absolute: There are quite a number of familiar, intermediate effects that have the potential to enrich and complicate the sound track and its relation to the image track. These additional categories have been added along the sides of the triangle in Figure 1-1b along with an example for each. In the following sections, we discuss each of the sound track components in turn in relation to narrative design, touching on the intermediate categories where they are relevant.

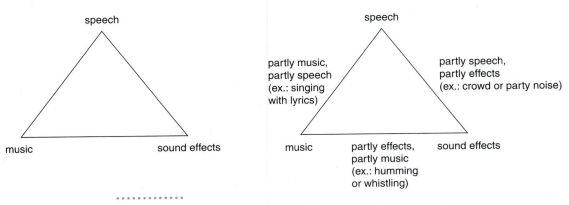

a | b   **Figure 1-1.** (a) The three sound track elements. (b) The elements with combinations.

Sound Track Components and Narrative

SPEECH

The most obvious way in which the sound track serves narrative is through speech, whose semantic dimension supplies a great deal of information that we either cannot get from the image track or could get only with considerable difficulty. In *Catch Me If You Can*, for example, we learn about the courtship of Frank Abagnale's father and mother through dialogue. Speech, however, can also organize (clarify) and interpret the frame for us. If we see a crowd on the screen, but the voice we hear is the voice of a person who is one of several standing in the foreground, our attention is turned to that person—the sound of speech interprets the image, telling us where to focus. Without that speech, a crowd may simply be a crowd making "generic noise." From speech we also often get a sense of the emotion of the speaker, which may confirm or supplement what we see in his or her face or bodily movements. This emotional confirmation is also a basic narrative function of sound in feature films. (A lack of such emotional confirmation is one reason silent film, especially when screened without music, can seem quite disorienting.)

Consider this short scene from *The Fellowship of the Ring* (2001): After a harrowing journey, Frodo awakens in Rivendell and talks with the wizard Gandalf; the scene ends as Sam enters (DVD ch. 18). At the outset, in bright white light, we see a close-up of Frodo's head on a pillow; Frodo speaks in a muffled voice— "Where am I?"—and Gandalf's voice (we do not see him) answers, first clouded by reverberation then in natural acoustics as all traces of the white light disappear and Frodo awakens. A conversation between the two is shown in a typical way, with the camera jumping back and forth, staying on the speaker (this method is called **shot/reverse shot**). Frodo asks questions, and Gandalf supplies information about recent events. Partway through this conversation, Frodo asks why Gandalf did not arrive to help his friends escape from their pursuers (ghostly horsemen of the evil Sauron), and Gandalf hesitates to answer, saying only, "I was delayed" (Figure 1-2). This brief comment prompts a flashback that briefly recounts how Gandalf escaped from the traitorous Saruman (the flashback itself includes speech that explains the reason the two wizards are now enemies). We return to the conversation in Rivendell, and shortly thereafter Frodo's companion, Sam, enters (we first hear his voice offscreen) to greet his friend warmly. Thus, it is speech that interprets the opening (awakening), which is obviously the point of the first conversation, and that invokes the flashback. Only once is speech missing—at the end of the flashback, as Gandalf speeds away on the eagle's back and orchestral music is foregrounded in the sound track.

The example shows that speech can supply new information, offer clues to emotion, and explain and direct plot elements (as with the flashback). The

Figure 1-2. *The Fellowship of the Ring.* Gandalf hems and haws.

extreme case for the control of speech is **voice-over narration** (or just "voice-over"): A person we cannot see (and who may not belong to the physical world shown in the film) talks directly to us, and the image track shows us the story he or she is telling. On the other hand, although speech typically controls scenes (that is to say, it is foregrounded), it can be moved to the background, literally by the reduced **volume** of persons speaking in the distance, or by the only partially grasped speech of guests at a party or of persons in a crowd (partly speech, partly sound effect—this is called "generic sound" or "generic noise"). Early sound films often used this procedure as a means of introducing human speech without the added difficulty of close **synchronization**: Two examples are the diners in *Coffee Dan's* night club just before Al Jolson sings his first songs in *The Jazz Singer* (1927) and the noise of people entering a train station, then on the street outside a hotel, and then the diners in the hotel restaurant in Hitchcock's *Blackmail* (1929), starting at about 00:10:50.

Because speech occupies such an important place in the narrative feature film, its absence is often notable (for example, in the Rivendell scene, Gandalf hesitates before answering Frodo's question about Gandalf's late arrival—we hear only the non-speech sounds of Gandalf's hemming and hawing—and this, more than anything, triggers the "visual" answer of the flashback **sequence**).

Presence or absence is an aspect of the treatment of each of the sound track elements, but it is perhaps most acutely felt when persons are onscreen and there is no speech. In *Psycho* (1960), for example, Marion Crane (Janet Leigh) is in her room packing before she runs off with $40,000 of her employer's money (updated to $400,000 in the remake (1998); see Figure 1-3; DVD 00:10:40; a few seconds earlier in the remake). In most of the scene she is still uncertain whether she will go through with it. Several cutaways to close-ups of the envelope containing the money confirm for the viewer that the money is the source of her dilemma. This is not new information—something we could not know

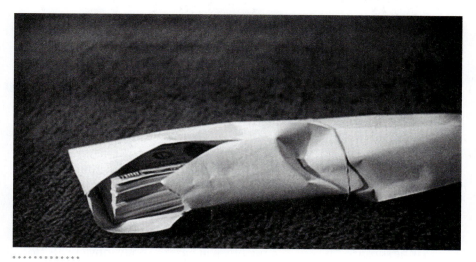

Figure 1-3. *Psycho.* Close-up of the money.

without the close-ups—but the redundancy of the close-ups concentrates our attention securely on the money. Normally, attention is drawn to persons in the frame—human characters are naturally foregrounded, and thus we focus on Marion, not the bed, the pictures on the wall, or even the shower that we can see through the open bathroom door (presaging Marion's fate). In this case, however, the money is made to share the foreground with Marion, and everything else (including the quietly nervous orchestral music that accompanies the scene) is in the background. In this scene, there is no speech, and it is left to other elements to guide our evolving understanding: the worried look on Marion's face, the small, repeated hesitations of her body, the cutaways to the money, and the slightly unsettled music.

SOUND EFFECTS

Sound effects ("sfx" or "fx") can also supply new information. This is sometimes in the simple form of non-speech human noises such as crying, groaning, or laughing (recall Gandalf's "hmm's"). More often, effects are used to "create" objects, animals, or even persons that we can hear but cannot see—an offscreen sound whose **source** we are able to identify: the bird sounds at the beginning of *Atonement* (2007); the call of the eagle that rescues Gandalf in the flashback; the bark of a dog and the croaking of frogs in a night scene from *Impromptu* (1991) as George Sand walks across a yard, returning, bruised, from a riding accident. Ambient sound (or generic noise) can create this same effect: in *The Big Sleep* (1946), the sound of (many) crickets in the nighttime as Philip Marlowe (Humphrey Bogart) walks up to the door of a casino club situated outside of town (DVD 01:05:56; see Figure 1-4), or the noise of water-fall or stream and birds during the conversation between Gandalf and Frodo discussed earlier. In this way, ambient sound extends the physical space depicted in the frame.

Ambient sound can be offscreen, as in the examples cited in the previous paragraph; or onscreen, as with typical daytime urban noises while we see their usual sources onscreen (cars, trains, crowd noises, etc.). In this way, the ambient sounds are not "creating" objects but confirming their expected characteristics. Sound effects operate primarily within the conventions of the sound film by confirming rather than creating physical space and significant action. In classical Hollywood sound film, sound effects were carefully marshaled and sparingly used, so much so that Michel Chion complains that, in a classical film "between the music and the omnipresent dialogue, there's hardly room for anything else."[2] If you watch a typical scene in a mid-1940s American film, you may be surprised at how infrequently you hear the body movements (footsteps, clothes swishing) of even the foregrounded actors. Background speech (except for crowd noise) is rare, and even ambient sounds in outdoor scenes are limited. The result is that the sound track contains only those sounds we are supposed to hear, those that give us significant narrative information.

Reel 1, Part 2, just after the refugee realizes his wallet is gone: "Aero-plane imitation" and note: "Somewhat like the Main Title—they'll keep the aeroplane effect down in the dupe room!!"

—Max Steiner, marginal note in his musical sketches for *Casablanca*[3]

Figure 1-4. *The Big Sleep.* Marlowe approaches Eddie Mars's casino at night.

In classical Hollywood cinema, in other words, sound effects are generally governed by pertinence to the narrative. We might put it this way: Synchronized sound cues us that some object or some person is important. This is obvious with dialogue. When Sam wheels his piano over to Ilsa's table in *Casablanca* (1942), we hear neither squeaking of the piano wheels nor Sam's footfalls—we hear only speech from the two actors, and as soon as their conversation gets underway in earnest, voices and sounds from the rest of *Rick's Café Américain* drop away. Advancements in sound technology have made it possible for the sound tracks of films in the past thirty years to be much more "live"—filled with sounds, especially ambient noise—but the same principle applies: Sound effects help to extend or confirm the physical environment of the scene and to identify the actions, objects, or events important to the narrative. In this scene from *Casablanca*, the absence of sound effects sends a message that dialogue (and music) are the focus—there is, in fact, not a single sound effect in the 4 min sequence from the point Ilsa asks for Sam (Figure 1-5) until a car engine starts very near the end of the scene, despite a group of four people going to a table, sitting, ordering drinks, getting up, leaving, and (three of them) going outdoors.

(By the way, for our purposes here we are making no distinction between sound effects that are direct recording of the events we see and those that are

Figure 1-5. *Casablanca.* Sam approaches Ilsa's table.

the result of **foley**; that is, sound effects created apart from the filming of the scene and added to the sound track. Indeed, it is the task of the foley artist to make effects as natural sounding as possible.)

The presence or absence of sound effects in itself can be significant, as can their foregrounding or backgrounding—that is, whether effects are prominent or "neutral." In some genres, sound effect "accents" (sharp or sudden loud sounds or **stingers**) are exaggerated for suspense or humor, as in the seemingly unmotivated slamming of doors, crashing of tools or canned goods, and so forth in teenage horror films (such as *Scream* (1996)), or in the enclosed, reverberant metallic environments of spaceships or space stations.

Silence, or the complete absence of effects and ambient sound, is not commonly used in films because it tends to instill doubts about the film's physical world. We might make an analogy with the image track, where black or white backgrounds have the effect of destroying all depth cues. In the unusual case of Stanley Kubrick's *2001: A Space Odyssey* (1968), this effect of eliminating depth is mitigated by the fact that silence defines the background of space just as the hum defines that of the space station. In the world of the film, silence *is* the sound of space. More important, it matches the depth-destroying black background of space. Although this can be justified by an appeal to realism—space *is* black and silent—it also serves to define the depth of space as unfathomable. To regress into the "space" of the background is to be removed from and to lose contact with the place of the film, which is constrained by the limits of the station. Every trip to the black silence of space is fraught with the possibility of death. Silence, too, serves as the analogue to death. In terms of sound, this is emphasized in the first instance by the loss of radio contact and in the second by the intense, sound-track consuming breathing of Dave as he returns from silent space and moves through the station to disassemble (and kill) HAL.

To summarize, sound effects can provide new information, but more often they aid narrative by directing attention to and confirming existing image track elements.

MUSIC

In general, speech and sound effects do a better—or at least a more specific and concrete—job than music can in providing narrative information. Music can provide narrative cues, but these tend to be fairly general and are usually used in an overdetermined way, confirming with the music what we already know from the visuals or dialogue: "Indian" music in the classical western; military marches or national anthems in war films; romantic foxtrots, ballads, or classical *andantes* with violins for love scenes; older popular tunes for nostalgia (as in *Casablanca* or in Nora Ephron's romantic comedies); threatening low strings and brasses for the entrance of the villain; or rapid, rhythmic "hurry" music to accompany a chase. Such uses of conventional music are known as **style topics** (see the sidebar for Aaron Copland's comment on how these can be an aid to composers).

When a musical theme (usually short) is created for a film and then developed (varied, reorchestrated) within that film, the theme acquires some of the properties of a word or symbol, with independent meaning or associations that can be called up when the theme is repeated. In such a case, the theme is sometimes referred to as a **leitmotif** (a term invented by 19th-century opera composer, Richard Wagner). At the simplest level, the information garnered from hearing a leitmotif is redundant (that is, overdetermined), as when two lovers are together and we hear a melody earlier presented as the love theme. On the other hand, a leitmotif can also be used to indicate absence rather than presence, as Erich Korngold does in *Captain Blood* (1935), where the love theme occasionally appears to signal Peter Blood thinking about Arabella. The leitmotivic method is mainly associated with early sound film and composers such as Max Steiner, Korngold, and Alfred Newman, but it has remained an essential tool for orchestral underscoring practice to the present day. John Williams is often credited with deliberately reviving the elaborate leitmotivic networks in *Star Wars* (1977) and its sequels.

The use of themes for narrative reference shows that music can provide new information under certain circumstances. In comparison with the other sound track elements, however, music is especially good at two things: (a) adding emotional specificity and (b) influencing and organizing time. Music can give the underlying or implied emotions of a scene direct expression; this is not mere redundancy—rather, it foregrounds the emotional content of a shot or scene, encouraging us to "read" the image or scene in a particular way. At one level this can be quite direct and abrupt, as when we hear a sudden musical chord (a stinger) on a cut to a close-up of a person whose face shows surprise or sudden fear. At another level, it can be much more subtle, as happens, for example, in *Casablanca* when the power of memory builds up during the unusually long close-up on Ingrid Bergman's face while Sam sings, "As Time Goes By"—her face changes minimally (a slight glistening in the eyes that might suggest imminent tears) but the music, by its presence and its persistence throughout the close-up, increases the emotional tension significantly.

Composer Aaron Copland refers to this effect of music as "underlining psychological refinements—the unspoken thoughts of a character or the unseen implications of a situation."[5] Another example is the theme for Frank Abagnale, Jr. in *Catch Me If You Can*—the restlessness of the rhythms, furtiveness of the lowered dynamics, hint of whimsicality, and perhaps even the repetitiousness all portray the character very well (Figure 1-6). These traits in the music are used later in the film to undercut Frank's appearance of self-assurance and daring. Although both of the examples here have referred to musical themes, the sound

Having to compose music to accompany specific action is a help rather than a hindrance, since the action itself induces music in a composer of theatrical imagination, whereas he has no such visual stimulus in writing absolute music.[4]

—Aaron Copland

Figure 1-6. *Catch Me If You Can.* Frank's theme (transcription from the sound track).

of the music (its **timbres** and **tempo**) is often enough to establish mood, as composer Franz Waxman observes:

> The immediate establishment of a particular mood is one of the most important functions of motion picture music. This usually can be done most effectively through expert **orchestration** and scoring rather than through melodic and harmonic development, [so that] the same melodic statement may serve many moods through a variety of orchestrational treatment.[6]

Music is by no means alone in articulating time in a film (linear time is the foundation of any narrative, after all, and associations can be created by stylistic devices such as showing the same image for the start of each day, returning to locations, etc.). Speech can be repeated or direct references can be made to earlier events in the story. Speech can even unify a scene simply by its continuous presence or absence, but in general speech is not deliberately exploited for this purpose. Instead, effects and music (and especially the latter) are used.

Music in particular may promote what Claudia Gorbman calls "formal and rhythmic continuity"[7] by framing the whole (for example, with music for beginning and end credits) or by presence or absence throughout a scene. In *King Kong* (1933), for instance, the absence of orchestral music under the opening sequence in New York City allows music to emphasize the fantastic Skull Island, Kong's home, as an enchanted place (orchestral music enters when we see the fogbound ship slowly approaching the island). Music is also characteristically used to establish continuity by overlapping and thereby connecting otherwise unrelated scenes. It was a routine practice in early sound films, for example, to extend the main-title music into the first few seconds of the film's first scene to smooth the viewer's path from the formal frame of the opening credits to the world of the film. The reverse—a **sound advance**—can function in the same way: Early in *Casablanca*, Sam's performance of "It Had to Be You" begins while we see the café from the outside, as customers enter (00:06:30); it takes more than 30 sec before Sam finally comes onscreen. This long, slow visual path makes the viewer familiar with the café and comfortable with the transition to it.

The simplest example of music shaping a scene, however, is a direct on-screen performance. Music is unquestionably foregrounded, and the form of the music dictates—it "becomes"—the form of the scene. Such radical presence is routinely expected in musicals, of course, but occurs in dramatic feature films and comedies, too; as if to compensate, music's absence elsewhere is not generally significant. In one of several performances during *To Have and Have Not* (1944), Hoagy Carmichael, playing a hotel pianist, begins to play and sing, then invites "Slim" (Lauren Bacall) to join in, as the rest of his band gradually does also—see Figure 1-7 (DVD timing 00:14:40). With the exception of one cutaway to Humphrey Bogart sitting at a table, the performance controls the film for its duration (not much more than 1 min, as it happens).

It is important to distinguish between "background music" and foregrounding or backgrounding of visual or aural elements. Although background music is a common term, other terms used for the same musical effect include "underscoring," "accompaniment," "commentative music," "dramatic scoring," or just "scoring." The basic characteristic of this music is that it belongs to a film's narrative register (like a voice-over narrator) rather than the fictional (diegetic) world. To avoid confusion, from this point on, we refer to either "underscoring" or "nondiegetic music," the term commonly used by film music scholars (it means music not belonging to the physical world shown in the film). Underscoring can be foregrounded, as when we hear loud, dramatic music accompanying a chase, battle, or ceremony, but it can also be backgrounded: Indeed, this is perhaps the most common situation for underscoring, to which

Figure 1-7. *To Have and Have Not.* Lauren Bacall sings "Am I Blue?," with Hoagy Carmichael.

The music has a certain control over the images, and there are places in the film where the scenes become a bit autonomous or simplistic or even vulgar, like in a few of the love scenes between the protagonists, and then the music comes and takes over as if it were saying, "Come on, let's go, let's go on, this is serious. . . ."

—Jean-Luc Godard, speaking about his film *Prénom Carmen (First Name: Carmen,* 1983)[8]

we as viewers generally pay little attention but in which narrative cues, mood setting, themes, and so forth are often embedded. Onscreen performances, of course, can be foregrounded, but they, too, can be backgrounded, as when a band plays in a club but the sound track's attention is given to a conversation between customers sitting in a booth.

To summarize, music can provide new information through narrative cues or through themes and leitmotifs. It can also define emotional states and situations, as well as influence and direct our perception of time in the experience of a film (see the sidebar for director Jean-Luc Godard's comment about music's capacities). Music moves easily between **foreground** and **background** and can take over the screen entirely during onscreen performances.

Example for Sound Track Components and Narrative (1): *Sleepless In Seattle*, Second Botched Meeting

Sleepless in Seattle, a romantic comedy directed by Nora Ephron and released in 1993, stars Tom Hanks as Sam Baldwin and Meg Ryan as Annie Reed. Annie has recently become engaged, although she is uncertain about the relationship; she hears Sam, a widower, talk about grieving for his wife on a call-in radio show, and Annie becomes obsessed with meeting him, convinced that he may be her "destiny." Eventually, she travels to Seattle, where he lives with his young son. After at least two "close calls" (botched attempts to meet Sam) she returns home; in the meantime, her friend Becky (Rosie O'Donnell) has mailed a letter that is intercepted and answered by Sam's son, who in turn sets up a meeting that finally takes place in New York, on the observation deck of the Empire State Building.

The sequence we are interested in here is the second—and more embarrassing—of the botched meetings in Seattle. Immediately afterward, Annie will return to the East Coast. In the preceding scene, Annie is in a hotel room talking by phone to her friend Becky; Annie has decided she will certainly meet Sam the next day.

For reference, here is a shot list. (Note: For definitions and illustrations of shot types, such as "point-of-view shot" or "**medium close-up,**" please see the glossary that follows after Part III.):

0. Hotel room, Ryan falls back on bed after hanging up phone (DVD 01:10:30)
1. Cut to outdoors; car moves into a parking place, seen from across the street (shot lasts 8 sec).
2. Ryan inside car, seen from outside front.
3. Point-of-view shot: She sees Hanks's vehicle arrive at marina (**extreme long shot**).

4. Ryan gets out of car (Figure 1-8).

5. Back to 3.

6. Long shot of Ryan, seen from across the street.

7. Medium close-up of Ryan.

8. To 3, but seen from behind Ryan's back.

9. Hanks and son, seen a bit closer; "wife" (actually his sister) enters frame from the left.

10. **Medium shot** of Ryan.

11. To 9, but closer still.

12. To 10.

13. Medium shot of Hanks and sister: "Where's Greg?"

14. Cut back to **medium long shot** of the two; truck horn sound starts during this shot; music out briefly.

15. Truck.

16. Medium close-up of Ryan.

17. To 14.

18. To 16.

19. Truck.

20. Hanks and sister, with truck passing by in foreground (blurred).

21. Street from more straight-on, with truck going off left side of frame; truck horn finishes during this shot.

22. Ryan; ambient sounds mostly gone.

23. Cut back to long shot of Ryan; music in again.

24. Hanks and sister; he approaches.

25. Medium shot of Ryan.

26. Ryan, from behind; Hanks approaches (Figure 1-9).

27. To 25.

28. Medium shot of Hanks: "Hello."

29. Medium shot of Ryan: "Hello."

30. To 28.

31. To 29—car horn noise.

32. She looks offscreen.

33. Cab.

34. Cab from over Ryan's shoulder.

Figure 1-8. *Sleepless in Seattle.* Annie (end of Shot 4).

Figure 1-9. *Sleepless in Seattle.* Annie and Sam (Shot 26).

First, we describe the sound track elements, their balance (foreground and background), and the dominant or striking events (or *accents*). A concise version of the description can be given in the form of a list:

0:00 Music enters with the cut to outdoors; the music actually started in the final second or two of the previous scene, but a new *scherzando*—playful, upbeat music—comes in with this cut (Figure 1-10). Outdoor sound effects: automobile noises. Music, however, dominates. (The sound level of passing cars is reduced to an improbably light "swish.")

0:50 The volume of the music comes down (Figure 1-11), but sound effects do not replace it—the general level of sound is reduced.

0:55 Speech—a few words from Sam, his son, and sister, who has just arrived. These words "poke out" of the music, as if they are fragments heard by Annie from a distance.

1:07 Truck horn (loud)—a stinger or *hit* (Figure 1-12, left).

1:20 Music in again, even softer and slower than before; sound effects out.

1:30 "Hello"—Sam and Annie speak one word, in turn.

1:40 Scene out with another stinger, this time a taxi screeching to a halt (Figure 1-12, right); music immediately answers with its own stinger over the cut, and speech follows closely with the suddenly foregrounded voice of Becky offscreen (actually a sound advance for the next scene).

This is a modern, multitrack stereo sound track: live, active, with wide low- and high-frequency definition. The first and most obvious thing to notice about the balance of the three elements is that speech plays a small—if narratively crucial—role in this scene. Even in genres like romantic comedy, which

Figure 1-10. *Sleepless in Seattle.* Music at beginning of the "Second Botched Meeting" scene (transcription from the sound track).

Figure 1-11. *Sleepless in Seattle.* Music in the middle of the "Second Botched Meeting" scene (transcription from the sound track).

Figure 1-12. *Sleepless in Seattle.* "Second Botched Meeting": two strong sound effects stingers.

tend to have a lot of talking, speech does not necessarily dominate in every scene. Because this is a modern sound track, "speech is no longer central to [the composition of the sound track],"[9] as Michel Chion put it. "Speech tends to be reinscribed in a global sensory continuum that envelops it, and that occupies both kinds of space, auditory and visual." Simple although our scene is, it is a good example of what Chion describes: Certainly, the two "Hellos" are weak, tentative speech very much "enveloped" by their sound environments; and, of course, for the sake of the narrative, that is exactly how we are supposed to hear them, as "weak and tentative."

As we think back over it, it is not hard to recognize that the three sound track elements in this typical scene from *Sleepless in Seattle* were woven together in a detailed, careful way—"composed," as it were—that is the essence of **sound design**. To bring out this "compositional" quality of the sound track, let us imagine for a moment that it is a piece of concert music or a CD track. Our "musical composition" consists of two main sections with an introduction: The introduction is the phone conversation, which leads into a more substantial musical section with clear design (music that easily enfolds the rhythmic swishing we guess belongs to passing cars); the section seems to slow down rather than stop, as if making a transition rather than a clear cadence (that is, a formal musical close)—it is interrupted by the huge articulation of the blaring truck horn and the sounds swirling quickly and loudly around that; the second part of the scene is characterized by a much duller sound environment with most of the ambient noise gone or greatly reduced in volume; the two accents in this section are the two "Hellos"; and this scene has an ending that is parallel to the first scene—this time, a car horn and its attendant quick

crescendo of sounds. Tom Hanks's voice is heard in both sections: "Where's Greg?" is balanced by his "Hello"; Meg Ryan is mute in the first section—her "Hello" gives her a voice and allows the scene to finish once it is rounded off by Hanks's answer. Mood and expression in the two sections are sharply different—positive, rhythmic, *allegretto* in the first (Figure 1-10); subdued, slow, tentative in the second (Figure 1-11).

If we want to add more detail to our description of the sound track, we can pay attention to the physical sources of the sounds in this scene. This matching of sound and source can be very specific (locating speech in Tom Hanks's body as we see it onscreen or connecting the sounds of passing cars to cars we see onscreen), or it can relate more generally to a category of sources (in this scene, women's voices; a man; automobiles; horns), or even more generally to a category of sound classes (swishing, harsh and loud, white noise), or to a temporal "history" of a sound's evolution regardless of category or class (for example, the truck horn, which is relatively long and changes quality and level over time).

The music, on the other hand, is clearly nondiegetic (there is no orchestra standing behind Meg Ryan or hiding in the boats behind Tom Hanks), and we need to describe the music in terms of how it functions in relation to the characters and events. One of the most obvious things to notice is that composer Marc Shaiman's music follows closely in tempo and mood the changing feelings of Meg Ryan's Annie Reed character, but the slowing tempo and more tentative affect in the moments before the truck horn tell us something the image track does not do very well—we see in Ryan's face and posture a few doubts or questions but no sharp collapse of her positive mood equivalent to what we hear in the music. This mood change is new; music supplies it and so "adds value" to the image track that helps us interpret it the way the film-makers want us to. This focus on mood, or empathic treatment of music, was typical of classical Hollywood film, and it obviously survives as a basic element of contemporary practice, too. Matching mood does not mean that music has to be closely synchronized to action, as in a cartoon; instead, it can create an overall mood for a scene, or, as it does here, follow shifting moods or feelings as they unfold.

Another way in which music clearly adds value is in the move from an external reality to subjective or internal sound. Once the truck horn blares, much of the outside world is shut out. This happens not in the image track, where we are seeing the same things (there are no close-ups of Ryan or Hanks—the usual cue for what is called point-of-view); it happens in the sound track, where the ambient sound—the outdoor noises—almost disappear, and we are there, perhaps in Ryan's mind, perhaps in the momentary private world she and Hanks share. Then comes the cab horn and, "poof," we are back in reality, almost as physically startled as Annie. It is the sound track that creates the impression of that subjective world.

There are two ways of writing film music. One is that in which every action, word, gesture or incident is punctuated in sound. . . . The other method of writing film music, which personally I favour, partly because I am quite incapable of doing the first, is to ignore the details and to intensify the spirit of the whole situation by a continuous stream of music.

—Ralph Vaughan Williams[10]

Finally, the pacing of the shots in the image track is quite fast—almost the whole scene is in a flurry, rushing by us. There are thirty-four shots in 1 min and 40 sec—that is an average of just over 3 sec each. The pacing matches the emotional excitement, the uncertainty, and the disruption in the story during this scene. We are set up for it by a long take in the hotel scene beforehand, and we remember it in the following scene, whose first four shots last 15, 10, 11, and 56 sec, respectively. What music accomplishes here is to slow down the pace, especially in the second part of the scene, so that the chaos of the quick sequence of shots for the truck and cab horns, and the quick rhythms of scene change, music stinger, and offscreen voice, stand out even more.

Music adds affect, empathy, and subjectivity while slowing down the pacing of the sequence; and sound (the truck horn) strongly articulates a scene whose parts are not all that different—in the second part, we are still on the street, we are seeing the same characters, and shots are still from the same angle, although the camera has moved in somewhat closer.

Example for Sound Track Components and Narrative (2): *Good Will Hunting*, Boston Common Scene

The Boston Common scene from *Good Will Hunting* uses a conventional pattern of framing (what is shown in the camera frame in terms of space and distance) that streamlines narrative priorities in dialogue scenes. Discussing this conventional design will not only help refine terms like "long shot" and "medium close-up" but will also relate sound to those image track conventions.

Good Will Hunting (released in 1997) was jointly written by Matt Damon and Ben Affleck. Damon and Robin Williams are the principal actors; Affleck, Minnie Driver, and Stellan Skarsgård play the main supporting parts. The film combines qualities of romantic comedy, the coming-of-age film, and character drama, as it follows a series of parallel plot lines whose common factor is Will Hunting (Damon). The basis of romantic comedy is the formation of the couple, and *Good Will Hunting* ends appropriately as Will follows Skylar (Driver) west (she has gone to California for graduate school). At the same time, Will's drive west is the final step in his coming of age, his outgrowing of his childhood environment, the south Boston embodied especially in his group of young male friends. The trip also represents his overcoming the psychological obstacles posed by the dissonance between his background and the situations he finds himself in due to his uncanny mathematical abilities—here, his therapist, Sean (Williams), and a math professor (Skarsgård) are the principal figures. In all areas of his life, Will finds it hard to make positive decisions and act on them.

Will has been assigned to therapy as part of probation. After some false starts, his therapist, Sean, decides to take Will out of the office and talk to him in a neutral setting. The preliminaries to the scene (in Sean's office) begin at about 00:46:00, the scene proper at 00:47:00, with a simple cut to the outdoors—although not identified as such, it is the Boston Common (a large park in the center of the city) on a pleasant autumn afternoon. Will and Sean are seated on a park bench and talk. The scene goes out a few seconds after 00:51:00.

The following shot list does not include notes about sound, but it does have additional terms (as headings) that relate to a prototypical design for dialogue scenes (that is, scenes where the main burden of the action is on the interactions of two (or sometimes several) characters, usually carried out mostly in conversation.

Prologue:
1. Indoors; Will coming down stairs (backlit); camera moves down to show him entering Sean's office.
2. Sean in medium shot (as if point-of-view shot: what Will sees), grabs jacket, and walks past the camera.
3. Back to 1, with Sean walking behind Will.

Establishing shot:
4. Two on park bench, seen from behind; pond beyond them (Figure 1-13).

Reverse angles or shot/reverse-shot sequence (Figure 1-14):
5. Close-up of Sean.
6. Close-up of Will.

Figure 1-13. *Good Will Hunting.* Will and Sean on Boston Common.

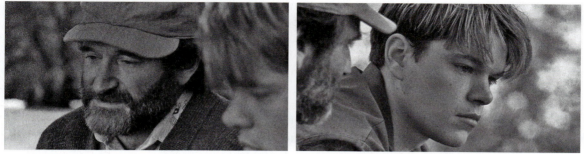

Figure 1-14. *Good Will Hunting.* Will and Sean on Boston Common: shot/reverse-shot sequence.

7. Back to 5; later in the shot, camera pans very slightly to the left, then to the right, stopping as part of Will comes into the extreme right side of the frame (this shot is unusually long, at 2:43).
8. Back to 6, but now with part of Sean's face at the extreme left side of the frame (this shot lasts a bit over 1 min).
9. Back to 7 (as it stood at the end).
10. Back to 8 (music enters quietly near the end of this shot and continues to the end of the scene).
11. Back to 7 and 9.
12. Back to 8 and 10.
13. Back to 7 and 9; Sean stands up and walks out of the frame; camera adjusts slightly to show more of Will's face.

Reestablishing shot:
14. Back to 4, but Will sitting alone.

Consider this note on scene design: The prototypical scene design begins with a general view of the physical space; this is referred to as an establishing shot. (In this case, the first three shots, marked "prologue," are actually a miniature scene unto themselves that makes reference to a preceding scene and motivates the change of venue for the therapy session.) Here, the long shot of Sean and Will on the park bench lets us know that the scene will take place in the park and positions them in that physical space. A common series of transitions moves gradually inward to close views of the conversing persons—a master shot (commonly showing a room for indoor scenes) is the frame of reference to which we return occasionally after a series of closer shots, and a medium **2-shot** (or set of them) focuses in on a pair of characters but in an emotionally neutral way (the medium shot shows characters from below the knees—or sometimes from below the waist—to the tops of their heads).

Both master shot and medium 2-shots are missing from this scene: When you watch it, notice how abruptly the film cuts directly from the establishing shot to a standard (collar bone-up) close-up of Sean. After a shot/reverse-shot series, all carried out in close-up with some small but telling horizontal shifts by the camera, a scene commonly closes as this one does, by briefly pulling back out to the establishing shot (or at least to the master shot). The complete series, then, is as follows: establishing shot, master shot, medium 2-shot, medium close-up (or close-up) in alternation, and reestablishing shot to end. In the section on description and evaluation that follows, we link common features of sound to this scene design schema.

Sound in the prologue section is muted: We hear a little speech and faint indoor **ambient sounds**, the most distinctive being the click of the office door opening. With the cut outdoors and the establishing shot of the two sitting on a park bench, outdoor sounds are strong—traffic, dogs, birds, and the faintly heard speech of adults and children. With the close-up, dialogue takes over. Not surprisingly, in dialogue scenes the dominant element is usually speech, in terms of sheer amount, prominence (loudness and accent), and narrative significance.

The Boston Common Scene is an extreme case because it is essentially a monologue by Sean; after his initial sarcastic remarks, Will is mostly silent (the few words he speaks are almost all offscreen as well [during Shot 7]). Sean speaks for some time as a sharp foreground/background distinction is maintained in the sound track; an essential element of this moment is that the background sounds, although by no means loud, do not decrease in volume either (as they typically would in a classic film to ensure clarity of the dialogue). Near the end of Shot 7, the sound of a low-pitched motor (airplane?) is added to the ambient sound under Sean's reflections on his wife's losing fight against cancer. Shortly thereafter, Shot 8 reverses to a close-up of Will with Sean at the edge of the screen, as Sean begins to home in on Will's vulnerabilities; in the background, we hear car horns and sirens throughout this segment, until a reverse again in Shot 9.

As Sean connects and Will is clearly affected, an emotive but not tuneful orchestral music enters very quietly (00:50:25; in Shot 10; the music is by Danny Elfman, who appears in another context in Figure 1-15) and gradually displaces most of the ambient sounds except that of birds, which fill the silences between Sean's sentences (Figure 1-16). He leaves at 00:50:52, and speech is gone; music takes over as Will sits silently, then overlaps into the next scene and dominates through its 2-min montage of the following day(s?). (We hear only occasional sound-effect accents and little, if any, speech until the final segment): A friend picks Will up for work, a brief view of the construction site, a phone call in the rain, the interior of a car with Will and his friends. During the phone call, speech, music, and effects (rain noise) are equal, but music goes out as Will climbs into the car.

Figure 1-15. *Meet the Robinsons* (2007) director Stephen Anderson (right) with composer Danny Elfman (photo: Dan Goldwasser).

The physical sources of sounds are kept very clear throughout the pro-logue and the park scene proper. The effect of this, paradoxically, is to support the concentration on close-ups by isolating the characters from their environment—we are made continually aware that the two men are having a very private conversation in a public space (the "stereo" effect of the relatively crisp background sound and somewhat muffled close miking on the two characters only exaggerates this contrast). Another result is that, when the music enters, its role as depicting Will's rising emotions is unmistakable, not only because its nondiegetic status is so blatantly obvious, but also because the opposition of external sound to the music's "internal sound" of emotion is so stark. Thus, sound supports a sense of distance yet emotional connection that is this scene's contribution to the larger narrative: Sean has figured out how to reach the well-barricaded psyche of his reluctant patient, who is talkative and seems self-confident at the beginning, but who is silent and brooding at the end. The foreground/background opposition serves to sharpen the unexpected intensity of the conversation, and the music confirms the emotion that begins to register in Will's face in Shot 13.

Apart from its specific functions for this narrative, the sound does have characteristics that fit the expectations for the typical dialogue scene, as we listed them earlier. An establishing shot is most often accompanied by some

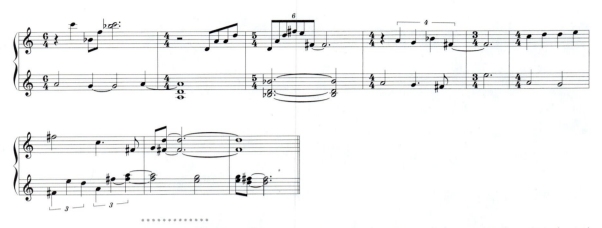

Figure 1-16. *Good Will Hunting.* Will and Sean on Boston Common: nondiegetic orchestral music near the end of the scene (transcription from the sound track).

kind of sound, either ambient sound that confirms and qualifies the physical space in the image or music that is somehow referential (in classical Hollywood cinema, it was a commonplace to insert a few bars of a national anthem or a song with relevant title or lyrics, such as "New York, New York" for a Manhattan skyline shot). Music that cites a theme or a musical **texture** that was heard earlier in the film as associated with a particular physical space is also common (a famous early example is the "Tara" theme in *Gone with the Wind* (1939)). Ambient sound in this situation can also be called "**establishing sound**," but we should note that the term "establishing music" is not used.

In the typical dialogue scene, we expect effects and music to drop off gradually, in line with the gradual movement into the physical space and toward the intimacy of the characters' conversation, at which point, of course, speech takes over and continues to dominate throughout, until the reestablishing (or other closing) shot, where conversation might cease and music or effects might make a final comment, a final spatial or narrative reference, or a transition into the next scene. In this scene from *Good Will Hunting*, as we have seen, effects do not drop back as much as they would normally, but we have also seen the narrative motivation for that atypical usage. The music, on the other hand, does serve a role as transition into the next scene (which it dominates, as is typical of montage sequences). Music, in fact, more often than not will enter—or rise in prominence if it is already been present, underscoring the dialogue—at the emotional crux of a conversation and then serve a double role: representing emotion but also acting in the formal function of transition sound.

Summary

Almost all films are narrative, and their elements are ordered to present the narrative in particular ways. The classical model, which continues to dominate contemporary filmmaking, favors narrative **clarity** over fidelity to the real world. This preference extends to sound, as well as image, with the result that the sound track is often called on to shape our understanding of the image track, to interpret it for us. The individual sound track elements—speech, effects, and music—typically work in concert, but each has characteristic or conventional ways in which it contributes to narrative.

EXERCISE 1: MASKING

Michel Chion promotes a simple but powerful tool to prove his point about **added value**—he calls it "**masking**,"[11] which is simply watching the image track of a scene without the sound, or, vice versa, listening to the sound track of a scene without the images.

Seeing the image track alone can alert one to both the richness and the ambiguity of the frame, but also to the rhythms of action within the frame and the rhythms of cutting (relative shot lengths and the transitions between shots). (See the sidebar for a composer's take on this exercise.) Similarly, hearing the sound track by itself can bring out its "musical" qualities, the shifting of volume (loudness) in toto or relatively among the three sound track elements, textures (sharp, soft, metallic, dull, etc.), register (high, middle, low) emphases, and sound track rhythms.

When we return to normal audio-viewing after a masking exercise, we can see how, for example, many image track rhythms tend to be suppressed by sound track rhythms but others stand out when the rhythms are in sync, how (previously) disembodied speech is anchored by the images of people, how some sound effects are anchored by their sources (such as telephones), how effects or speech can create offscreen space, how visual and auditory backgrounding and foregrounding interact, and so on.

Because you have probably watched the conversation scene from *Catch Me If You Can* and the "Second Botched Meeting" from *Sleepless in Seattle* several times already in the course of reading this chapter, a masking exercise will not be very effective. (Recall that we already asked you to consider the sound track for the scene as if it were a piece of concert music or a CD track.) You might try audio and video masking for the next scene in each of the films: Hanratty discovers an important clue (DVD timing 01:06:29–01:07:50); Annie continues her conversation with Becky (DVD timing 01:12:03–01:14:45). On the other hand, you can turn masking into something of a game by choosing a DVD chapter at random from a movie you have not seen before and trying to guess how the sound track is shaped from the clues in the image track, or how the

When well contrived, there is no question but that a musical score can be of enormous help to a picture. One can prove that point, laboratory-fashion, by showing an audience a climactic scene with the sound turned off and then once again with the sound track turned on.

—Aaron Copland[12]

image track editing is likely to feel after the rhythms and balance (foregrounding/backgrounding) of the sound track are added.

EXERCISE 2: USING AN ANALYSIS CHECKLIST

From the "Second Botched Meeting" example, we can assemble a preliminary checklist for analysis of sound in a film or film scene. In the analysis of an entire film, of course, the statements we make will be much more general, but the processes and effects we are describing are no different: (a) presence or absence of sound track elements and balance between them, (b) design of the sound track (that is, how it is mapped out over time or how the balance changes over time), and (c) relation to the narrative (how are sound track elements tied to characters and action, and how does design of the sound track relate to the articulations of the narrative).

In the "Botched Meeting" example, we began with a synopsis of the film (genre, director, release year, summary of the plot with principal actors) to set a minimal context for the film and the scene being analyzed ("*Sleepless in Seattle*, a romantic comedy directed by . . ."). Moving down to the scene itself, we briefly described its action (synopsis of the scene) to set the framework of the narrative ("The sequence we are interested in . . ."), and provided a shot list to anchor the description in detail ("For reference, here is a shot list"). Next, to turn attention specifically to the sound track itself came a list of timings with description of the sound track elements and their balance ("First, we describe the sound track elements . . ."). The two lists—shot list and timings with descriptions—could easily be combined if a scene is not too complicated.

After that, the prose paragraphs describe and evaluate the sound track from different angles: This description and evaluation is necessary because the shot list and timings list gives mostly raw information for each individual shot—it is the prose paragraphs that tie this information together, that create something like a "story" of the sound track design. The first of the seven paragraphs evaluates speech as not dominant ("This is a modern, multitrack stereo sound track . . ."), and the second tests this idea by masking (that is, listening to the sound track as if it were a musical composition to help make a better determination about the balance; "As we think back over it, it is not hard to recognize . . ."). The third paragraph is devoted to the physical sources of sounds ("If we want to add more detail . . ."); whereas the fourth, fifth, and sixth paragraphs describe music's narrative functions, taking up, in turn, emotion and characterization, the external/internal opposition, and pacing ("The music, on the other hand, is clearly nondiegetic . . .," "Another way in which music clearly adds value . . .," "Finally, the pacing of the shots in the image track is quite fast . . ."). The seventh and final paragraph offers a summary ("Music adds affect, empathy, and subjectivity . . .").

Our checklist for scene analysis in terms of sound, then, looks like this:

> 1. Background and general information as needed for context:
>   This might include genre, director, release year, principal actors,
>   summary of the plot or story with attention to describing the
>   context of the scene you are analyzing
> 2. Synopsis of the scene
> 3. Shot list
> 4. Description of the sound track elements and their balance
> 5. Description and evaluation of the sound track from different
>   angles: physical sources of sounds, music's narrative functions
>   (emotion and characterization, the external–internal opposi-
>   tion). Here we might also look more closely at sound and rep-
>   resentation (What does sound tell us about the kind of person
>   Annie is?, etc.)
> 6. If needed, a summary statement about the sound track in the
>   scene

Here, in list form, is the sequence for the Boston Common scene from *Good Will Hunting*:

Background and general information: "*Good Will Hunting* (released in
    1997) was jointly written . . ."
Scene synopsis: "Will has been assigned to therapy as part of proba-
    tion . . ."
Shot list: "The following shot list does not include notes about sound . . ."
Continues shot list with some specialized information: "The prototypical
    scene design begins with a general view of the physical space . . ."
Description of sound track elements and balance: "Sound in the pro-
    logue section is muted: We hear . . ."
Description and evaluation of the sound track from different angles:
    "The physical sources of sounds are kept very clear throughout . . ."
Continued: "Apart from its specific functions for this narrative, the
    sound does have characteristics that fit the expectations . . ."
Continued: "In the typical dialogue scene, we expect effects and music
    to drop off gradually . . ."

The analysis checklist is the basis for the analysis reports and reaction papers described in the interlude after Part I. We refine our methods of analysis in
the intervening chapters to include a wide range of specific techniques in the
sound track (such as sound advance, offscreen sound, etc.), common techniques and uses for music (**audio dissolve**, narrative reference, pacing, etc.),
and music properties (in particular, diegetic/nondiegetic, synchronization/
counterpoint, and **empathetic/anempathetic**).

2

The Musicality of the Sound Track
Concepts and Terminology

Introduction

As you may have discovered from doing a masking exercise or during class discussion of sound track details, describing what you hear is often difficult, not just because the task of sorting out the various elements can be exacting but because for the most part we lack a common vocabulary for talking about sound. Sound designer Mark Mangini notes that even among professional sound personnel communication often relies on onomatopoeia: "boink, boing, twang, squidge, zip, rico, whibble, wobble, wubba—I can go on for hours. There's thousands of them, and every sound editor uses different ones."[1]

The fact that every sound editor uses different terms suggests the limits of an onomatopoeic vocabulary. This is where music terminology can be of value to the student of the sound track: Musical terms are limited in number and well understood by everyone who uses them. Musical terminology also has an added benefit: Like the image-masking exercise, it draws our attention to the many ways the sound track itself is organized along musical principles.

Language has certain limiting factors in terms of sound. Describing a blooming explosion may not mean anything to you but sounds bloom. They are strident, they have a rizzz quality, they have a boomy quality, they have a piercing quality, they have a stinging quality.
—Wylie Stateman (sound designer)[2]

Music and Sound

Music in the broadest sense is an art of sound (not just an art of musical notes or musical performance), and a complex set of terms has been developed to describe it. For those without formal training in music, these terms can seem daunting, perhaps even a little mysterious. Some of them are, in fact, difficult to understand without the ability to read music, but a great many are readily accessible to any listener. For instance, most of us have a good idea of what words like *melody, tempo, dynamics, range,* and *beat* mean. These terms may seem relatively basic, but they do divide the material of music into specific categories that allow us to highlight certain attributes.

The same can be said for sound. Take the terms mentioned earlier. Melody certainly seems to be a specifically musical term, but the others extend easily to the domain of sound in general. Footsteps, for example, can be described in terms of tempo as fast or slow (as in running vs. walking), in terms of dynamics as loud or soft (stomping vs. tiptoeing), and in terms of range as high pitched or low (the crunch of gravel vs. the heavy thud of unseen footsteps on wood floors overhead). Beat is related to tempo but designates some kind of regular pattern: Thus, walking might be fitful (involving repeated stops, as might happen when two characters engage in conversation while walking in a garden or along a street), but soldiers marching are obviously highly regular, as are the pistons of a train or the ticking of a clock.

Musical terminology helps us focus on the abstract qualities of sound so that we can draw distinctions of this sort. This terminology does not cover all aspects of sound, of course, but it does give us a general strategy for proceeding: Instead of following the basic mode of human cognition to look for the causes or sources of the sounds, as much as possible we try to describe the sound itself. As this suggests, in cinema the causal relation between image and sound can be broken; that is, it is not necessary always to insist on realistically anchoring a sound in a physical source or requiring a particular naturalistic sound to represent an onscreen object in the sound track (Jack Warner makes a point about this in the sidebar).

To cite one very common example, footsteps on a quiet street can be rendered by all sorts of sounds: music for a highly stylized effect, coconuts for a humorous effect, or a highly "realistic" tap-tap-tap. In addition, realistic footsteps might sound loud or soft, heavy or light, dull or hollow; they might have an echo added; the echo might be subtle or pronounced, and so forth. Each of these choices will affect our understanding of a scene. Louder footsteps, for instance, will emphasize the act of walking, encouraging us to follow the moving figure and underscoring that character's importance. Likewise, through their use especially in film noir, echoing footsteps have accrued connotations of loneliness and even existential despair. Thus, something as seemingly mundane as the sound of a footstep can be raised to the level of a thematic element of the narrative.

Once we recognize the extent to which the sound track presents filmmakers with choices, we will realize that the sound track is crafted, that is, designed in a more or less conscious way. We might even think of the sound track as "composed," much like a piece of music. Applying musical terminology can help us hear a continuity between the design of a sound track and music. In essence, it allows us to hear, recognize, and describe how musicality—an artful organization of sound—extends beyond a film's music to the sound track as a whole.

Music has, among the arts, the most, perhaps the only, systematic and precise vocabulary for the description and analysis of its objects.
—Stanley Cavell[3]

The real sound is not necessarily the right sound. Sound is an element that is easy to apply abstractly. Once you realize the capability, you're really painting with sound.
—Jack Warner (supervising sound editor)[4]

*The varying tempi
and volumes of each
set of footsteps render
the nearness of the
respective threats,
and carry essential
information about each
of the steppers. Their
bodily dimensions, their
gender, and even their
fearful mental states
are rendered through
pitch and irregularities
of rhythm—stumblings,
shufflings, trippings,
and the segueing of
walking-into-running.
The patterning of the
footsteps also renders
the surfaces of these
cinematic streets.*
    —Helen Hanson,
    writing about 1940s
    horror films[5]

TEMPO

Tempo is the perceived rate (beat or pulse) of sound or musical events. (In non-musical contexts, tempo is often used interchangeably with pace.) Recognizing the beat is fundamental to the way we organize and hierarchize musical sounds in consciousness. Cognitive scientists who have studied how humans recognize tempo differences have found that an "average" or "moderate" tempo lies in the typical range of the (resting) human heartbeat, or from about 60 to 75 beats per minute. A "slower" tempo has fewer than 60 beats per minute, a "faster" tempo more beats per minute. It should not be surprising to find that the same is true for sound in general.

A persistent, foregrounded sound can strongly focus a scene and increase tension, often dramatically, as in the creation scene of *The Bride of Frankenstein* (1935), where gradually louder drumbeats are heard as a sound effect representing the beating of the Bride's heart. Regularly recurring sounds can also be put into the **background**, in which case **foreground** elements determine the overall tempo of the sound track. For example, if we are outdoors or near an open window at night, the chirping of crickets creates a lively tempo—their sound dominates because, more than likely, other sounds will be intermittent and irregular (a car drives by, an owl hoots, a dog barks, etc.). In a film sound track, on the other hand, the cricket sounds may in fact be rather quick, yet the overall tempo of the nighttime environment may seem relaxed, almost slow. This effect is a function of context. Typically, the ambient sound of crickets is isolated, especially at the beginning of a scene that uses them to establish an atmosphere of pastoral night. Other sounds that do occur are generally sparse, meaning not just that there are few of them but that they tend to be relatively spread out in time. As a result, the ambient sound of the crickets tends to fade into the background (because it is continuous), and it is the pace of those other sounds that determines the perceived tempo.

The musical conception of tempo encourages more precise description of the sound track, although more often than not there is not a clear, regular beat of the kind we find in music. Even without that, we can profitably think in terms of gradations of tempo: Just how fast or slow do the sounds seem to be coming in this scene? How do these affect the way(s) we are asked to interpret characters' actions and narrative unfolding?

Dialogue, for example, establishes a tempo that generally conforms to the tempo of the rest of the sound track (or else determines that tempo if dialogue is especially dominant). A moderate tempo of speech suggests the "everyday," or a calm but attentive mood. Rapid (and perhaps overlapping) speech can be either excited and happy or tense and nervous, depending on the situation—a condition that also applies to slow speech, which can be relaxed and inviting or sad and detached. In addition, characters are frequently defined by the tempo of their speech. In *Star Wars IV: A New Hope* (1977), Luke Skywalker and

Han Solo deliver dialogue at relatively quick tempos, whereas the tempo for Obi-Wan and Darth Vader is relatively staid. In addition, through the course of the *Star Wars* films, Luke's delivery becomes slower, suggesting that measured dialogue is associated with command of the Force.

Actors, too, usually have tempos that define their voice. Jimmy Durante, for instance, speaks at a relatively rapid tempo. The characteristic pace of John Wayne, on the contrary, is much slower. Some of the humor of the films of Jerry Lewis and Dean Martin comes from the marked difference in tempo (and pitch) between the actors. Indeed, the exasperation of Martin's characters at the antics of Lewis's has the effect of accelerating the tempo and raising the **pitch** of Martin's voice toward that of Lewis as he tries to gain control of the situation. The same can be observed in many other classic comedic pairings, such as Abbott and Costello or Lucy and Ricky in *I Love Lucy* (1951–1957). Something similar happens between Cary Grant and Katharine Hepburn in *Bringing up Baby* (1938)—both of these actors are masters at modulating the tempo of their voices.

Finally, a useful pair of musical terms related to tempo is **accelerando** and **ritardando**, a smooth, usually gradual speeding up or slowing down of tempo. Returning again to the example of footsteps, changing from walking to running produces the effect of an accelerando, although a fairly rapid one. A train pulling away from a station is an example of a more gradual one. Action sequences often consist of a series of accelerandos, each marking an intensification of the action. Scenes can also be initiated through an accelerando or ritardando before settling into a basic tempo.

RHYTHM AND METER

Closely related to tempo is the concept of **meter**. Meter is a regular, recurring unit of time corresponding to groups of beats—in other words, meter is a higher level organization of beats. There are two basic types of meter, duple and triple, reflecting the number of beats in each group. Each repetition of the group is called a measure or bar. Most popular music is written in duple meter, as are marches. The waltz, by contrast, is the prototypical example of triple meter.

Because of the way it organizes beats, meter can be an important factor in determining tempo. Music can produce meter almost effortlessly. In fact, the effects of meter are so strong that music can easily alter the perceived pace of a scene significantly. When directors count on music to "save" a scene, they often have in mind music's ability to affect the pacing through the strong patterning of meter.

Rhythm is closely connected with meter, but it usually refers to distinctive groupings of notes rather than to the regular groups of meter (the famous da-da-da-duh that opens Beethoven's Fifth Symphony is a rhythmic figure, not a meter). Rhythms can produce a metrical feel if they repeat at

There's a lot you can do very subtly with sound tracks. It doesn't have to be in-your-face, traditional, big sound effects. You can especially say a lot about the film with ambiences—the sounds for things you don't see. You can say a lot about where they are geographically, what time of day it is, what part of the city they're in, what kind of country they're in, the season it is. If you're going to choose a cricket, you can choose a cricket not for strictly geographic reasons. If there's a certain cricket that has a beat or rhythm to it, it adds to the tension of a scene. In Rush *(1991) some bad guys break into Jason Patric's house. They get into a fight and break a window. Once the window's broken, there's a cricket sound that comes in. It's this really rapid, machine gun-paced cricket chirp, very low on the sound track. The audience doesn't have to be aware of it, but it adds a subtle, emotional sense of tension to the scene.*

—Gary Rydstrom (sound designer)[6]

regular intervals, as they often will in dances: Genres such as the tango, the Charleston, and swing are defined through recurring characteristic rhythms, as well as an underlying meter.

Rhythm and meter in general are important for other aspects of sound as well, even when they are not strictly defined. The cadence and beat of dialogue, for instance, set up a basic framework within which vocal rhythm works. Timing is intimately bound up with rhythm: whether to stay ahead of the beat, on the beat or behind it; and whether and where to increase or decrease the tempo. We might also speak of the "rhythm" of a machine, where the meter is triple but the recurring rhythm long-short|long-short|long-short . . . , as shown through musical notation in Figure 2-1. Approached from the standpoint of meter and rhythm, each repetition here defines a measure. In terms of sound, such regularity is usually associated with machines and manual labor.

The placing of sound effects is determined as much by rhythm as by the need for synchronization. In a martial arts fight sequence, for instance, the choreography of the sounds is as important as the choreography of the images. Indeed, Michel Chion suggests that many of these fight sequences are comprehensible only because sound helps us parse a visual image that is moving too fast for the eye.[7] Moreover, many such scenes and action scenes in general have a substantial amount of offscreen sound. This allows considerable freedom in making decisions about how to render the sound track. Sound designer Gary Rydstrom notes the interplay between image and sound rhythm in gun battles:

Figure 2-1. Machine rhythm.

> Guns are hard. You do have to follow along with how they've designed the scene. The rhythm or pattern to a scene is due to the picture editor, but a lot of the action in a gun battle takes place offscreen, so that gives the sound people more flexibility to give it shape and rhythm. You can use it just like music. I always think of film sound in terms of rhythm. That's sound happening over time, so it's the rhythm of the sound effects over time that people remember.[8]

VOLUME

Volume is the physical strength of the sound we perceive, its loudness. Strictly speaking volume is defined by amplitude, which is the power of sound (normally as measured in decibels). The correlations between perceived loudness and amplitude are inexact, however, so decibel levels are only approximations for our impressions of volume. In any case, it is usually sufficient to distinguish three levels: normal, loud, and soft. Extremes are rendered as "very loud" and "very soft." Musical terminology uses eight generally accepted sound levels, the two basic ones being *p* (*piano*)—soft—and *f* (*forte*)—loud.

In recording, dynamics are often referred to as "levels," quantified in decibels (dBs). The dB is a logarithmic measure, where +10 dBs signifies 10 times the amplitude. This means that perceived volume of sound doubles approximately every +3 dBs. The standard dynamic range of mixing for cinema is 0 to 105 dB (0 is threshold of hearing), although in practice the full range is rarely if ever used (see Walter Murch's comment in the sidebar). By way of comparison, normal conversation is about 65 dB; dialogue in a film is mixed at roughly 75 dB.

Considerations of dynamics and recording level come into play at nearly every stage of sound production, from the object that first makes the sound to the sound as it leaves the loudspeaker in the theater. At a minimum, there are four points along the way where the volume of the sound can be altered: (a) the initial unrecorded sound, (b) the recording of that sound, (c) the mixing of that recording to the print (see Richard Portman's comment on this in the sidebar), and (d) its output through the speakers of the theater. In practice, there are actually several additional, intervening steps where the sound is mixed down to intermediate tracks before the final mix.

Dynamic levels can be altered at any one of these stages. A whisper might be mixed at a very high level (as occurs during Galadriel's Elvish narration that opens *The Fellowship of the Ring* (2001), or a ninety-piece orchestra might be recorded or mixed at a much lower level. A good example of the latter is the music in the sound track for *Foreign Correspondent* (1940): Despite an extensive and complex orchestral score rich in referential melodies, the music is mixed so low that its complexities are mostly lost. In a more recent film, most of the orchestral underscoring is mixed unusually low in *Four Weddings and a Funeral* (1994).

In addition, volume need not remain constant—and historically it has not: In classical Hollywood, a device known as the **up-and-downer** automatically raised and lowered music levels inversely with the presence of dialogue. Musicians use the terms *crescendo* and **diminuendo** or *decrescendo* to refer to the gradual increase or decrease in the volume of sound (for one use of this device, see Figure 2-2). In mixing, the fader is the device that changes the levels for a recording. Fading up and fading down refer to increasing and decreasing from one volume level to another; fading in and fading out, by contrast, take the beginning and end level, respectively, as zero. As with the relation between dynamics and sound levels previously mentioned, fading need not coincide with a crescendo or decrescendo of the recorded sound source. The aesthetic effect of the fade out of a pop song, for instance, depends in large measure on the fact that the musical performance maintains its dynamic level while the actual sound of the recording dissipates. In this way, we are left with the impression that the song has passed out of the range of hearing rather than ended.

The clichéd fade out of the typically constant-volume pop song points to one of the most important practical questions in using preexisting music in film: How is the music to be introduced onto and removed from the sound track? When the music is played by a band or is heard from a radio there is usually no problem because the story world justifies the entry and exit of the

We've actually got too much dynamic range. We have to control it in the mixing or else we will blast people out of the theaters.

—Walter Murch
(sound designer)[9]

It's very simple: you play the music up when they kiss, down when they talk.

—Richard Portman
(rerecording mixer)[10]

Figure 2-2. *Das Boot* (*The Boat*, 1981). Pursued by a destroyer, the crew listens as the sound of the enemy ship's propeller slowly increases in volume. The crescendo here is an effective means of raising the tension, and it culminates in the explosion of depth charges and the resulting aural confusion on the ship.

music. On the other hand, when it is treated as underscoring, the music will sound like a fragment, and, unless carefully controlled, the effect can be awkward. In *There's Something About Mary* (1998), Danny Wilson's "Mary's Prayer" covers the transition between Ted talking with his friends and his arrival at Mary's for their date (Figure 2-3). The entrance and exit of the music here is

Figure 2-3. *There's Something About Mary.* Awkward Ted.

handled in a very clumsy manner, the fragment seemingly chosen only as a forced method of knitting the two scenes together while also using another song with "Mary" in its title. On the other hand, this awkwardness might be justified as underscoring the awkwardness of the "first date."

Timbre

Think of the difference between a baseball hit by a wooden bat and by an aluminum one. Although it might begin with a "crack," the wooden bat gives a relatively round sound. The metal bat produces a sharp ping, full of high frequencies. Musicians call such distinct coloring of sound *timbre*. Timbre is also one of the most important categories for describing the sound track.

FILTERS AND "DISTORTION"

Common effects such as the fade out are examples of purposeful recording distortion, which might be defined as the difference between the sound produced by the original output (for example, the orchestra in the recording studio) and the sound produced in its final reproduction (the speakers in the movie theater). Any departure is, by this definition, a distortion of the original.

Despite the negative connotation of the word, distortion is basic to sound editing. Telephone sound, for instance, is generally represented by compressing the frequency response. The same is true for television, radio, or public address. Such filtering marks the technological mediation as distinct from sounds present in the physical space depicted in the frame. The effect is to reinforce the appearance of presence, so that face-to-face dialogue is clearer and more direct (and therefore seemingly more "authentic") than communication through technological media. In this sense, the lack of distortion in "real" sound is symbolic.

A change of level in mixing will also produce a change in tone color. In particular, sound that is output at a level below what it was recorded will lose disproportionate strength in the lower frequencies; and, vice versa, sound output at a higher level will increase it. These transformations are part of what effects a change in tone color. Microphone placement has similar timbral effects. A close microphone placement will emphasize direct sound and high frequencies. A more distant placement will capture more reflected sound and fewer high frequencies. Due to the presence of the reflected sound, distant placement also gives a better sense of the space in which the sound was produced.

Similarly, the sound of the same "sound" varies with the dynamic level at which it was produced in the first place. For instance, the tone color of a trumpet playing *fortissimo* (very loud) is quite different from the trumpet playing *piano*. If we compare the sound of the subdued trumpet under the credits of *Glory* (1989) or in the opening scene of *Saving Private Ryan* (1998) to the brash sound of a trumpet signaling "Charge," we can get some sense of what volume contributes to tone color.

Overt signal processing is often used for timbral effects. Adding artificial reverb is one common device used to render the illusion of a large space. Somewhat differently, *Laura* (1944) manipulates the recording of a piano playing the main **theme**; here the reverb alters and unsettles the familiar sound of the instrument. This distortion accompanies Detective McPherson's passage into dream, whereas the musical theme itself suggests that his thoughts are on Laura. In still another treatment, a trumpet motive in *Patton* (1970) is processed through an Echoplex to produce a distinctive, almost unworldly timbre that helps endow General Patton with a seemingly mythical status.

PITCH

The musical measure of frequency is called pitch. Particular ratios of frequency define intervals as between pitches, and these intervals in turn fix the positions of pitches as notes within a musical scale. Most musical systems recognize the octave as the primary interval that contains the scale, meaning that once the octave is reached, the scale seems to repeat, only at a higher pitch level twice the original frequency.

To hear how pitch affects timbre, try an experiment. Play two notes on the piano relatively close in pitch, and you will find that they sound more or less the same (except for the frequency difference). Now play a low note on the piano and another in the same position within the octave but several octaves higher (the higher the better) and you should find that they sound quite different (except that they are octaves). The similarity you hear in the first case and the difference in the latter are the domain of what musicians generally refer to as timbre, whereas the difference you hear in the first case and the similarity in the second are the domain of pitch. You can hear a similar effect by speaking in a very low voice or in a very high voice (*falsetto*) and then comparing that to your normal voice. The timbre characteristic of pitch levels is called **tessitura**, which in typical usage is divided into registers: high; middle or normal; low.

Another element that colors sound is harmony, which is the sounding of more than one pitch at the same time. We call any groups of simultaneous notes "chords" or "sonorities," although musicians tend to restrict these terms to complexes of three or more notes. If you hear any two notes played simultaneously, you should recognize a difference: some of these combinations will sound "sweet," some "hollow," whereas others will seem "harsh." These differences are also timbral, but they are so important to music that musicians have special terms for them: "consonance" refers to the first two categories and "dissonance" to the last. As more notes are played together, you will hear that some combinations seem very consonant, others very dissonant indeed, but there will also be many gradations in between. For our purposes, the main thing to pay attention to is how each combination gives a particular color to the sound.

Individual sounds are constructed along similar principles to harmony. Musical sounds tend to sound musical on the basis of their harmonious quality, that is, they vibrate with primarily consonant intervals—so-called "harmonic" overtones—beyond the basic note we perceive. This series of overtones consists of simple ratios of that basic note, which is called the "fundamental." Noise, by contrast, is characterized by jumbled, "inharmonic" overtones, so that noises sound "harsh" by contrast to a musical pitch. An intermediate stage would be represented by a "humming" motor, which would have some discernible pitches but not the clarity of a musical sound (the sounds of many percussion instruments are similar).

As suggested earlier, volume also affects timbre because the strength of the individual harmonics does not always vary equally with volume. This is particularly true at the extremes of the dynamic range. It is important to recognize that this is true of most sounds: the timbre of a shouting voice differs from that of a normal voice, although much of the difference may be attributable to a markedly different way of using the vocal instrument. We know that this difference is timbral rather than simply a product of mere volume because these voices sound quite different when recorded and played back at the same volume.

ORCHESTRATION

Another, more characteristic example of timbre would be something like the difference between the sound of the oboe and that of the flute. In its middle register, the flute has a sweet, rather smooth sound, whereas the oboe is more nasal. As the instruments go higher in their range, the flute becomes brighter, almost piercing. The oboe, on the other hand, generally mellows in its upper register, especially at moderate dynamic levels.

The timbres of musical instruments can be mixed. We might have a flute and oboe playing the same tune in unison, for instance. Such combinations often blend to produce a tone color quite different from the timbres of each taken individually. In this sense, combining instruments is somewhat analogous to blending paints, where colors mix in ways that nonprofessionals might not expect they would. The traditional symphony orchestra (the model for a studio orchestra) can produce a surprising variety of timbral combinations (see Figures 2-4 and 2-5 for orchestral images).

Orchestration is the term musicians use to designate this art of choosing and combining instruments to produce a particular sound. Tone color in music is not used indiscriminately any more than is pigment in painting (indeed, orchestration is regarded as a specific professional skill in the commercial film industry—see Figures 2-6 and 2-7). Timbre sets an underlying "mood" to the music, much as the palette does for painting. In addition to differences in sound, the instruments carry many connotations inherited

Figure 2-4. Recording studio, view from within the orchestra (photo: Dan Goldwasser).

Figure 2-5. Composer George S. Clinton conducts a studio orchestra (photo: Dan Goldwasser).

Figure 2-6. Orchestrator Brad Dechter and composer James Newton Howard (photo: Dan Goldwasser).

Figure 2-7. *Firewall* (2006) orchestrator Conrad Pope, director Richard Loncraine, and composer Alexandre Desplat (photo: Dan Goldwasser).

from opera, operetta, melodrama, program music and so forth: the oboe and flute, for instance, are pastoral instruments; the trumpet is associated with military and heraldic functions; the horn suggests hunting; and so forth. These connotations are not always obvious—in fact, generally they are not—but they are always latent, so that something will seem wrong when for no apparent reason the orchestration calls for an instrument to play too far against type.

TIMBRE AND SOUND

Much like the sound of a flute differs from that of an oboe, footsteps on gravel sound markedly different than those on grass or concrete. Likewise, the sound of the footstep of a large animal in the distance differs from that same footstep in close-up, even if the sound levels remain the same. (This has to do with the fact that distant sounds have primarily low frequencies, whereas the close-up contains many more high frequencies as well—the strength of high frequency sound diminishes greatly with respect to distance.) Also like musical instruments, many sounds have specific associations. A low rumble is often ominous, suggesting a distant danger (such as the previously mentioned large animal); a bright, crunchy sound puts us on alert, indicating close proximity and danger (the close-up of the large animal); crickets have pastoral associations, suggesting a calm, peaceful night; a dull thud often fills us with dread (body hitting floor); and so forth.

As Walter Murch explains, the particular timbre of a sound is often chosen with extreme care to ensure an appropriate filmic effect: The image of a door closing accompanied by the right "slam" can indicate not only the material of the door and the space around it but also the emotional state of the person closing it. The sound for the door at the end of *The Godfather* (1972), for instance, needed to give the audience more than correct physical cues about the door; it was essential to get a firm, irrevocable closure that resonated with and underscored Michael's final line: "Never ask me about my business, Kay."[11]

Tessitura also can serve as an important concept for thinking about the sound track in general, especially issues of the voice. As we noted earlier, the regular speaking voice, *falsetto*, and whisper are quite different in timbre. Furthermore, if we listen to how an angry voice sometimes grows shrill as it stretches into the upper register, we can start to hear that "raising a voice in anger" is more than a matter of a change in volume. Tessitura arguably plays as great a role in characterization as dialogue. Voices themselves have characteristic tessituras. Jimmy Stewart's voice is generally placed relatively high and Jerry Lewis's very high; whereas John Wayne's voice is pitched much lower. Similarly, Ginger Rogers and Betty Grable both have voices that are placed in the upper range; whereas Lauren Bacall, Marlene Dietrich, and Greta Garbo all have relatively low voices.

Finally, as in the orchestration of music, sounds can be produced through blending a number of individual sounds together. For instance, a tiger's roar was added to jet sounds of *Top Gun* (1986), giving it a ferocious personality. The sounds of the dinosaurs in *Jurassic Park* (1993) are also composites created by combining various animal sounds. Such **sweetening** of sounds through combination is extremely common.

Texture

In music texture designates the functional relation of musical lines to one another. This concerns the number of musical strands or layers occurring simultaneously and the type and nature of the connections among them.

DENSITY AND LIVELINESS

A "thick" texture refers to a relatively large number of strands, but the strands are fairly well coordinated, like a thick string of yarn. The strands in a "busy" texture, by contrast, are generally more active and more discrete, the effect being that they compete for attention.

In music, a texture can be thickened by doubling a strand (as by adding an instrument), especially at intervals other than the octave or unison. Thickness is also influenced by spacing. When strands occur in approximately the same register, the sound will be thicker than if the strands are separated by register. The impression of thickness is also influenced by registral placement, as lower notes seem to have more "mass" than higher ones and so create a much denser aural impression.

In recording and editing, the creation of sound texture is often called "layering," each layer being more or less equivalent to a musical strand. The thickness of the texture in this sense would be determined by the number of discrete layers but also by the overall volume. We might call this thickness the "density" of the mix. As with music, low frequency sounds tend to increase the impression of density. Busyness, by contrast, is a measure by the total amount of activity. We might term this busyness the "liveliness" of the mix. In this respect, liveliness does not refer to the absolute number of layers but to the perceived level of activity (and, secondarily, the amount of high frequencies).

Density and liveliness of the mix do not necessarily correlate with scene type. Walter Murch notes that "Sometimes, to create the natural simplicity of an ordinary scene between two people, dozens and dozens of sound tracks have to be created and seamlessly blended into one. At other times an apparently complex 'action' sound track can be conveyed with just a few carefully selected elements."[13]

Density and liveliness are useful terms for describing a sound track mix but they offer little help in determining the functions of the various layers of a

If something is clear but isn't dense enough, if it doesn't have any heft to it, I try to find something to make it have heft. If something is as dense as you want it but you can't understand anything in it, what do I have to take out to make it clear? So I'm always looking for that balance point between density and clarity.

—Walter Murch[12]

mix. Musicians, however, do have terms that refer to the means of controlling functional relations among various lines, especially in terms of foreground and background. We describe and illustrate these four textures below: (a) **monophony**, (b) **homophony**, (c) **melody and accompaniment**, and (d) **polyphony**. To these four categories, we add a fifth that is understandably rare in music but common in film: (e) accompaniment without melody (or **"a-melodic"**). As we see, each of these textures has important correlates in sound design.

MONOPHONY

Monophony is the simplest texture. Strictly speaking it consists of a single melodic line. Obviously, this melodic line will occupy the foreground, as the "background" is absent, consisting only of silence. A familiar example is the singing of medieval chant. In film, a person singing without any accompaniment creates a monophonic texture, as do several persons all singing the same melody. In most writing, the meaning of the term monophony is expanded to include a single melody against a pedal point, that is, a pitch or sonority held without change in the background. A good example would be the drones of bagpipes or of certain types of Tibetan chant.

In terms of sound, a monologue—even a dialogue—can be considered "monophonic" if it occurs with no sound effects (see Figure 2-8 for an example with commentary). When the ambient sound field is relatively thin and inactive, the overall effect might still be considered to be monophony. In other words, the important consideration for a monophonic sound design is that the background be absent or minimally defined. When dialogue is rendered with a monophonic sound design, the emphasis falls squarely on the words, allowing for maximum clarity. That is one reason this texture was commonly used for dialogue sequences, especially in the 1930s and 1940s, whenever clar-

Figure 2-8. *Trois Couleurs: Bleu* (*Three Colors: Blue*, 1993). Olivier (Benoît Régent) and Julie (Juliette Binoche) talk on the phone. The lack of ambient sound in the sequence places strong "monophonic" emphasis on dialogue in the scene. The silence of the sound track here also underscores the long gaps of silence between the lines.

ity of dialogue was the absolute value of the sequence. On the negative side, a lack of well-defined background cues to establish time and place is the primary drawback of this kind of sound design.

HOMOPHONY

In music, a strict homophonic texture consists of more than one line, but each line moves with more or less the same rhythm. This is a style you may be familiar with from hymns. In homophony, the tune is supported by the other lines, so in that sense there is a separation into foreground and background function. The fact that the lines do not have distinct rhythms, however, considerably diminishes the differentiation of the functions. For this reason, homophonic texture is not frequently encountered as a textural component of sound design—although it may, of course, be used for music within the sound track. One instance of such a texture might be when two or more sounds are causally connected, such as punches and grunts in fight scenes of martial arts films, or in military charges, where a single voice (the commander's or sergeant's) nevertheless needs to emerge above the others.

MELODY AND ACCOMPANIMENT

Melody and accompaniment is probably the most common texture in music. As the name implies, the tune is supported by its accompaniment, making for a strong functional separation of melodic foreground and background accompaniment. Because the accompaniment is rhythmically distinct from the melody, foreground and background functions are better defined than in homophony.

One of the most powerful functions of accompaniments is establishing the "setting" (genre) or "mood" (affect) in which the melody will appear. Tunes certainly have generic and affective qualities in themselves, but an accompaniment can augment, diminish or even transform the character of a melody.

If we think about how filmmakers distinguish foreground and background on the sound track, we should quickly recognize that melody and accompaniment texture also dominates in sound design. In almost any dialogue scene, the voice will be set off as foreground. Music and ambient sound typically serve as a background that supports the voice, clarifies meaning of the dialogue and gives a scene direction by "setting" the mood, establishing location, providing emphasis, and so forth.

POLYPHONY

In music, polyphony is characterized by an independence of musical lines. In other words, polyphonic texture exhibits a relatively shallow hierarchy between foreground and background. The term polyphony is often used as shorthand for imitative counterpoint, such as a fugue or canon, where musical lines achieve musical independence through imitation. Familiar examples of imitative counterpoint include the rounds "Row, Row, Row Your Boat," and "Are You Sleeping, Brother John." The independence of line in the case of these simple canons is clearly not between the lines themselves, which are identical; rather the independence refers to the lack of functional differentiation between the lines: the lines do not establish a clear hierarchy but rather compete for our attention. Which line is primary? As a rule of thumb, the more we feel obliged to ask this question, the more likely it is that we are dealing with a polyphonic relation.

It should be remembered, however, that polyphony is not restricted to imitation. For our purposes, polyphony is a measure of hierarchy: the shallower the hierarchy between foreground and background layers, the more polyphonic or "contrapuntal" it will be.

Polyphonic textures are quite common in sound design. Action sequences, for instance, often set music and sound effects off against one another in such a way that neither seems to dominate the other—at least not over long stretches. Even at moments when sound effects mask the music almost to the point of obliteration—for example at the beginning of *Star Wars IV: A New Hope* where laser blasts in the corridors often make it impossible to hear the music—the sound design does not set up a real hierarchy between the elements. It is more like they are set one against the other in a somewhat antagonistic manner (counterpoint literally means "point against point"). As with music, the sounds need to be controlled if they are not to simply produce cacophony. Sound designer Skip Lievsay puts it this way:

> When you attack a film with a volume of work, it tends to muddy up the issue unless you're trying to create something [that] is a conflagration of sounds. Even then it is almost always more meaningful to isolate certain sounds that will play on a given shot in a very succinct way, and will go ten times farther psychologically and emotionally than all of the other ninety-seven other elements that you're not listening to.[15]

Overlapping dialogue—for instance in screwball comedies—is also a form of counterpoint. As the name implies, the beginning of one line of dialogue begins before another line ends, and at times several people may be speaking entire sentences simultaneously (see Figures 2-9 and 2-10 for examples with commentary).

A-MELODIC (ACCOMPANIMENT WITHOUT MELODY)

The a-melodic texture is similar to monophony in that it diminishes the foreground/background distinction, but whereas monophony occupies only a foreground, an a-melodic texture has only background. In music, the a-melodic texture occurs most commonly at the beginning of a piece or section

There are many kinds of counterpoint, and each has varying degrees of complexity. I think this can be evaluated only by the final effect it makes. I have used the fugato, for instance, very frequently. Now I don't expect an audience to stop looking at the picture and say, "Ah, Waxman has written a fugato." But I think an audience will notice that somehow the music is growing in tension and excitement because the reiteration of a single short motif, in a contrapuntal style, is a fairly obvious way of driving toward a climax. The technique of a fugato is strictly my own business. The dramatic effect is the audience's business.
—Franz Waxman[14]

Figure 2-9. *M*A*S*H* (1970). Radar O'Reilly (Gary Burghoff, second from right) closely echoes—sometimes even anticipates—Col. Blake's (Roger Bowen, far right) commands, suggesting dialogue in close canon. This gives the effect that Radar is running the unit as much as Col. Blake.

where it serves to introduce an accompaniment pattern. In musical theater, jazz, and popular music, this is called a "vamp" (as in "vamp till ready") and functions to set tempo, mood, and genre or occasionally just fill time between melodic statements. The primary characteristic of the vamp is that the reduction to background alone is only temporary, that is, it presumes the eventual appearance of melody and so also a restoration of the foreground/background

Figure 2-10. *Brigadoon* (1954). In this shot, there are two conversational groupings, one on the left and one in the center, as well as a man on the phone toward the right. Dialogue from each is simultaneously presented on the sound track. As the camera moves through the crowd, other conversations of this sort are briefly isolated. With ambient sound of background chatter mixed at an extremely high level, the impression is one of utter confusion. This sense of confusion underscores the disorientation and alienation of the modern city, which the film opposes to the pastoral utopia of Brigadoon.

distinction. (In the past two decades, certain types of "ambient" music styles can hold a-melodic textures over the course of an entire track.)

Something akin to introductory vamping is common in sound design. It is not at all unusual for scenes to begin with background alone. This observation applies to sound as a whole as much as to music (see Figure 2-11 for an example with commentary). Ambient sound especially is often used this way. One reason for using an a-melodic texture as an introduction is that it permits us to concentrate on the details of the background, which allows us to absorb the details of setting and place, which can be particularly useful if we need to orient ourselves to a marked change of tempo and mood. Like the establishing shot, it "sets the scene" before initiating action or dialogue.

The a-melodic texture is occasionally used as an ending as well, where the return to background serves as a means to disperse the energy of the scene, to allow reflection, and to buffer the transition to the next scene. In *Impromptu* (1991), for instance, George Sand (Judy Davis) rushes into the woods on a horse as Chopin's Prelude in G# Minor plays on the underscore. She is ultimately thrown from the horse, and the scene ends with a thud (00:24:38) and then only ambient sounds. This is followed immediately (00:24:44) by a slow **dissolve** to George stumbling back to the house at night, again with only ambient sound accompanying the shot. The ambient sound in this case is a kind of "reverse" or "mirror" vamp: it

a | b   **Figure 2-11.** *Rashômon* (1950). The sound of rain is prominent at the beginning of each episode under the ruined Rashômon gatehouse. In each case it serves as a prelude to the scene (a), where it settles into the background for the generally sparse dialogue (b). Although it is a-melodic in itself, and it serves consistently as an introductory figure, rain—along with sunlight and the baby—is a prominent symbol in the film. This symbolic status is marked not simply through recurrence but also through the length of each introductory sequence and its continued presence as background for the dialogue.

comes after the main part of the sequence; it serves as a transition; and its mood contrasts quite markedly with the scene that precedes it. (For another example, see the graphic with commentary in Figure 2-12).

TEXTURE AND FOREGROUND/BACKGROUND FUNCTIONS

Texture offers a useful way of thinking about and describing the functional relations among components of the sound track. The terms should not, however, be taken as absolutes—for our purposes, making a correct identification is less

Figure 2-12. An interesting use of a-melodic texture can be found in the opening scene of *Aguirre, der Zorn Gottes* (*Aguirre: The Wrath of God*, 1972). After a brief set of explanatory titles with no sound, the film opens with a shot of people snaking their way along a narrow mountain pass (00:00:36). Atmospheric synthesizer music evocative of voices enters at the very end of the titles and continues throughout the scene, which plays silent (meaning that it contains no **diegetic sound**). A voice-over narration is added (00:00:49), suggesting that the music has been functioning as a vamp because the voice-over establishes a foreground relationship with respect to the synthesized music. Yet, when the voice-over ends about 15 sec later, the music continues alone until the beginning of the next scene (00:04:53). Because the voice-over is comparatively brief, and the music amorphous, the music in the sequence ultimately seems to function as an extended accompaniment lacking melody (i.e., the voice-over). In a sense, the long continuation of the music serves as a rejection of the foreground/background hierarchy and, therefore, also of the clarity offered by the voice-over.

important than using the terms to make sense of foreground and background; and, in any case, scenes frequently fluctuate from one texture to another as the dramatic action plays out.

Monophony emphasizes foreground to such an extent that background cues to setting are all but eliminated. Homophony offers a richer texture but is little different in function. Melody and accompaniment occupies a middle point between monophony and polyphony. What separates it decisively from the other textures and what makes it the most common texture is that it establishes a clear hierarchy between foreground and background and thus allows the formation of strongly demarcated functions. Polyphony introduces multiple conflicting foreground elements that confuse the foreground/background distinction. Finally, the a-melodic texture asks us to pay attention exclusively to the details of the setting, that is, it directs attention to background but without fully transforming that background into a foreground: it leaves an unfilled space.

In distinguishing between monophony and melody and accompaniment, setting and mood are paramount. The more redundant or less narratively pertinent information the background conveys, the more the texture will seem monophonic. In distinguishing a-melodic texture from melody and accompaniment, the delineation of a foreground figure against the background is most important. When a foreground is well defined against a background, we will understand the figure as significant. In short, melody and accompaniment situates the foreground within a context determined by the background. Polyphony differs from melody and accompaniment in terms of clarity. The relative lack of hierarchy coupled with a multiplicity of layers creates confusion, which need not be construed negatively. Action sequences, for instance, often benefit from such aural confusion because the aesthetic of spectacle that drives these sequences depends on sensory overload.

Few scenes rely exclusively on one texture or another except in a broad sense. As noted earlier, accompaniment alone often functions as a vamp, that is, an introduction to a scene that will be characterized primarily by the foreground/background relation. As in this case, texture generally fluctuates, generally centered around melody and accompaniment so long as dialogue dominates, for instance, but drifting now and then toward the other textures. Likewise, chase scenes may fall more on the polyphonic side, but there will inevitably be moments where, say, dialogue comes forward accompanied by a suspension of the "contrapuntal" field.

Finally, we need to bear in mind that we can apply the idea of texture to different levels of the sound track. For example, an a-melodic musical texture—music without a strong melodic component—might easily function as an "accompaniment" to dialogue. The repetitions of the distinctive marimba figure at the beginning of *American Beauty* (1999), for instance, are essentially an a-melodic texture. On the larger level of the sound track, however, they serve as an accompaniment to Lester's voice-over. Something similar happens between the music and voice-over in *Double Indemnity* (1944). Each time Walter Neff begins to narrate, an agitated musical figure accompanies his speech.

Example for Sound Track Analysis Using Musical Terms (1): *Trzy Kolory: Bialy (Three Colors: White)*, The Shooting

The checklist for scene analysis introduced in chapter 1 can easily be edited to emphasize analysis of sound track elements and functions using musical terms. In the following version, Steps 4 and 5 have been combined to avoid redundancy and the specific musical terms discussed in this chapter are listed, along with the background-foreground functional relation:

> 1. Background and general information.
> 2. Synopsis of the scene.
> 3. Shot list.
> 4.–5. Description of the sound track elements and their balance; description and evaluation of the sound track (tempo, rhythm & meter, volume, timbre [distortion, frequency, register], texture [density & liveliness, background/foreground]).
> 6. If needed, a summary statement about the sound track in the scene.

In the following text, the steps are identified in parentheses at the beginning of the paragraph or section.

(Background and general information) *Trzy Kolory: Bialy (White,* 1994) is the second film in director Krzysztof Kieslowski's *Three Colors* trilogy. *Bleu (Blue), Bialy (White),* and *Rouge (Red,* 1994) were released in a space of less than two years and are based on the colors—and their symbolism—in the French flag. *Bialy* (Polish for "white") thus addresses equality (*egalité*)—or, more accurately, the struggle for equality in a poisoned relationship based on great inequality. Karol (Zbigniew Zamachowski) is a Polish hairdresser working in Paris. His wife, Dominique (Julie Delpy) not only divorces him for his inability to consummate the marriage but also hounds him with legal maneuvers until he is driven out of France. A pathological desire to prove himself equal to her (or is it really just revenge?) drives Karol to become a successful businessman (albeit partly by devious means) and to initiate a scheme whereby Dominique is eventually convicted of Karol's (faked) murder and is imprisoned. In the context of the trilogy, *Bialy* is the comedy (where *Rouge* is the romance and *Bleu* the redemption drama), but these genre labels in themselves cannot capture the complexities of identity, morality, and motivation that Kieslowski explores.

(Synopsis of the scene) Having returned to Poland, Karol is befriended by a professional card player, Mikolaj (Janusz Gajos), whose world-weariness leads him to hire Karol to shoot him. They agree to meet in an underground train station. A brief prelude to the scene (at 00:48:00) shows Karol spinning a coin (music starts under this), then Dominique in her Paris apartment, apparently pulled emotionally by desire for the absent Karol. Then cut to Karol descending a wide stairs into an empty train station (00:48:30) and looking for Mikolaj, who emerges abruptly from behind a pillar. They talk to settle terms, Karol fires the gun (whose bullet is a blank), and the two sit to talk afterward. A simple cut outdoors initiates the subsequent scene.

(Shot list) Rather than give a complete shot list, as we did for the analysis examples in chapter 1, we group the shots according to action:

1.–3. Prelude
4.–5. Karol walks into the train station (Figure 2-13).
5b.–18. Mikolaj appears (00:49:20); the gun shot (00:50:35) (Figure 2-14). This segment is made up of 2-shots and shot-reverse shot sets.
18b.–30. Conversation after the gun shot (end with cut to outdoors 00:52:56). This segment is also made up of 2-shots and shot-reverse shot sets.

(Description and evaluation of the sound track) In the Prelude, the basic tempo of the sound track, including that of the music, is slow. Each of the four

Figure 2-13. *Trzy Kolory: Bialy (White)*. Karol enters the underground train station.

Figure 2-14. *Trzy Kolory: Bialy* (*White*). Karol shoots Mikolaj.

sound "moments" has its own speed, emphasizing a sense of parallelism but separation: the coin toss is fast (whirring), Karol's inhale–exhale is deliberate, the silence in the first moments of Dominique's shot is "empty," and her exhale vectorized, increasing in speed to the end. It also increases in volume, like a musical crescendo. The coin spinning on the wood table is a mid-register, relatively loud sound that has a hollow quality, as if the microphone were lying on the table and catching the sound as much through the table as through the air. The coin's abrupt stop under Karol's hand has the effect of a stinger, but music picks up almost immediately with a slightly nervous figure in a very high register, and a distinct, plainly foregrounded melody in a low oboe register (low for the oboe, that is; it is still a middle register overall) sounds against Shot 2, just making room enough that we can hear Karol's subdued inhalation of breath.

As the Prelude continues, the melody overlaps into Shot 3, and Karol's exhalation persists, too. The music is alone for a few seconds as Dominique begins to walk to camera left but, then, in parallel to Shot 2, pauses during her strong inhale and exhale, which distorts to something like a hiss. The texture in the Prelude, then, is initially monophonic—all we hear is the coin spinning. The oboe melody dominates so strongly that we might say that the monophony continues, but the pattern of breathing eventually puts effects into (polyphonic) competition with the music.

After Dominique's exhale, music picks up again and overlaps for 1 or 2 sec into the next segment, competing with loud, sharp, reverberant sounds of Karol walking down the stairs into the train station. After a brief pause, music starts again, but this time, after an initial stinger (an oddly dull sound against the harsh effects sounds), the music is mostly a-melodic, although its registers are very distinct (low clarinet sounds, high string and wind notes). The tempo of the music is slow, its mood suspenseful. The exaggeratedly reverberant footfalls continue, the last of them coming in the form of a stinger as Mikolaj emerges from behind a post (music goes out with it). Throughout this segment, music and effects are separate-but-equal layers—again, an essentially polyphonic texture.

Once the two men begin talking, the sharp footfall effects disappear (after two or three "hangers-on"), music is gone, and dialogue is strongly foregrounded (its volume at or above the level of the oboe melody earlier), although several strong intakes of breath early in the conversation recall the previous high-register noises. The environmental echo is greatly diminished. From this point until the gunshot, the texture is again functionally monophonic: dialogue is alone (nor is there any competition, as the speakers never overlap—in fact, there are silences between most of their sentences). Within that dialogue, we could also speak of differences in tempo (Karol speaks more quickly—and says more—than Mikolaj, suggesting nervousness) and in register (Karol's voice is higher than Mikolaj's).

With the sharp sound of the gunshot and the strong, echoing reverberation in its aftermath, the harsh, high-register hissing sounds of the locale return in force, continuing until the two sit down, then for most of the remainder in Karol's loud intakes of breath, the dropping of the gun, and the envelope with money. Given how persistent these sounds are, we can speak of melody and accompaniment texture in this segment: dialogue is clearly foregrounded, but a continuing pattern of sound effects "accompanies" it. In the final seconds music enters quietly but its vamping is in a tempo noticeably faster than anything we have heard in recent minutes; the music rises in volume and speed very quickly, rushing into the cut to outdoors for the next scene.

(Summary statement) The restrained (slow) tempos in all the sound track elements are consistent with the narrative situations (Karol's strange, long-distance emotional effect on Dominique; Mikolaj's intention to carry out his wish to die, Karol's uncertain participation), as is the simplicity of the texture overall (predominantly monophonic with some variation). Volume and timbre, on the other hand, combine to make both Prelude and the shooting scene slightly unnerving, suspenseful.

Example for Sound Track Analysis Using Musical Terms (2): *Atonement*, Main-Title Sequence and First Scene

In the recent film *Atonement* (2007), the first sounds are effects—birds chirping, heard against the last two of four studio credits and quickly joined by a sharp mechanical sound (something like "zzzzt"), which viewers recognize in

---

A good clean recording of the way a gun sounds normally on the firing range is great, but it doesn't have that much emotional impact. Often what works is recording a gun where there's an interesting reverberant space and letting it echo. For the parking garage gunshots [in Terminator 2 (1991)] we actually went to the parking garages under Skywalker and recorded the gun which was loud but wasn't all that interesting. Finally we took two-by-fours, slapped them together, and recorded the slapping echo in the garages. Then we added that to the sound of a real gunshot. It fattens the sound and makes it much more interesting.

—Gary Rydstrom[16]

retrospect as the carriage return of a manual typewriter. The letter-by-letter presentation of the main title against the sounds of typing is no surprise, then, nor is the typing out of "England" during the "establishing shot" of a large English country house (the house is a scale model of the actual house in which the action takes place). Typing, strongly rhythmic and foregrounded, continues as the camera pans slowly across what is clearly a child's room until it reaches Briony (Saoirse Ronan; see Figure 2-15). The typewriter sounds continue undiminished and unchallenged, then music enters to compete, in the form of a single repeated piano note not rhythmically synchronized with the typing (an obvious counterpoint).

As the scene continues, the typing stops, Briony gathers her papers and walks out of the room in a determined, march-like gait. As soon as the typing stops, the music takes over (moving at a similar pace) and we hear Briony's theme over her procession through the house to her mother's drawing room. All the while, typing sounds continue, now synchronized with the music (indeed, rhythms within the music—note that the melody moves at a slower pace than the elements of the accompaniment (including the typewriter), suggesting a certain disjunction in mood. All stop abruptly with two loud chords, both stingers tightly synchronized, the first with a door closing, the second with a jump cut to Briony and her mother seated inside the room.

The charming anachronism of the manual typewriter does help to suggest time and place before the opening titles are past, and the volume and tempo are plausible. The typewriter is also strongly linked to the character of Briony herself: single-minded, brisk, and one might imagine slightly "brittle," like the

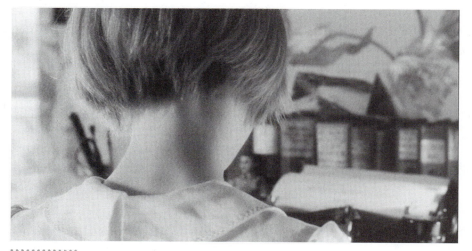

Figure 2-15. *Atonement.* Briony types.

sound of the typewriter key striking. Like the disparity between melody and accompaniment, this brittleness suggests both the charming and the slightly disturbing, a premonition of the flaws that have tragic consequences not only for Robbie (James McAvoy) and Briony's older sister Cecilia (Keira Knightley) but also for others in the household, including Briony herself.

Summary

Musical terminology is much more specific and concrete than most terms for sound analysis. In this chapter, we introduced a number of musical terms, defined them, and then extended their meanings to sound in general. The terms cover broad distinctions in musical materials, including rhythm, meter, volume, timbre, and texture.

EXERCISE 1: ANALYSIS OF SOUND TRACK ELEMENTS (AFTER ALTMAN, JONES, AND TATROE)

Rick Altman, McGraw Jones, and Sonia Tatroe have developed a method of graphic notation for the close analysis of sound track elements in the context of film scenes. As they describe it, the "method involves plotting . . . relative volumes for the various sound components[, along with] a shot-by-shot breakdown, plot description, and important dialogue." They assert that "this configuration encourages a new kind of analysis by subordinating image data to the representation of sound and therefore foregrounding the relationship among sound components."[17] A small portion of one of their graphs is reproduced in Figure 2-16. This is for the opening scene in *Backstreet* (1932).[18]

Note that the authors have chosen a single sound track element, volume. That is because they are interested in showing the development of the complex, continuous-volume sound track. The graphing method could, as they say, "easily be applied to other variables, such as frequency or reverberation."[19] At the left, shots are listed, with a description of what's represented and internal motion in the shot, if any. The numbers running down the center of the figure are seconds, measured from the beginning of the scene. Numbers on the horizontal axis are relative volume, from silent (0) to the loudest (and presumably distorted) sounds in the sound track (7). As the authors put it, "Volume levels are based solely on careful listening; because individual sound components are not presented on isolated channels, they cannot be analyzed with oscilloscopes or computer software." On these axes of time and volume, then, the three sound track elements are measured.

The results: Dialogue is always audible over effects and music (as in Seconds 1–17), but both music and effects are both present throughout and are "dialed up" once the speech stops (Seconds 18–20), so that the total volume of the sound track remains more or less constant (at Level 4 or 5) throughout.

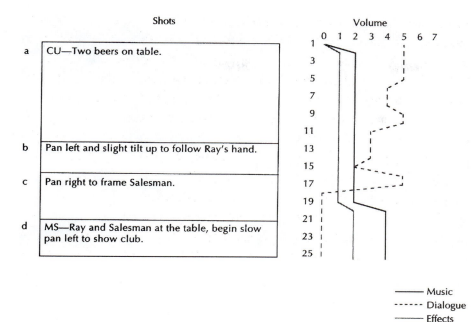

Figure 2-16. Altman, Jones, and Tatroe, beginning of a graph of sound track elements (for volume) in *Backstreet*, opening scene.

EXERCISE 2: USING GRAPHIC DISPLAYS FOR SOUND (AFTER WIERZBICKI)

Film music scholar James Wierzbicki has developed a method of graphic nota-tion for sound track events in connection with his study of Alfred Hitchcock's *The Birds* (1963).[20] This film is a special case, to be sure, because its sound track has no music—instead, it includes musically constructed sound effects tracks consisting of bird sounds developed from electronic sound sources. Neverthe-less, the manner of graphic notation that Wierzbicki uses here could also be employed effectively as a way to represent more traditional sound tracks, even those including music.

The scene is the birds' second attack on the house (DVD timing 01:40:32–01:41:30)—screen stills from the beginning and end of the scene are given in Figures 2-17 and 2-18; in the former, Mitch (Rod Taylor) and the others wait after boarding up the house, in the latter Mitch fights off a gull trying to enter through the broken window pane. Basing his comments in part on production sketches for the sound track, Wierzbicki describes the sound track as "a series of clearly distinguishable sonic events each of which has a measurable dura-tion." He lists the elements of this progression for the first minute of the scene (Table 2-1) and then converts them into graphic form (Figure 2-19). Finally,

Figure 2-17. *The Birds.* Waiting for the birds to attack.

in Figure 2-20, the progression is reduced to its basic, "musical" effects. Figures 2-19 and 2-20 are essentially simple time and pitch level graphs in which the horizontal x axis is time and the vertical y axis is pitch from low to high.

The sounds listed in Table 2-1 were converted into unique symbols mapped out on these coordinates in Figure 2-19 ("chirping" sounds are indicated by dashed horizontal blocks, "flutter" sounds by tremolo marks, "chorus" sounds

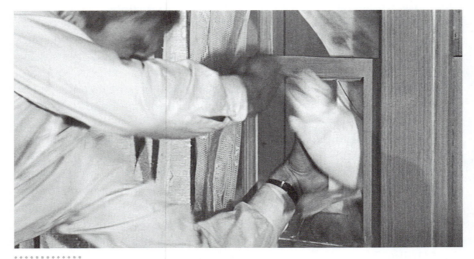

Figure 2-18. *The Birds.* Mitch fights off a gull.

Table 2-1 *The Birds*, Sonic events, second attack on the house, 0:00–0:60 (James Wierzbicki).

Chirping sound	0:00–0:03	Steady noise	0:21–0:32
Flutter of wings	0:03–0:05	Distant "bark"	0:32–0:33
"Distant chorus"	0:08–0:12	Wooden knocks	0:38–0:39
Flutter surge	00:12–0:13	Loud "yelps"	0:39–0:40
Soft "barks"	0:15–0:16	"Strangle" sound	0:41–0:43
Flutter surge	0:16–0:17	"Strangle" sound	0:45–0:46
Flutter surge	0:17–0:19	"Chorus" swoop	0:50–0:53
"Yelps"	0:19–0:20	Breaking glass	0:54–0:55

by vertical blocks, "barks" by standard quarter notes, "yelps" by **accent**-headed notes, "wooden knocks" by note heads without **stems**, "strangle" sounds by X-headed notes, and the sound of breaking glass by a jagged-edged oval). In Figure 2-20, a reduction of the sequence to its broadest effects, the vectorized increase in sound (or musical crescendo) and the "breaking glass" effect near the end are the only elements remaining.

In constructing graphics of this kind, it helps to have the variety of the symbols available in musical notation, for their compactness as much as for their widely understood meanings, but their use is not absolutely necessary: *pp* could be rendered by "very soft," for example, and crescendo by "getting louder."

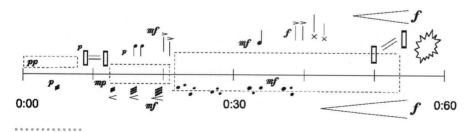

Figure 2-19. *The Birds*. Graph of the events listed in Table 2-1 (James Wierzbicki).

Figure 2-20. *The Birds*. Reduction of Figure 2-19 (James Wierzbicki).

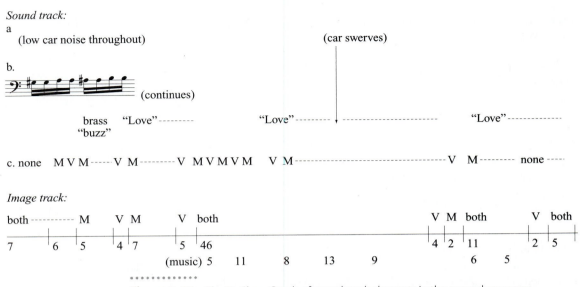

Figure 2-21. *The Big Sleep.* Graph of sound track elements in the second car scene.

At the same time, because standard musical notation is itself a time/pitch-level coordinate graph, it would be quite easy to introduce melodic fragments into the analysis, as we have done in Figure 2-21. The design of this graph, for a brief scene near the end of *The Big Sleep* (1946; 01:43:54), is somewhat different from Figure 2-19, however, as we have replaced the y-coordinate with three linear strands, each representing one of the sound track elements (a = effects track, b = music, c = speech). The **image track** is articulated by shots and durations in seconds. Within the extended Shot 7 (46 sec), the articulations in the music are marked. In the music line, "br." is "brass instruments," and "love" is the film's love theme (which we heard for the first time during a parallel car scene earlier, when the outcome was somewhat rancorous). In the speech line and in the image track line, "M" is Marlowe (Humphrey Bogart), and "V" is "Vivian" (Lauren Bacall). As the chart shows, the car effect and the underscoring are continuous throughout the scene, which is a conversation between the two characters (by the end of it they admit a romantic attraction to each other).

CHAPTER 3

Music, Sound, and the Space of Narrative
Concepts and Terminology

Introduction

Under normal circumstances, sound is closely tied to physical space. The basic human cognition of sound is to "anchor" it in an object—a person speaks, a door creaks, a dove coos, the radio plays. Those objects necessarily reside in some physical space (the space of the real world). Narrative complicates matters, however. A storyteller speaks and in that sense is the object-source of that speech, but he or she also conjures up a fantasy world whose own "objects" can be the sources of sound, as when the storyteller attributes dialogue to a character ("Then George said, 'I don't know what you mean'").

The cinematic narrative complicates things still further because it directs most of the attention to that conjured-up fantasy world, so that the primary vehicle of narrative is no longer speech but visual representation. In film, the role of a storyteller is sometimes taken over by voice-over narration, someone unseen who speaks on the sound track, but there is always an "implied narrator" (because narrative films tell stories, there must be a storyteller "somewhere"). Therefore, the viewer-listener's cognition of sound is obliged to operate at two levels: the level of the narration (implied or spoken) and the level of sound in the fantasy or screen world.

"Background" and "source," respectively, are terms commonly used for sound in these two levels, but as we noted in chapter 1, "background" is too easily confused with the subordinate element in the foreground/background pair. (You'll see what we mean if we say that in most cases of voice-over narration background sound is foregrounded.) The terms "onscreen" and "offscreen" do not solve the problem because "screen" refers simply to the part of the film world that is within the camera's frame at any particular moment. "Offscreen," then, is whatever part of that filmic world we cannot see in the frame but may already have seen or may imaginatively project from the part we can see (recall those chirping bird sounds in the opening minute or so of *Atonement* (2007)). Partly to solve this problem, but also partly to draw attention to the fundamental importance of visual representation in film, scholars have borrowed the term "diegetic" from literary theory to refer to the world of the narrative, the screen world or world of the film. Thus, "nondiegetic" refers to the level of narration: voice-over narration is nondiegetic—and so is underscoring.

In this chapter, we first consider the diegetic/nondiegetic pair, which is essential to the analysis and interpretation of sound and music in film but from which all kinds of ambiguities arise. Then, we will cover a number of specific traits and devices of diegetic sound related to the **onscreen/offscreen** pair and to sound perspective. Finally, we will discuss some specialized but commonly used devices that exploit the boundaries between diegetic and nondiegetic space.

Diegetic/Nondiegetic Music and Narrative

At its most basic level, diegetic sound refers to everything that can be heard by characters in the film. Nondiegetic sound, by contrast, cannot be heard by the characters. Consider, for example, the conversation scene from *Catch Me If You Can* (2002) that we discussed in the Introduction to Part I and have mentioned several times since. The radio on Carl Hanratty's desk produces sounds (Bing Crosby singing "Mele Kalikimaka") that Carl can hear and that Frank also hears through the telephone receiver. The melancholy underscoring near the end of the scene, on the other hand, is heard only by the audience—if we understand this music as mimicking Frank's mood, we do not assume that it is literally going through his mind at the time (in fact, that would be highly unlikely because the music continues when Frank speaks). Similarly, in the Boston Common scene from *Good Will Hunting* (1997), the dialogue and ambient sounds of birds and traffic are diegetic but the music that enters near the end is nondiegetic; and again the same in "The Shooting" from *Trzy Kolory: Bialy* (*White*, 1994): All the noises in the underground train station could plausibly be heard by the characters, but the music could not.

The typewriter sounds in *Atonement*, on the other hand, pose a problem. We can assume in retrospect that Briony can hear the diegetic sounds that actually first appear behind the opening titles, but what about the typewriter sounds that continue after she stops and walks away? Have they simply been transferred to the underscoring, or are they sounds of typing still mentally resounding in Briony's ears? The music's marchlike gait, which seems synchronized with her walking, also threatens to lose its nondiegetic independence and join in the action, so to speak—not to mention the stinger chords at the end, which are not so much music as sound effect.

It is by no means uncommon for ambiguities of this kind to arise, especially in connection with rhythmic mechanical sounds such as a typewriter. In

Shall We Dance (1937), Pete Peters (Fred Astaire) is sailing to America to make his debut as "Petrov," purportedly a Russian ballet dancer. To conceal his identity, Pete must refrain from openly dancing in the vernacular "jazz" style that he prefers. He therefore descends to the engine room, where the pistons of the ship's engines establish the rhythm so that the song "Slap That Bass" seems to emerge from it. Something similar occurs at the beginning of *Love Me Tonight* (1932). Here, Paris in the early morning slowly awakens in rhythm. We hear the sound of a bell chiming the hour, a lone bicyclist, then the sound of a pick ax, all laying down a basic rhythm. The hammering of cobblers, the beating of rugs, the sounds of a factory all join in rhythm, suggesting the vitality and common purpose of the city. This symphony of sound ultimately dissolves into Maurice Chevalier singing "That's the Song of Paree."

Where *Love Me Tonight* moves from sound to music, another early sound film, *Das Testament des Dr. Mabuse* (1933), essentially reverses the procedure. The film starts with very dissonant music over the title only to dissolve into the oppressive rhythm of the machine stamping out a triple meter. The opening scene, furthermore, begins *in medias res*: Hofmeister has slipped into the Forger's factory and has been forced to hide in a room (Figure 3-1). The scene plays essentially as silent film, the machine being the only noise on the sound track.

Underscoring, then, can move with ease—and speed—between diegetic and nondiegetic functions. If we are not bothered by music that lacks anchoring in the diegesis, equally we are not bothered by music that begins onscreen and then wanders offscreen or even hovers uncertainly between. This is business-as-usual in musicals: in *Meet Me in St. Louis* (1944), for instance, one number has Judy Garland singing a verse and chorus to accompaniment of a piano that we see (initially anyway), but then she sings a second chorus to the accompaniment of an invisible orchestra. This technique of passing from one to the other scholar Rick Altman has named "audio dissolve."[1] Although common in musicals, the audio dissolve occurs in dramatic films as well, as we shall see later in this chapter while discussing the lead-in to Rick's flashback in the after-hours scene from *Casablanca* (1942).

EXAMPLE FOR DIEGETIC AND NONDIEGETIC MUSIC: *GLORY*, BOSTON PARTY SCENE

A scene from early in the Civil War film *Glory* (1989) will illustrate both the distinction between diegetic and nondiegetic music and some of the ambiguities that can arise from them. The city (Boston) is the same one depicted in *Good Will Hunting* and the scene is probably just a few blocks away at most from the Common (because both films use location shooting, this could be literally true), but in *Glory* the time is about 130 years earlier. A party is underway to honor Massachusetts officers who fought in the recent battle of Antietam (September 1862). It is one of the few "non-military" scenes in the film, which stars Matthew Broderick, Denzel Washington, and Morgan Freeman and recounts

Figure 3-1. *Das Testament des Dr. Mabuse.* A distressed Hofmeister (Karl Meixner) tries to think amidst the din of the machinery in the Forger's factory.

the early history of the 54th Massachusetts Infantry, the first regularly formed African-American regiment in the United States Army.

The party scene begins at about 00:09:30, lasts just over 5 min, and is heavily scored—only about 30 sec are without music. Up to this point, more than half the film has had nondiegetic orchestral music: music begins with the opening titles and runs about 3½ min until the beginning of the Antietam battle scene; a second cue begins at 00:05:30, as Captain Robert Gould Shaw (Broderick) rises from the ground after the battle, and continues until he enters the field hospital (1 min and 45 sec in all).

The extended party scene that follows breaks down readily into three parts, the first being Shaw's decidedly self-conscious entry into the party, the second a conversation with the Governor and others about forming the regiment, and the third a final conversation with his friend Forbes (Cary Elwes) carried on outdoors. We will be concerned here only with the first part and its transition into the second.

The scene opens with a shot of a rose window, which is quickly revealed as a skylight providing illumination to the upper end of a staircase (top frame in

Figure 3-2). Music is heard from a piano, a pastoral piece stylistically appropriate for the era (by early 19th-century composer Franz Schubert; Figure 3-3). Our first reaction, then, is to regard the music as belonging to the physical environment, as diegetic, but the volume level is quite unrealistically high. Eventually we will learn that the music *is* meant to be diegetic—we see the pianist briefly in the general shot of the room (Figure 3-4), but sound levels are never quite appropriate (even when we see the piano close by in the background of segment two). The transition to this scene was achieved by a short lap dissolve (overlapping images) from an Army field hospital where, among other things, an amputation was being performed—sound participates, as the hospital sounds mingle briefly with the music. In the course of the shot, the camera pulls back, moves down and to the left to reveal Shaw (in medium shot) descending the stairs (middle frame of Figure 3-2). He is in his parents' upper-class Boston house on his way to join the large party in progress.

After a point-of-view shot (from the staircase looking down on people below and traveling across them as if Shaw is scanning what he sees below him) and a sudden, **insert**ed close-up of a plate of food, with a woman and an older man talking (the man takes and is about to eat a small tomato), comes what we will take as an establishing shot, a general view of a large room with partygoers. Sound, on the other hand, is oddly unsettled. The piano music does provide a suitable aural counterpart to the establishing shot: its unrealistic sound levels and broad stylistic-chronological reference would work just as well as nondiegetic music. A generalized sound of party conversation is appropriate, but it is undermined by odd moments (particularly by unusually loud laughter and whispering in the close-up mentioned earlier), and the result is that we begin to suspect that the sound is subjective—specifically, it is ambient sound as filtered through Shaw's mind and emotions. This is still diegetic—unlike the generalized sense of emotion in the scenes from *Catch Me If You Can* and *Good Will Hunting*, we are hearing diegetic sounds as filtered, distorted, by Shaw's own hearing and attention.

All this is confirmed in subsequent shots: (1) Shaw in medium shot as he walks through the doorway (lower frame of Figure 3-2) (at this point, the crowd sounds begin to mingle with a wordless (and nondiegetic) boys chorus

Figure 3-2. *Glory.* Boston Party Scene: (a) Dissolve from previous scene; (b) Shaw descending the staircase; (c) entering the main room of the party.

Figure 3-3. *Glory.* Boston Party Scene: Franz Schubert, *Drei Klavierstücke*, D.946, No. 2.

Figure 3-4. *Glory.* Boston Party Scene: A pianist plays on the far side of the room.

(as the piano fades out)—this music continues, mixed with bits of conversation, and gradually grows louder); (2) another extreme close-up, now of two women talking as they look at Shaw; (3) cut back to a close-up of Shaw (another soldier enters the room behind him), then (4) away to another close-up of a woman laughing, (5) again back to Shaw, (6) then a medium shot of an officer in a wheelchair entering the room, (7) back to one last close-up of Shaw before the nondiegetic music goes abruptly out and the diegetic piano music returns as Thomas (Andre Braugher) addresses him (we see Shaw in medium shot over Thomas's shoulder).

Until the greeting from Thomas, Shaw maintains his distance from the crowd, the shot/reverse-shot series emphasizes that distance (it jumps back and forth between close-ups of him and of people who seem to be at some physical distance from him), and the disjointed quality of the sound track corresponds. The uncertain diegetic status of the piano music is followed by Shaw's mental filtering of room sounds, and the intrusion of nondiegetic music over them. The crux of the scene is reached, not in conversation, but in Shaw's rapidly increasing discomfort (Figure 3-5a; music here, as in the scene from *Good Will Hunting*, contributes much of the emotional intensity). Rather than concluding and making a transition to another scene, this first part is simply cut off by Thomas's greeting (Figure 3-5b). There is a strong sense in which this moment explains everything before it as subjective: with a sudden return to the real world comes a normal mode of hearing.

The basic categories are defined easily enough: the piano, crowd, and speech are all diegetic; the wordless chorus is nondiegetic. Before Thomas's

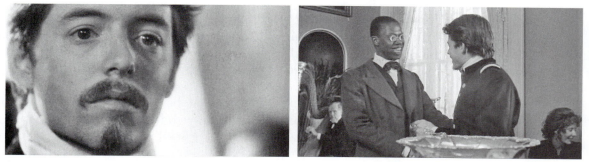

Figure 3-5. *Glory*. Boston Party Scene: (a) Shaw is deep in thought, disconnected from the   a | b
party; (b) Thomas greets Shaw.

greeting, however, the diegetic sounds, including the music, were interpreted, filtered, as if they were sounds "narrated" for us by Shaw.

See Figure 3-6 for an example of a particularly subtle interplay between diegetic and nondiegetic within the continuously playing music for a dance.

Figure 3-6. *Shakespeare in Love* (1996). The de Lesseps' dance (00:27:58–00:30:30). The music is diegetic, mostly restricted to the historically accurate ensemble seen in the background—flute, lute, harp, viols and tambourine. As Will (Joseph Fiennes) integrates himself into the dance (00:28:47), the viols are subtly augmented by modern strings, with a tremolo growing ever-more pronounced until Viola (Gwyneth Paltrow) says: "Master Shakespeare" (00:29:07), when the tremolo is transferred upward to the violins. The scoring retreats to the diegetic ensemble as she moves on to Lord Wessex (Colin Firth) (00:29:18). When she returns to Will (00:29:29), the scoring shifts again, now dominated by modern strings. The style of the music is also transformed. Lord Wessex drags Will away (00:29:58) and the modern instruments again recede, although not as far as before and the musical style also remains the new one, emphasized by drum fills at the ends of phrases. With the shot of the exterior of the house (00:30:30), the orchestra takes over completely.

Onscreen/Offscreen Sound and Music

The diegetic/nondiegetic pair refer to the status of sounds within (or without) the physical world depicted in the narrative, or the set of relations induced specifically by what is presented to us in the frame and the sounds that occur in the sound track.

The basic categories of these relations can be expressed by combinations of the terms. The first of these, diegetic-onscreen, is certainly the default case: we see within the frame what we expect to see in the film world (Will and Sean talking on a park bench, not a view of Sean's empty office or an insert of, say, the Voyager I spacecraft while they talk). Diegetic-offscreen is also common: a room is shown onscreen but we hear someone speaking or music playing with the correct volume and other sound qualities that would match another room connected to the one we see. Nondiegetic-onscreen, on the other hand, is much less common but is likely to be invoked when it is clear that an on-screen character imagines or remembers speech or music and the performance of that music is visualized. Nondiegetic-offscreen is the default case for voice-over narration and underscoring, but it can also apply to characters such as ghosts whose voices can be heard but who have no definable place in the physical world.

In this section, we will first stress offscreen sound and then several ways in which offscreen and onscreen sound interact.

OFFSCREEN SOUND

Without evidence to the contrary, we will take offscreen sound as simply an extension of onscreen space. For example, dialogue scenes that utilize the shot/reverse-shot syntax will often cut away at some point in the conversation to the non-speaking character. During this reaction shot, clearly, the speech that continues will be offscreen. The reaction shot is so common that we seldom pay attention to the fact that the shot itself creates offscreen sound, which has the effect of also binding offscreen and onscreen space more tightly together.

A brief but narratively important scene late in *The Big Sleep* (1946) provides a simple example (01:43:54). Philip Marlowe and Vivian Sternwood, characters played by Humphrey Bogart and Lauren Bacall, have escaped from one dangerous encounter and are heading toward another (the final scene of the film). They are shown in a car (Figure 3-7), and they discuss their situation (although Marlowe, in fact, does most of the talking). They were clearly attracted to one another early on in the film, but here they admit, for the first time, genuine romantic feelings.

The scene lasts less than 2 min and consists of twelve shots. (This scene, by the way, is the one that we graphed under Exercise 2 at the end of ch. 2.) Three of the twelve are 2-shots of Vivian and Marlowe: at beginning and end,

This overrunning of one person's image with another person's voice is a method peculiar to the talkies; it is one of the devices which help the talkies to tell a story faster than a silent film could tell it, and faster than it could be told on stage.

—Alfred Hitchcock, on the significance of offscreen sound to the reaction shot.[2]

Figure 3-7. *The Big Sleep*. Second car scene, Vivian and Marlowe.

as well as one in the middle. The others are alternating close-ups of the two characters. At several points one character is shown in close-up while we hear the other speaking. The effect is not only to bind offscreen and onscreen space (limited although those differences are in such a situation) but in this case also to highlight the emotional resonance in this newly forming couple. (See Figure 3-8 for another example of offscreen sound.)

When offscreen sound is localizable as an object that *could* be shown but is not—that is, a sound that suggests an object is more than simply background—we refer to it as "**sound-off**" (short for "sound offscreen"). Examples include doors, footsteps, telephones, and so forth. Such noises are commonly used as a means of establishing a scene, either at the beginning of the sequence itself, where an offscreen sound can motivate a cut to the location, or to introduce new characters (and so also a new direction) to the scene. Off-screen bomb sounds, for example, are used this way in *Lawrence of Arabia* (1962) (at 00:37:58). The sound of the bombs interrupts a conversation between Lawrence and Colonel Brighton; a cut to an encampment of Arabs being attacked by Turkish planes follows.

As a "noise" in the diegetic world, music can also be used in this manner. In the opening of *The Broadway Melody* (1929), for instance, music wafts from

Figure 3-8. *Trois Couleurs: Bleu* (*Blue*, 1993). Julie (Juliette Binoche) listens as a man, evading thugs, runs through her building knocking on doors (00:34:48-00:36:04); the scene is rendered wholly in offscreen sound.

a window of a music store before a cut shows the interior of the shop. In *The Bride of Frankenstein* (1935), the monster hears the sound of a violin and gradually finds his way to the house of its blind player; and the main-title sequence of *The Birdcage* (1996) includes (apparently) nondiegetic underscoring that is revealed as a stage performance of "We Are Family" after the camera moves gradually across the water, beach, and street into the interior of the club.

A sound-off can also be used to signal the end of a scene. In *42nd Street* (1933), the offscreen sound of a door closes to signal Julian (Warner Baxter) leaving the office, which sets up the tagline: "New York will see its first triple funeral."

The **voice-off** is similar to the sound-off, except that it highlights the voice. A simple voice-off will occur with a cut to a reaction shot. More characteristic, perhaps, are introductory words, like "hello," that announce the presence of a new character before we see him or her. A voice-off will sometimes involve a clear mismatch in sound scale (that is, linking sound volume and timbre to shot scale).

The film in *Emma* (1996) contains several excellent examples of the voice-off technique. At 00:13:58, Emma (Gwyneth Paltrow) and Harriet (Toni Collette) are walking along a creek, where they are presented in an extreme long shot, often even obscured by trees. Nevertheless, their dialogue is rendered with the clarity of a normal 2-shot, into which they eventually move. Another example appears shortly thereafter (00:15:16). Emma and Harriet are doing embroidery under a canopy. Again, they are first shown in extreme long shot but with the dialogue suggesting much closer proximity. The mismatch encourages a series of cuts that will eventually bring the image in line with the sound. At the end of this sequence, we are once again shown an extreme long shot, but this time the dialogue declines in clarity, moving in tandem with the distance as framed. A pattern of mismatched scale of image and sound continues throughout the film and seems calculated to coincide with the mismatched romantic pairings that Emma attempts to bring about.

ONSCREEN/OFFSCREEN SOUND INTERACTION: EXAMPLES

Filmmakers are very sensitive to the play between onscreen and offscreen sound. One of many striking examples we could cite occurs in *The Apartment* (1960). Bud (Jack Lemmon) has just been promoted and is settling into his office (00:43:00). As he is hanging up his overcoat, an offscreen voice offers congratulations. He finishes putting away his jacket, and responds, "Hi, fellows." Only at this point is there a cut to four men entering his office. This, then, initiates the scene proper where the men remind Bud that he is beholden to them for his promotion.

As everyone moves further into the office, the camera reframes to incorporate Bud into the group. In a sense, the camera here entertains the perspective of the men: "all for one and one for all." Nevertheless, the desk intervenes to keep Bud somewhat apart from the group (Figure 3-9a). When he is accused of not having the right "attitude," he is separated from the group with a cut for his response. There is another accusation, this time delivered completely offscreen with the camera locked on Bud through his response. A reverse shot of the four men brings a third accusation. The shot is reversed again for Bud's response. Another accusation begins offscreen before cutting back to the man to complete his line. One of the men complains of the trouble he's been having because Bud no longer lets him into the apartment. Bud's response occurs in another reverse shot.

Next comes a cut back to the full group, with the four men now clearly separated from Bud, and one of the men delivers a threat. Bud responds briefly, but this is followed by a more pointed threat. At this moment (00:44:03) Jeff (Fred MacMurray) enters, he and Bud begin to converse, and the other men leave. Bud closes the door and returns to his desk, sits down, and a relatively uncomplicated shot/reverse-shot sequence follows, but without reaction shots and offscreen sound. One exception is an odd moment with the close-up of a mirror (00:45:01): Bud delivers a line while being somewhat out of focus (Figure 3-9b) and

Figure   3-9. *The   Apartment.* a Sound and the dynamic play of b onscreen and offscreen space. c

Jeff's face appears in the broken mirror for his response (Figure 3-9c). The lack of departure from onscreen sound emphasizes the strangeness of this particular exchange, the distorted image of each man suggesting each character's relation to the mirror—or rather to Fran (Shirley MacLaine), its owner.

In *Lost in Translation* (2003), Bob (Bill Murray) is jetlagged, having just arrived in Tokyo. He is in the hotel bar where a woman is singing. The sound track is filled with ambient chatter and on the first shot of Bob some of the chatter grows more distinct. Offscreen voices indicate that they have recognized him. As they address him, the camera pans from Bob to reveal two young American businessmen. The two continue talking on a cut back to Bob, where he briefly responds, then gets up while the other voices carry on. The overall effect of the exchange is Bob's refusal to engage the other characters, who remain defined almost entirely by their offscreen voices. The fact that the voices remain offscreen minimizes the importance of these characters, while also suggesting a narrative direction that the film will not follow. (See Figure 3-10 for an additional example with commentary.)

Figure 3-10. *Lara Croft: Tomb Raider* (2001). In this scene (00:07:34–00:09:30), Manfred Powell (Iain Glen), who has been charged with finding the Key, stands before the Council of Illuminati to report his progress. Despite a large amount of offscreen dialogue and wide shifts of shot scale, the dialogue remains at a constant level and squarely centered in the stereo field. The large space is cued, however, through the use of pronounced reverb.

Partly due to the reverberant space, the tempo of the dialogue is quite slow, appropriate for the formal setting and to the gravity of the discussion. Much of the head of the Council's dialogue is delivered offscreen, which coupled with the lack of any sound perspective has the effect of disassociating his voice from his body, allowing the words to transcend the limits of the character. (It should be noted in this respect that offscreen dialogue is not always rendered thus in the film.) The use of apparently nondiegetic singing voices at the opening of the scene and bells tolling periodically throughout reinforce the ecclesiastical setting suggested by the exterior shot of the Santa Maria Della Salute (Venice) in the establishing sequence. The interior, however, is the Painted Hall at the Old Royal Naval College (Greenwich), a secular space appropriate to a secret society. The mysterious quality of the quest for the Key is emphasized by the brooding strings and especially the thrice stated piano figure that displace the voices from the sound track later in the scene as talk turns to the Key itself. The crackling thunder interspersed with the instrumental music adds to the effect, portending that the Key will unlock something ominous and supernatural.

AMBIGUITY OF OFFSCREEN SOUND: UNDERDETERMINATION OF SOUND

Sound is often underdetermined, that is, not defined down to all its possible naturalistic details. Depending on how it is rendered, a waterfall, for instance, sounds very much like applause, which is also similar to the rustling of leaves or the crackle of fire. Crumpling paper might likewise be mistaken for fire or fallen leaves in autumn. The crack of a baseball bat can sound like a tree branch snapping; the buzz of an insect like an electric saw or a malfunctioning radio tube. Indeed, the production of sound effects often depends on misrecognitions of just this sort: the hitting of high tension wires for the sound of a laser blast, or coconuts for horses' hooves.

A scene from *King Kong* (1933) plays with precisely this ambiguity. As the ship sails into the fog surrounding Skull Island, amorphous nondiegetic music enters, the first music heard since the opening credits. Gradually, a soft crackle can be heard. Jack says, "Listen. Do you hear anything?" The sound grows louder and an offscreen voice shouts "Breakers ahead!" A moment later, Jack says, "That's not breakers—that's drums." This confusion helps to establish the sense of Skull Island as a mysterious place. (Figures 3-11 and 3-12 give additional examples from other films, along with commentary.)

Figure 3-11. *Lawrence of Arabia*. After a beating at the hands of the Turkish army, Lawrence (Peter O'Toole) has gone to Jerusalem, abandoning his Arab comrades and vowing to be nothing more than a regular man. The establishing shot shows a marching band. As Lawrence enters the military compound, there is a cut to the interior of the compound and the music begins to echo rather significantly, to the point where the echo separates into its own channel, lagging significantly behind the source. Lawrence himself is almost stooping as he walks through the courtyard, even as the echo separates further and further from the source. The sound seems to split, go out of focus, representing Lawrence's own divisions and self-doubts. The importance of the music is emphasized by its continuation throughout the sequence as Lawrence moves through the building. It only goes out when Lawrence reaches the office where General Allenby (Jack Hawkins) and Prince Feisal (Alec Guinness) are waiting.

Figure 3-12. *The Apartment.* Ambiguity of offscreen sound: Near the end of the film, Fran (Shirley MacLaine) has come to realize that she loves Bud. As she is rushing up the stairs to his apartment she hears what sounds like a gunshot coming from Bud's apartment (02:03:11). Fearing the worst, she rushes to the door. Bud opens it to reveal a bottle of bubbling champagne. Here Fran's reaction to the offscreen bang allows us to see just how deeply she feels for Bud.

POINT OF VIEW SOUND

Point of view sound is rendered from the perspective of a character in the film. The effect is generally to increase our identification with that particular character whose hearing the sound track mimics. A very common example is a conversation heard over the telephone when a shot/reverse-shot structure is not used. The filtering of the voice to render a realistic telephone sound underlines the distance between the characters and in so doing increases our focus on the character we can see.

The first part of the Boston party scene from *Glory* clearly is point of view sound, as we hear speech and music filtered through Captain Shaw's ears and mind. A more recent film, *Lost in Translation*, contains a short example that effectively illustrates point of view sound. Bob is swimming laps while a water aerobics class is also taking place. The short scene all takes place from Bob's aural perspective, with the characteristic tone of his gentle sound and music dulled.

"Imagined sound" is a special case of point of view sound. Here, the sound track presents what a character is hearing in his or her head. A good example of this occurs in *The Bourne Ultimatum* (2007). Here Jason Bourne's numerous flashbacks are presented with distorted sound (and image). Such imagined sound may be a dream, memory, or hallucination; an internal monologue; or hearing something like music in one's head. For obvious reasons, the latter case is especially common in films about musicians. Another typical use is for an individual reading a message, letter, or passage from a book silently. A potentially more complex instance is when a character in a film also acts at one or more points as a voice-over narrator. Once we have associated the voice-over narration with a character in the diegesis, the sound can no longer be unambiguously nondiegetic. Instead, we hear a simple imagined sound if the character is onscreen, not shown speaking but nevertheless speaking in imagination.

Point of view sound, like the basic distinction between diegetic and nondiegetic, is open to many ambiguities. A good example to illustrate this point occurs in *The Graduate* (1967), where it is coupled with a sound advance. In this scene, Ben (Dustin Hoffman) is decked out in scuba gear that he received as a gift from his parents. As he reluctantly leaves the house to go to the pool to show off the equipment, all we hear is his heavy breathing, a point of view **sound match**ed to the image, which also has been matted to give the impression of seeing through a scuba mask. The matched perspective of image and sound continues into the water, separating only when the image changes to an external reverse shot. After the cut, the sound continues with what at first seems to be a return to point of view, but the sound of bubbles gradually dissolves into an externalized perspective as we become aware that a decrescendo in the sound is accompanying a slow tracking back of the camera. As the camera finally comes to rest on Ben in long shot, we hear his voice speaking in normal tones over this image of him isolated in the pool. With the cut we recognize that he is speaking on the phone with Mrs. Robinson (Anne Bancroft), whom he has agreed to meet for their first rendezvous. The **sound bridge** here serves to tie these scenes together, his isolation in the pool being literally answered by companionship with Mrs. Robinson.

The animated feature *Madagascar* (2005) manages the linking of the sound bridge with point of view sound in a somewhat different manner. In this case, the protagonist, Alex the Lion, is tranquilized and experiences a hallucinatory production number to the strains of "Candyman" (sung by Sammy Davis, Jr.). We easily recognize that at this moment we are perceiving things from Alex's perspective; ultimately, everything goes black and silent, a sign that Alex has fallen unconscious and probably a sign that the scene has ended. Because the screen is black we recognize that the next scene will emerge out of this dark silence and a sound bridge seems a likely way to make this transition. We do in fact hear voices: a sound bridge seems to be taking shape. As a shot opens with a wipe from the bottom revealing a matted half oval, however, we understand that the voices we had heard were not a sound bridge but a representation of Alex beginning to wake up, that is, a continuation of the point of view that had led into the silence to begin with. In this way the dark, silent join between the production number and the awakening is rationalized. After Alex is shot with the tranquilizer gun again, and the sequence repeats, this time with a highly sped up version of the production number follows. The screen goes momentarily dark, but this time we hear Alex speaking at the same time that we see big eyes—the same shape as the previous matte shot—floating in the darkness. It quickly becomes clear that these eyes belong to Alex, the continuity of shape with the previous emergence out of the dark silence cleverly allowing a seamless reversal here to the normal, external shot.

Offscreen Sound and Music in Relation to the Diegesis

In the following sections, we will discuss three of the most common conventions of sound design that take advantage of the ambiguity in diegetic/nondiegetic and onscreen/offscreen relations. These are voice-over narration, the audio dissolve, and **mickey-mousing** as "sweetener" for sound effects.

VOICE-OVER

Along with music, narration also serves to direct viewer attention and, through intonation and pacing, lets the audience know how they are supposed to understand the image. The voice-over is often used in documentary film, where it serves to provide context for the images as well as to fill in other pertinent information that is either not present or not obvious in the image. The voice-over thus serves to clarify, even determine, our understanding of a sequence. In *Letter from Siberia* (1957), for instance, an identical sequence is shown three times but with different narration. In each case, the narration frames the sequence of images, marking certain details for attention, and encouraging us to interpret them in a particular way—for the first, celebration; for the second, demonization; and for the third, a more measured response.

Documentary is the genre most likely to be dominated by the voice-over, and an audience's knowledge of this convention can therefore be exploited to create a documentary "atmosphere" in narrative films as well. Morgan Freeman's work for the English language version of *March of the Penguins* (2005) is an excellent recent example of straightforward, detached narration. In this film, the narrator seems simply to relate to us the information we need to make sense of the sequence of images. Similarly, even if we understand the lesson that *Letter from Siberia* teaches us about the interpretive malleability of a sequence of images, the detached quality of the narration nevertheless allows it to seem authoritative and objective.

In fictional film, as we might expect, voice-over generally serves the function of narration, that is, voice-over is often narration belonging to a character in the film. *Laura* (1944) and *The Name of the Rose* (1986) are examples of films in which the narrators are intimately connected with the story. In the former case, Waldo Lydecker (Clifton Webb) is a rather unreliable narrator (as he tries to conceal his own responsibility for what he mistakenly thought was Laura's murder); in the latter case, Adso of Melk (Christian Slater) is recounting an episode in his life. Many voice-overs operate under this conceit of describing a significant episode of the narrator's life. This does not mean that there need be anything "realistic" about the narration. Fiction works by its own rules: both *Sunset Boulevard* (1950) and *American Beauty* (1999), for example, feature dead narrators. For a recent example of diegetic music performances used for a similar narrative function as the voice-over narrator, see Figure 3-13 and its commentary.

Voice-over can also be used to establish character or as a plot device. Cher's irreverent monologue at the beginning of *Clueless* (1995) immediately captures her self-centeredness but also her charming naiveté. In *Million Dollar Baby* (2004) (Figure 3-14), the voice of Morgan Freeman's character, Eddie "Scrap-Iron" Dupris, is very prominent as a voice-over narrator in the first 20 min—even when he is also onscreen—but then appears only intermittently in the remainder of the film, until the very last moments, when his final words in voice-over reveal that the entire film has been an elaborate visualization of a letter he is writing to the estranged daughter of Frankie (Clint Eastwood).

In addition to delineating character and structuring the plot, the voice-over is frequently used for informational prologues. In these cases, the voice-over does

Figure 3-13. *Good Night and Good Luck* (2005). The sound track is notable for the exclusive but sparing use of a jazz combo evoking the film's setting in the 1950s. Six songs are performed once each by the combo and a female singer. "When I Fall in Love" plays during the prologue and opening credits, as very faint chatter is heard from the party scene in the background. Throughout the film, the musicians act like a quasi-Greek chorus, as they perform four songs in a television studio: in each case, the camera cuts back and forth between the principal actors and the musicians, while the lyrics of the songs link to action. End credits roll with the sixth song, "One For My Baby"; a brief reprise of "When I Fall in Love" comes at the very end.

Figure 3-14. *Million Dollar Baby*. Frankie and Eddie ("Scrap") talk in the office of Frankie's gym.

not belong to a character in the story but to some unknown, extra-diegetic in-dividual who relates the general background that allows us to understand the significance of the actions in the story. Good examples include the prologue to *Casablanca* and *King of Kings* (1961). The recent film *Le Fabuleux Destin d'Amélie Poulain* (*Amélie*, 2001) demonstrates that such detached voice-over narration can be used to comedic effect as well.

AUDIO DISSOLVE

A dissolve is a means of joining two shots, the one briefly overlapping the other so that we momentarily see both shots simultaneously, one fading as the other becomes visible. Generally, the dissolve is used to signify an ellipsis, that is, a marked change of time and (usually) place. By analogy, the "audio dissolve" can function as a transition from the primary level of the diegesis to another level (such as a dream), but it finds its most characteristic treatment in the musical, where it is serves as a transition to song and dance.

Rick Altman proposed the term "audio dissolve" to describe how musicals operate on principles that are different from other narrative films, in particular, the fact that song in a musical generally does not lend itself to direct interpreta-tion in terms of diegetic or nondiegetic. The character seems to know very well that he or she is singing, and thus (especially with musicals written specifically for the screen rather than close adaptations of stage musicals) the song begins diegetically, just as it normally would in any other narrative film (one very common device in classical Hollywood musicals is to show one or more char-acters gathered around a piano). As the song progresses, however, nondiegetic orchestral accompaniment enters, replacing the piano. It is this displacement, or dissolve of one accompaniment into another, that Altman defines as the audio dissolve.

This formal feature of the musical sets it apart from other narrative films. Musicals do not maintain the clear separation of diegetic and nondiegetic registers and so cannot define the boundaries of the diegetic world, which seems to constantly dissolve under the force of song. For Altman, this is the very point of the musical: the world of song is a world apart from mundane reality.[3] We should remember that, aside from the song performances, musicals are essentially romantic comedies and so are governed by the "normal" strictures of narrative film. The function of the songs, then, is to intensify the romance to the point where it can constitute and sustain an idealized world. The audio dissolve is the process by which this transformation occurs.

For Me and My Gal (1942) provides an exceptionally clear example of the audio dissolve, because it takes place fairly slowly and in distinct stages (the scene begins at 00:19:54 or DVD ch. 8). It begins with Harry (Gene Kelly) clumsily pounding out the title song at the piano (Figure 3-15a). Jo (Judy Garland) then comes over to the piano and relieves him (b). As she sings the verse, the orchestra comes in under the piano, which at first remains audible. By the end of the verse, although the orchestra has completely taken over, she continues to play at the piano. Harry then joins her as they sing a duet on the second chorus, with Jo still at the piano (c). She stands up (d) and they stroll across the room still singing. Finally, they move into dance (e). (Curiously, part of the dance itself is accompanied by a solo piano.) Of course, the orchestra continues through to the end of the song, when Jo and Harry sit down at the table and laugh (f). The laughter itself serves as a transition, reversing the dissolve and bringing the characters back into the mundane world.

Although the audio dissolve appears most frequently in the musical, it can occur in other sorts of narrative film, where it generally retains the function of a bridge, or a passage to a different, usually idealized world. As we might expect, in non-musicals (and especially in classical Hollywood cinema), the audio dissolve requires strong narrative and psychological motivation. That motivation is perhaps easiest in romantic comedies, which occasionally deploy the gesture of the audio dissolve to help define the world of their romance, especially, interestingly enough, to help signify blockages to it. In *The Apartment*, for instance, a piano begins to play as Bud and Fran leave their table (00:40:51). The piano continues until they reach the door, at which point nondiegetic strings enter under the piano (00:41:16). Once in the street, the tune continues in the strings until the cut to Bud standing in front of the theater, where he is waiting for Fran to join him to see *The Music Man* (00:41:44). The lonely saxophone associated with Bud enters with this cut—Fran has broken their date. Here, the collapse of the audio dissolve represents the deflation of Bud's hopes.

Another, more complex example occurs during "the Sacrifice of Faramir" sequence of *The Return of the King* (2003). Denethor, Faramir's father, has ordered Faramir to lead a suicidal attack on Osgiliath. As Faramir begins the

a | b
c | d
e | f

Figure 3-15. *For Me and My Gal*, title song. An illustration of an audio dissolve.

attack, there is a cut back to Denethor eating noisily with Pippin standing in attendance. Denethor demands that Pippin sing. As Pippin does, there are cut backs to Faramir's attack in slow motion. With the cut back to Pippin on a climactic **phrase** "on the edge of night," his voice is given more reverberation. The charge is depicted once again as Pippin returns to the original vocal register, quieter dynamic but continued reverberation. After two brief shots of Orcs, there is another of the charge, this time with the prominent whinnying of a horse. Strings sneak in under this, at first seeming simply a part of the reverberation of Pippen's voice. This accompaniment grows more dissonant and intense across a series of cuts—Denethor, Faramir, Orcs, Denethor, Orcs, Faramir, Pippin, and Orcs—reaching its peak as the Orcs unleash a flight of arrows.

Then comes a surprise: a sharp cut to Denethor coincides with the sound track falling shockingly silent as Pippin takes a dramatic pause for the end of his song. What emerges from this silence is nothing but Denethor's chewing, relieved only when Pippin haltingly intones the final word of the song, "fade," once again without accompaniment. Throughout the song we hear sound effects—horses, Faramir drawing his sword, the shooting of the arrows and most of all Denethor's eating—but no voice other than Pippin's, although both Faramir and the Orc captain are shown yelling. In that sense, the "dissolve" here is a transition to anything but an idealized world. Instead, it would seem to represent a fall from an idealized world into the hostile, fully mundane world of things. Pippin's song is a lament, and this case suggests that the audio dissolve in the context of the lament can serve an inverse function to that of the musical.

MICKEY-MOUSING: MUSIC AS EFFECTS "SWEETENER"

The voice-over and audio dissolve generally affect our perception of film form and narrative at the level of a performance scene, scene transition, or even the plot design of an entire film. At times, however, the ambiguity of the diegetic and nondiegetic can be felt at the opposite extreme, at the level of close synchronization within a shot or short series of shots, when music closely mimics screen action, cartoon style, blurring the boundary between music and sound effects. This is called mickey-mousing, and, although generally denigrated as a gimmick by most composers and theorists of film music and tolerated only in comedy, it can be extremely effective in dramatic contexts.

Mickey-mousing was employed on a regular basis in Hollywood film scores during in the 1930s and 1940s. Of the composers who were fond of this device, Max Steiner stands out. *The Informer* (1935), for instance, makes extensive use of mickey-mousing. In one scene, Gypo has informed on a friend, a member of the Irish resistance, to get money to help his destitute girl friend. Wracked with guilt, Gypo moves through the neighborhood, his every step falling heavily to the beat of the music. The mickey-mousing here seems like a metaphor for the weight of his conscience.

Close synchronization did not disappear in later film sound tracks. In the famous shower scene of *Psycho* (1960), the percussive hits of the high, screeching violins match the physical gestures of the stabbing. One reason the scene is so terrifying is the way the music couples screaming with physical pounding while also substituting for sound effects. The result seems to shock the scene out of the world into an almost supernatural domain. This potential was realized systematically in slasher films of the late 1970s and later. In these films, the monster's attacks are nearly always associated with music—here, too, music shocks, sets the monster in a supernatural dimension, and in some sense seems to emanates from the monster or even constitutes its point of view. The killing of Annie in *Friday the 13th* (1980), for instance, is accompanied by music very reminiscent of *Psycho*.

The prior examples still give primary importance to the narrative function of music, but we can reverse the relation and construe mickey-mousing as a way of sweetening a sound effect, thereby making the world "other," or different from our own. By sweetening, we mean that a sound is rendered so that it seems to violate the conditions of verisimilitude. Increasing volume above expected levels, adding unmotivated distortion, and otherwise altering the expected timbre of the sound effect are some of the ways in which sound can be sweetened. As might be expected, this device is useful for emphasizing a particular action or thing, especially one that is fraught with significance but might otherwise go unmarked and so unnoticed. Generally the effect is humorous (see Figure 3-16 for an example with commentary). Often the very idea is one of mismatch, an

Figure 3-16. *The Apartment.* Near the beginning of the film, Bud (Jack Lemmon) watches his electronic accounting machine as it moves through its task. As Bud's head bounces up and down to the stuttered rhythm of the carriage movement, the music mickey-mouses those movements with a series of low-pitched notes that are almost noise. The effect here is one of sweetening the sound effect, drawing our attention to the curious rhythm of the odd work task and setting the comedic tone of the film.

absurd sound that matches the absurd world of slapstick comedy, as in the substitution of a timpani glissando or a cymbal crash for a fall, for instance.

Sweetening is often coupled with a verisimilar close-up. Although this might seem overly redundant, in fact the disjunction between the realistic image and the less-than-realistic sound allows us to understand that we are aware of a significance that is not apparent to those in the diegetic world. See Figure 3-17, where Will (William Shakespeare, played by Joseph Fiennes) throws his manuscript on the fire. To signify its importance, the sound of the fire is sweetened by introducing it offscreen, placing it in the center channel, and mixing it at an abnormally high level. The sound increases in intensity (crackling of the paper) and volume once the manuscript ignites.

A special case of this sort of sweetening effect is the stinger, a sharp, usually dissonant musical chord (although we should note that effects, such as doors slamming or gunshots, can be used the same way). Stingers are particularly common in underscoring as a means of punctuating dialogue, but they can also provide multiple sound accents in an action sequence). When used under speech, stingers can be thought of as psychological sound effects. In other words, they are audible metaphors of particular psychological states and as such greatly aid in reading expressions, especially facial ones. Composers are precise about the timing of stingers so as to "catch" just that right moment that opens the expression of the face to the fullest. Stingers are also used as a means of emphasizing psychological shock. As such, they are often reserved for turning points in dialogue and scenes. An excellent example of this technique occurs at a critical moment in the reunion scene from *Casablanca*, where Rick first sees Ilsa. The stinger here renders his absolute shock of recognition, whereas the fact that the chord is held manages to convey in a short span of time the extent of attraction between the two (Figure 3-18).

Figure 3-17. *Shakespeare in Love* (1998). Will's manuscript burns in the fire.

Figure 3-18. *Casablanca*. The stinger chord that sounds when Rick first sees Ilsa (transcription from the sound track).

We call a stinger that is used this way "internal" because it is motivated by the inner psychological state of the character. "External" stingers are also possible. For example, a stinger can be used melodramatically, especially as a means of demonization. An example of this occurs near the opening of *Hangmen Also Die* (1945), where a sharp stinger accompanies a shot of a portrait of Hitler. The dissonant stinger that underscores Darth Vader's initial entrance in *Star Wars IV: A New Hope* (1977) serves a similar function.

THE ACOUSMÊTRE (ACOUSTICAL BEING)

Michel Chion notes that sound film makes possible a special kind of character, one who exists in the diegetic space but is placed consistently offscreen. He calls such a character an **acousmêtre**,[4] a French neologism that means "acoustical being." Being heard but not seen, such a character is defined wholly in terms of diegetic sound. This situation is distinct from narration because the voice of the acoustical being is taken to occur in the same timeframe as the diegesis, whereas narration is necessarily after the fact, even when the voice of the narrator is also that of a character in the diegesis. The *acousmêtre* is also distinct from a radio voice, which may be defined solely through sound and in that sense is "acousmatic" but lacks any expectation of being visualized: the world of radio is an acousmatic world consisting only of sound, and so no character can have other than an acoustical presence.

Neither onscreen diegetic nor offscreen nondiegetic music or sound pose any real obstacle to our attempts to make sense of what we see and hear. Onscreen diegetic testifies to the reality of the diegetic world. As typically used, offscreen nondiegetic sound (especially music) testifies to the inner psychology of the character. One of the most common functions of nondiegetic music, for instance, is to give us some sense as to how a particular piece of dialogue or incident affects a character. "Underscoring" thus operates in two senses: technically, it is music that is scored under dialogue; but figuratively, it is also music that *underscores*—that is, emphasizes—gestures and moments that are particularly psychologically fraught and revealing.

Whereas the typical character lives by the rules of psychological reality, the acoustical being lives outside them. A typical character has no awareness of and so no control of the camera and what the camera shows. The acoustical being, on the contrary, seems aware of the camera inasmuch as it has the mysterious ability to avert the camera's gaze, to be always just outside the frame. This ability to sense the frame so as to avoid being shown seems to endow the character with almost god-like powers. On the other hand, the acoustical being is typically represented as malevolent. The loss of its powers, through revelation of its body onscreen, that undoes and destroys the malevolent *acousmêtre*. Chion points to such pathological or even psychotic characters as the child murderer in *M* (1931), the Mother in *Psycho*, and Mabuse in *The Testament of Dr. Mabuse* as the common type of acoustical being. Mabuse is a prototype of the evil genius that appears frequently in later films. Those films in the James Bond series dealing with threats of world domination or destruction often have antagonists who are revealed and gradually lose power through the process of de-acousmatization (becoming visible). Likewise, horror films often introduce their monsters as acoustical beings, and the more we see the more vulnerable they become—it is the unseen monster that is most terrifying.

Acoustical beings are not absent from musicals or comedies, where they often appear as authority figures who rule or assert control despite absence. In such cases, the process of de-acousmatization is often the process by which comedic deflation, subversion, or inversion of authority occurs, allowing the individual to escape the determinations of authority. Although represented by a giant head floating translucently in space among flames and smoke, the Wizard in *The Wizard of Oz* (1939) is in many respects an acoustical being; certainly, the revelation of the "man behind the curtain" is a particularly direct example of de-acousmatization.

The opposite procedure, or what we might call the acousmatization of a character, can also have the effect of rendering that character impotent, especially when it occurs near the end of a film. In *The Robe* (1953), for instance, the Emperor Caligula's voice desperately cries out offscreen as Gallio and Diana leave "to a better world." Similarly, at the end of *A Face in the Crowd* (1957), Marcia (Patricia Neal) walks out on Larry "Lonesome" Rhodes (Andy Griffith). As she exits the building onto the street, Lonesome calls to Marcia from a window far above. As her taxi pulls away his voice grows fainter, disappearing into the sounds of the city as "The End" fills the screen. To render the effect even more poignantly, the camera does not follow the taxi as it disappears but instead shifts to general shots of the city. The sound changes similarly so that Lonesome's voice has become just another sound of the city, and the city, like Marcia, has become indifferent to his cries.

As might be expected, actual filmic representations of God or Jesus, although typically acousmatic, are treated somewhat differently. Here, the character is understood as belonging to a different world. In *The Robe*, for instance, Christ is either not shown or seen only from a great distance, and his presence is marked by a prominent shift to nondiegetic choral music. *Cabin in the Sky* (1943), by contrast, allows the diegetic appearance of an angel, but God is acousmatic in the extreme, sounding as "otherworldly" bell-like music that only the angel can understand. Such films as *King of Kings* or *The Greatest Story Ever Told* (1965) dealing directly with the life of Christ must necessarily treat Jesus as a diegetic character, but the representation generally follows a scenario of de-acousmatization near the beginning of the film, which is reversed at the end, with the ascension. Whereas God exists *beyond* the diegesis so that the sound or music that represents God is usually understood as a peculiar mode of the nondiegetic (as in *The Robe*) or as an intrusion in an extraordinary diegetic space (*Cabin in the Sky*), the acoustical being exists *within* the diegesis.

Summary

In this chapter, we paid particular attention to the (surprisingly complex) relations between sound in the sound track and the physical world or diegesis represented through the narrative. The distinction between diegetic and nondiegetic refers to this anchoring of sound in the filmic world (or, in the nondiegetic, the failure to be anchored in that world). Another pair, onscreen/offscreen, refers more narrowly to sound anchored in what the camera frames for us at any given moment (onscreen) or that we can reasonably assume belongs to space we can extend from what we see (offscreen).

EXERCISE 1: USING AN EVENTS TABLE

Instead of a prose description or list (modeled on our analysis checklist), you could use the following template (or your own variant of it) as a quick way to describe the sound track in a film scene (Table 3-1). The template has been

Table 3-1 Sound track elements and functions in the opening of *42nd Street*.

Sequence	Time	Music ND	D	sfx	Dia.	Comments	General comments
Titles	0:00	√				Music high on mix	Title music: "42nd Street"; new tune for cast.
Establishment	1:28	√		√	√	Music levels remains high; sfx mixed; dia. added near end	Music provides continuity for montage; sfx present "life" of city in contrast to static images; dia. used more as sfx (audio collage).
Abner and Dorothy	1:59			√	√	Dia. pre-dominates; minimal sfx	Emphasis on dialogue; only prominent sfx is rustling paper, which underscores importance of the "contract."

ND = nondiegetic; D = diegetic; sfx = sound effects; Dia. = dialogue (speech)

filled in for the opening minutes of *42nd Street* as an example. Use column 1 to segment the sequence or scene (we did something similar by grouping shots in the analysis of the Shooting scene from *Trzy Kolory: Bialy (White)* in ch. 2). Start points for each segment can go in the second column. Use columns 3 and 4 to indicate presence or absence of that sound component on the sound track. Use the "comments on mix" field to make more nuanced observations, such as the predominance of dialogue, music sneaking in and out, use of ambient sound, and so on. Use the "general comments" field to note items of particular interest, such as whether sound is onscreen or offscreen; musical genre, tempo, or mood; **point-of-view sound** or music, and so forth.

EXERCISE 2: USING AN (UPDATED) ANALYSIS CHECKLIST

In chapter 2, we updated the analysis checklist to include description of the sound track in terms of tempo, texture, and other musical terms. We can do the same for the topics discussed in this chapter:

1. Background and general information
2. Synopsis of the scene
3. Shot list
4. Description of the sound track elements and their balance
5. Description and evaluation of the sound track (diegetic/non-diegetic; onscreen/offscreen; point of view sound; voice-over, audio dissolve, mickey-mousing, the *acousmêtre*)
6. If needed, a summary statement about the sound track in the scene

Music, Sound, and Time

Introduction

Films, like pieces of music, unfold in linear (or clock) time. Temporality is thus fundamental to the experience of film, including film sound. At the broadest level, the basis of a narrative film is the story, or the chronological ordering of a series of related events, and the plot presents a particular arrangement—again temporal—of these events. The temporalities of story and plot, then, can be set against one another. At the level of the scene, time can interact with image and sound in multiple ways. In chapter 2, we discussed sound using musical terms such as tempo, meter, and rhythm. In this chapter, we will discuss three distinct but related ways sound impacts on the perception of time in and between scenes: the formal treatment of transitions, synchronization (or "playing with the film"), and "counterpoint" (or "playing against the film").

Transitions: The Sound Bridge and Hard Cuts

The sound bridge and the **hard cut** may be understood as opposed terms: the sound bridge effects a smooth transition by means of different kinds of overlaps, whereas the hard cut is a simple, direct cut from one scene to the next in which the change in the sound track is as abrupt as it is in the image track, sometimes disconcertingly so.

The sound bridge is obviously related to the very brief overlaps that arise from an editing rule of thumb: image and sound should not be cut at the same point unless a particular effect is called for. The sound bridge can be understood as simply a longer version of these overlaps, long enough to reach the immediate consciousness of the viewer, sometimes even long enough to focus one's main attention on the overlap, thus raising questions about its narrative function. Like a simultaneous cut of image and sound, in the system of **continuity editing** the bridge and the hard cut are specialized devices, for both draw attention to the act of editing and therefore cannot be used freely: they need to be motivated by the needs of filmic narration.

Sound bridges are now a relatively common way to make a transition from one scene into the next. Generally speaking, bridges are most striking when they are diegetic, especially when they consist of dialogue. Nondiegetic music and voice-over narration often perform a similar function, but perhaps because they have a long history of doing so, the effect is usually less noticeable. Montage sequences, for instance, almost always use music to organize a disparate set of images into a single unit, and even films that otherwise have no music will typically employ its bridging effects for montage.

In the following sections, we will distinguish between five different kinds of bridges and discuss each in turn: the advance, the lag, the **link**, the match, and the substitution.

SOUND ADVANCE

A sound advance occurs when we hear a sound before we see its associated image. This device can be used equally well in connection with a cut or a dissolve into a new scene and may be anywhere from less than 1 sec up to several seconds—in unusual cases (like two to be discussed later), the advance may run much longer. Although we concentrate here on their formal use as transitions between scenes, where it involves temporal or spatial displacement of sound and image, we should also point out that sound advances can be used within scenes, as well. By far the most common instances are offscreen speech or sound whose source is then revealed onscreen as the speech or sound continues; perhaps the most common use is in shot/reverse-shot sequences when one person is speaking while we see the other onscreen—if the person continues to speak when the cut returns to him or her, that is technically a sound advance so long as a line of dialogue is heard before the person speaking it is shown.

Although rare before the 1960s, advances used as transitions between scenes have since become a fairly frequent occurrence. Nevertheless, the most famous single example is from the 1930s: in Alfred Hitchcock's *The Thirty-Nine Steps* (1935), a woman discovers a dead body and screams, but a train whistle is substituted for her natural voice. With a hard cut, the scene changes and we see a train blowing its whistle. Because music has commonly been used as a transition device, it was also not unusual in classic Hollywood sound film for diegetic music to be appear in anticipation of the scene with which it was associated. The rehearsal scene for "It Must Be June" in *42nd Street* (1933) begins with the chorus singing over black briefly before the images appear. Likewise, the introduction to Kathy recording "Would You" in *Singin' in the Rain* (1952) occurs over the end of the preceding scene where Don (Gene Kelly), Cosmo (Donald O'Connor) and R. F. (Millard Mitchell) devise a plan to save "The Dueling Cavalier" by turning it into a musical, "The Dancing Cavalier. "

You may have noticed, in connection with the "Second Botched Meeting" from *Sleepless in Seattle* (1993), which we discussed in ch. 1, that the map-like graphic insert that appears just after the scene ends is accompanied by speech that anticipates the next scene. The first scene ends with the cut to the graphic at 01:12:02; within 1 sec or so, we hear Rosie O'Donnell's voice asking "So then what happened?" followed by Meg Ryan's answer; at 01:12:06, the graphic "rolls up" as if it were on a map stand; the screen is black for 1 sec, then cuts to the two getting out of a car—their conversation continues at the same sound level. The suggestion created by this sound advance, combined with the dialogue, is that the "Second Botched Meeting" scene itself was a visualization of Annie's account as she told it to Becky in the car before they stopped and got out. The effect, then, is to smooth over what is, after all, a considerable break in temporal continuity (Annie had to leave Seattle and fly back to Baltimore, of course, before the conversation in the car with Becky could take place).

The opening of *Atonement* (2007) offers a lengthier instance in its bird sounds and typing noises during the opening credits. Both of these anticipate diegetic sounds: in the one instance, Briony's typing, in the other, birds heard (but not seen) singing or chirping outside the open windows to Briony's room. Note that it is possible, therefore, to have a sound advance for what eventually turns out to be offscreen diegetic (even ambient) sound.

An especially extended and particularly striking example of diegetic dialogue used as a sound advance occurs in another Nora Ephron film starring Meg Ryan: *When Harry Met Sally* (1989). In this sequence, we first hear Harry (Billy Crystal) talking to Sally on the phone (00:35:29). As they talk, a series of brief scenes shows them apart, then together. Only at the end of the sequence (00:36:57) do the voices finally synchronize as we see both Harry and Sally in split screen, each watching *Casablanca* with telephone receivers in their hands. This sound advance is nearly 90 sec in length!

SOUND LAG

A **sound lag** occurs when sound from one scene lingers over into the next. Lags are much less common than advances, probably because they tend to retard the plot rather than push it forward. The continuation of the sound across a scene change makes a connection between the scenes, to be sure, but it seems to force us to retain the old scene even as the new scene appears, creating a sense of nostalgia for the "lost" scene.

The lag is particularly effective when used to color the following scene, as in one place near the end of *Lawrence of Arabia* (1962), where Lawrence's ironic laughter (03:37:39) persists, generating what amounts to a voice-over commentary on the opening of the subsequent scene.

In *De-Lovely* (2004), the applause following "Let's Fall In Love" carries over into a scene at the Murphys' house (00:39:14). This scene also ends with a performance ("True Love") and applause, but the song and setting are much more domestic. Here the bridge ties these two scenes together, in the process asking us to draw a comparison between the public Cole Porter (played by Kevin Kline) and the private Cole. This is made evident by the stylistic juxtaposition of "Let's Fall In Love," which is one of his most distinctive tunes, and "True Love," a simple waltz about which Cole says, "it doesn't sound like me."

Near the end of the film, applause is once again used in a sound lag, this time moving from Cole's success with *Kiss Me Kate* to Gabe (Jonathan Pryce) and old Cole watching the scene play out in front of them (01:41:23). The old Cole's reaction to Gabe's insistence that they "move on" underscores the nostalgic aspect of the sound lag: "Please, please, let me enjoy this." (The "So in Love" sequence that precedes this (01:34:19–01:40:48) is particularly rich in the sound track qualities and devices explored throughout this chapter. Note especially the frequent use of various kinds of sound bridges and the complicated play between diegetic and nondiegetic music occasionally mediated by audio dissolves.)

Goodfellas (1990) uses an extremely long sound lag to move from the Copacabana, a nightclub where Henry (Ray Liotta) and Karen (Lorraine Bracco) are having dinner, to Henry pulling off the heist of money at the airport. The scenes are connected through a routine by Henny Youngman, which begins in the nightclub (00:34:22). The performance continues on the sound track over the cut to the airport (00:34:35) to the point where Henry picks up the key (00:34:56) that allows him access to the bag with the money. Although this sound lag is certainly prominent as a formal element, the reasons for it unusual length and prominence are obscure at best.

The film *Munich* (2005) has many sound overlaps, including a number of important sound advances and lags: see Figure 4-1 for examples. In the first instance (a), a particularly striking lag occurs at 02:01:48, where a high-pitched train whistle lingers, slowly fading over a cut to men riding bikes. Under the whistle, ambient nature sounds appear along with this visual of two bikers. Here the point of the lag is not so much nostalgia as a means of marking the significance of the scene in the train station, urging us to remember what was said there. It also has the effect of unsettling the pastoral scene, leading us to suspect that the peaceful environment is only an appearance. A long sound advance follows in the next scene (b), which opens with

Figure 4-1. *Munich.* (a) Sound lag over bike riders.   a
(b) Sound advance over chopping vegetables.   b

shots of Avner's (Eric Bana's) hands chopping vegetables immediately after the assassination in the previous scene. Hans (Hanns Zischler) watches Avner throughout the sequence without moving his lips. Nevertheless, we hear Hans deliver a long monologue recounting the activities. It seems like a voice-over until later in the sequence we finally see Hans speaking and recognize that we had in fact been hearing a sound advance. Yet precisely because it is revealed as a voice belonging to the story, the effect is very unsettling, as if it were dividing Hans' voice from his body.

SOUND LINK

A link is the use of sound to bridge a series of cuts, transforming what might otherwise seem a collection of unrelated shots. *Emma* (1996) contains an excellent example of this procedure. Emma is speaking with Mrs. Weston (Greta Scacchi) about how to tell Harriet about Mr. Elton's marriage. At the end of the scene (00:44:26), she says, "I suppose I'll just say, 'Harriet,'" where there is an immediate cut to the next scene with Emma and Harriet. Emma's line simply continues across the cut, "I have some bad news about Mr. Elton."

Links are quite common with music. We are already familiar with the stereotyped use of music behind montages in classical cinema. As one of many possible examples, *The Glenn Miller Story* (1953) uses a continuous rendition of "Pennsylvania 6-5000" over a montage of the band playing at various venues. Here the device is used rather simply to represent the band on tour. So-called passed-along songs in musicals, such as the opening title number from *Meet Me in St. Louis* (1944) or "Isn't It Romantic" from *Love Me Tonight* (1932), work similarly. Radio is often used in this way as well. In *American Graffiti* (1973), the radio broadcast is a ubiquitous presence, often continuing across cuts from one scene of action to another. The effect in this instance is to stitch these scenes together in terms of time: Although the scenes happen in different places, they occur at the same time.

As mentioned previously, the "Would You" sequence from *Singin' In the Rain* begins with a brief sound advance, where the introduction of the song begins over the end of the scene of Don, Cosmo, and R.F. discussing how to save their film by turning it into a musical. A cut to Kathy (Debbie Reynolds) singing closes off the sound advance, but this moment of synchronization only initiates a series of links: Kathy records the song, Lina (Jean Hagen) rehearses to it, Lina syncs to playback, and the filming dissolves into the finished film. The continuity of the sound track, in this case the song, serves as a means of tying together into a single thread the discontiguous space and time of the images.

SOUND MATCH

A sound match is made possible when a sound belonging to one scene can be followed by a similar or identical sound belonging to the next. For instance, near the beginning of *The Big Broadcast* (1932), Mr. Clapsaddle (George Barbier) complains to George (George Burns), the owner of a radio station, that Bing Crosby has failed to appear for the show Clapsaddle sponsors. He demands that Crosby be fired and emphasizes his point by pounding on the desk three times. A cut to a taxi driver sounding his horn three times (in the same beat) immediately follows. The continuity of sound serves to bridge the two scenes in an unequivocal way and adds an element of humor as well.

The sound match is not only used for comedy. In *De-Lovely*, Cole and Linda finish singing "You'd Be So Easy To Love." During the applause that follows, the sound of a galloping horse is faded in, which serves as a brief sound advance to the next scene, where Cole has a rendezvous with Boris, a dancer in Diaghilev's *Ballet Russe*. The match between the applause and the horse serves to tie the two scenes together as his two different loves.

For another example, see Figure 4-2. Early in the film, Cole sits at the piano and begins playing the introduction to "In the Still of the Night" (a). As he lands on the chord to begin the song proper, a substitution match brings a shot of hands (b) and a sound match that acts as a bridge to what appears to be a rehearsal (c). The cut here is the first of many confusions where Cole looks back on his life as though it were a musical.

HARD CUT

A hard cut uses sound to further mark an abrupt shift from one place and time to another. Because such moments tend to be memorable, the hard cut will probably seem familiar to most film viewers, as will the fact that sound often contributes. The alarm clock that abruptly shifts a nighttime or dream sequence to the next morning, the loud factory or ship horn that suddenly shifts location, the scream of jet plane engines on take-off or landing, a diegetic musical performance (or radio or phonograph) that enters without warning and probably *in medias res*—all these are common treatments of the hard cut intensified by sound. For an example from *Trois Couleurs: Bleu* (*Blue*, 1993), with commentary, see Figure 4-3.

Figure 4-2. *De-Lovely*. An example of a substitution match: the hands in the middle frame, although motivated by the first image, belong to the younger Cole of the third image.

a
b
c

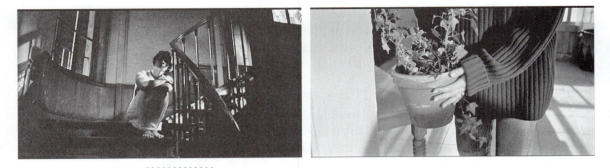

a | b   **Figure 4-3.** *Trois Couleurs: Bleu* (*Blue*). The music Julie (Juliette Binoche) is hearing in her head during the first shot (a) is interrupted by a loud door buzzer belonging to the second (b). The jarring effect is like an alarm clock wrenching one from sleep. (Note the shift from nighttime to daylight as well.) Julie is as startled by the noise as are we, and she drops the plant in response. You should also notice that in and of itself the door buzzer is not particularly loud; its effect of loudness comes from the contrast with the quietness of the previous scene. This should remind us that absolute volume is not a particularly good measure of perceived loudness—a lesson often lost on contemporary sound track design.

Synchronization ("Playing with the Film")

The default case for sound in relation to the image is synchronization, or the appropriate temporal linking of sound to image. Synchronization plays an important role in the process of sealing our identification with a film: it aids the impression that the sound emanates from the world of the screen, an effect that is essential to orienting our relation to the screen. This function is very similar to the carefully managed fluctuations of onscreen and offscreen sound, which also reassure us that the diegetic world exists and that the space beyond the edge of the frame can be represented.

Synchronization stitches the diegetic world together, convincing the film viewer that it might be possible to see all of that world; sight is limited only by what is relevant to narrative at any particular time. That is to say, synchronization is a means of enabling clarity: Its redundancy of image and sound aids us in determining pertinence because, as a general rule, characters and objects with narrative significance (whether at the local or global level) are synchronized. (We most likely wouldn't care if sea gulls in the distance failed to be synchronized with the sounds of their squawking, but we would care, and take it as a technical flaw or at least a matter of filmic significance, if performers in a foregrounded musical performance or conversation are not in sync.)

The effect of synchronization is especially strong in dialogue sequences. Whatever the setting defined by the background, nothing appears so natural in film as characters in conversation. This seeming naturalness of synchronized dialogue serves to convince us that the characters we see conversing possess real bodies, although the bodies these characters occupy are actually what film theorist Mary Ann Doane calls "phantasmatic." They are, she notes, "reconstituted by the technology and practice of the cinema."[1] That is to say, from the standpoint of the technology taken by itself, the voice need not occupy a particular body, or indeed any body at all: filmmakers actually must do work to achieve the transparent effect of synchronization. In the image track, a cut could in principle take us anywhere, so that rules of continuity editing are needed to constrain the possibilities and rationalize the joins between shots as a unified space contained by and placed at the service of narrative. Similarly, what compels synchronization in the sound track is this need to represent the diegesis as if it were real.

The degree of synchronization can vary depending on circumstances, however. Loose synchronization is usually adequate for groups of people talking at a party or in a crowd (the **generic sound** or generic noise we mentioned in ch. 1). Given the mechanical limitations of recording in the early years of sound film, generic sound often lacked any attempt at close synchronization, as, for example, in the boat arrival scene early in the Greta Garbo vehicle *Wild Orchids* (1929) or the previously mentioned conversation of café customers and the silverware tapping in advance of Al Jolson's first two songs in *The Jazz Singer* (1927). On the other hand, we expect close synchronization in dialogue scenes, that is, a match on the movements of a character's mouth and the words that we hear. It is true that, once rerecorded dialogue (**ADR** or **automated dialogue replacement**) became common practice, standards for dialogue syncing relaxed a bit (films in the 1950s and 1960s, in the United States and in Europe as well, sometimes test the limits of this relaxation), but the principle of close synchronization remained in force—indeed, in recent years, with digital editing technology that allows sound editors to stretch and compress the length of phonemes at will, synchronization is generally very tight, even with rerecorded dialogue.

Nevertheless, the possibility of the phantasmatic body is embedded in sound-film production, which, because it must address the separate reproductive technologies of the screen and the speakers, necessarily places the image and voice on separate tracks. Dialogue editing in postproduction presupposes this possibility of separation because one of the tasks of the dialogue editor is to sort through the vocal track of the various takes and shots of a scene and decide which one works best. The take the dialogue editor chooses is often not the one that was recorded with the image it accompanies in the finished film. ADR— also called "looping"—is even more telling. Only if the voice is disembodied can it be edited this way, separate from the image: a character is created through the illusion of re-embodiment, and it is the way this illusion convinces us of the unified body of the character that constitutes its phantasmatic quality.

Occasionally, a film uses this effect of synchronization as part of its narrative theme. *Singin' in the Rain*, to cite one of the most famous examples, acknowledges the fictional unity of synchronization and foregrounds the technical work that is required to obtain that synchronization. Technology and technique both falter in Don and Lina's first attempt to make a talking picture. In terms of technology, the recording apparatus proves inadequate and at the screening the film slips out of synchronization. In terms of technique, the screenplay is inappropriate, and Lina has difficulty mastering the microphone. These deficiencies prove to be inspirational. When Cosmo lip-syncs Kathy singing "Good Morning" he demonstrates that "faulty" synchronization can be used to create its own fiction. Cosmo's "performance" allows us to recognize that the technology does not in any sense compel a body to sing with its own voice. Nothing in the technology in and of itself constrains a particular relation between image and sound.

The surprising ability of technology to split body and voice only to reassemble them otherwise is demonstrated in the previously discussed sequence built around the song "Would You." Here, we see (1) Kathy recording the song, (2) her performance displaced to a phonograph record to which Lina attempts to synchronize her lips, and finally (3) the perfect mating of Lina's body to Kathy's voice in the finished film. In other words, Kathy's voice must be disembodied before it can be placed on Lina's body, thereby creating the heroine of "The Dancing Cavalier." Despite this feat, the film ultimately suggests that proper synchronization must exclude the appearance of the phantasmatic body; the unity of body and voice in the character should naturally reproduce that of the actor. In other words, the fact that Kathy's voice can be moved and shifted into Lina's body is less troubling than the splendid appearance of that phantasmic body, the perfect success of the synchronization in "The Dancing Cavalier" (the first talking picture with Lina and Don). If technology allows the voice and body to be separated and reassembled in essentially any way, *Singin' in the Rain* ultimately asserts a *moral* obligation to reproduce a proper, natural unity. (The moral point of the film is extremely ironic given that Hagen rather than Reynolds looped in Lina's character's spoken lines in "The Dancing Cavalier" and that "Would You" was sung not by Reynolds, but by Betty Noyles.)

Another way of thinking about synchronization is in terms of empathy, or emotional engagement. When the sound track is coordinated with the image track, following and emphasizing the mood of onscreen characters and action, we can describe the effect as empathetic or engaged. Like synchronization itself, the empathetic is the default case for most narrative cinema. Certainly we expect that voices will speak in ways appropriate to the apparent emotions of the characters and that ambient sounds will help rather than hinder (quiet effects in subdued scenes, accents in scenes of tension, etc.).

Overwhelmingly, music in both classic and contemporary Hollywood sound film is empathetic and coordinated with the scene. In one now very familiar example, the "Second Botched Meeting" from *Sleepless in Seattle* follows closely in tempo and mood the changing feelings of Meg Ryan's character (note, however, that dialogue synchronization is questionable for the other characters in that scene—do Tom Hanks's lips move at all when he says "Hello"?). In a very different situation, the sudden, harsh and shrieking violins in the bathroom murder scene from *Psycho* (1960) closely follow the sense of shock and fear in Janet Leigh's character; and, more broadly speaking, in the genre of science fiction thrillers, the tight interweaving of music and effects mimics the sounds of a space-ship environment but also creates the sense of strangeness and always-being-on-edge that is appropriate to, for example, the *Alien* series.

On the other hand, music can be empathetic yet threaten to lead us out of the scene by adding new information or, more likely, by so exaggerating its presence that it defamiliarizes the action, turning mythic. Near the end of Scarlett's soliloquy that closes Part I of *Gone with the Wind* (1939), the orchestral music becomes very loud (intrusive) and, by quoting the "Tara" theme, pushes us out of the immediate surroundings to the mythic realm of the hope for a revival of the South (although we are left in doubt about whether this is a progressive change or a reactionary restoration). Similarly grand, in *Empire of the Sun* (1987), the final scene at a Shanghai stadium, as British citizens prepare to depart "upcountry" near the end of WWII, brings the death of one of their number, a Mrs. Victor, and the young Jim at that moment sees a bright light flash across the sky. He takes this to be Mrs. Victor's soul departing into the ether, and the music does nothing to dissuade us from believing him. Not long thereafter, we learn that the light came from the second of the American atom bombs dropped on Japan. This suggests that irony is not only the property of music that "plays against" but can emerge in an even more powerful way from (deceptive) empathy.

Another, less obvious example is the music for the main-title sequence in Hitchcock's *North by Northwest* (1959). A more or less conventional series of establishing shots goes on behind the titles: we see the side of a skyscraper, then the streets below, then move down to several shots at street level, and finally to the front of a hotel, from which Roger Thornhill (Cary Grant) emerges. Against this, however, is a rhythmically vigorous, angular, and frequently dissonant fandango played loudly in a full orchestra. We might speculate that the music is meant to suggest a busy urban environment, but the pace of the music noticeably outmatches the movements of cars on the street or people rushing to the subway entrance. It is only in retrospect that we realize this music warned us that something is "out of whack," that Roger Thornhill's world will shortly be upended when he becomes a victim of mistaken identity. Thus, although

The "overplaying" by which is meant playing so loud that it attracts the ear more than the picture attracts the eye, has killed many a good picture.

—Erno Rapee (music director)[2]

the music initially seems at odds with the images, eventually we realize that it has provided a strong narrative cue—not at the level of a single scene (or even a shot within a scene) but at the level of the film as a whole.

EXAMPLE FOR SYNCHRONIZATION: *CASABLANCA*, RICK AND ILSA MEET

We have two ways to think about synchronization, then: the temporal synchronizing of image track and sound track elements, and the emotional or empathetic synchronization of image with sound.

In the famous scene from *Casablanca* (1942) where Rick (Humphrey Bogart) and Ilsa (Ingrid Bergman) meet in Rick's café, temporal synchronization is consistently close throughout. The scene may be said to begin when Ilsa, seated by herself, asks a waiter to tell Sam (Dooley Wilson) to come over to her table. Sam does so, bringing his piano with him; he plays something but at her insistence plays, then sings, "As Time Goes By." Rick emerges from the casino room, starts an angry reprimand to Sam, then sees Ilsa (Figure 4-4) (nondiegetic orchestral music enters with the cut to her (Figure 4-5) and continues to the end of the scene). Note that the reaction shot (showing Ilsa) is matched by a shot of Rick (Figure 4-6). Captain Renault (Claude Rains)

Figure 4-4. *Casablanca*. Rick challenges Sam for singing "As Time Goes By."

Figure 4-5. *Casablanca*. Ilsa reacts to seeing Rick.

Figure 4-6. *Casablanca*. Rick reacts to seeing Ilsa.

intervenes, and he, Rick, Ilsa, and her spouse Victor Laszlo (Paul Henreid) sit down for a four-way conversation (Figure 4-7). After a short while, everyone leaves, Rick is left to sit down again dejectedly, and Renault talks briefly to the others outdoors.

Following our expectations for the classical Hollywood cinema, sound synchronization is tight throughout this scene. Given the large number of medium close ups and close ups (an especially long one of Ingrid Bergman occurs early in the scene [Figure 4-8]), dialogue synchronization is especially tight. There are very few sound effects and none of substance. We discuss music later in terms of empathy, but the famous stinger chord that accompanies Rick's reaction to seeing Ilsa is not timed with the cut to Rick—it enters 1 sec later, on the reaction shot of Ilsa, almost mimicking a sharp intake of breath that might naturally accompany the shock; and, as an aside, we should mention that, although Sam's singing is synchronized, his piano playing in the beginning of the scene is not: that is, he is not playing exactly the notes that we hear (observe that we never see his hands on the keyboard during this scene).

In terms of empathy or emotional engagement, dialogue follows expected paths and by and large is quite informative about the emotions behind the

Figure 4-7. *Casablanca*. Rick, Captain Renault, Ilsa, and Victor Laszlo.

Figure 4-8. *Casablanca.* Closeup of Ilsa while Sam plays "As Time Goes By."

speech. Like the music, inflections in the speech throughout follow the shifts in emotion of Rick and Ilsa, not in Captain Renault (who, however, makes plain that he is learning something about his friend Rick's character) and Laszlo (whose speech throughout is guarded).

As for the music, composer Max Steiner said that his ideal for underscoring was that the music "fits the scene like a glove," and "seamless" is undoubtedly the best way to describe this cue: it accompanies, comments on, and amplifies every turn in the action.[3] The stinger chord is a powerful narrative cue ("Look!" "Pay attention!"); "point of view" music immediately follows as we "hear" the sudden encounter register in the minds of Rick and Ilsa; the plaintive oboe suggests sadness, loneliness, isolation; the reinforcement of specific time-place references in quotations of "As Time Goes By" in waltz form as Ilsa make a reference to Paris, then the German national anthem when she mentions the Germans; the "sinking" emotions and movements near the end (Figure 4-9). The only exceptions are the neutral "walking music" (just after Laszlo says that it is time to go) and the unexpectedly loud, formal cadence at the end (we cannot tell from this scene alone, but this is the end of the film's first large section, which has consisted mostly of one evening in Rick's café).

Figure 4-9. *Casablanca.* Rick sits alone after the others leave.

Counterpoint ("Playing against the Film")

If sound can play "with" a scene, in synchronization, then one has to assume that it also has the potential to play "against" a scene, an effect that is sometimes referred to by the term "counterpoint" (not to be confused with the same word used for texture: we prefer to reserve "polyphonic" for references to a lively, complex texture). As with synchronization, we can think of counterpoint in two different ways, but in this case, we are speaking of the *failure* of temporal synchronizing of image track and sound track elements, or of the emotional *distance* of sound from image.

The first of these—inadequate temporal synchronizing—is amusingly familiar from overdubbed, translated dialogue in Japanese horror films of the 1950s; but "failed" synchronization of dialogue and mouth movements can also be used to defamiliarize speech, as in Elia Kazan's *East of Eden* (1954) and, rather later, in Clint Eastwood's spaghetti westerns, such as *The Good, The Bad, and The Ugly* (1967) and, especially, *Once Upon a Time in the West* (1968).

These two effects—humor and defamiliarization—are the two primary results of failed synchronization at this level. Music and sound effects can do this, too, but they require unusual emphasis and perhaps for that reason are employed for this purpose far less often than speech. Examples include inappropriate sound effects (a sheep quacking), a delayed rimshot for humor, and an obvious and prolonged mismatch of a performer's physical motions and the resulting music (although this last is perhaps more often the result of production failures—the inability of actors to imitate performers' motions accurately—than it is a deliberate device). Consider the sound advance from *The Thirty-Nine Steps* that we mentioned earlier in this chapter: the initial moments, while we see the woman screaming but hear the train whistle, are counterpoint: the image and the sound don't match, even if the latter is similar to what we would have expected naturally. Jean-Luc Godard often uses sounds in this way, as when an apparently unmotivated boat horn blares out against a shot of a young woman on a Paris street (it turns out this is a sound advance but we do not realize that until 30 sec later) in *À bout de soufflé* (*Breathless*, 1960), or when we hear sounds of seagulls' cries against an image of a nighttime Paris street in *Prénom Carmen* (*First Name: Carmen*, 1983).

Sounds or music that are emotionally distanced are **anempathetic**, or not in empathy with the image track. A simple example would be a sad or distraught person in the midst of a happy, celebrating crowd—clearly, the generic sounds of the crowd do not match the mood of the character. A nondiegetic pop song in a mood, or with lyrics, that contradict a character's feelings or speech would be another common example. Near the end of *Catch Me If You Can* (2002), Frank has escaped from the airplane as it lands in New York and has made his way to his mother's house, where she lives with her second husband and their young daughter. It is Christmas and Frank approaches the house in the snow; inside, the house is well-appointed, and out of its warmth the daughter gazes at him with silent curiosity. He sees his mother sitting on a couch, and her contented pleasure when the spouse enters. Christmas music plays, rather too loudly; with one barely noticed exception, the camera jumps back and forth between inside and outside views, as if to emphasize Frank's isolation. Here, the music plays strongly against Frank's emotions, but it is important to note that the sharp dissonance between music and image is closely tied to narrative, as he (and we) quickly realize that his mother is happy and that he cannot be a part of her new life.

This example from *Catch Me If You Can* shows the active sense of "playing against" the image: the music not only contradicts Frank's feelings but seems to mock them. It is also possible to have "**neutral**" **music**, or music that is indifferent to the scene, neither significant to its narrative nor emotionally engaged—in other words, music that functions much like ambient or environmental noise. A band playing in the background of a club scene will often act neutrally (as in those parts of the casino scene from *The Big Sleep* (1946) other than Bacall's numbers, or many of the numbers in the lengthy first part of

The ballet sequence [in An Affair to Remember (1957)] was a film clip from some musical. Lord knows how long ago it was made, and it was all in a long shot, which was in 2/4 [meter]. And I had my music editor make me a click track in 3/4 because I wanted a kind of a Tchaikovsky-Glazounov waltz feeling in the thing, which I fortunately got. And it worked out just fine in that way.

—Hugo Friedhofer, interviewed by Irene Kahn Atkins[4]

Casablanca, which consists of a series of scenes all taking place in one evening at Rick's *Café Américain*): minimally necessary to establish ambience, such music contributes little if anything to narrative and follows it own affective path, separate from dialogue and action.

A neutral music, whether diegetic or nondiegetic, can continue without paying any heed to emotional nuance; if it continues long enough, we are encouraged to ignore it as a kind of aural wallpaper. On the other hand, neutral music can turn in a flash into aggressive counterpoint with the image or close empathy. For example, neutral carnival (circus) music can suddenly turn empathic if a melody strongly associated with a character or couple appears in the music, or intrusive and even unnerving if the volume suddenly rises substantially or if a familiar and upbeat melody is played against some emotional anguish in a character or couple or against physical violence. For some treatments of music in circus scenes, see *A Streetcar Named Desire* (1951), *Strangers on a Train* (1951), *Tarnished Angels* (1958), and *Der Himmel über Berlin* (*Wings of Desire*, 1987).

Summary Example for Synchronization and Counterpoint: *Casablanca*, After-Hours Scene

We now have a total of four possibilities: (1) the temporal synchronizing of image track and sound track elements, (2) the emotional or empathetic synchronization of image with sound, (3) the temporal or logical mismatch of sound and image, and (4) an emotionally distanced or anempathetic sound track.

The first after-hours scene in *Casablanca*, which immediately follows the meeting discussed earlier, is obviously intended to be parallel to that earlier scene. The scene begins with Rick pouring himself a drink in his empty, darkened bar. The sound track is exceptionally, indeed painfully quiet, with neither music nor ambient sound. Sam enters and attempts to pull Rick out of his depression. At first, Sam tries talking to Rick but soon sits down and begins to play, apparently seeking to soothe Rick's pain. This music, identified by Sam when Rick challenges him as "a little something of my own," is not temporally synchronized (3), because the music we hear doesn't quite match Sam's playing. Rick rejects the song and insists that Sam play "As Time Goes By," the song that Rick and Ilsa associate with their old romance in Paris. Reluctantly, Sam plays. (Of course, as we would expect, all dialogue is closely synchronized (1).) Sam's "something of my own" could be considered neutral (4)—its mood is indistinct (though it does sound reminiscent of Jerome Kern's "Can't Help Lovin' Dat Man") and it only becomes significant at all when Rick draws attention to it ("What's that you're playing?")—see Figure 4-10. "As Time Goes By," on the other hand, plays against the scene emotionally (4), because the moods

Figure 4-10. *Casablanca*. Rick and Sam after hours in the café.

of music and characters are not in sync: the sweet sentimental love ballad is sharply contradicted by Rick's bellicose drunkenness and anger at Ilsa's appearance earlier that evening ("Of all the gin joints in all the world . . .") and by Sam's nervousness about the situation and about the potential consequences of Rick's bad mood.

The dissonance of moods between the two characters serves the narrative very well, and thus we can say that music and scene fit together, are well-coordinated to advance the story: the supposedly unsentimental Rick wants to hear the song he associates with Ilsa, and this, combined with the fact that the aloof and professional café owner has become drunk, reveals for the first time the depth of his feelings for Ilsa. As here, in most cases, sound—and especially music—that actively plays against the scene is forwarding the narrative somehow by doing so.

What immediately follows is one of the most famous audio dissolves outside of musicals, used here as a transition to Rick's flashback that visualizes for us his memories. Soon an orchestra sneaks in under the piano, at first seeming to sweeten the sound of the piano but soon displacing it altogether. As the image dissolves from Rick to the Arc de Triomphe, the music mutates, leading to a statement of the opening of the Marseillaise, which coincides with the shot

a | b **Figure 4-11.** *Casablanca.* Transition to the flashback of Paris.

of Paris and the beginning of the flashback (see Figure 4-11). Here, music becomes a bridge to that earlier and—for Rick at least—happier time. The Paris of the flashback is therefore also a time that Rick idealizes, and the audio dissolve here marks it as such.

Summary

In chapter 3 we covered sound in relation to the physical space of the filmic world. In this chapter the attention turned to the temporal relations of sound and image, specifically the formal effects of scene transitions that manipulate sound (sound bridge) and the close (or loose) coordination of sound and image (synchronization)—and its opposed term, the deliberate juxtaposition of sound and image (counterpoint). We also discussed synchronization and counterpoint in terms of what we might call narrative or emotional dissonance (another common meaning of "playing with" or "playing against" the film).

EXERCISE: THE COMMUTATION TEST

There is no easier way to confirm our explanation of music's role in the sound track and its narrative functions in a scene than by seeing (hearing) what happens when we substitute other music. In fact, this kind of exercise is very closely allied in its method and even in its goals to the spotting process that is used to decide on music for a film: you can feel much more comfortable that you "got it right" by considering alternatives.

Commutation tests are easily made for any film by simply playing music on a CD player while the film runs without sound.[5] The disadvantage is that you lose the dialogue and effects, so that the overall character of the sound track is altered (unless you have editing software available, of course). You might try an experiment with main titles, which are often accompanied by music only. For scenes without music, on the other hand, you can judge what music does by playing both CD track and film audio simultaneously. More frequently nowadays, DVDs are released with alternate tracks, for example, *Dracula* (1931) with a new string quartet score by Philip Glass.

Suppose that we removed the quiet, slightly nervous music from the bedroom scene in *Psycho*, discussed in chapter 1, where Marion Crane packs her suitcase before running off with her employer's money (Figure 4-12). Now, replace that music with a much more obviously ominous cue from a recent horror film. The empathy we feel for Janet Leigh's character as she mulls over an all-too familiar human dilemma about how to balance behavior and desire would be lost—we would immediately be sharply distanced from her ("Is she about to become a victim already?") but still wanting to communicate, to warn her about the danger that awaits her in a closet, perhaps, or in the shower we see in the background. What this substitution confirms, by negative example, is how effectively Bernard Herrmann's music makes us empathize with Marion, despite its rather sparse and understated quality.

More radically, if we substituted a popular song sung by a woman, such as the classic 1970s-era "Get It While You Can" (Janis Joplin) or the more recent "Cornflake Girl" (Tori Amos), there would suddenly be an extra semantic layer whose meanings we would take to be emanating from Marion (because

Figure 4-12. *Psycho*. Marion hesitates for a moment about whether to take the money.

the soloist is a woman) or else from the singer as a confidante or mentor for Marion. This substitution confirms, again by negative example, that Bernard Herrmann's music emphasizes the immediate problem of desire in Marion— "Should I take the money or not?"—rather than the sexual desire that is the root motivation for her stealing the money (Figure 4-13). (Sexual desire here is best understood in the more abstract sense of wanting to establish the couple: Marion steals the money so that she and her lover, Sam, can move away and establish a life for themselves.) Alternatively, the stylistic anachronisms provoked by these songs might seem to put the singers at a distance from Marion, encouraging an interpretation of them as narrators or commentators (voice-over narration or "Greek chorus") and perhaps unsympathetic (anempathetic) commentators at that.

Finally, if we used an electronic dance track (say, early 1990s house, with volume level set lower than normal (for its style), although still prominent in the sound track), the music would pass over and ignore the very subtle shifts of emotion that occur every few seconds in this scene. What such an overbearing but neutral music confirms is that Bernard Herrmann's cue is firmly set in the classical tradition of empathetic, synchronized music. That in itself is an important observation about film style, as Herrmann is not necessarily known for closely adhering to that tradition, especially in his later film scores.

Note that the issue is not whether the music we substitute has an effect on the scene—thanks to the cognitive process that Chion called the **"audiovisual contract,"**[6] *any* music added to the sound track will have *some* kind of effect,

Figure 4-13. *Psycho.* Marion takes the money.

leading us to draw connections among the things we see, even if those connections provoke confusion and therefore "play against" (what if we tried the opening of Beethoven's Fifth Symphony?). The issue is the narrative coherence of those connections—our ability to judge easily the appropriateness of the music to the characters, emotions, and actions of a scene and our understanding of its narrative contexts.

Writing About Film Sound
Analysis and Description

Introduction

The chapters and exercises of Part I have supplied some tools for basic analysis of the sound track. This "interlude" between Parts I & II presents advice and models for gathering and presenting information gained from analysis in the form of reports and response papers.

As with any other kind of writing, the way an essay on film sound or film music is shaped—in its design, in the information it provides, and in its argument—will vary according to the author's goals. In general we can say that essays will usually fall into one of three broad categories: analysis, criticism, or interpretation. For a class, you might be asked to produce an analysis report that gives the kind of information generated by the analysis checklist in ch. 1 (updated in ch. 2 and in the second exercise at the end of ch. 3). Or you might write a short response paper (similar to an essay question on an exam) that characterizes the sound track in a scene or a whole film, summarizes music's narrative functions in a film (or, more narrowly, describes music in a scene) or compares the treatment of sound or music in two scenes. (Less likely is a response paper that asks for your personal opinion of a film.) The published critical literature includes evaluative reviews of sound track CDs and, occasionally, significant mention of sound and music in journalistic film reviews. The general literature also includes interviews with sound designers, composers, and other film professionals. Finally, scholarly articles range from archive studies to historical narratives to interpretive essays that may be informed by theoretical, literary, or narratological models. The advanced student who wants to make sound or music the focus of his or her work needs to know something of narratology, literary theory, and the historical and interpretive traditions of film studies and music studies.

There are many readily available examples of reviews and journalistic writing on film music, but fewer on film sound in general. In that connection, it is important to understand that the term "sound track recording" does not in fact refer to a recording of the film's sound track but to a recording of some or all of its music. When LP recordings of film sound tracks became common in the early 1970s, they normally consisted either of a film's nondiegetic orchestral music or of its songs in popular or jazz idioms, but rarely ever both. In more recent years, the contents of sound track CDs have become more diverse, consisting sometimes of the orchestral cues, as in earlier decades, sometimes of a mixture of orchestral cues and songs (or older recordings quoted in the film) that were used either diegetically or nondiegetically, but sometimes only of songs and related performances.

The purpose of a CD review of a sound track recording is the same as a film reviewer's task in a review of current theater or video offerings: to give a lively, brief account of the contents, to assess the technical quality of performance and recording, and to offer an evaluation that might guide the reader's decision to purchase the item. One of the curious features of CD reviews is that they often make little mention of the film from which the music is derived. Although that may seem strange at first, it becomes understandable if you remember that the average fan does not need a review of the recording—he or she will buy a sound track CD based on a liking for the film. It is the sound track collector who typically reads CD reviews, and he or she buys sound tracks for reasons that might include fondness for the film but are more likely to be related to building a broad-based or carefully specialized but comprehensive collection, or else preference for a composer, genre, or even orchestra and conductor (in the case of newly performed suites or re-recorded classical sound tracks).

We will not discuss the writing of CD reviews further in this book. Instead, we will concentrate on class reports and papers, including descriptive and interpretive essays that approach their topics in ways similar to the articles found in scholarly journals. Our first category, the "analysis report," is a succinct description of a film's sound track or music, often including tables of detailed information. The "response paper" may be a prose version of the analysis report, typically for one or more scenes, or a short essay that responds to questions (such as "How does music articulate narrative structure—or highlight narrative priorities?" "Are sound track (or music) treated conventionally or in a distinctive, stylized manner? etc.) or that compares sound or music in two different scenes. Another broad category, the interpretive essay, will be discussed in the Interlude after Part II.

Analysis Report: *Catch Me If You Can*

OVERVIEW

An analysis report is a short descriptive paper that demonstrates you can follow a film's narrative and can analyze and make general statements about some specific aspect of the film (such as comparing plot and story, following character development, observing features of lighting or framing, etc.). Usually an instructor will assign particular features to be analyzed. In our case, of course, the analysis report takes as its topic for analysis the sound track as a whole, or some element of it (music, dialogue, or effects). Alternatively, an analysis report may chart in detail the balance and functions of the sound track elements in a single scene or set of closely related scenes.

To write an analysis report, it is almost always necessary to take written notes on the film. These notes in many cases are likely to be extensive enough that they themselves could constitute the bulk of the analysis report in a film music course, to which you might add one or two sentences of comment and summary. You should expect to watch the film in its entirety at least twice, and some individual scenes one or more additional times. Applying the checklist for analysis in chapter 1 (or as updated in ch. 2 and ch. 3) will give an efficient and thorough method of compiling notes. The checklist is designed for detailed analysis of a single scene and you can use either version for that purpose. If we want to apply the checklist to an entire film rather than just to a single scene, however, we must update it again:

1. Background and general information for context: genre, director, release year, principal actors. To this you might add the production company or companies, and principal personnel for the sound track (usually composer, sound designer, and perhaps also effects supervisor)
2. Synopsis (3–4 sentence summary of the narrative)
3. Table of music cues
4. General description of the sound track elements and their balance
5. [if appropriate to the exercise; might also be included under #4] General evaluation of the sound track
6. Summary or description of music's narrative functions: music's codes, diegetic/nondiegetic, synchronization/counterpoint, emotion and characterization, and the external/internal opposition

To show this edited checklist in action, we will apply it to *Catch Me If You Can*.

1. Background

> *Catch Me If You Can* (2002). DreamWorks SKG. Produced and directed by Steven Spielberg; written by Jeff Nathanson based on a book by Frank Abagnale Jr. and Stan Redding. Principal characters: Frank Abagnale Jr. (Leonardo DiCaprio), Carl Hanratty (Tom Hanks), Frank Abagnale, Sr. (Christopher Walken), Roger Strong (Martin Sheen), Paula Abagnale (Nathalie Baye). Supervising sound editors: Charles L. Campbell, John A. Larsen. Score by John Williams. Other music is listed in the music cues table below.

Credits and other information can usually be acquired from online sources (in particular the *International Movie Database* (or *IMDb*)) but should always be double-checked against the credits on a DVD or VHS print of the film. (On the other hand, *IMDb* often provides information not available on the DVD or VHS tape.)[1] The information supplied in the report can vary, but at a minimum should include title, year, production company, director, screenwriter, principal actors, and all original music contributions (for a report concentrating on music). Music reuses (existing recordings that are incorporated into the film) generally are better placed in the music cues table. If you plan to focus on details of any one scene, make sure that secondary characters who appear in that scene are listed here, too.

2. Synopsis

> This film tells the story of Frank Abagnale, Jr., who runs away from home rather than face the trauma of his parents' divorce and his father's slow financial ruin. Frank is a risk-taker, who discovers that he has innate talent for imitating professionals (airline pilots, doctors, and lawyers), and he develops great skill in forging checks. The story, told mostly in flashback, is about FBI agent Carl Hanratty's campaign to capture Frank, who spends several years in prison but eventually works for the FBI cracking check forgery cases.

A synopsis should generally run from 75 to 200 words. This one (you may recognize it from the opening of ch. 1) follows the story. We could have shaped the synopsis in terms of the plot, instead, beginning with the release from a French prison, because that would have aligned better with our list of music cues later—but, in general, a simple and brief account of the story line is enough. If you plan to focus on details of any one scene, make sure that the synopsis provides enough information for the reader to understand the context of that scene.

In a more detailed analysis report, you might break the film down into narrative segments (chapters and scene sequences). Remember that DVD tracks do not always reliably follow narrative segmentation, so do not assume that you can simply use track labels as scene titles. If you are asked to carry out this kind of sequence breakdown, you should be careful to collate it with the labels used in the cues table (see #3, which follows).

3. Music Cues
See Table Int-1 for a listing of music in *Catch Me If You Can*. The musical themes named in the table are given in Figures Int-1, Int-2, and Int-3.

Figure Int-1. *Catch Me if You Can.* Main theme.

Figure Int-2. *Catch Me if You Can.* Frank's theme.

Figure Int-3. *Catch Me if You Can.* Frank's father's theme.

Table Int-1 *Catch Me if You Can*, music cues.

DVD track	Scene (titles in square brackets are from the sound track CD)	Timings and notes
1	Main title sequence ["Catch Me if You Can" theme (Figure Int-1)]	Out 00:03:00. Alternating thirds theme; visual and musical imitation of graphics-based main-title sequences from 1950s–1960s movies; jazz orchestrations mixed with traditional orchestra
1	Song behind *To Tell the Truth* introduction	In 00:03:10; out 00:04:15. "To Tell": Paul Alter and Robert Israel
3	Dance music on phonograph "Embraceable You"	In at 00:11:00 with closeup of phonograph; out 00:12:42 with cut. "Embraceable": Gershwin, sung by Judy Garland
3	Sad music for the move from house to apartment (saxophone solo)	In at 00:16:00; out 00:18:30 under chimes. Shifts mood near the end when Frank is given book of checks—intimation of Frank's theme

4	Phonograph (offscreen; mother and male visitor)—brief: "Put Your Head on My Shoulder"	In at 00:22:50. "Put Your Head": Paul Anka
5–6	He runs from divorce [A Broken Home]; cut to Paris; into Chapter 6 for first check scam	In at 00:26:40; out 00:28:55 with cut to Paris; in again at 00:29:20; out 00:32:55
7–8	He fakes co-pilot (Frank's theme—upper register, undulating [Deadheading] (Figure Int-2)	In at 00:35:00; out in ch. 8 at 00:38:30
8–9	Plane trip (Frank's theme; second section is [The Float])	In at 00:39:45 out 00:040:50; in again at 00:041:15; out in ch. 9 with FBI at 00:42:55
9–10	Several pieces in a row: Low-volume neutral diegetic piano music in background under restaurant scene with Frank and father; quick cut to FBI car (big band on radio); to hotel in Hollywood (phonograph? "The Girl From Ipanema"); "Catch Me" theme; Frank escapes	In at 00:44:25; out 00:55:40—Music is continuous; "Girl" enters at 00:51:30, to underscoring ("Catch Me" theme) at 00:52:40; out briefly, back in at 00:55:00. Neutral piano music is "Body and Soul," John Green et al., perf. Errol Garner; "I've Got the World on a String," Harold Arlen, perf. Teddy Wilson. Car radio is "Take the A Train," Billy Strayhorn. "Girl" credits are Antonio Carlos Jobim, performed by Jobim with Stan Getz and Joao Gilberto.
11	"James Bond" sound track in theater; then "The Look of Love" and visual joke with Hanratty in laundromat	In at 00:57:44; "Look" at 00:58:40; out 00:59:45; back in at 01:00:00; segue to next cue. "Bond": Monty Norman. "Look": Burt Bacharach, sung by Dusty Springfield
12	Hanratty and Frank on phone with song ["Mele Kalikimaka"] on radio; cut to restaurant and radio: "He's So Fine"; at word "Flash," the "Catch Me" theme	In at 01:03:30; to underscoring at 01:05:45 (Frank's father's theme (Figure Int-3)); very briefly radio and underscoring together, then to restaurant at 01:06:30; "Flash" at 01:07:02; out 01:07:45. "Molo": Alex Anderson, perf. Bing Crosby. "He's so fine": Ronald Mack
13	"Catch Me" theme (short)	In at 01:09:25; segue
13	Party in Atlanta (rock and roll) "You Really Got Me"	In at 01:10:00; out about 01:10:50. "You Really": Ray Davies
13	Doctor (Frank's theme)	In at 01:13:20; out 01:15:20
13	Father and Hanratty ("Catch Me" theme)	In at 01:19:10; out 01:19:55
13–14	Engaged (Frank's theme changes to "Catch Me" with FBI); Mozart behind dinner with Brenda's family; cut to hospital office ("Catch Me" theme); Frank (Frank's theme)	In at 01:21:05; Mozart at 01:22:20; "Catch Me" at 01:24:50, then back to Mozart; out at 01:27:40 with cut to bar exam. Mozart is the slow movement from Piano Concerto no. 11 in D major
14–15	Frank becomes a lawyer; family watches TV (Mitch Miller: "Anybody Here Seen Kelly?") and phonograph (reprise of "Embraceable You"), continues under meeting of father and son in bar, then "The Way You Look Tonight"; underscoring briefly after father says "You can't stop"; Frank calls Hanratty (lush orchestral setting of "I'll be Home for Christmas"—recorded, in hotel bar)	In at 01:28:55; lawyer out 01:30:35; then family at TV; "Embraceable" at 01:34:30; "You can't stop" at 01:35:40; phone call at 01:36:00; out 01:37:50. "The Way": Jerome Kern. "I'll be home": Walter Kent

16-17	Background music for engagement party ("I Can't Give You Anything but Love, Baby"; then " I'm Shooting High"); to underscoring, Frank escapes, at 1:44:15 segue to airport (Frank's theme)	In at 01:38:15, to underscoring at 01:42:05; out 01:45:45. "I Can't" and "I'm Shooting": Jimmy McHugh
17	Brief underscoring	01:46:20.
17	Brief diegetic music: "Leaving on a Jet Plane"	01:47:05. "Leaving": John Denver
17	Background voice with piano "Come Fly with Me"	In at 01:47:25; out 01:49:35 under noise of plane taking off (song synchronized to end with scene)
18-19	Hanratty thinks; goes to printer; cut to children's choir in France, then low bass and percussion sounds in printing building	In at 01:50:35; at 01:51:50 "Catch Me"; choir in at 01:52:50, out about 01:53:15; choir in near the end at 01:56:30; out at 01:57:48 with return to the plane. "Angels We Have Heard on High." (Choir credits read "Los angos danos nos campagnos" and "Peuple fideles")
19	After Hanratty says "your father is dead"— theme from divorce scene; "Christmas Song" at mother's house, continues as Frank is placed in jail cell	In at 01:59:00; out at about 2:00:00; song at 2:01:05; out 02:03:40. "The Christmas Song: Mel Tormé, sung by Nat King Cole (song synchronized to end with scene)
20	Frank arrives at FBI office	In at 02:07:10; out 02:09:10
21	FBI Monday morning; music based on Frank's theme; end credits feature "Catch Me"	In at 02:12:25; out 02:13:35; in again at 02:14:10, and into end credits at 02:15:45; ends at 02:20:17.

This table was compiled from a DVD print, and thus the basic time marker is the track (DVD chapter). Depending on the number of chapter divisions on the DVD and how closely those divisions accord with sequences, you might find it more convenient to use time codes. If you are working from a VHS print, you will have to use the player's digital timer to determine your markers. You may designate either the main title or (preferably) the studio logo before the main title as time point 00:00:00; include this time point in the cues table so that your choice is clear. Be sure to include both time-in and time-out for all cues. It is not necessary to be absolutely precise—a time within 5 to 10 sec is usually good enough. (You have to improve the accuracy if you are timing the details of an individual scene, of course.) If something striking or notable happens in the action or in the other elements of the sound track at the point music comes in or goes out, add a comment in column two (for action) or three (with the timings). In column two we used scene labels or descriptions; you could also use DVD chapter titles or even music cue names, if you have a complete sound track list (usually from a recording). The third column here provides timings and names of composer and performer for music reuses, but you could also use it for comments on tempo, mood, recurrent material, sound track mix, etc.

It is not necessary to have access to formal cue lists or song lists like those in this chapter to develop a description of the music in a complete film. Listing entry and exit times, collating these with scenes, and then describing or summarizing the character and function(s) of the music works quite well for many purposes. This can, however, become tedious in films with very large amounts of music, especially when one wants to list and label recurrent themes.

A reuses list can usually be taken from the song credits, especially in recent films. A reuse is existing music that is cited—by reproducing the original recording or by a new arrangement—in the course of the film; these are listed near the end of the credits and are almost always listed in order of appearance in the film, a fact that can be very useful in making identifications. (A studio **cue sheet**—which is the legal document accounting for all music uses and reuses in a film—would resolve all this with precision, but cue sheets are generally not available unless you have a commercial or legal interest in the music licenses.)

Sound track CDs can sometimes help with cue titles and song titles and, of course, music tracks that you can collate with the film's music. Be aware, however, that sound track CDs vary widely in their contents: very few contain all the music in a film and many do not have the music in the same order that it appears in the film. It is common, for example, to delete popular songs from CDs that highlight the symphonic **background music**—and vice versa for films with several featured songs. Thus, it can be a tedious task to collate a sound track CD with the music of a film. Likewise, major online resources rarely have complete sound track listings, but they can serve as good resources for titles of popular songs, standards, and quotations from historical music that appear in a film. Bill Wrobel's website "Film Score Rundowns" (*http:// www.filmscorerundowns.net/*) has a small but growing collection of cue lists and descriptions for classical American films, in particular those with music by Bernard Herrmann.

4. General description of the sound track elements and their balance

This is a sound track dominated by speech and music. Sound effects occasionally play a role (more so in the first part than later), but much of the story takes place indoors in sound-deadened institutional environments. Furthermore, the plot is advanced in considerable part through conversation: Frank's family becomes dysfunctional, Frank tries to maintain his relationship with his father, Frank talks with people to gain information he needs to talk his way through his scams, Carl talks to agents and to Frank as the FBI works through its case. Relatively speaking, the music track is also quite active: music is present in roughly 90 of the film's 141 minutes, although it is only foregrounded on a few occasions.

With the conventional exceptions of the main-title cue and end-credits composition, the nondiegetic orchestral music is not foregrounded; it is songs that sometimes receive this treatment, whether they are obviously diegetic (or even a performance, as in the case of the Mitch Miller sing-along), uncertainly diegetic, or nondiegetic.

This description constitutes a brief statement (about 150 words) that summarizes how the sound track as a whole operates in the film. It stresses the first level of analysis—the sound track elements and their balance—but you might extend the statement to include a description of how the sound track contributes to the narrative point of the film (and perhaps also an evaluation of how well it makes its contribution). Items you might discuss under this rubric include narrative associations of music or sound effects, the use of music and sound to articulate narrative structure, etc.; but you should always include a summary statement of the narrative work that the sound track is doing on the more general level of the film as a whole.

5. General evaluation of the sound track

If you have not already made a comment under #4, then draw up a short statement of opinion about the effectiveness of the sound track—in terms of a satisfying acoustic experience and in terms of success in contributing to the narrative. Our description under #4 carries an implied criticism: "This is a sound track dominated by speech and music. Sound effects occasionally play a role. . . ." We could make that explicit by complaining about an over-reliance on speech and music—the under-utilized effects track shortchanges suspense elements in the film, forcing more work onto music, which results in a somewhat romanticized effect overall (an effect considerably exaggerated by the many nostalgic song quotations). We might also connect our evaluation of the sound track with evaluative statements made by film critics. Our complaint about the routine and conventional nature of the sound track fits very well, for example, with Roger Ebert's summary opinion: "This is not a major Spielberg film, although it is an effortlessly watchable one. Spielberg and his writer . . . don't force matters or plumb for deep significance. The story is a good story, directly told, and such meaning as it has comes from the irony that the only person who completely appreciates Abagnale's accomplishments is the man trying to arrest him."[2]

6. Description of music's narrative functions

Music here is equally divided between original orchestral music and re-uses, the music passing freely among musical styles and the diegetic and nondiegetic spheres. John Williams' music, which is scored for a small traditional orchestra whose prominent saxophone solos suggest jazz colorings, is heavily dependent on recurrences of three themes: "Catch Me If

You Can," the Father's theme, and Frank's theme. These uniformly function empathetically. The reuses are more complex: (1) simple diegetic
cues are anchored in their physical spaces by onscreen radios and phonographs; (2) truly neutral diegetic background(ed) music; (3) apparently
diegetic cues continue, at the same volume, through two or even three
scenes; (4) strongly foregrounded nondiegetic cues (such as "Come Fly
With Me"). Most of the reuses also serve a definable narrative function—
confirming a venue (a diner, an elegant hotel dining room, a mid-1960s
youth party in an upscale house), acting as the pure code of performance,
making culturally coded references to musical styles and genres, and establishing associations within the film (as with the reappearance of "Embraceable You" and the recurring style topic of popular Christmas songs,
but more often through references in the lyrics or song titles: "Embraceable You" for the two moments when Frank's mother dances; "Come Fly
with Me" and "Leaving on a Jet Plane" for Frank's last aerial escape; "I
Can't Give You Anything But Love, Baby," when Frank tells his fiancée the
truth about himself; etc.).

A prose description of these details could become quite long. As an alternative, you might gather notes under headings. In the "notes" column of the
shot list or in the parallel place in the analysis template, you could remark on
examples of the type cited in the previous paragraph, then collect the notes
under main headings such as "diegetic/nondiegetic," etc.

Response Paper that Describes Music's Narrative Functions

The response paper is most likely to be a course assignment, like the screening report. A response paper is a short essay (typically between 300 and 800
words) that is roughly the size of a newspaper film review. Like any essay, the
response paper may veer in the direction of analytic description or evaluative
opinion, or it may strike a balance between the two. For a course in film music
or film sound, it is most likely that the instructor will ask that the paper summarize how the sound track as a whole contributes to the narrative point of
the film, in which case you should discuss the narrative associations of music
or sound effects (speech, too, if there is something unusual about it), the use
of music and sound to articulate narrative structure, and the narrative work
that the sound track is doing on the more general level of the film as a whole.
If there is room (or as an alternative assignment), you might also compare the
use of sound and music in this and another film.

Items under headings 4, 5, and 6 in the analysis checklist will probably
supply most of the information—and perhaps much of the text—you need for

a response paper. The first paragraphs under each of those three headings in the previous section total just over 600 words. We have reworked those texts as a paper that responds to the question, "How does music work in the sound track of *Catch Me If You Can*? Answer in a paper of 500 to 750 words."

(response paper example, paragraph 1) The sound track of *Catch Me If You Can* is dominated by speech and music. Sound effects occasionally play a role (more so in the first part than later), but much of the story takes place indoors in sound-deadened institutional environments.

(response paper example, paragraph 2) Furthermore, the film follows the simplest conventions of the sound film in that speech dominates over music: the plot is advanced in considerable part through conversation. Frank's family becomes dysfunctional, Frank tries to maintain his relationship with his father, Frank talks with people to gain information he needs to talk his way through his scams, Carl talks to agents and to Frank as the FBI works through its case.

(response paper example, paragraph 3) The music track is actually quite active, in the sense that there is music in roughly 90 of the film's 141 minutes, but it is only foregrounded on a few occasions. With the conventional exceptions of the main-title cue and end-credits composition, the nondiegetic orchestral music is not foregrounded; it is songs that sometimes receive this treatment, whether they are obviously diegetic (or even a performance, as in the case of the Mitch Miller sing-along), uncertainly diegetic, or nondiegetic.

(response paper example, paragraph 4) Music is about equally divided between original orchestral music and reuses, and it passes freely among musical styles and the diegetic and nondiegetic spheres. John Williams' music, which is scored for a small traditional orchestra whose prominent saxophone solos suggest jazz colorings, is heavily dependent on recurrences of three themes: "Catch Me If You Can," the Father's theme, and Frank's theme. These uniformly function empathetically. The reuses are more complex: (1) simple diegetic cues are anchored in their physical spaces by onscreen radios and phonographs; (2) truly neutral diegetic background(ed) music; (3) apparently diegetic cues continue, at the same volume, through two or even three scenes; (4) strongly foregrounded nondiegetic cues (such as "Come Fly With Me"). Most of the reuses also serve a definable narrative function—confirming a venue (a diner, an elegant hotel dining room, a mid-60s youth party in an upscale house), acting as the pure code of performance, making culturally coded references to musical styles and genres, and establishing associations within the film (as with the reappearance of "Embraceable You" and the recurring trope of popular Christmas songs, but more often through references in the lyrics or song titles: "Embraceable You" for the two moments when Frank's mother dances; "Come Fly with Me" and "Leaving on a Jet Plane" for Frank's last aerial escape; "I Can't Give You Anything But Love, Baby," when Frank tells his fiancée the truth about himself; etc.).

(response paper example, paragraph 5) The under-utilized effects track short-changes suspense elements in the film, forcing more work onto the music, a situation that results in a somewhat romanticized effect overall (considerably exaggerated, of course, by the many nostalgic song quotations). Overall, the sound track (and its music) are treated in an effective but routine and conventional manner, a conclusion that seems to be consistent with Roger Ebert's summary opinion of *Catch Me If You Can*: "This is not a major Spielberg film, although it is an effortlessly watchable one. Spielberg and his writer . . . don't force matters or plumb for deep significance. The story is a good story, directly told, and such meaning as it has comes from the irony that the only person who completely appreciates Abagnale's accomplishments is the man trying to arrest him."*

Compare and Contrast Paper Focusing on Music

The device of compare and contrast provides an alternative format for an essay or response paper. At its most straightforward, a compare-contrast essay is simply an interpretive essay that studies two films (or scenes from two films) instead of one.

Martin Marks' scholarly article "Music, Drama, Warner Brothers: The Cases of *Casablanca* and *The Maltese Falcon*,"[3] is a very extended (10,000+ words) exercise in compare and contrast. He does not choose his two films arbitrarily: they were released within one year of each other by the same studio, both involve international intrigue and feature the same (male) actors. Their composers are different, however, and this is Marks' entry point: the background music for *Casablanca* (1942) was composed by Max Steiner; the composer for *The Maltese Falcon* (1941) was Adolf Deutsch. The thesis, then, is "the scores by Deutsch and Steiner follow similar formal schemes, [but] they offer sharp contrasts in style and function, owing partly to the inclinations of the composers, partly to fundamental differences in the filmic narratives." Although the article is generally an appreciation of both works, Marks is critical of details in Deutsch's score, which leads to a broader evaluation: "In summary, we might say that one of these scores [*Casablanca*] sings, the other [*The Maltese Falcon*] doesn't; that one speaks a language we can easily understand, the other whispers secrets; and that, following pathways both parallel and far apart, each finds a different way to move with its film, from beginning to end."[4]

For *Catch Me If You Can*, you might write a paper that compares it with another recent film having a score by John Williams, your goal being to articulate common treatment or differences in terms of music's role in the sound

---

* Always remember to credit sources for material in course papers: see the Notes for the citation to Ebert's review.

track and its narrative functions. You can also argue, if you choose, that one film is better suited to Williams' style and methods. Another possibility would be to make an historical comparison with a Williams score for a similar film—perhaps another coming-of-age film such as *Empire of the Sun* (1987). In this case, you might choose to focus on the development of—changes or improvements over time in—Williams' practice. Still another possibility, of course, is to adopt Marks' device of comparing two recent films with scores by different composers. It is usually best to use his criteria, too: the films and their scores should show some strong commonalities, so that comparison has a plausible basis—it would be difficult to make much out of a comparison between, for example, *Catch Me If You Can* and *The Lord of the Rings* (2001–2003).

Concluding Comments

Just as in any writing you do, you may also bring to bear specialized knowledge you have: about film production, film history, actor or other personnel biography, the repertoire of a certain film genre or national film tradition, cultural studies, or music theory and history. We have tried to cover modes of description and models that will be useful to most writers, but you could certainly enrich an analysis report with transcriptions of the themes in music notation or more systematically listed connections between the sound track and continuity editing. Similarly, comments on style and genre can benefit from a broad grasp of the common historical narratives, cultural analyses can be better grounded through a knowledge of critical or music theory, and any study of narrative film can make use of some basic skills in narratology. Nevertheless, as we have tried to demonstrate throughout this book, it is not necessary to have specialized knowledge or terminology to hear music in the sound track and to write about it productively.

At the same time, be careful not to distort your descriptions and interpretations by misjudging the role of music—or other sound track element—or the sound track as a whole. Because you are trying to pay attention to it, music may become decidedly more prominent in your perception of a film than would be the case if you had approached viewing the film in a "normal" way, with typical expectations for narrative films. By paying attention to *any* one element of a film for an extended period of time, you threaten to inadvertently "stylize" that film, to skew its hierarchy and flow of materials and events. (The easy fast forward and recall of the VHS tape and DVD only make the problem more acute.) One of the most important skills for film music and film sound study is the ability to alternate—jump back and forth—between a "normal," open but critical mode of film viewing and a biased mode that gives particular attention to music or other elements of the sound track (or to the sound track as a whole). Even the scholarly literature has too many case studies that make exaggerated claims for music's influence in a film because the analyst-author became so focused on the music that he or she was no longer able to position that music appropriately within the context of the film's mode of presentation.

Finally: *always* go back and double check information you write up from memory. As we have said in chapter 1, films put a great deal of information out at the viewer, and it is extremely difficult to retain an accurate memory of scene details, including the specific interactions of music and action. As a cautionary example, one of us wrote about the "Christmas Song" scene in *Catch Me If You Can* for chapter 4, under the heading "counterpoint." A draft version of this text was written from memory of classroom viewing and discussion about four months earlier. Memory dictated that all shots but one were from the outside of the house and that the music came from a phonograph visible in the background. Neither of these things is true, and both are significant errors that could result in poorly grounded interpretations of this scene. (Michel Chion gives similar examples of faulty memory in ch. 10 of his book *Audio-Vision*.[5])

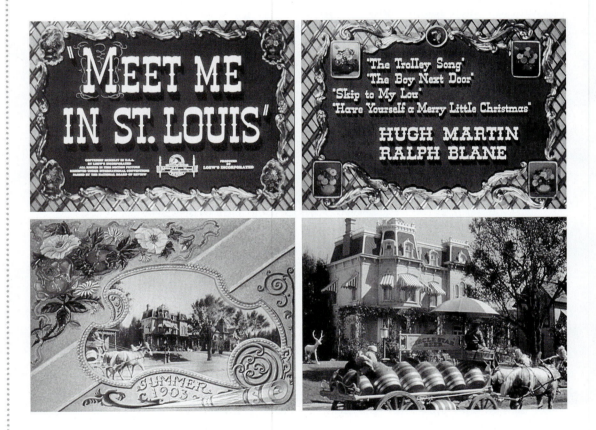

PART TWO

Music, Film Form, and Film Style

In Part II we direct attention especially to music's roles in film form and film style.

Film form refers to the overall design of a film, or the temporal articulations of its running time in relation to the deployment of conventional units such as establishing sequences, scenes, chapters (or acts), and so forth.

Film style also refers to the treatment of conventional expectations, but the basis of film style is the collection of techniques, practices, aesthetic preferences, and cultural and cinematic expectations that constitute the distinctive way narrative is "delivered" in any individual film. The term can also be generalized to groups of related films: in that broader sense film style means the various conventions and figures that have evolved over the course of time as films have been made by production teams, exhibited in theaters and via home media, and responded to by audiences. By calling on these conventions and figures (and the codes they form), film scholars can develop descriptions of the ways that film elements, including the sound track, are presented and manipulated and can make comparisons of the ways these basic materials are treated in different national or regional cinemas. Using these comparisons, one can also construct style histories, that is, accounts of the ways these treatments have changed over time within a single tradition (or, on a grander scale, multiple cinematic traditions).

The term film style, thus, can apply to any level of discussion and analysis. We can refer to national or regional styles (Hollywood, European, etc.), to schools, movements, or genres (film noir, Italian Neo-realist, New Wave), to studio styles (Warner Bros. or MGM in the 1930s), or to individual directors, sound designers, or composers. In the same way as other components, music participates in and helps shape film style.

Chapter 5 gives an overview of ways to mark the units of film form and to position music in relation to them. Six films from different periods and different genres provide extended examples. The formal functions of establishing and end-credit sequences, performances, and fantasy montage scenes are explored in chapters 6 and 7, mainly through sets of examples with commentary. These will demonstrate that aspects of film form and film style inevitably interact with and overlap one another, as the sequences also show marked variation due to historically distinct patterns of practice and to the individual aesthetic choices of directors, composers, and sound designers. Chapter 8, then, turns to specific aspects of film style that refer to music, especially musical themes and style topics, and chapter 9 follows this up with another series of scene examples, this time scenes that especially exploit musical style topics, either characteristically at the level of the scene itself (action scenes and love scenes) or in more complex ways (as commonly happens in dialogue underscoring).

Music in Film Form

Introduction

The time of a film may be manipulated in many ways, as story elements are reordered, given more or less emphasis, or even deleted, but the most basic experience of watching a film is the same as it is with a piece of music: movement through linear or clock time. A symphony may last 45 min, a CD album may last 1 hr, a feature film may run 2 hr. Articulating or segmenting that time line is the process of breaking down the continuous flow of clock time into graspable units. By convention we refer to this as analyzing form in music and as segmentation in film. Although terminology differs, the articulation of musical form and film segmentation work in much the same way. The units do not correspond in terms of clock time (for example, we do not have a simple equivalent in musical form to the scene in film), but both modes of analysis segment time hierarchically, that is, into smaller units contained inside successively larger units. Of course, because narrative is the driving force in all traditional feature films, the test for descriptions of film form at any level is how well they fit plausible narrative units.

Runtime Segmentation

In music, the smallest significant time unit is the measure (or bar), a group of two to four beats with an initial accent (recall from ch. 2 that it is the recurring patterns of musical meter that make the measure or bar-length units recognizable). Measures are grouped by articulation into increasingly larger segments: motive (or "basic idea"), phrases, periods, sections, movements. The most familiar of these terms is probably "phrase." More or less aligned with short-term memory, phrases are typically 6- to 10-sec segments articulated by means of devices such as a clichéd cadence, a slight slowing down, a drop downward or stop on a long note in the melodic line, or starting over with the same melodic figure in the immediately following bar.

Consider the title song from *Singin' in the Rain* (1952). The title text is sung first (its music is a motive or basic idea), then repeated, the last note being held a little longer the second time than it was the first. Then a new text follows, its musical line dropping to a long note at the end (and a text rhyme is coordinated with it): rain, again. This entire unit, which most people would sing in 7 to 8 sec, is a phrase. Thus, the musical phrase is more like a sentence in language than like a phrase, which usually refers to an incomplete grammatical unit; and there is a sentence-like "grammar" to the musical phrase: it is composed of smaller units (the motives or ideas), and it typically concludes with punctuation (cadence, in musical terms) that effects closure. Like language, which offers commas, semi-colons, periods, etc., the strength of a musical closure can vary. The phrase from "Singin' in the Rain" includes a very weak stop (after the second repetition of the title text) and a more conclusive stop (at its end), or what is sometimes called a half cadence. As the song continues, its second phrase—which eventually repeats the title text at its very end—has an even more conclusive stop, or full cadence. The two phrases together, lasting roughly 15 sec, form a section, which might have its own designation, in this case the chorus of the verse-chorus form that was standard for popular songs (and many numbers in musical theater, as well) until about 1960.

Here is another example using musical notation. The song "Meet Me in St. Louis, Louis," which figures very prominently in the film musical of that name (1944), is also written in the verse-chorus form. Its chorus (almost always the better known part of a popular song) is a rather fast waltz whose first motive or basic idea is four bars long, setting the title text (see Figure 5-1). The next four bars finish the phrase, which would take about 7 to 8 sec in all to sing. Notice the longer note at the end of the phrase, the settling on a lower note after some higher notes, and the starting over in a second phrase. The first two phrases together form a period, and the entire thirty-two bars would be a sec-

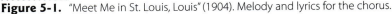

Figure 5-1. "Meet Me in St. Louis, Louis" (1904). Melody and lyrics for the chorus.

tion (although, in this case, we call the section a chorus, as we did with "Singin' in the Rain" earlier).

Unfortunately, there is no simple analogue to "phrase" in film analysis. The *shot* is the basic unit of continuity editing, but the length of a shot can vary greatly, from 1 to 100 sec (or more). A single very long shot (often called a "long take") or, more likely, a number of shots gathered together in terms of unity of time and space is a *scene* (we understand clock time in the diegetic world and usually a single place, such as a room, a garden, etc., along with a unified, cause-and-effect based narrative progress). Screenwriting textbooks typically dictate that a new scene starts whenever there is a change of either time or place (or preferably both). Thus, scenes, like shots, can vary greatly in length, although we can still venture to say that, on average, scenes typically last from 1 to 5 min.

A series of shots related as a narrative unit is a *sequence*. The term is generally reserved, however, for large segments encompassing several scenes. Strictly speaking, "sequence" is short for "sequence of shots" and thus can refer to any series of shots that are related by some criteria that is important to the person doing the analysis. Such a series could be five contiguous shots of a face, a dialogue scene in a room or café covering twenty shots, or a major segment of the film running 10 min with perhaps one hundred shots. The last of these is still the most common way to use the term, not only in reviews and similar writing about films but also in most scholarly writing. We will follow this usage and, thus, the sequence is a "sequence of scenes" roughly equivalent to a chapter in a book—and just as the number (and length) of chapters in a book can vary widely, so can sequences.

The term **act** is used to gather several sequences in a common broad narrative grouping, using the same general criterion of unity of time and place. Typically, a film would not have more than three or four acts. (Here again, screenwriting conventions refer to "three-act," "four-act," or even "five-act" models.) It is not absolutely necessary to use the word "act" because most 2-hr films can easily be understood in terms of a relatively small number of sequences (perhaps 10–12), but, as shall see in the extended examples later in this chapter, many films naturally fall into a smaller number of major narrative units. Finally, although the term *chapter* is a synonym of sequence, we suggest avoiding it, because the word is commonly used to designate individual DVD tracks, which are more likely to cover the dimensions of one or two scenes. (The mechanical division of a DVD into chapters, however, can sometimes be a useful place to start in sorting out the segmentation of a film because chapter articulations normally coincide with *some* significant level of film articulation.)

Thus, the filmic analogy to music's hierarchy of motive, phrase, section, and movement is shot, scene, sequence, and act, respectively. As a simple example, Alfred Hitchcock's *North by Northwest* (1959), whose runtime is 2 hr

Essentially, the logic here is the logic of the screen, which happily does not preclude musical logic. Poets manage to think within the sonnet form, philosophers within the essay. So composers can think within the film scene.
—Lawrence Morton[1]

and 16 min, can easily be partitioned into four acts, which coincide with geographical locations of the action: (a) New York, (b) between New York and Chicago (the train trip), (c) Chicago, and (d) South Dakota (Mount Rushmore). In the Chicago act, which lasts 40 min, there are five sequences. These are listed in Table 5-1, along with timings and the method of marking or defining the beginning. The last sequence is broken down further into scenes, with notes about music, in Table 5-2.

At all levels from scene through act, the change from one unit to the next is typically demarcated clearly, by a change in the physical location (from town to country, indoors to outdoors, etc.), by a change in time (to the next day, morning to night, flashback), or by a formal marker in the film (fade to black, dissolve, an establishing shot of a different location)—or by any combination of these. These articulations are much more reliable indicators than any temporal marker (such as "scenes equal x minutes," "sequences equal y minutes"), but the latter are still generally applicable: A scene is unlikely to run for more than, say, 10 min, and sequences are commonly between 10 and 30 min long. In *Casablanca* (1942), for example, the first evening in Rick's café is depicted in a continuously running filmic unit of nearly 30 min, with a dissolve into the sign outside the café to begin and another dissolve just after Rick and Ilsa's reunion defining the end. Time and place are unified by continuous chronological time and the café building itself. It might be possible to refer to this as one enormous scene, but most of us would refer to these 30 min as a sequence because of the length and because of the large number of smaller but substantial segments, including the rigged roulette wheel, Ugarte's arrest, at least two song performances, Rick's first encounter with Major Strasser, and the reunion, among others. Along with the establishing sequence and early outdoor scenes, the café sequence forms the first act of *Casablanca*, running just over 36 min

Table 5-1 *North by Northwest* (1959), Chicago act, breakdown.

Sequence	Timing	Marker	Scenes (in sequence 5 only)
Train station	Begins at 1:00:15; lasts 6:00	Fade to black, fade in	
Corn field	Lasts 9:41	Dissolve	
Hotel	9:27	Dissolve	
Auction	8:30	Dissolve	
Airport	Sequence lasts 6:40; first scene is 2:00	Cut (to exterior of auction building)	Police car
	Lasts 0:55	Dissolve	Airport lobby
	3:45	Cut	Airport exterior

Table 5-2 *North by Northwest*, Chicago act, airport sequence breakdown.

Sequence	Scene	Scene segment	Shots (#)	Music
Airport	Police car	Auction house—exterior	1	In at 1:33:40 in auction house lobby, overlaps to beginning of car interior, then out
		Police car—interior	1 (with several s/rs• pairs)	
		Airport—exterior	1	Music in with dissolve
	Airport lobby	Thornhill with policemen	1	Music continues, gradually quieter, and goes out shortly after the shift outdoors
		The Professor arrives and takes charge of Thornhill	1	
	Airport exterior		6 (with s/rs* pairs in 2–6)	

*s/rs = shot/reverse shot

total. (One could even argue that the after-hours scene belongs to this first act, as well, because its action is closely related to the previous scenes (closing is even mentioned during the reunion scene), and there is a clear break in time and place afterwards.)

Two examples from recent films will serve to show different scales and levels of complexity in the articulation of film form. The first example is a pair of scenes from *Million Dollar Baby* (2004) in which veteran boxing trainer Frankie (Clint Eastwood) very reluctantly agrees to train Maggie (Hilary Swank). Frankie's gym manager, "Scrap" (Morgan Freeman) and Maggie share a "night out" at a diner (00:59:12). This scene is not long (4½ min) and is simply structured with obvious transitions. The initial shift is abrupt and direct: a simple cut from Maggie training late at night to an establishing shot of the diner seen from across the street. Maggie and "Scrap" enter; a bit later another man enters, greets Eddie, and sits at the opposite end of the counter; the camera moves in and "Scrap" tells Maggie about his final fight (see Figure 5-2); "Scrap" leaves and Maggie talks with the other man (who is a boxing manager "Scrap" has invited there); she leaves and as she closes the door, a cut (not fade) to black precedes the door of Frankie's house opening. The sound track divides the scene in half. When Eddie leaves the diner, his voice continues in voice-over narration and the music changes from a fairly plausible backgrounded diegetic status to a plaintive, nondiegetic acoustic guitar (music we have heard in the main-title sequence and occasionally since then).

The second example is the opening sequence of *The Birdcage* (1996). In a diegetic performance of a song or other piece, scene (or scene segment) and musical form can coincide, but, perhaps more often, film music adapts itself to cinematic form: that is, a performance will not be a scene—it is far more likely to form a sub-scene within a larger scene, as, for example, Lauren Bacall's two

Figure 5-2. *Million Dollar Baby.* Eddie ("Scrap") and Maggie talk in a diner.

consecutive performances in Eddie Mars's casino in *The Big Sleep* (1946): these are obviously sub-scenes of the larger casino scene that begins with Marlowe's arrival and ends with the two of them leaving. In *The Birdcage*, on the other hand, we see a considerably more complicated treatment of performances (none of them seen completely onscreen).

The opening sequence moves fluidly through the main titles and an opening stage number—the ambiguously nondiegetic singing over the titles turns into the singing of the transgendered chorus (although the volume barely changes) as the camera moves over the ocean, onto Miami Beach, lingers on the street outside the club, and then goes inside. Cutaways during the number introduce Robin Williams' character, Armand, the owner of the club, and, indirectly through the backstage manager doing a stage call, Albert (Nathan Lane) or Starina (his stage name). Through Armand's walking about the club greeting guests and talking with employees, we are introduced to the physical and cultural environment of the club; through the stage call, we can anticipate the first narrative complication. The stage number ("We Are Family") ends at 00:04:20, and with it the first scene. In this case, the change of physical environment is minimal and not unequivocal—essentially attention shifts gradually from the club audience and stage to backstage. It takes the conclusion of the musical number and a subsequent narrative complication, the announcement by an assistant, Agador, that Starina–Albert will not perform tonight, to confirm the change. An abrupt shift further into the building—upstairs to the penthouse that Albert shares with Armand—announces another scene shift. Music, stage, and club noise are cut off, but a brief cutaway will confirm that another, Native-American themed, performance has begun.

Whether the backstage segment is a sub-scene of the confrontation between Albert and Armand that follows or whether it is a (transitional) scene unto itself is difficult to say: the motivation for the confrontation comes from backstage but since the beginning of the film there has also been a steady "geographical" progress from exterior deeper and deeper to and into the interior of the building. In any case, Albert and Agador talk, then with a cut back to the stage area we see Armand heading up the stairs. He bursts in the door (about 00:05:45) and calls out "Albert!" There follows a series of yells, screams, and banging on doors, as Albert tries to prevent Armand from entering his dressing room. An exchange of accusations, with Albert doing most of the talking, is interrupted by the stage manager. Through the open door we hear low level club sounds (including the continuing performance). Confronted with an ultimatum, Albert agrees to go on. Armand instructs the stage manager to insert a mambo number. Agador leaves, and Albert and Armand continue the conversation at a lower level. Close to the end (about 00:10:00), Albert suddenly interjects a loud word (he is suspicious of Armand), and a bit later another sound accent (his scream as Armand pushes him) abruptly ends the scene as it merges with a sharp cut and loud music for the mambo number.

So far then, an initial scene lasting about 4 min was followed by a transitional scene, at about 1½ min, then another scene at about 5 min. As the mambo finishes, Armand announces Starina's number (at 00:10:45) and then goes upstairs shortly after the performance begins: we hear it at a very low level as Armand prepares for his son Val's arrival. At this point, the narrative direction shifts toward the principal narrative complication in the film, as we learn that Val (Dan Futterman) wants to get married. One might decide that this starts a second sequence, except that when this last, extended scene ends (at 00:20:50), an abrupt shift in time and place makes it clear that everything before has belonged to one large segment, a night in the club. The cut is simple but it does not need to be subtle: Albert is shown outdoors the next day, shopping for groceries.

SYNC POINTS AND AUDIOVISUAL PHRASING

Another way to think of the segmentation of clock time in a film is the temporal coordination of sound and image in terms of points of synchronization, or **sync points** (sometimes spelled "synch point"). Michel Chion defines these points as "a salient moment of an audiovisual sequence during which a sound event and a visual event meet in synchrony."[2] By synchrony he means the general psychological effect of the combination of sound and image; because this operates at every level of time, from the immediate moment to the level of scene and sequence, there are in fact "thousands of sync points," but for practical purposes of sound analysis, "only certain ones are important, the ones whose placement defines what we might call the **audiovisual phrasing** of the sequence." A simple example is the "stinger chord," a sudden, accented musical chord (or short figure) that "hits" screen action such as a surprised look or a fall. Gunshots, a knock on the door, a loud cry, or clapping hands are also natural sound accents or stingers.

Thus, *sync point* and *audiovisual phrasing* refer to the dramatic or expressive articulation of a sound film's time line, not to its formal segmentation. Yet both can be understood as instances of a more general process of synchronization. The end of a scene is in many ways a *negative* articulation of time—something comes to an end, whether it's a conversation, a cause-and-effect action sequence, a period of time, or an event. The techniques used will reflect this negative articulation: the screen fades to black or dissolves to another time and place, conversations cease and the sound track goes quiet, a musical performance stops, the dynamic level (loudness) of the background music falls. Thus, one can say that the image, music, and plot are synchronized in this "negative" effect of ending. These "low points" are the opposites of our usual meaning of sync point, a *positive* articulation of time where image and sound are active, expressive, and usually louder than their temporal surroundings.

Effects of ending and sync point can coincide (for example, the cliffhanger of the old serials—and some contemporary television shows—requires it), but in general they are distinct: at the level of the scene, the major sync point is most likely to coincide with the scene's climax, not its beginning or ending. A sync point, no matter the level, creates a before–after effect: the "before" seems empty as we forget it under the newly raised attention forced by the sync point, and an "after" or reaction follows.

For examples, let us return to the diner scene in *Million Dollar Baby*. Overall, the sound track is subdued, but the voices are foregrounded in the typical manner to make sure the conversation is clear. The establishing shot of the diner only lasts about 3 sec and includes an undifferentiated whir of nearby traffic movement, except for a car horn that sounds a fraction of a second before the shift indoors, as if prompting the cut itself. Although not literally happening together, the sound and the cut are so near another that they create a sync point. The sudden spike in the sound track catches our attention—whether we are immediately conscious of it or not—so that we briefly focus more intensely on the image track. In this case, the effect seems gratuitous: it remains a mystery why we should pay *extra* attention to Maggie and "Scrap," beyond what we are already giving them thanks to the cut and the camera framing, which places them together at the center of the image.

(Note also the equally odd coincidence of the sound lag, which keeps the outdoor traffic noise going for several seconds after the cut (cars can be seen going by out the windows but the sound level is far too high). The effect is to set off more strongly the intimate, personal nature of the conversation—the first of its kind in the film—but the handling of it still seems a little clumsy.)

"Watch Picture. Might have to stop earlier— break it off any place."
—Max Steiner, marginal note at the end of his sketch for one cue in *Casablanca*[3]

Roughly at the same level is a series of effects syncs or "hits" behind "Scrap"'s telling of the final part of his story: the sound of the cook scraping his metal spatulas together after "Scrap" mentions his wounds (01:00:34— this is even repeated later), sustained car sound that is almost like a drum-roll as he begins to talk about his last fight (01:00:40), a car door closing just after he says that he and Frankie were alone (01:00:52). These are much like the mickey-mousing effects of music and effects in classical film. We know why the effects are present—as ambient or environmental sounds of the diner—but their repeated coordination, or synchronization, with speech events is obviously planned. One has to surmise that they were meant to keep the emotional level of the conversation down, to keep it from seeming *too* intimate.

Music and effects are clearly subordinate to speech throughout the scene, as we would expect. The accents they create (except at the most local level, that is, judged in units of a few seconds) are not potential sync points but functional: to forward the continuous sound track by filling gaps in the moments when there is no speech in the sound track. There are only two exceptions: together they create the largest temporal articulations in the scene.

The first of these articulations is the coincidence of effect and speech when a man (Mickey Mack, the boxing manager) enters the diner. A loud squeaking and clicking sound accompanies the door opening in the background, and "Scrap" immediately says "Fought. . . ." The narrative impact of this is substantial—in fact it announces what the rest of the scene is about, although most of the scene's time is actually taken up by "Scrap"'s story of his last fight. The second of the large sync points occurs just after "Scrap" finishes his story and leaves. When his voice-over enters (01:03:05) the loudness level of speech is suddenly higher: the first text being "it's the rule: always protect yourself." The voice-over lasts about 15 sec, but the entry moment is a strong sync point: we hear "it's the . . ." during a 2-shot of Maggie and Mickey Mack at opposite ends of the counter but the more heavily emphasized "rule" and "always protect yourself" with a quick cut back to her (oddly, we can also still see "Scrap" in the background, just out the door, although he is already speaking in voice-over).

The scene, thus, divides expressively into three parts: before the door opens, after it opens ("Scrap"'s story), and after "Scrap" leaves.

Beyond the level of the scene, the sync point—as a specific, significant point in time—is increasingly less likely than is the more abstract narrative category of the crux or climax: tension and narrative complications accumulate to a moment—or segment—of greatest conflict and (usually) resolution, after which the sequence, act, or entire film "winds down" in a denouement or final scene(s). In the opening act of *Casablanca*, we can assert that there is a specific, highly localized sync point: when Rick sees Ilsa and we hear the stinger chord. In the film as a whole, on the other hand, the "moment" is more diffuse, if no less dramatic overall: the second after-hours meeting between Rick and Ilsa, in which she argues with him over the visas (letters of transit) that she and Laszlo need to escape. (The stinger chord does reappear in this scene but with nothing like its earlier effect.) A similar example is *Sunset Boulevard* (1950), where the climax occurs very near the end of the film in Norma Desmond's famous descent down the staircase, accompanied by Franz Waxman's distorted tango music. The climax is the descent, not some specific synchronized moment within that scene; and, in *Psycho* (1960), the climax of the film's first half is the murder of Marion Crane, an intense minute-long "sync point."

Romantic films typically position the climax near the end of the film, either at the moment the couple is formed or in the scene with the greatest level of conflict just before the couple is formed. It is not necessary for the climax to occur near the end, however. Composer and film music scholar George Burt writes, for example, that "The [initial] attack on Pearl Harbor in *Tora! Tora! Tora!* [1970] was . . . the focal point or moment of dramatic release, in which all elements within the story converged. Music was not used for the battle, nor was it needed. . . . The [essential] drama was over at that point."[4] More radically, in *Atonement* (2007) the climax comes very early, indeed, with Robbie's mistaken arrest for sexual assault: the great majority of the film is a long, slow, and sad denouement; and *Psycho* doubles its climax points: the murder of Marion near the end of the first half and the discovery of Norman's mother near the end of the second half.

Examples for Music in Film Form

Distributing music across a film is by no means a simple mechanical task, even if there clearly were some characteristic historical practices, many of which persist into the present day. In this section, we provide detailed cue lists, or lists of the music keyed to a film's runtime, for six films from different decades and genres. Commentary on each of these lists points out conventional features as well as treatments specific to the film at hand. Overall, the examples should suggest the variety of music's uses and formal positioning in film, at the same time they show preliminary instances of scene categories that will be discussed in greater detail in the following chapters (music in establishing and end-credit sequences, performances, and montage fantasy scenes).

LADY WINDERMERE'S FAN
Released in 1925, during the "**picture palace**" era, the heyday of the silent feature film, *Lady Windermere's Fan* was a major (and as it turned out very successful) production of the Warner Bros. studio. The most prominent member

of the production team, however, was not an actor, but the director, Ernst Lubitsch, who took the remarkable step of removing all the dialogue (which would otherwise have been displayed on intertitles) from his film version of Oscar Wilde's play. Lubitsch explained that "playing with words is fascinating to the writer and afterward to the reader, but on the screen it is quite impossible."[5]

The play is part comedy of manners, part domestic melodrama, and Lubitsch successfully balances the two aspects in the film version. The best known actor is Ronald Colman, who plays Lord Darlington, infatuated with the married Lady Windermere (May McAvoy). Her husband Lord Windermere (Bert Lytell) has agreed to pay money to Mrs. Erlynne (Irene Rich) to keep quiet the fact that she is Lady Windermere's mother (presumably the child was born out of wedlock). After starting an affair with Lord Augustus Lorton (Edward Martindel), Mrs. Erlynne insists on an invitation to Lady Windermere's birthday party. Lady Windermere finds the check intended for Mrs. Erlynne, misunderstands its significance and agrees to go away with Lord Darlington, but is intercepted in the latter's apartment by Mrs. Erlynne. Having hoped to break into society through the birthday party (which she had attended with great success), Mrs. Erlynne now sacrifices her chances by staying in the apartment as her daughter escapes unnoticed. In the end, the Windermeres are re-united and so are Mrs. Erlynne and Lord Augustus.

The film is readily divided into three acts. In the first, the characters are introduced and the central narrative problems are presented in a series of four scenes. The second act (beginning at 00:32:27 or DVD ch. 5) could be understood as one large scene because it concerns the events of a single day and a specific place, but it is probably better to think of it as an act comprised of two sequences: the preliminaries to Lady Windermere's birthday party and the party itself. The third act (beginning at 01:11:30 or DVD ch. 11) takes place at Lord Darlington's apartment, as Mrs. Erlynne arrives to find Lady Windermere already there, the men arrive to continue the festivities after the party, and Mrs. Erlynne diverts attention while she escapes but permanently ruins her reputation in the process, as the men find Lady Windermere's fan and she is obliged to claim that she took it by mistake. The final scene, the film's denouement, takes place next morning (01:23:04 or DVD ch. 13), as Mrs. Erlynne visits Lady Windermere to return the fan and explain as much as she can (without divulging her parental status). As she leaves, she encounters Lord Augustus on the street, and the two go off together.

We will focus here only on the first act, which divides readily into four scenes: the Windermere's house (conversations between Lady Windermere, Lord Darlington, and Lord Windermere); Mrs. Erlynne's apartment (including a conversation with Lord Windermere); the racetrack; and Mrs. Erlynne's apartment (including a conversation with Lord Augustus).

Table 5-3 *Lady Windermere's Fan* (1925), music cues in the first act.

0:00:00	Credits	1. J. S. Zamecnik *The Sacrifice* beginning. (see music in Figure 5-3) [with the main title] Marks Fan Motive ad lib (see second half of Figure 5-3)
0:00:33		2. V. Herbert *The Only Girl* Overture Waltz
0:01:15	T. *Lady Windermere faced . . .*	3. Trad "Oh, Dear, What Can the Matter Be?"
0:01:27	Scene in Drawing Room	4. Thomas *Mignon* Gavotte beginning (see Figure 5-4a)
0:02:47	Lord Darlington enters	5. Mozart *Don Giovanni*: "*Là ci darem la mano*"
0:03:38	Lord Windermere at desk	Variation of #1 (*The Sacrifice*) (from Figure 5-3)
0:04:24	Lady W enters	Fan Motive ad lib (from Figure 5-3)
0:04:35	Lord D enters	Continuation of #4, strain 2 etc. (*Mignon* Gavotte; see Figure 5-4b)
0:06:12	Lady W & Lord D alone, long shot	New version of #5 ("*Là ci darem la mano*"), leading to
0:06:32	T. "*Lady Winderemere, I have . . .*"	6. W. Goodell, *Dreaming* until pause at fade
0:07:29	*[beginning of DVD Chapter 2]* T. After a life of adventure	Continuation of #1 (*The Sacrifice*), several strains ad lib (from Figure 5-3)
0:13:48	Lord W takes out check book	7. Zamecnik, Theme "Madeleine" (see Figure 5-8)
0:15:12	Photograph of Lady W	#1 (*The Sacrifice*) final strain to cadence at fade (from Figure 5-3)
0:16:42	*[beginning of DVD Chapter 3]* T. *Thanks to Winderemere's cheques . . .*	8. Allusion to Loewe *My Fair Lady* "Ascot Gavotte"
0:16:56	Racetrack scenes	9. Offenbach "Can Can" as 6/8 march
0:17:08	Scottish band marching	10. A. Sullivan *Pirates* "With Catlike Tread"

For the recent DVD release of *Lady Windermere's Fan*, silent-film music scholar and performance specialist Martin Marks provided a piano accompaniment very much in keeping with silent-film era performance practices. As he explains, "I created a **compilation score**, using preexistent music of the sort that a pianist or an orchestra could have played at the time of the film's original release. I also employ the silent-film pianist's methods for varying and developing this music in accordance with the story." In keeping with that spirit, the seventeen pieces of music played, quoted, or alluded to in Act 1 include only one that is Marks' own: the "fan motive" that first appears in the main title (see the cue list with timings for the opening credits and Act 1 in Table 5-3). All the other music, except for an anachronistic reference to *My Fair Lady*, could very well have been performed by a theater pianist or organist in 1925.

The lead character in the story is clearly Mrs. Erlynne, not Lady Windermere, and Marks immediately presents her theme in the opening credits: see

0:17:25	Mrs. Erlynne surrounded by men	11. Allusion to Arne *Rule, Britannia*
0:17:43	Mrs. E leaves, ascends stairs	12. Herbert, *The Only Girl*: Overture March
0:18:18	Montage: looking at Mrs. E	Variation of *#7* ("*Madeleine*")
0:18:51	Ladies sitting in box	13. A. Czibulka *Stephanie* Gavotte str 1 & 3 (see Figure 5-5)
0:20:46	T. *The Duchess of Berwick* . . .	14. L. Gautier *Le Secret,* strains 1-2 (see Figure 5-6)
0:21:54	Duchess looks at Mrs. E.'s hair	13a. *Stephanie* strain 2 ad lib (from Figure 5-5)
0:22:47	After T. "*She is getting gray*"	14a. *Le Secret* strains 3-4 ad lib (from Figure 5-6)
0:24:11	After T. "*Why gossip about a woman*	Variations of #13 & #13a (*Stephanie* Gavotte) (from Figure 5-5)
0:26:04	Horse race	Ad lib
0:26:18	Mrs. E followed by Lord Augustus	Variation of #12 (*The Only Girl*: Overture March) as tango, cadence at fade
0:26:51	*[beginning of DVD Chapter 4]* T. *A gentleman's relation to a lady*	15. G. Clutsam *Billet-doux*, Intro & str 1
0:27:54		Ad lib
0:28:12	Maid leaves, Lord A alone	16. F. Dougherty *Waltz* (Eb) (see Figure 5-7)
0:29:05	Maid returns to Lord A	Ad lib & Variation of #15 (*Billet-doux*)
0:29:50	T. *But when the relation becomes*	16a. *Waltz*, Strain 2 & ad lib (c#) (from Figure 5-7)
0:0:53	CU Cigar, Lord A becomes jealous	16. *Waltz* Strain 1 (E)
0:31:25	T. "*If you really loved me*"	16a. Variation of *Waltz* Strain 2 (c#)
0:31:45	Mrs. E. goes over to Lord A with cigar	Ad lib with Variation of #15 (*Billet-doux*)
	T. "*I am sorry my maid forgot*"	

the melody in Figure 5-3 (the "fan motive" is near the end of the example). As Marks explains, the theme is "intense [and] conveys the emotions Mrs. Erlynne displays from scene to scene. . . . I like to imagine that [its composer] had such a woman in mind when he composed (or at least titled) his piece—especially because her 'sacrifice' of social position for her daughter's sake is the climactic action in the film." Both *The Sacrifice* and the "fan motive" reappear in the first and second scenes (and, of course, at a number of other significant moments later in the film, as well).

Figure 5-3. J. S. Zamecnik, *The Sacrifice*, opening melody (mm. 1–8), plus Marks, "Fan Motive" (mm 8–12).

Of the other music, Marks says that the works he chose "speak in accents of wit and romance. Several are stylized dances that bring to mind comic images of formal behavior and ritualized social interactions, such as constrain the film's aristocratic characters." Among these are a gavotte (an old-fashioned dance already before 1800) from a 19th-century French opera, *Mignon* (first entrance at 00:01:27; see Figure 5-4 for the melody); two characteristic piano pieces that were originally meant to be played in the home but are equally suitable to film accompaniment, *Stephanie* (another gavotte; at 00:18:51; see Figure 5-5), *Le Secret* (at 00:20:46; see Figure 5-6); and a waltz written specifically for use in "photoplays" (at 00:28:12; see Figure 5-7). A more serious exception is *Madeleine*, the second melody associated with Mrs. Erlynne (at 00:13:48; see Figure 5-8). As Marks explains, "Mrs. Erlynne is too complex a character to be pictured by only one piece of music. . . . This I took from [a] 1921 set of *Sam Fox Motion Picture Themes*, for female characters only. It plays like a moody fox-trot of the era, although it eventually puts on a happier face."

Music that plays continuously throughout a 2-hr feature is necessarily complex and varied, but the unifying associations that come with recurring themes and motives remain typical of classical sound-film practice as well.

a **Figure 5-4.** Ambroise Thomas, "Gavotte" from *Mignon*: (a) melody only for the first section;
b (b) melody for the second section.

Figure 5-5. Alphonse Czibulka, *Stephanie* (gavotte).

Figure 5-6. Léonard Gautier, *Le Secret*, melody of section A.

Figure 5-7. Frank C. Dougherty, *Waltz (For General Use)*.

Figure 5-8. J. S. Zamecnik, *Madeleine*, melody.

Unlike later practice, however, Marks's music tends to emphasize the film's temporal articulations much more consistently, a tendency that makes sense not only because a continuous music needs some articulation (which the film aids) but also because the film, in turn, lacks dialogue and effects and thus relies more heavily on music.

MILDRED PIERCE

In many ways, *Mildred Pierce* (1945) is a characteristic product of Warner Bros. in the period before about 1950—it is focused on action and its narrative is fast paced, with an editing style adjusted to match and a large number of relatively short scenes. Nevertheless, its overall design is very clear: two long, chronologically consistent flashbacks embedded in a frame of current time. The studio had long been known for its gangster and detective films, but had also found a niche by the later 1930s in melodrama or women's films, thanks largely to a cycle starring Bette Davis that includes, among others, *The Sisters* (1938), *Dark Victory* (1939), *All This and Heaven Too* (1940), *The Letter* (1940), *In This Our Life* (1942), *Now, Voyager* (1942), and *Old Acquaintance* (1943). (For all but the last of the titles listed here, Max Steiner wrote the orchestral score.) Starring Joan Crawford in the title role, *Mildred Pierce* combines the two genres: melodrama is evident in the two extended flashbacks that make up most of the film's 111-min runtime; the detective story is the framework of "current" time, from Monty's murder in the opening minute to the exposing of the murderer in the final minutes—from about 11:00 pm one evening until sunrise the next morning.

A detailed cue list with notes on the music is given in Table 5-4. "Current time" is really a single act that is interrupted by the flashbacks, each of which forms an act as well. Act 1, then, is from the beginning to 00:20:15, 1:05:45 to 1:08:00, and 1:44:12 to the end. Act 2 (the first flashback) runs from 00:20:15 to 1:05:45, and Act 3 (the second flashback) from 1:08:00 to 1:44:12. Subheadings in Figure 5-12 identify sequences and isolated scenes.

Note that diegetic and nondiegetic music appear in current time as well as in the flashbacks. The two are strongly tied together through parallel performances in Wally's club: the band and an unnamed singer at 00:03:55 and Mildred's daughter Veda (Ann Blyth) at 01:27:45. Diegetic music outside of the club consists only of two fragments of Chopin (00:26:39 and 00:38:49) and a phonograph record playing in the beachhouse as background for the only romantic scene between Mildred and Monty (Zachary Scott) (after 00:52:00). There is no ambiguity about the status of the diegetic music (the music on the phonograph is by Steiner but it is arranged in a popular lyrical style); this theme does appear a few times in the nondiegetic music later, but that is the only crossover between the diegetic and nondiegetic music. The parallel performances are stylistically striking but not really significant to the narrative: the viewer who did not already know the James Cain novel on which the film is based would not catch the bitter, ironic reference as we hear "You Must Have Been a Beautiful Baby" from a singer in the scene background while we see Mildred in the foreground, but it becomes clear when Veda performs on the same stage later in the film.

The burden of music's narrative work is borne—and one has to assume, happily—by Steiner's orchestral underscoring, which covers about 50 min of the film. As we have written earlier, Steiner preferred to write extensive scores, and in this instance we can add that such scores were expected in women's films, which focused on family and other personal relationships and on the emotional responses of the protagonist(s). Furthermore, as Claudia Gorbman explains, nondiegetic music was associated not only with emotion but with fantasy and the irrational, and the fact that the bulk of the film focuses on memory, on recounting in imagination, was an invitation to long passages of empathetic underscoring.[6]

Steiner's music relies more on thematic statement and development than on timbral or other qualities. In fact, as Gorbman says, "The lion's share of *Mildred Pierce's* score consists of statements or variations of . . . five themes. The melodies are treated in conventional ways to fit each narrative context in which they appear. Variations in tonality, register, harmonic accompaniment, time signature, rhythm, and instrumentation alter their sound and mood."[7] The beginnings of these five themes are notated in Figure 5-9, and the first appearance of each is marked in the appropriate place in Table 5-4. In structuring his score this way, Steiner was firmly in the center of a classical tradition that he himself helped to create: "[He] clearly bore in mind the difference between the referential function of a musical theme, 'understanding a melody,' and the theme's emotive function: 'if it gets too decorative, it loses its emotional appeal.' It almost goes without saying that both functions of themes in the film score are 'subordinated . . . to the picture,' to the narrative discourse."[8] (In this quotation from Gorbman, the internal quotes are from Steiner himself.)

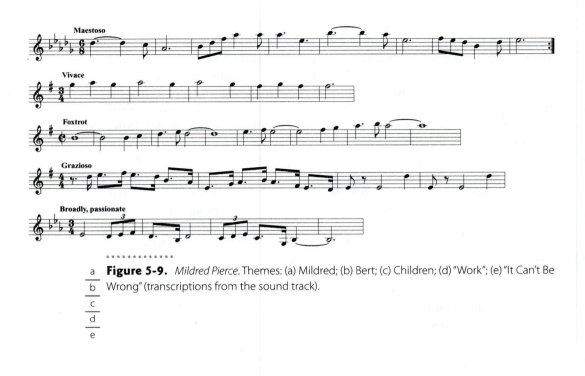

a
b
c
d
e

Figure 5-9. *Mildred Pierce.* Themes: (a) Mildred; (b) Bert; (c) Children; (d) "Work"; (e) "It Can't Be Wrong" (transcriptions from the sound track).

Table 5-4 *Mildred Pierce* (1945), timeline and cue list.

ESTABLISHING SEQUENCE

    1. 0:00–0:01:38. Logo, main title, and credits, with an overlap into the opening scene (music out under sound of gunfire about 0:01:45). Theme #1 is heard with the main title and throughout the rest of the sequence.

"CURRENT TIME"; LATE EVENING

—Murder 0:01:35 Monty's beach house.

    2. 0:01:48–0:03:20. Music in with the cut inside the beach house; continues into the next scene, till shortly after the policeman raps his baton on the metal railing at 3:15; music is replaced by dialogue and low-level ambient sound.

—Suicide? 0:02:15 cut to wharf; Mildred considers suicide.

—Mildred and Wally 0:03:55 cut to front of Wally's wharf-side cafe; Wally comes out; they go inside to talk; 0:05:57 cut to the beach house; 0:08:46 Wally realizes something is wrong; 0:10:45 police car appears.

    3. 0:03:55–0:06:00. Diegetic cue: band and a singer, "You Must Have Been a Beautiful Baby."

    4. 0:08:52–0:14:30. Music in with a soft stinger chord as Wally realizes something is wrong; music continues into the next scene (see below).

—Mildred, Veda, and the police. 0:12:05 Mildred arrives at her house/police/Veda; 0:13:35 at police station; several characters come in and out; 0:16:40 Mildred in Inspector Peterson's office.

    (4. continues to 0:14:30, just after Mildred enters the back area of the police station)

FIRST FLASHBACK (DIVORCE THROUGH OPENING THE RESTAURANT)

—Family life. 0:20:15 flashback; real estate office/Bert—Mildred as narrator; 0:25:00 children, outside. then in the house; 0:28:20 Mildred doing bills; 0:29:00 Wally appears; 0:32:00 Mildred talks to Veda upstairs.

5. 0:20:15–0:21:25. Music in with the dissolve to the flashback. Theme #2 is heard the first time.

6. 0:24:25–0:26:07. Music in as conversation ends and Bert resolves to leave. Theme #3 is heard for the first time at 0:25:00, with cut to children playing outdoors. Music out as Kay and Veda enter the house.

7. 0:26:39 and 0:27:25. Veda at the piano plays the opening of Chopin, Waltz in Eb Major, Op. 18, twice (off-screen, then onscreen).

8. 0:28:13–0:29:04. Music in as Mildred reacts to Veda's spiteful remark; out as Wally arrives at the house.

9. 0:32:05–0:34:40. Music in as Mildred goes upstairs to talk with Veda; music continues into the next scene (see below).

—Mildred; restaurant. 0:34:05 Mildred job hunting; restaurant; 0:39:00 Mildred. Veda argue; 0:40:30 Mildred visits Wally; 0:42:45 Wally/Mildred/visit Beragon beach house.

(9.–continues to 0:34:40, just after Mildred enters the restaurant)

10. 0:36:12–0:37:38. Montage cue as Mildred starts restaurant work. Theme #4 is heard first at the beginning of this cue. Music out as Mildred arrives home, talks to Lottie (Butterfly McQueen).

11. 0:37:38–0:38:12. Diegetic cue slips under the end of cue 10. "South American Way" played and sung by the girls.

12. 0:38:49–0:40:28. Initially, a diegetic cue: Veda briefly plays Chopin, Mazurka in Bb Major, Op. 7 no. 1; blends into nondiegetic cue from about 0:39:08; music out as Mildred and Veda's argument heats up.

13. 0:42:35–0:43:30. Music in to overlap; out as Monty enters the room.

—Death of Kay. 0:46:05 home, Mildred and Bert talk about divorce—Bert, children, preparing for trip; 0:48:15 new restaurant, Mildred/Monty; 0:49:40 beach house, Mildred/Monty; 0:53:15 home, Bert, rain.

14. 0:48:05–0:48:25. Short transitional cue. Music in as Mildred watches Bert and the children leave; out in the restaurant.

15. 0:49:40–0:50:00. Another transitional cue: in with kiss; out with cut inside the beach house.

16. 0:50:48–0:53:15. Music in for swimming; out under loud waves effect but diegetic cue follows without a break: phonograph plays an arrangement of "It Can't Be Wrong" (this is Theme #5, heard the first time—the song is based on Steiner's main theme for *Now, Voyager* (1942)). The song finishes and we hear noise of the phonograph needle for several seconds.

17. 0:54:08–0:57:40. Music enters as Bert says "pneumonia"; overlaps into the next scene (see below).

—Back to restaurant. 0:57:25 restaurant opening; 01:03:40 Mildred/Monty talk after restaurant, then Bert arrives.

(17. Overlaps for a few seconds into the first scene.)

18. 0:57:45–0:59:05. apparently diegetic cue: low-level music from an unseen sound system; out with cut to the kitchen.

19. 0:59:48–1:02:55. Diegetic cue again with cut back to the restaurant—this time, however, the music continues through a brief cut back to the restaurant; overlaps and fades into nondiegetic cue at 1:01:45; then suddenly back to a diegetic cue with cut to bar area at 1:01:53 ("Please Think of Me" played on foregrounded jukebox, later sung by Wally).

20. 1:03:44–1:05:50. Music in at "Kay died"; out during the whip dissolve to the next scene.

BACK TO CURRENT TIME

      1:05:45 Back to Inspector Peterson's office; near the end Mildred says, "I killed him."

SECOND FLASHBACK CONTINUES STORY (SUCCESS THROUGH RE-MARRIAGE)

—Mildred's success in business 1:08:00 to restaurants; success; 1:09:40 Mildred's office; Mildred/Wally argue over Monty; then Mildred/Ida; then Monty and Veda enter; 1:13:00 Veda receives car as present.

    21. 1:08:00–1:09:40. Music in with dissolve for montage, overlaps with diegetic dance music cue, which in turn overlaps cut to Mildred and Wally talking in restaurant office.

    22. 1:13:25–1:16:00. Music in as Kay goes outside to drive the car, out under the diegetic cue with cut to Wally's club (see below).

—Veda's marriage 1:15:55 Wally's club, with Ted and Veda; 1:16:50 Mildred's office, Mrs. Forrester; 1:18:24 Mildred's house/Wally/Veda; 1:19:50 Forrester lawyer's office.

    23. 1:16:00–1:16:52. Diegetic cue (band in background playing "You Must Have Been a Beautiful Baby"); out abruptly with cut to Mildred's office.

    24. 1:18:24–1:19:50. Music in with Mildred's return home after conversation with Mrs. Forrester; briefly out at 1:18:51; out with dissolve to lawyer's office.

—Veda leaves 1:21:38 house; Mildred/Veda; they argue; 1:24:35 Mildred returns to restaurant after travelling; 1:27:45 Wally's bar/Bert/Mildred; 1:29:30 dressing room.

    25. 1:21:38–1:24:35. Music in with the scene change, continues through argument and brief travel montage, going out as Mildred arrives back at the restaurant.

    26. 1:27:45–1:32:08. Diegetic music in (heard from outside Wally's bar, then inside): introduction, then "The Oceana Roll" sung by Veda. Band immediately goes to "Sweet Georgia Brown" when she finishes; heard offscreen during dressing room scene. Music finishes and cut coincides.

—Mildred and Monty; Veda returns 1:32:08 Monty's large house/Mildred; 1:35:45 marriage; redecorated house/Bert visits; 1:38:00 Veda returns; 1:39:40 Monty enters.

    27. 1:35:45–1:36:05. Transitional cue—music in with effect "gag" (music imitates sound of clinking glasses).

    28. 1:37:05–1:40:10. Music in when Bert asks if Mildred loves Monty, goes out with change to Veda's birthday party.

—The fatal evening 1:40:00 Veda's birthday party (evening of the "present"); 1:41:10 Mildred calls from the office; 1:42:40 "Monty" (it's revealed that the financial crack-down is his idea); 1:44:03 beach house.

    29. 1:42:40–1:44:15. Music in with quiet stinger chord, builds in intensity till the end, overlapping slightly with return to present time.

CLIMAX AND CONCLUSION

      1:44:12 Peterson's office; 1:45:20 beach house/Mildred, then Monty/Veda; 1:49:23 Peterson's office; 1:50:20 outside. sunrise/Mildred/Bert; end credit in at 1:50:34.

    30. 1:44:36–1:46:00. Music in with the door opening as Veda is brought in; out as Veda speaks when Mildred finds Monty and her together in the beach house.

    31. 1:46:06–1:50:40. Music in with Mildred's reaction, out for a few seconds, then in as Veda is taken away.

RASHÔMON

With the enigmatic *Rashômon* (1950), which tells four different versions of a single event without making an ultimate judgment about the veracity of any of them, director Akira Kurosawa won a grand prize at the 1951 Venice Film Festival and immediately became a familiar figure to Western film audiences. Often considered the most "Western" of Japanese directors of his generation (which also includes Mizoguchi and Ozu), Kurosawa worked with musicians who were trained in European classical music traditions but who also were familiar with, and sympathetic to, Japanese traditions. Fumio Hayasaka was trained at a Western-style music conservatory (with strong Russian influence) as a modern European musician, not a traditional Japanese musician; and the means (Western orchestra, piano, and so on) and techniques of his film scores are essentially European. In *Rashômon*, Hayasaka only adds some Japanese features, such as melodies, rhythms, or imitation of traditional instruments or ensembles, for example, in the medieval gagaku (court music) of the main titles and the Priest's music, which the composer himself described as a "study in gagaku rhythm."

Hayasaka was familiar with the scoring conventions of Hollywood films and follows many of them,[9] including the assumption that a film should be heavily underscored with a standard orchestra, that careful plotting of music's functions in relation to narrative is necessary, and that music's presence alone can represent fantasy or, more precisely for this film, the unreliable irrational. The film is just over 87 min long and contains roughly 43 min of music in fourteen nondiegetic cues (the cue list appears in Table 5-5); there is no diegetic music (although the status of drumming at the beginning of the scene with the medium might be considered ambiguous).

Table 5-5 *Rashômon* (1950), timeline and cue list.

MAIN TITLE SEQUENCE
  1. 0:00:25–0:00:58. Music for the titles (beginning with the Main Title).

OPENING SCENE
  —At Rasho Gate Three men (the Priest, the Woodcutter, and a Thief) talk.

THE FOUR STORIES
  —The Woodcutter's Story (told to the others at the Rasho Gate, then from 0:11:45 to the trial judge)).
    2. 0:07:50–0:11:56. Music for the Woodcutter's story; begins immediately; goes out shortly after he begins his testimony before the judge.
  —Testimony of the Priest (0:12:35) and the Policeman (0:14:00) before the judge
    3. 0:12:50–0:13:38. Priest's flashback to encountering the samurai and his wife on the road.
    4. 0:14:25–0:15:15. Policeman's flashback to capturing Tajomaru.

—Tajomaru's Story (0:15:40)

    5. 0:15:40–0:16:15. Tajomaru's version of his encounter with the Policeman.

    6. 0:17:00–0:20:00. Music starts just before the beginning of the flashback; Tajomaru meets the couple; they pass on; music overlaps with return to Tajomaru speaking to the judge.

    7. 0:20:24–0:21:24. Tajomaru runs after them, talks to husband.

    8. 0:22:10–0:26:50. Music in as the husband looks at a sword Tajomaru shows him, continues through fight with and defeat of the husband and return to the wife; overlaps slightly with cut back to courtyard.

    9. 0:27:10–0:31:10. Tajomaru and the wife run to the husband sitting bound in the woods; she fights Tajomaru and he seizes her; music overlaps slightly with cut back to courtyard.

    10. 0:31:29–0:36:00. Tajomaru and husband fight; husband cries; cut back to courtyard at 0:35:07; music out at 0:36:40 with cut back to Rasho gate.

—Back to Rasho Gate The three men continue talking; the Priest begins to recount the Wife's story.

—The Wife's Story

    11. 0:39:07–0:49:00. Music begins immediately with the cut to the wife in the courtyard, continues into the flashback at 40:40 and through the continued courtyard testimony; out with the cut back to Rasho Gate.

—Back to Rasho Gate. The three men continue talking.

—The Husband's Story (told through a medium).

    12. 0:51:00–1:00:10. Percussion only immediately with the cut to the medium in the courtyard; orchestral music at 0:52:40 with the flashback; several cuts back and forth between the medium and the flashback; music out several seconds after the final cut back to the courtyard.

    13. 1:00:23–1:01:17. Final statements of the medium (the Husband speaking about the moments after he died); out with abrupt cut back to Rasho Gate.

THE TRUTH?; DENOUEMENT

—Back to Rasho Gate.

—Second version of the Woodcutter's story.

—Back to Rasho Gate; the Thief finds a baby; the Woodcutter takes the baby home.

    14. 1:26:30–1:27:53. Final shots & end title.

In general, the way Hayasaka handles the scoring is what we would expect by the standards of the conventional practice of Hollywood narrative film as established in the 1930s. Music is, of course, used for the titles, beginning and end. The scenes at the Rashó gate—the film's diegesis or "current time"—have no underscoring, except in the latter part of the final scene. These scenes are heavy with dialogue that contains quite a bit of story information; they are, furthermore, accompanied by the persistent natural sound of heavy rain (except for the film's closing scene, which is accompanied in part by the sound of a crying baby, although the music for the end title comes in early to initiate the conventional dramatic–dynamic swelling toward the final shot and the end title).

The flashbacks to the trial generally have no music either (nor, by and large, even natural sounds), but music repeatedly comes in under dialogue to smooth over the transitions from the trial to the forest, and vice versa. By using this particular film-scoring convention, Hayasaka helps establish the trial as a kind of secondary "reality": Although it is reached only in flashbacks from the scenes at the gate, the trial is thus more readily accepted as present time, the starting point for flashbacks to the forest. In this context, the presence or absence of music in and of itself has strong narrative connotations, for, as Claudia Gorbman says, "in classical cinema, . . . above and beyond . . . specific emotional connotations, . . . music itself signifies emotion, depth, the obverse of logic."[10] Hayasaka clearly builds his score on this principle—of the 43 min of music, 2 min and 40 sec are used for the titles, and all the rest is used in the several forest scenes.

In summary, then, the formal uses of music follow the conventional practices of Hollywood narrative film. Music is used for the titles, beginning and end, and otherwise it follows narrative and dramatic principles, setting up a contrast between reality (or present time) and fantasy (or memory) through its presence or absence and, in most cues, following the turns in action and emotion fairly closely.

The greatest amount of conventional dramatic underscoring occurs in Cues 3 to 10, during the bandit Tajomaru's story. Unlike the music elsewhere, these cues are filled with short passages of varying styles that accompany closely, and reinforce, changing events and actions on the screen—in short, conventional dramatic underscoring in the manner of major Hollywood composers of the 1930s, such as Max Steiner, Alfred Newman, or Franz Waxman. (We should note, however, that Hayasaka also understood conventions of Japanese film perfectly well: as the wife sits quietly on the ground posing for the camera (Cue 8), he introduces an innocuously sweet, otherwise irrelevant tune, exactly in the manner of (silent) Japanese film melodramas in the 1930s.) Finally, Hayasaka also makes some use of thematic devices. The samurai and his wife, for example, are given two kinds of identifying "walking" music—both "modern" melodies with motives obviously derived from the opening court music, an association that very efficiently confirms the couple's social status. As the bandit and the husband walk back to inspect a fictitious cache of swords the former uses as a ruse, there even reappears about 45 sec of walking music from the first forest scene (Cue 2). Cue 11 (for the wife's story) stands apart from the others in its melodies and simple tonalities, but its repetitious rhythms are obviously related to those of Cue 2, and the percussion music that opens Cue 13 (to accompany the medium) is clearly a metrically-disfigured expansion of the rhythm from Cue 2.

PSYCHO

A glance at Table 5-6 will confirm that, although Hitchcock's *Psycho* has quite a bit of music, like both *Mildred Pierce* and *Rashômon*, that music is laid out quite differently. First of all, the number of music cues is large (thirty nine, as opposed to thirty one—including the diegetic music—for *Mildred Pierce* and fourteen for *Rashômon*), and yet almost all of these cues are relatively short—seventeen are less than 1 min in length (as opposed to seven such nondiegetic cues in *Mildred Pierce*), and only seven are more than 2 min (this number includes combined cues when one cue segues immediately into the next). In *Mildred Pierce*, fourteen diegetic and nondiegetic cues last more than 2 min. Second, there is no diegetic or **source music** of any kind. (That is also true of *Rashômon*, but the imitation of court music in the opening and similar music later do establish a reasonable connection to time and place.)

Table 5-6 *Psycho* (1960), timeline and cue list.

ESTABLISHING SEQUENCE
   —main title sequence
      1. 0:00–   (length = 1:50)   (cue title = Psycho Prelude)
   —establishing shots of Phoenix and hotel
      2. segue   (length = 1:02)   (cue title = The City)

MARION CRANE STEALS $40,000 AND FLEES
   —Marion and Sam
      3. 4:25–   (length = :49)   (cue title = Marion)
      4. 5:50–   (length = :40)   (cue title = Marion and Sam)
   —Marion takes the money
      5. 10:44–   (length = 1:45)   (cue title = Temptation)
   —on the road to California (1): overnight
      6. 12:50–   (length = :41)   (cue title = Flight (A))
      7. 16:08–   (length = 1:20)   (cue title = Patrol Car)
   —on the road to California (2): buying a new car
      8. 17:38–   (length = 1:14)   (cue title = The Car Lot)
      9. 21:52–   (length = :55)   (cue title = The Package)
     10. 23:04–   (length = 3:03)   (cue title = The Rainstorm)

THE MOTEL; MURDER
   —arrival; conversation with Norman
     11. 30:28–   (length = 1:28)   (cue title = Hotel Room)
     12. 32:40–   (length = :55)   (cue title = The Window)

13. segue   (length = 1:32)   (cue title = The Parlor)

14. 40:25–   (length = 1:45)   (cue title = The Madhouse)

—Norman contemplates, carries out the murder

15. 43:05– (length = 2:24)   (cue title = The Peephole)

16. segue (length = :45)   (cue title = The Bathroom)

17. 47:07–   (length = :56)   (cue title = The Murder)

—Norman "finds" the body and cleans up

18. 49:32–   (length = :09)   (cue title = The Body)

19. 50:17–   (length = 1:13)   (cue title = The Office)

20. segue   (length = 1:06)   (cue title = The Curtain)

21. 52:45–   (length = 1:20)   (cue title = The Water)

22. segue   (length = :48)   (cue title = The Car)

23. 55:42–   (length = 1:24)   (cue title = The Swamp)

SEARCH & INVESTIGATION

—Marion's sister talks with Sam, Arbogast; the latter goes to the Bates motel and is murdered

24. 63:22–   (length = :37)   (cue title = The Search (A))

25. 69:47–   (length = :45)   (cue title = The Shadow)

26. 71:24–   (length = :48)   (cue title = Phone Booth)

27. 73:35–   (length = :58)   (cue title = The Porch)

28. segue   (length = 2:17)   (cue title = The Stairs)

29. segue   (length = :14)   (cue title = The Knife)

—Lila and Sam talk; they continue the search (he goes to the motel; they talk to the sheriff); Norman and his mother

30. 78:09–   (length = 1:12)   (cue title = The Search (B))

31. 84:25–   (length = 1:51)   (cue title = The First Floor)

—Lila and Sam go to the motel

32. 88:27–   (length = :53)   (cue title = Cabin 10)

33. 91:29–   (length = 1:26)   (cue title = Cabin 1)

—Lila goes up to the house; finds Norman's mother

34. 94:32–   (length = :52)   (cue title = The Hill)

35. 96:22–   (length = 1:03)   (cue title = The Bedroom)

36. 97:57–   (length = 1:00)   (cue title = The Toys)

37. 99:34–   (length = 1:36)   (cue title = The Cellar)

38. segue   (length = :10)   (cue title = Discovery)

DENOUEMENT

39. 106:57–   (length = 1:16)   (cue title = Finale)

out 108:13

Film music scholar and critic Royal S. Brown explains that the lack of music in everyday circumstances and with familiar styles is one of a number of ways in which "*Psycho* cuts its audience off from normal reality." Because there is no music at all coming from, say, a radio, a phonograph, or via singing or even humming, this absence "has the function of heightening the effect of the film-music convention whereby the appearance of nondiegetic music generally 'means' that something out of the ordinary is happening," or that the emotional or psychological implications of a scene or situation have special significance, that the viewer-listener should pay attention to them. As a result, "since *Psycho* has no diegetic music to somewhat 'rationalize' music's very presence in the film, the nondiegetic music gets an even stronger weighting on the side of the irrational."[11]

Third, although many of the *Psycho* music cues do offer some kind of emotional enhancement to a scene (for example, Cue 5, which accompanies Marion's mulling over whether to go through with the theft; or Cue 6, which reprises the frenetic music from the main-title sequence to accompany Marion's frenzied rush out of town; or, of course, in far more dramatic circumstances, Cue 17, which plays with the murder of Marion and is briefly heard again with the murder of Arbogast [Cue 29]), but their formal roles in smoothing transitions between scenes often seem at least as important as their affective qualities. A number of authors have pointed out this trait in Bernard Herrmann's film scores and have traced it to his work in radio during the 1930s. Finally, the whole textures of music cues, not just their themes, are often repeated, and the cues themselves are internally repetitious (an excellent example is the Prelude that accompanies the main-title sequence—for its first few measures, see Figure 5-10). Film music scholar Graham Bruce has called this a "cellular" method of composition,[12] and most writers now consider working with motivic cells as a defining trait of Herrmann's musical style. The technique is not unique to *Psycho*, but, according to film music composer and scholar Fred Steiner, it "assumes special importance" in this score and "[imparts] to it a special, disturbing quality [which contributes] much to its overall effectiveness."[13] Motivic cells and cues built on them can readily serve all the functions of a more traditionally thematic underscore, including motivic unity (where the cells act like themes) and the formal unity imparted by

Figure 5-10. *Psycho.* Prelude, opening (transcription from the sound track).

the repetitions. Herrmann's technique had a substantial influence on what are sometimes called "minimalist" orchestral scores in the past twenty years.

THE BIRDCAGE

As its opening sequence suggested by its staged performances and its confusion of the diegetic and nondiegetic realms, *The Birdcage* has a number of affinities with film musicals. Performances are prominent, there is relatively little underscoring, and often diegetic music substitutes for underscoring in backgrounded functions. Unlike *Psycho* (or even *Rashômon*), the music of *The Birdcage* is entirely (or almost entirely) based on songs or dance music. The nondiegetic music, even the underscoring, is all apparently based on songs or popular Latin dances. In addition, the very prominence of performances and nondiegetic songs and dances accentuates the starkness—or at least the simplicity—of the sound track in scenes or segments without music. Finally, like some traditional musicals, the roles of diegetic and nondiegetic music become more ambiguous—or mixed—as the film proceeds.

The film is easily partitioned in terms of time: an evening and two full days (see the headings in the cue list; Table 5-7). The first evening is dominated by the club, the Birdcage (see Figure 5-11), but parallel narratives also begin here, alternately showing us family conversations involving Val (Dan Futterman), and his father, Armand (Robin Williams) and mother, Albert (Nathan Lane), on the one hand, and Barbara (Calista Flockhart) and her parents, on the other. The parallel narratives continue throughout the first full day and into the second, until the families meet.

Figure 5-11. *The Birdcage.* Exterior shot.

Table 5-7 *The Birdcage* (1996), timeline and cue list.

(EVENING)

ESTABLISHING SEQUENCE & OPENING SCENE

    0:00:00   song [production number] with chorus, possibly nondiegetic at first, eventually revealed as diegetic when we see the stage and singers ["We Are Family"]

    0:04:20   trumpet fanfare, followed by an Indian-themed dance [Rossini, William Tell Overture in arrangement]

    0:05:40   same, cuts back in

    0:07:28   heard in the background again

    0:10:15   Latin number ["La Virgen Lloraba"]

    0:10:30   orchestra introduces Starina; at 11:00 orchestra plays behind her monologue — the same standard that she eventually sings ["Can That Boy Fox Trot"]

Family conversations

—VAL AND ARMAND TALK

    0:12:30   diegetic Latin music on cut to upstairs (Agador cleaning the kitchen, listens to a radio visible in the foreground) ["Conga"] (after about 0:14:00 muffled sounds of the club can be heard from downstairs)

—Barbara talks to her parents (in at 0:17:30)

—cut back to the penthouse

    0:20:00   nondiegetic piano music as Albert looks in on Val, who is sleeping

(NEXT DAY)

Morning

—Albert shops for groceries; breakfast in the penthouse

    0:20:50   Latin music, nondiegetic ["Lady Marmalade"]

—morning in the Keeley's house

—cut back to Armand and Albert

    0:26:45   on cut, Armand works on "Little Dream" at the piano

—cut back to Keeley's house (news organization set up outside)

Later that day

—rehearsal

    0:30:27   rehearsal piano with "Little Dream"

—cut back to Keeley's house at night

    0:38:10   orchestral underscoring (backgrounded)

—back to the club (after closing)

    0:41:15   piano with "Little Dream" (nondiegetic?)

(FOLLOWING DAY)

Early the next day

—Keeleys on the road; Armand and Albert on the beach; penthouse is cleared out; Armand and Albert return

0:43:00 orchestral; nondiegetic ["No Pain for Cakes"]— music continues over beach scene, morphing into Latin rhythm, and through subsequent segments; out with Albert's cry

—Albert and Armand talk outside and in a restaurant

0:47:40 Latin dance music heard faintly in the background — diegetic or nondiegetic?

0:52:43 orchestral music back in again with cut back to back to Keeleys on the road; goes out just after cut back to Armand and Albert (0:53:15)

Back to the penthouse; decision to ask Val's mother for help; in Katherine's office; Armand and Albert talk outside

1:00:50 low level diegetic music (radio) in the office

1:00:55 Armand and Katherine dance and sing ["Love Is in the Air"]

1:01:20 return to low level diegetic music in the office

1:08:25 low level diegetic music again on cut to the office

Back to the penthouse, the time approaches; the Keeleys arrive; dinner

1:12:40 Agador sings while working ["She Works Hard for the Money"]

1:14:45 music outdoors as Keeleys approach the club

1:18:49 same briefly again

1:20:00 Latin music as Katherine waits in traffic (enters just before the cut)

1:27:00 low level music from the club or from outdoors (as newsmen look at name on the door)

1:31:07 again, then to piano and singing with cut back to penthouse ["I Could Have Danced All Night"]

Finale: the press arrive; the Keeleys escape; end credits

1:47:05 low level music again with newsmen outside; continues to be heard during subsequent conversation indoors

1:48:48 Latin performance in the club, goes directly into "We are Family"; overlaps with Latin music heard outdoors at about 1:53:25 (after cut outside)

1:53:45 overlaps with Latin music for credits and wedding ["Family Salsa" followed by "Conga"]

Music follows a steady path from beginning to end, with clearly divided functions that give way to more complex treatments before resolving suddenly into a framing repeat performance at the end. We hear only diegetic performance in the first 10 min, then, briefly, radio sounds. Music, which has been very prominent so far, drops out entirely for the first conversation between Barbara and her parents, thus even further accentuating the divide between the young couple's families—and also the very prosaic character of Barbara's parents. Plainly nondiegetic music appears at 00:20:00, as Albert looks in on the sleeping Val. With the cut to the next scene (and next day), the status of the

Latin music seems only a little less secure (are we hearing it playing from somewhere outdoors and nearby?). Rehearsals involving the song "Little Dream" reassert performance in the sphere of the club, but nondiegetic underscoring appears in the Keeleys' scenes (at 00:38:10 and 00:43:00) as the dramatic situation intensifies (they are hounded by reporters and try to escape).

From this point on, the diegetic performances are brief and personal (Armand with his former spouse Katherine at 01:00:55; Agador at 01:12:40; Armand and Mrs. Keeley at 01:31:07) and other diegetic music is decidedly backgrounded until the finale, when Armand and Albert help the Keeleys escape in disguise during a reprise performance of "We Are Family." As a final touch, the diegetic music transforms into (prominent) underscoring for the wedding scene that closes the film—and overlaps with the end credits. For this, arranger Steve Goldstein created an instrumental salsa version of "We Are Family."

THE HOURS

The Hours (2002) is based on a novel by Michael Cunningham that self-reflexively focuses on the writing of a novel and the wide-ranging influences of reading it. Three parallel stories play out in the years 1923, 1951, and 2001: during a day in each of these years, respectively, Virginia Woolf (Nicole Kidman) writes a novel *Mrs. Dalloway* and ultimately commits suicide; a housewife, Laura Brown (Julianne Moore), reads the novel, contemplates suicide but eventually abandons her family instead; and an editor, Clarissa Vaughan (Meryl Streep), prepares a party honoring a poet (and former lover), who is, coincidentally, Marion Brown's son Richard (Ed Harris) and who commits suicide before the party.

In an interview included among the DVD's special features, composer Philip Glass comments that his task was to try to hold together a film that jumps frequently from one of the parallel stories to another.[14] Whether the film truly required that kind of help at unification is open to question: the **mise-en-scène** for each period is visually distinctive, the focus on a female lead in each story is obvious, and connections are frequently drawn between the stories, including (among others) the motif of the novel *Mrs. Dalloway* and the themes of lesbian love and of suicide.

Some but not all of Glass's nondiegetic orchestral cues overlap scenes—the simplest and most direct way to tie them together (see especially the cues for the Morning and Lunch segments listed in Table 5-8). Instead, it is the remarkable homogeneity of the music that allows the sound track's musical element to lend a sense of cohesion to the film at the level of the whole. Most of the cues, in fact, can be heard as more or less subtle variants or developments of the first one. Glass's minimalist style emphasizes repetition and small changes within generally homogeneous textures. In a sense, this reduces the "cell" method of Herrmann to its bare essentials and, usually in slightly less radical forms, has become a common method of film music composition in recent decades (composers who have employed it at one time or another include James Horner, Thomas Newman, Mychael Danna, and Dario Marianelli, among others). At the same time, Glass's cues do satisfy the classical requirements of non-diegetic music, in the formal work of transitions and thematic unification, as mentioned earlier, and also in establishing mood and, in a few instances, even in following shifting moods and circumstances within a scene (for example, see Cue 10, which follows Laura Brown's emotional crescendo as she leaves her son with a babysitter and checks into a hotel, resolved to kill herself—or so she thinks). A striking—and unique—moment is a "hit" or stinger: a sudden flurry of loud and rapid piano notes as Richard falls out of the window to his death.

Table 5-8 *The Hours* (2002), timeline and cue list.

PROLOGUE & CREDITS	
1. Virginia Woolf's suicide	
0:02:00 [CUES 1 & 2] Music in: 1. "The Poet Acts" and segue to 2. "Morning Passages"; continues to 0:09:20	
2. 0:03:40 Opening credits combined with prologue-style introductions of the three time periods	
MORNING	
3. 0:08:54 Woolf and her husband Leonard in the morning; "Flowers" parallel between the three periods	
0:09:20 Music goes out	= 7:20
4. 0:11:38 Breakfast in the Browns' house	
0:13:20 [CUE 3] Music in (6. "'I'm Going to Make a Cake'")	
5. 0:14:16 Clarissa plans the party; buys flowers; "One day" parallel at the end	
0:15:30 Music out	= 2:10
0:16:30 [CUE 4] Music in (12. "Escape!")	
6. 0:17:31 Clarissa visits Richard	
0:18:53 Music out	= 2:23
0:21:25 [CUE 5] Music in (variant of 1. "The Poet Acts")	
0:23:58 Music out	= 2:33
0:26:50 [CUE 6] Music in (6. "'I'm Going to Make a Cake'")	
LUNCH	
7. 0:27:40 Back to Woolf writing, household, walk ("She's going to die")	
0:28:14 Music out	= 1:24
0:31:20 [CUE 7] Music in (latter part of 9. "The Kiss")	
8. 0:32:02 Laura Brown and her son make a cake; Clarissa and Sally talk about the party for Richard	
0:33:24 Music out	= 2:14
9. 0:35:38 Back to Laura Brown working on the cake; a friend Kitty visits	

AFTERNOON

10. 0:43:29 Woolf's sister Vanessa and her children arrive early; Woolf and Angelica hold a funeral for a bird; Laura Brown makes a decision

    0:43:32 Music out

    0:45:40 [CUE 8] Music in (8. "Dead Things")

    0:50:10 Music out   = 4:30

11. 0:50:11 Louis Waters (former lover of Richard's) arrives at Clarissa's apartment, very early for the party

    0:50:16 [CUE 9] Music in: diegetic music, recording of Richard Strauss, "Beim Schlafengehen" (from "Four Last Songs")

    0:51:32 Music out

12. 0:59:25 Laura Brown finishes the cake, then goes to a hotel, intending suicide; back to Woolf with the sister and children, with cuts back and forth to Laura Brown in the hotel; Vanessa and the children leave; Louis leaves; Woolf returns to writing

    0:59:25 [CUE 10] Music in (11. "Tearing Herself Away"); 1:04:35 music out   = 5:10

    1:05:15 [CUE 11] Music in (3. "Something She Has to Do"); 1:08:23 Music out   = 3:08

    1:09:35 [CUE 12] Music in; 1:11:58 music out (from 6. "I'm Going to Make a Cake'")   = 2:23

13. 1:12:11 Clarissa's daughter Julia arrives

LATE AFTERNOON/EVENING

14. 1:17:02 Virginia Woolf leaves the house; Leonard looks for her, finds her at the train station, they argue

    1:23:15 [CUE 13] Music in (4. "'For Your Own Benefit'"); music out 1:26:30   = 3:15

15. 1:25:56 Laura Brown returns; she and Richard talk on the way home; Richard upends his apartment, he jumps to his death; dinner and party at Browns; Clarissa in the hospital; Leonard and Virginia by the fire discuss the book; late night at the Browns and parallel with Leonard and Virginia

    1:27:40 [CUE 14] Music in; 1:30:05 music out (variant of 1. "The Poet Acts")   = 2:25

    1:31:50 [CUE 15] Music in (12. "Escape"); 1:34:30 music out   = 2:40

    1:37:15 [CUE 16] Music in 10. "'Why Does Someone Have to Die?'"

16. 1:39:42 Taking down the party at Clarissa's; Laura Brown arrives and they talk

    1:41:14 Music out   = 3:59

    1:44:10 [CUE 17] Music in (13. "Choosing Life"); 1:48:00 music out   = 3:50

EPILOGUE

17. 1:47:59 End of the night; drowning reprise: end credits

    1:48:44 [CUE 18] Music in (beginning of 12. "Escape," then 14. "The Hours"); music out 1:54:22

We have laid out Table 5-8 somewhat differently from the previous cue lists to show how one can make use of DVD chapter numbers and CD sound track recordings. The film's large segments, its acts, are given as headings, as usual. Within each of these, the DVD chapter numbers are given, along with a description of the chapter's contents. This layout works for *The Hours*, as scene changes coincide well with chapter changes. Musical cues are labeled and numbered ("CUE"), and in parentheses the corresponding CD track is identified by number and title. Note that the CD tracks do not appear in order (three are missing, as well): despite titles that evoke the narrative sequence of the film, the CD is not simply a compilation of the recorded cues. Instead, the cues were newly performed and recorded (and some of them apparently revised, as well), with the result that the CD is more like a suite of music from the film than it is a reproduction of the film's music.

The title "suite" has commonly been used for selections of concert music derived from films. The term has been used since the 19th century for concert compositions that draw selections of music from larger, usually stage, works—familiar examples are the "Carmen" suite of Georges Bizet (from his opera) and the two "Peer Gynt" suites of Edvard Grieg (drawn from his incidental music for a production of the Ibsen play). In this case, the basic progressions and themes for the film's music cues were derived from *earlier* concert works by Glass. The publication credits for the CD read:

> Music published by Famous Music Corporation (ASCAP), except the following, published by Dunvagen Music Publishers, Inc.: the first section of track 6, "'I'm Going to Make a Cake,'" based on the theme from "Protest" (Act II, Scene 3) from the opera *Satyagraha*; track 11, "Tearing Herself Away," based on "Islands" from the album *Glassworks* (not contained in the motion picture); and track 12, "Escape," based on "Metamorphosis Two" from the album *Solo Piano*.[15]

To complicate matters even further, the reference to track 11 as "not contained in the motion picture" is incorrect: almost the entirety of it, with no orchestrational or other changes, is heard as Cue 10.

The DVD and the CD, the film and the "suite," are different artistic works, no matter how much of their material they share. In general, for recent films, a CD recording is not necessary for a study of the film and can, as here, even introduce some obstacles. For classical films, on the other hand, sound track CDs, especially those issued in the past decade or so, frequently *are* compilations of the film's musical cues from the original studio recordings and therefore can often be helpful in sorting out and collating the nondiegetic music.

Summary

The segmentation of a film's running time produces a flexible hierarchy of units: shot, scene, sequence, and act. Listening to concert or other instrumental music also involves a hierarchy of grouping—motive, phrase, section, and movement—but these units do not correspond, one-on-one, to filmic units.

Musical motives, for example, are always short (a few seconds) but shots can range anywhere from 1 sec to many minutes. Note also that, in *The Hours*, a complete movement from the CD suite ("Tearing Herself Away") accompanied a single scene in the film (Laura Brown's trip to the hotel).

Music, whether principally diegetic or nondiegetic, is laid out over the segments of a film. The six case studies in this chapter offered opportunity to examine these filmic units in individual films and to get a sense of the formal and stylistic variety in the ways music has been deployed.

Music in Main-Title and End-Credit Sequences

Introduction

In the context of production, making decisions about the placement of music is referred to as "spotting." In the context of reception (watching or analyzing a film), we match our expectations against the decisions made by the director, sound designer, and composer (except as backstory, it does not matter to the viewer-listener which of these three might have been responsible for the spotting). In this chapter, we identify two of the most characteristic—and predictable—categories of music placement in film form: the establishing sequence and end-credits music.

Establishing Sequence

One of the most powerful roles for music is in the formal framing of opening titles and end credits. These conventions have been manipulated in many ways over the years (see the sidebar for silent-film era music director and composer Erno Rapee's comments on openings), but their function as buffers between the outside world and the diegetic world (time, space) of the film has remained constant. Music has traditionally played an essential role in this framing. The traditional "overture" of the musical theater was central to exhibition practices of the silent-film era, when live concert-style or song performances were normally also part of the program and, in theaters that could afford orchestras, overtures were often played before the main feature. (Appropriately to the occasion, these overtures frequently were taken from 19th-century operas.) The grand orchestral music making associated with these moments was transferred to music for the main-title sequences in

I [have] found the following a very satisfactory plan:—start your prologue with offstage singing drawing nearer and interrupting some kind of pantomime on stage:—this will prove particularly effective if done behind the scrim and when the picture [starts] let the singing and dancing continue by dimmed lights until the picture on the screen occupies the complete attention of your audience and your orchestra has drowned the singing on stage.

—Erno Rapee[1]

sound films as a way to frame the feature film that followed but also to give it due prominence in the theater's program. Alternatively, the opening credits would be covered with a recorded performance of a popular song, especially for musicals.

In the classical Hollywood sound film, the opening titles were often linked to the first scene of the film by means of music (other linking devices include prologue intertitles and background shots or drawings that anticipate the action of the film). For this reason, the "main-title sequence" is tied to the first scene in what we can call an "establishing sequence."

MEET ME IN ST. LOUIS, TITLES AND OPENING SCENE

Meet Me in St. Louis (1944) is usually taken to be the first characteristic product of what became known as the "Freed Unit" at MGM studios (after Arthur Freed, the producer who ran the unit). This group was well-funded by the studio and was able to create a series of musicals with very high production values; their titles include, among others, *Easter Parade* (1948), *An American in Paris* (1951), *Singin' in the Rain* (1952), *Brigadoon* (1954), and *Gigi* (1958). The Freed Unit also was also influential because of its focus on the "integrated musical," that is, a musical that drew its performances into the context of a narrative film, or that subordinated the musical's tendency to promote spectacle to the primary emphasis on narrative continuity and clarity of the traditional feature film.

In keeping with this emphasis, *Meet Me in St. Louis* employs what had already become by the late 1930s a conventional musical design for a feature film's opening credits, consisting generally of three or four functionally defined sections (see corresponding images in Figure 6-1): (1) a dramatic gesture begins, quickly announcing a musical theme whose beginning coincides with the main title (that is, the one that gives the film's name); (2) a very brief transition to a second, more lyrical, and usually quieter theme—this is normally not timed to match any particular title; (3) a slightly longer transition to a dramatic ending flourish or cadence—this normally plays against the credit titles with producer, director, and composer names but only because they are always placed at the end of the main-title sequence; and (4) a transition that "winds down" either to a prologue (with a text-heavy intertitle, voice-over narration, or both) or to an establishing shot for the film's first scene. Depending on how quickly the action of the film follows the director's credit, the functions of parts 3 and 4 may be combined because music is generally timed to go out at the moment of the first significant sound effect or speech.

In *Meet Me in St. Louis*, we hear all parts of this standard, two-theme design: the opening section surrounds the main title with a large orchestra-and-chorus

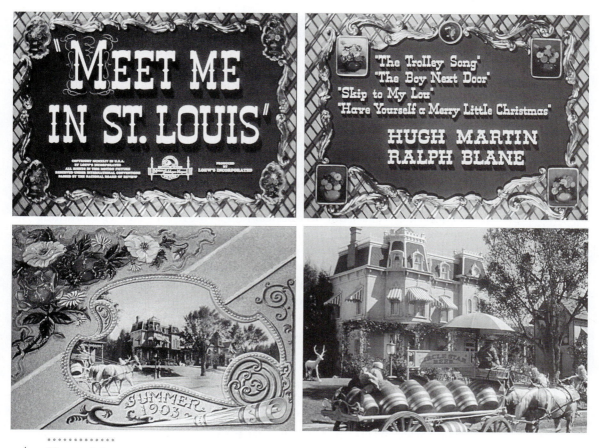

1 | 2
3 | 4

Figure 6-1. *Meet Me in St. Louis.* Establishing sequence.

rendition of the title song (1); the second, lyrical section quotes "The Boy Next Door" (2); and the third part tails off to merge with the brass motto that announces the "Summer" title (3). Finally, music goes out (4) as sound effects and generic speech take over during the establishing shot of Kensington Street. Everything we have heard announces a nostalgic costumer, either as romantic comedy or light family melodrama—not a musical. Only when Agnes starts singing several minutes later do the "unreal" traits of a musical start to come to the fore, not because she (or Grandpa shortly after) sings—something natural enough in a high-spirited household—but because the accompaniment is provided by a nondiegetic orchestra (it starts up in a quickly realized audio dissolve). Finally, we recognize this as a "number" when the song is completed after the camera moves outdoors to the street and Esther (Judy Garland) and Rose (Lucille Bremer), amazingly, pick up the song from Grandpa in a perfectly synchronized overlap.

RASHÔMON, TITLES AND OPENING SCENE

Our second example comes from *Rashômon* (1950), whose design and music we have already discussed in chapter 5. The studio logo is silent; music enters with the main title, as we would expect, but behind the credit titles is a series of filmed shots (not stills) showing different angles on the Rashômon gate, the ruins of an historic entrance to the city of Kyoto. (Although still photographs were sometimes used earlier, it was only in the later 1940s that it became common to overlay credits transparently on filmed scenes in title sequences.) We see but do not hear rain as the music and titles continue. After the director's credit, the music stops and, with a very slight audio overlap, a cut to a long shot of the gate brings the sound of rain that takes over the sound track at a loudness level nearly equal to that of the music we have just heard. The image track uses it own (classical) establishing sequence: a series of establishing shots—five of them here—that progressively bring the viewer in from a long shot of the environment to a much tighter shot showing individuals (who typically then begin to speak). The long shot of the gate is followed by a somewhat closer shot of same in which we can barely see two individuals sitting, then two cuts further in, each time with a clearer view of the two (but still at a distance), and finally a medium shot of the two seen from the side, at which point the sound of the rain is reduced somewhat and the man in front (the Woodcutter, played by Takashi Shimura) speaks. The background sound of rain persists throughout the first scene; music enters again when the Woodcutter begins his story and the scene switches to a flashback.

THE SOUND OF MUSIC, OVERTURE AND TITLE SEQUENCE

Beginning in the 1960s, the conventional design was frequently compromised (especially in films with popular music underscoring, where the music for an establishing sequence may simply be a recorded song), or the establishing sequence was even deleted so as to move immediately to action, but the formal establishing sequence did not entirely disappear—even today, it can be found, with a wide range of variations, in the majority of feature films, and in particular romantic comedies and dramas. More complex variants of the establishing sequence began to appear in the widescreen spectacles of the 1950s, such as historical epics (*The Robe* (1953), *Julius Caesar* (1953), or *Ben-Hur* (1959)) and lavishly produced musicals such as *Oklahoma!* (1955) and *My Fair Lady* (1964), which open, like theatrical productions, with formal overtures.

The establishing sequence of *The Sound of Music* (1965) is a good example of a complex variant. We can describe it most efficiently by making use of a timeline:

I. Studio logo
00:00:02   20th Century Fox studio logo with fanfare.
00:00:08   Screen fades to black.

II. Prologue A
00:00:14   (a) Grey clouds appear, mountains with snow, the sound of howling wind; (b) the camera pans over the mountains, and the wind sounds increase.
00:01:04   As the camera continues to pan, the season changes to spring, birds sing.
00:01:17   Music enters (Figure 6-2)— an introduction, nebulous, starts quietly and gradually builds, flute and other winds imitate bird sounds with trills and runs, then:

Figure 6-2. *The Sound of Music.* Establishing sequence. The moment when music enters.

00:01:43   The first phrase of the title song, "The Sound of Music," enters (played by orchestral horns), then the introductory music, interspersed with bells tolling and occasional phrases from "The Sound of Music" continues to 00:02:44. At 00:01:53, views of Salzburg, the lake, the von Trapp villa. At 00:02:25, a plateau on the mountain, with Maria walking toward the camera from the background.
00:02:44   Maria begins to sing "The Sound of Music" (Figure 6-3).
00:04:41   She finishes singing; bells toll, she realizes she needs to return to the abbey, begins to run, turns and runs back to pick up her wimple (exclaiming an exasperated "Oh!"), then turns and runs out of sight.

III. Main title and credits sequence
00:04:58   Credits begin with "A Robert Wise Production" and overture, which plays over various shots of mountains, churches, and steeples from 00:04:58 to

Figure 6-3. *The Sound of Music.* Establishing sequence. Maria sings.

00:07:35. At 00:05:14, the main title "The Sound of Music" appears. (Credits continue through all this.) At 00:07:25, a final shot of the city of Salzburg during the overture, with a superimposed title: "Salzburg, Austria, in the last Golden Days of the Thirties."

IV. Prologue B—Transition to first scene

00:07:35   Credits and overture end; new music begins: "Preludium" (three sections: "Dixit Dominus," Morning Hymn, "Alleluia"), with a view of the abbey. At 00:07:43, cut to the courtyard of abbey, nuns walking toward the cloister on way to chapel. At 00:07:56, cut to long shot of nuns walking down the cloister. At 00:08:07, cut to the chapel. At 00:09:27, cut to the cloister, nuns walking. At 00:09:32 comes the first line of dialogue: "Reverend Mother"; conversation among the nuns about Maria ensues.

00:010:02   "Preludium" ends; the conversation continues, leading after a time to the song performance "Maria."

The typical features are all there, but each has been greatly expanded, and an extra prologue has been inserted before the title and credits sequence. In classical Hollywood sound film, the establishing sequence typically ran to about 1 min. Even in *Gone with the Wind* (1939), the elaborate opening (which includes a prologue) runs to just a little over 3 min. In *The Sound of Music*, the opening would run 5 min even if we deleted Prologue A. In keeping with this pattern of expansion, Prologue A itself is at base a simple song performance, but the introduction alone lasts nearly 2½ min and includes a variety of visual and aural elements. Finally, note that what would normally be a short transition into the first scene is also very elongated here: the "Preludium" moves along for 30 sec behind dialogue before it finally ends.

OUT OF AFRICA, PROLOGUE AND TITLE SEQUENCE

Like *The Sound of Music*, *Out of Africa* (1983) begins with a long prologue—only after 5½ min does the main title appear; from that point on, the sequence is conventional; we reach the first scene at 00:07:30.

The prologue itself is quite complex. It begins ambiguously with a sunrise over an African landscape, the sound of a clarinet, a woman sleeping, a man profiled against the sun. Things gradually become clearer as a woman speaks in voice-over narration, reminiscing about her life in Africa and, in so doing, identifying each of the previous images for us. At about 00:01:30, cut to a room where the woman (Isak Dinesen, played by Meryl Streep) is writing; the voice-over narration continues and we now understand it to be the text of her memoir, spoken as she writes (Figure 6-4a and b). At a reference to her life

a | b   **Figure 6-4.** *Out of Africa* (1983). Prologue and establishing sequence.
c | d

in Europe, we see a preliminary scene set there (this acts as an extended flash-back). The main-title sequence follows. The body of the film is thus plainly marked as the staging of the memoir, as a visual analogue to the story told in the book. A text prologue might have accomplished the same thing but placing the prologue before the titles more forcefully sets the story off from present time, thereby emphasizing a quality of memory, "pastness," or even the sense of unreality or the mythic that always attends memory.

Action continues in the background of the title sequence as the credits are shown: behind the text elements, images of the Kenyan landscape track the progress of a passenger train. (See Figure 6-4c and d.) The film's main theme appears and swells at the appearance of the main title. This theme, however, has a definite musical form that continues until music goes out under the noise of the train (which we had previously seen but not heard) and the first scene begins.

The form of the theme is the standard AABA design of the popular song (the chorus of Gershwin's "I Got Rhythm" is one of literally thousands of examples of this design: a phrase of music (A) is literally repeated with different text, then there is a different phrase (B, or the "bridge"), followed by a final repetition of the first phrase (A) with yet another new line of text). Composer

John Barry distributes the elements of this design across the credits sequence: the theme phrase (A) is played in a robust, firmly expressive manner (part 1); the bridge (B) drops back to a quieter, tentative state (part 2); and the reprise of A swells again to provide the dramatic conclusion (part 3), its final moments tapering off as a quiet conclusion-transition (Part 4).

This single-theme or "monothematic" music for the main-title sequence does have precedents in classical practice, too, notably in Max Steiner's music for *Mildred Pierce* (1945) and David Raksin's score for *Laura* (1944). These two films are exceptions to the generalization for classical Hollywood that the two-theme design described earlier was more common for higher-budget productions ("A films"), but the single-theme model was routinely used for the more numerous lower-budget productions ("B films").

As the example from *Out of Africa* suggests, voice-over narration is sometimes used as a substitute for stationary or rolling text in prologues. Such narrated prologues often occur without music, but when music is added it typically supplies an emotional edge that may or may not be obvious in the disembodied voice. Familiar examples include the prologues after the main title and credit sequence in *Rebecca* (1940) and *Casablanca* (1942). (More recently, the beginning of *The Matrix* (1999) uses two voice-overs in a complex merging of the usual establishing sequence elements.) The same principle holds true when voice-over is used elsewhere in a film, as well, as, for example, when we see an insert with the text of a letter and that text is read in voice-over or by a character momentarily offscreen. The contemporary analogue is an insert of a computer screen (as, obviously, in *You've Got Mail* (1998), the *Matrix* trilogy and many others) or a cell phone (as in *Casino Royale* (2007), where repetition of such moments gives the cell phone text message the status of a motif).

TO KILL A MOCKINGBIRD, MUSIC IN THE MAIN-TITLE SEQUENCE

Unlike the grand opening of *The Sound of Music* or the orchestral expansiveness of the theme for *Out of Africa*, the opening of *To Kill a Mockingbird* (1962), like its score overall, is notable for its relative sparseness and intimacy; the tender use of chamber orchestra and emphasis on solo instruments struck a distinct contrast with other films of the period, but, as we will see, appropriately sets the stage for a film that portrays a small rural town in Alabama through the eyes of two children and depicts the events surrounding the trial of a black man who is defended by the children's father.

Composer Elmer Bernstein acknowledged that "in many ways, *To Kill a Mockingbird* was one of the most difficult scores to write. I distinctly remember procrastinating for weeks before committing a single note to paper."[2] His dilemma, in part, was caused by the fact that *To Kill a Mockingbird* is not a film of action or high drama. Many of its characters are children, and the situations are local, often domestic, and (with important exceptions) everyday. In such circumstances, simplicity and directness of expression are virtues, but simplicity in film music is an enigmatic concept; simplicity and conciseness are valuable in that they help a music cue make an effective emotional impact on an audience, but if the music is merely simplistic it can easily become too obvious and therefore distracting. After mulling this over, Bernstein finally came up with the concept that the music should "deal in the magic of the children's world." For the composer, "That was the whole key to the score, and it accounts for the use of the high registers of the piano, harp, and bell, things that I associated with child magic in a definitely American ambience." Through this subtle concept of giving the children's world a coherent voice and color, Bernstein allows the audience to tap into memories of childhood—not with "child-like" music, but with well-crafted "adult" music set within a melodic, harmonic, and orchestral framework that "addresses itself to children."

For reference, here is a complete shot list for the main-title sequence:

1. Black Screen.
2. Universal Studios Logo.
3. Fade to Black.
4. Old Cigar Box.
5. Child opens Box, which is filled with odds and ends, while she hums.
6. Child grabs a crayon out of the box.
7. Child begins to rub crayon on paper that creates a negative image of the film's title.
8. Main Title image as crayon relief.
9. Child draws line on paper.
10. Spiral shot of a pocket watch, which we can hear ticking, while credits begin.
11. Cross-Fade to a full shot of a safety pin and coins.
12. Pan across length of a pencil.
13. Child drawing with the crayon .
14. Child grabs another crayon out of the box.
15. A marble rolls away.
16. Camera dollies along following path of the marble.
17. The marble hits a second marble and the Child says "Ding."
18. Shot of box from above (see Figure 6-5).
19. Cross-Fade to Child drawing a squiggly line on the paper.
20. Shot of Crayon and Pen Nib.

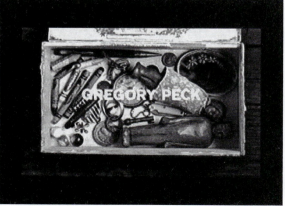

Figure 6-5. *To Kill a Mockingbird* (1962). Image from opening credits.

Figure 6-6. *To Kill a Mockingbird.* Image from opening credits.

21. Cross-Fade to the pocket watch, then pan across to . . .
22. A Harmonica.
23. A Marble, and a.
24. Blurry image of a whistle.
25. Image of whistle sharpens into focus (see Figure 6-6).
26. Line continues.
27. Child fills in a picture of a bird with the crayon.
28. Shot of interior of the box, child drops the crayon into the box.
29. Image of bird.
30. Paper is torn to show black background.
31. Fade to first scene.

In this main-title sequence, Bernstein presents the primary thematic material in an unhurried and quiet manner that places the listener into the children's world from the outset. A solo piano states what will eventually become the second phrase of the title theme, first under a black screen, then underneath the Universal Studios logo (Shots 1-2; see the music in Figure 6-7a). The entrance of the background music before the logo comes on screen firmly subverts the usual expectation of loud, grandiose music (for example, Alfred

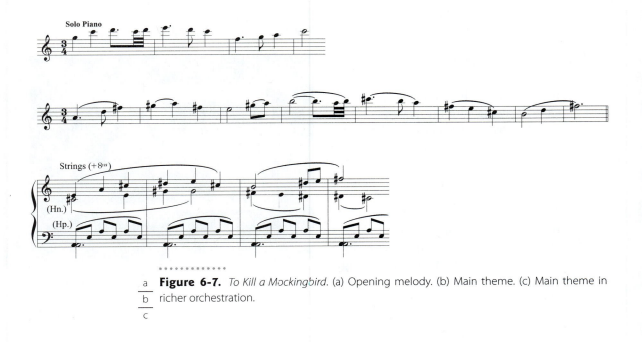

a
—
b
—
c

Figure 6-7. *To Kill a Mockingbird.* (a) Opening melody. (b) Main theme. (c) Main theme in richer orchestration.

Newman's well-known fanfare for 20th Century Fox). The phrase ends with the first image of the film, a cigar box (Shot 3); the subsequent six images are shown with no music, only the sounds of a child humming as she is blithely playing with her crayons. Immediately the sonic world of the film has been created by the solo piano and then the silence of the nondiegetic (that is, the nondiegetic is displaced by quiet, unprepossessing sounds of the diegetic). The majority of the film (and, particularly, any time adults are the focus of the action) has no music, so it is fitting that the main-title sequence also utilizes (nondiegetic) silence as a tool to establish what becomes a structural relation.

Once the title is established (Shot 8), the camera follows a crayon drawing a line downwards, followed by a shot slowly spiraling down toward the broken pocket watch in the cigar box; it is here that the main theme proper (that is, from its own beginning) finally enters with a solo flute over a light harp and accordion accompaniment (Figure 6-7b). After three images of items in the cigar box we see a pencil (Shot 12), not from an overhead vantage point, but from ground level, as it were. The audience has now been given a Lilliputian point of view of the items in the box (these images take up the entire screen), and a transformation is complete: the audience is drawn into the children's world through the cigar box, and the music's confirming formal status (as main theme) acts as reinforcement to that process.

The theme then unfolds in an unhurried way, its first phrase of seven bars finished as the camera's pan reaches the end of the pencil, its second phrase (identical to the piano's opening music) set mostly against the rolling crayon. As the child takes another crayon from the box (Shot 14), she sets in motion a marble that rolls through the final measures of the theme; the child announces "ding" as the marble clicks against another marble and the score gently blooms into the first phrase again (Figure 6-7c), for the first time balancing all three aspects of the sound track (music, child's speech, and noise from objects).

Throughout the orchestral version of the first and second phrases of the theme, the camera relaxes to meander through the box, slowly panning across images of crayons, watches and harmonicas (through Shot 23 and into Shot 24). As the second phrase is extended with lines in the flute and bells, a blurry image of a whistle sharpens into focus (acting as a visual accent to the composer's credit: Figure 6-6). The final statement of the theme (this time by the piano with a similar accompaniment as the flute previously) is combined with the sudden return of the diegetic sounds: the child, the crayon, and the ticking watch. When the child rips the paper she has been drawing on (Shot 30), the theme does not come to a full close but repeats the last phrase segment as the image of trees emerges through the torn page, creating a simple but effective musical fade-out.

ADDITIONAL EXAMPLES

To suggest the variety of treatments of the establishing sequence and its music, here are short descriptions of the openings of several films from the 1960s and later. In *Who's Afraid of Virginia Woolf?* (1966), the opening credits appear over an apparently (but only apparently) leisurely walk home by Richard Burton and Elizabeth Taylor's characters. The opening of *Sleuth* (1972) has a disconcertingly "stagey" feel thanks to music that reproduces the sound of a theatrical pit orchestra. *Witness* (1985) has a leisurely, 5-min establishing sequence that goes at a slow pace and without complexity through each of the conventional formal elements while it fails to engage as closely as one might expect with the image track action. *Gandhi* (1985), on the other hand, uses a surprisingly short establishing sequence (with very few titles) for such a long film (over 3 hr). The first 7 min of Robert Altman's *Fool for Love* (1985) uses an orderly succession of effects, harmonica music, a truck driving on the highway, and an acoustic country western singer on the radio, but then intermixes these sound elements, all the while giving surprisingly little mood information or narrative reference for the three characters, the Old Man (Harry Stanton), Eddie (Harry Connick, Jr.), and May (Kim Basinger). Finally, the establishing sequence in *Four Weddings and a Funeral* (1994) runs almost 5 min and is divided by the sound track into two parts: In the first, a song is performed in its entirety as background; in the second, speech and then effects dominate with rhythmic qualities of their own.

A main-title sequence without sound reverses the traditional "overture" or "framing" function of this segment of the film. In the rare instances when main titles were silent in classical Hollywood film, the effect was one of starkness, barrenness, or mystery. On the other hand, in European films, especially after about 1950, it was not uncommon to run the opening of a film to silence. A late, apparently ironic use of such a main-title sequence is in Woody Allen's romantic comedy *Annie Hall* (1978), where the silence throws off the viewer's expectations about what will follow: Because Allen is said to have regarded the film as a tribute to French director Jean-Luc Godard, the opening may be said to signal "art film," a narrative or interpretive gap in itself that the viewer can spend considerable time trying to explain (especially after a boring, self-centered film critic in the line of people waiting to enter a movie theater is roundly put down, with the assistance of two logic-breaking devices: Allen's direct address to the audience and his pulling in Marshall McLuhan from offscreen to rebut the critic).

The opposite procedure, where music appears in the "framing" elements but not within the film's narrative segments, can be equally striking. Even in recent decades, music has not lost its connotations of fantasy and the irrational, and deliberately minimizing music after the establishing sequence creates a strong effect of realism or of the everyday. In most sound films before about 1932, on the other hand, nondiegetic music was very restricted more for technological reasons than for aesthetic ones. For example, the early horror films of Universal Studios, such as *Frankenstein* (1931), *The Mummy* (1932), and *Dracula* (1931), have no music outside of the credits sequences. In all three of these films, there are many moments that would certainly have been scored with music even as little as one or two years later. Compare these three films with *The Invisible Man* (1933) from the same studio: this film has a background musical score that seems quite conventional by later standards, including the underscoring of dialogue.

End-Credit Music

End credits in early sound cinema were usually just a single title showing a cast list, and the music was typically not related to the film; instead, a bright foxtrot tempo encouraged the audience to shift their attention away from the film quickly and therefore, presumably, prompted them to get up out of their seats, as well. End-credits lists began to lengthen in the 1950s, and, especially since about 1990, they have become greatly elongated, often running to as much as 4 or 5 min. These long lists almost always have music, which can vary from unrelated pop tunes (analogous to the foxtrots of early cinema) to repetitions of songs or orchestral cues from the film to symphonically developed short compositions on the main themes from the background score—or a combination of all the above. The convention of music over the credits sequence is so powerful that a distinctive effect is made if the credits are run silently—an effect of solemnity, seriousness, or (if not done well) higher aesthetic pretension.

FILMS FROM 1939, END CREDITS

We will start with the statistics for several films from the year 1939, as examples of typical classical practice for end credits. By this time, the end-credit sequence normally consisted of an "The End" card followed by the cast list. It was expected that some minimal transition would be made between the final scene and this sequence. In *Intermezzo*, for example, the film closes with Holger (Leslie Howard) entering his house and closing the door, which remains onscreen as the background for the end card and a short rolling cast list. The sequence lasts 25 sec in all. The same method is used for *Stagecoach:* as the wagon carrying Claire Trevor and John Wayne's characters rides away into the night, "The End" and then a short cast list are superimposed.

Lower budget films at MGM followed a formula that is a variant of this model. *On Borrowed Time*, for example, separates the end-credit sequence with a short fade to black—then appears an end card with a spare, elegant graphic of a lion (the studio emblem) behind it; after another short fade to black, two cards with the cast list appear. The entire sequence lasts 30 sec. Music runs continuously from the final scene to the end (in this case orchestral underscore because of the film's subject (death and the afterlife)). *Honolulu* follows exactly the same model but uses the typical bright foxtrot rhythms. In the high-budget production *Gone with the Wind*, the end title is brief, superimposed over a final shot of Scarlett on a hillside looking at Tara. Then a simple card with the legend "Exit Music" appears (Figure 6-8), against which plays a 4-min composition made up of music heard earlier in the film (this piece is very much like a symphonically developed composition for end credits in contemporary films). There is no cast list. This "Exit Music" balances the Overture that begins the film and the "Entr'acte" between the two Parts.

At Warner Bros., Max Steiner emphasized continuity between film and credits more strongly, and end-credits sequences he scored are typically a bit longer, at 45 to 75 sec. For *Dust Be My Destiny*, music swells into the "End" card but then shifts to a foxtrot tempo halfway through the shot, overlapping with the first of two cast credits cards. This foxtrot is based on the same theme that Steiner used as the main theme for the film score proper. A brief swell brings the foxtrot, and the film, to an end at 45 sec. The pattern is almost identical in *They Made Me a Criminal*, another early John Garfield vehicle. For *Confessions of a Nazi Spy*, the design is different: a fade to black precedes "The End" but

Figure 6-8. *Gone With the Wind* (1939). This is an unusual announcement of exit music.

music actually overlaps into the fade and continues through a rolling cast list to the finish at 75 sec. The music is "America the Beautiful" played in a foxtrot or moderate march tempo.

OUT OF AFRICA, FINAL SCENE AND END CREDITS

The end-credit sequence of *Out of Africa* is an early example of the most common contemporary model. The last chapter of *Out of Africa* recounts Karen Blixen's final preparations to leave Africa and has the quality of a slow-moving final scene. There is no music for several minutes, until she begins a voice-over that brings us back to the present of the story (that is, her writing her memoirs in Denmark (refer to the section, "Main Titles")). In these final moments, she recounts one last nostalgic memory about Denys, then a superimposed legend tells us that she never returned to Africa, and a fade to black brings the credits. There is no "The End" card. The end-credit sequence runs just under 3 min with the familiar rolling credits against a black background. The music repeats the main theme from the beginning of the film, along with some cue elements heard elsewhere.

BRIDGET JONES'S DIARY, END-CREDITS SEQUENCE

In *Bridget Jones's Diary* (2001), the end-credit sequence lasts about 6 min and has three distinct components, defined by three popular songs. The first of these songs is "Have You Met Miss Jones"; the segment begins with a blackened screen, then within that a smaller-scale projection of a home movie appears. The home movie records a birthday party for Mark Darcy when he was a little boy. Among the guests is a young Bridget. Toward the end of the home movie a paddling (wading) pool is brought out, and the young Bridget is seen running through and splashing in the pool, wearing only her underpants, a reference to comments earlier in the film of how Bridget ran naked in Mark's paddling pool when he was eight and she was four. After this, the credits begin to run; these are limited to the cast and appear on a black screen, alternating with footage from the home movie. The home movie ends with a close-up on the young Bridget; the screen goes black and the remaining non-cast credits begin to roll. The song changes to "Killin' Time" (written and performed by Shelby Lynne) followed, 2 min later, by "Not of This Earth" (performed by Robbie Williams, written by Williams-Chambers), which fades out at the end of the credits. The final title is the studio—"Working Title"—with no music.

ADDITIONAL EXAMPLES

The two extremes of contemporary musical practices for end credits may be seen in *Four Weddings and a Funeral*, where we hear irrelevant pop songs, unconnected to the underscoring music or any of the diegetic music of the film, and *The Shawshank Redemption* (1994), which closes with a several-minute-long symphonic development of the film's main theme growing directly out of the music for the final scene.

Summary

Narrative conventions for the classical cinema, in place by the 1920s, subsumed sound and music once the sound film became the standard medium (by 1930 in the United States). Within this system, music also became codified with respect to film form. In this chapter, we looked at music's persistent but changing role in the formal framing of beginning and ending a film: the establishing sequence and the end credits.

Music in Performance and Montage Scenes

Introduction

In addition to the establishing sequence and end credits, certain scene categories involving music also have what might be called "formal" properties. First among these are musical performances, especially any highlighted or foregrounded performances. Another category is the montage or fantasy scene. Music enables montages to provide clear information while nevertheless rapidly shifting time and sometimes place, and dream or fantasy scenes to retain a sense of continuity in what is otherwise usually a disjointed visual sequence. Both performance and montage scenes are quite distinctive, set off from the "everyday," clock-time depiction of conversation and action.

Performance Scene

Musical forms are sometimes superimposed on film segments—the most obvious case being the diegetic performance of a song or other piece, where scene (or scene segment) and musical form can coincide. One of the most famous instances of this simultaneous treatment outside of the genre of musicals is the cantata performance that constitutes the climactic scene of *The Man Who Knew Too Much* (1956). In general, film music adapts itself to cinematic form, but we will see instances of both types in the sample analyses that follow. Musical performances naturally take over and structure a film's timeline, superimposing the music's design on the scene. It is possible, of course, to continue action over a performance, especially if the music is in the background (as neutral music such as a diegetic café band), but even in these cases classical practice tends to situate articulations of scene segments and music together. Here, we will focus on the extreme case of the highlighted performance, where musical design controls all the film's elements. As Claudia Gorbman puts it, "The stanzaic form of popular song, the presence of lyrics to 'compete' with the viewer's reception of film narrative and dialogue, and the cultural weight and significance of the stars performing the songs all work directly against classical Hollywood's conception of film music as an 'inaudible' accompaniment."[1]

Musicals, of course, have many such highlighted performances, in the form of songs, instrumental numbers, songs with dance, or large-scale production numbers. Dramatic feature films often have performances, too, but in musicals the narrative typically stops for performances (that is, we learn little if anything new about characters and narrative action is not forwarded, although the status of relationships may be confirmed, intensified, or undermined), in the dramatic film performances may structure the time of a scene segment but usually are obliged to share the viewer's attention with some kind of narrative-forwarding action.

TO HAVE AND HAVE NOT, "AM I BLUE?"

We look first at a relatively simple example from the best known of the sequels to *Casablanca* (1942): a café number featuring Hoagy Carmichael in *To Have and Have Not* (1944). Carmichael is a secondary character in the film, a hotel pianist nicknamed Cricket. We hear diegetic music in the background, mostly offscreen, in the early minutes of the film, but at 00:14:40, Cricket plays a short introduction and then begins to sing the chorus from "Am I Blue?", a song by Harry Akst and Grant Clarke. The chorus is in the standard 32-bar AABA design. Cricket sings and plays the two A phrases solo and the camera stays focused on him. At the bridge (B), the camera cuts to the band's drummer, who puts down his newspaper and begins a soft accompaniment with brushes. At the reprise of A, the bass and guitar players join in. Lauren Bacall's character (known only as Slim) approaches the piano as the chorus ends and Cricket tells her to "take over," at which they all shift back to the bridge with Slim singing. The reprise comes back one last time with Cricket joining Slim in the singing. The performance ends with audience applause, roughly 1 min and 40 sec after it began.

The scene actually begins a few seconds before Cricket starts playing: a dissolve indicates a change from the previous scene (in this case, passage of time, not locale, as both scenes are in the hotel), and we see Harry Morgan (Humphrey Bogart) at a table in a combined lobby-café area. The camera is on him as the piano intro starts offscreen. Cut to a long shot of the orchestra area as Cricket continues to play; cut to a nearby table on a repeated bar of music (Slim and an interested man sit there); cut back to a closer shot of Cricket on the next bar, and he begins to sing. During the two A phrases, cuts back to the tables make it clear that Slim is trying to get Harry's attention, and this is the apparent motivation for her walking up to the piano (the song's lyrics help, offering lines like "plans with your man falling through"). The end of the performance is clearly the end of the scene segment: we return to Harry's table as the hotel manager approaches and talks about a group of resistance fighters who want to hire Harry's boat to escape—the topic of the conversation in the previous scene.

Thus, we have two simultaneous strands: the musical performance and Slim's efforts to excite Harry's interest. The design of the music may constrain and channel the narrative events, but it does not stop them entirely.

THE SOUND OF MUSIC, "THE LAENDLER" (AS DANCE SCENE)

Following the familiar patterns of the musical, the Laendler scene in *The Sound of Music* (1965) is primarily a performance, a dance by Captain von Trapp (Christopher Plummer) and Maria (Julie Andrews). It does, however, succeed in contributing in a crucial way to narrative, as the moment in which the two realize they are becoming attracted to one other occurs within (in fact, near the end of) the dance and, one might say, as a result of the dancing itself. In this section, we will concentrate on the scene as a performance. In chapter 9, we return to it and describe its dynamics as a love scene.

Maria, the von Trapp governess, is on a large terrace of the von Trapp villa with the Captain's seven children. They are all looking into the ballroom, watching party guests begin the Laendler, an Austrian folk dance. One of the boys, Kurt, asks Maria to teach him the dance. After a few awkward bars, the Captain appears and cuts in.

To capture the details of the dance, we will once again use a timeline (as we did for the Overture and main-title sequence in ch. 6). The music has seven clearly defined phrases (in the terminology of the waltz, these are called "strains"), consisting of a first strain (A) that alternates with three others. The entire design, then, can be represented as (introduction)-A-B-A-C-A-D-A. The times given in the following are from the currently available DVD:

Figure 7-1. *The Sound of Music.* Laendler scene.

01:30:10 Introduction: Indoors, the dance begins; on the terrace, the children ask Maria what the dance is, and Kurt asks her to teach him. At the end of the introduction, Maria and Kurt bow to each other (Figure 7-1).

     A: Maria and Kurt dance half the strain, then the Captain cuts in. As Maria takes the Captain's hand, she has a surprised and unsure expression on her face (Figure 7-2).

Figure 7-2. *The Sound of Music.* Laendler scene.

Figure 7-3. *The Sound of Music.* Laendler scene.

Figure 7-4. *The Sound of Music.* Laendler scene.

Figure 7-5. *The Sound of Music.* Laendler scene.

Figure 7-6. *The Sound of Music.* Laendler scene.

B: Maria and the Captain dance: first a promenade, then a step-hop figure. Maria's face alternates between a social smile and continued uncertainty. [Note: In B through the final full repeat of A, each half of the strain (or each quarter in the case of C and D) is given a specific dance figure.]

A: Lady turns (spins), then skaters' arms (holding both hands across the front) (Figure 7-3). In this segment, we cannot see the dancers' faces clearly.

C: (This strain is twice as long as the earlier ones, or in musical terms, 16 bars rather than 8.) The most complex sequence of the dance, with figures using crossed hands, then 360° turns, the lady's turn, and finally a promenade. At first, Maria keeps her eyes demurely down. When they change lanes, the Captain cocks his head and grins in enjoyment and approval. She looks up to his face with a smile of ease as they go into the 360° turns.

A: He stands and claps while she dances around; then she stands while he walks around, still clapping. Maria smiles as she circles the Captain (Figure 7-4).

D: (Like C, this strain is twice as long.) He walks in front of her (Figure 7-5), then brings her around front, moving into hammerlocks (two-handed turns ending in one of the lady's arms behind her back). (In the middle of this strain, cut away to Baroness Eberfeld looking at them from the terrace door.) The Captain's gaze never waivers, but Maria shifts hers several times; at the end, Maria looks up, mesmerized, and they remain locked in each other's eyes.

A: (At 1:32:14.) Still in the second hammerlock, they stop, looking into each other's eyes (Figure 7-6). Maria blinks; the Captain's face has a slightly stunned look, then they release hands and Maria steps back, away.

A: Last half of the strain repeated to end the dance music. Brief
speech between Maria and Brigitte, another of the children.
01:32:34 Music ends.

Both the dance and its narrative elements are highly structured, according to the phrases of the music. The music's introduction and its ending capture the narrative elements: the motivation of the dance and the emotional
outcome of the pair's physical contact through the dance. Thus, once again,
narrative is able to proceed even within the confines of a performance scene,
although in this case the narrative information is part of the dancing itself, not
an interruption to a performance, as in "Am I Blue?"

THE SOUND OF MUSIC AND GREASE,
TWO LARGER PERFORMANCE NUMBERS

We have examined two small-scale performance scenes in detail. The same
general principles hold for scenes that consist of (or highlight) larger-scale
performance numbers. In most instances, even large performance numbers
are based on one song (or at most two), and each subscene corresponds to a
section (verse or chorus of a standard, strophe of a strophic song, A or B of an
ABA form).

In the performance scene of "Do Re Mi" from *The Sound of Music*, for example, there are five subscenes based on the two sections (A and B) of the song.
The subscenes are:

1. A, repeated three times, while Maria and the children are shown on a
   field in the mountains.
2. B, repeated three times—they are now on steps and a terrace overlooking the city.
3. A, again—now they are on bicycles.
4. B, in a carriage; and
5. A & B, in the garden and grounds of the villa.

As these brief descriptions suggest, the subscenes are clearly distinguished
from one another by their physical settings. (For readers with access to the
piano-vocal score of *The Sound of Music*, #s 1 & 2 above correspond to #9a
"Do-Re-Mi Encore.")

The famous closing scene in *Grease* (1978) is more complicated. Based on
two songs, "You're the One That I Want" and "We Go Together," it has six subscenes in all, three for each song. These are distributed over verses and choruses
but also include an interlude. For "You're the One That I Want":

1. First verse and chorus: Danny (John Travolta) and Sandy (Olivia
   Newton-John), along with respective groups of friends, on the carnival
   grounds.

2. Second verse and two choruses: Danny and Sandy in the funhouse.
3. Two more repeats of the chorus: Danny and Sandy with friends, coming out of the funhouse, the friends in photo boards.

At the close of "You're the One that I Want," Danny hammers a "Ring the Bell" game and we hear a bell. Dialogue follows, with the main characters wondering if they will ever see each other after graduation. At the end of this short dialogue transition, Danny hammers the game and the bell is heard again as the next song begins. For "We Go Together" (song in AABA design):

4. AAB: main cast with a few extras added in B.
5. Interludes (chant to nonsense words and instrumental (sax riff)): full cast dancing, pan of carnival rides.
6. A and refrain: full cast in lines with the main cast highlighted, Danny and Sandy drive away.

A central formal feature of both of these song-and-dance numbers is the contrast between the main characters and the full troupe of dancers (the graduating students): we repeatedly cut back and forth between relatively tight shots of the former and wide shots of the entire group.

ADDITIONAL EXAMPLES

It is probably not an exaggeration to say that in fact a majority of dramatic feature films include at least one performance of some kind, whether neutral or foregrounded, whether involved in narrative or simply part of the ambience of a venue—and the degree to which musical form dictates filmic form depends in great part on the importance of the characters involved and degree of foregrounding of that performance. (Compare the performance of "You Must Have Been a Beautiful Baby" by an unnamed singer early in *Mildred Pierce* (1945) with Veda's performance in the same venue much later, for example.)

Recorded songs or concert compositions played nondiegetically or diegetically on a radio or phonograph, similarly, will have a strong influence if foregrounded, but if not, they tend to recede to something nearer the commentative role of underscoring. (They can also be confusing, like the sudden eruption of a Strauss song from a CD player with a cut to Clarissa's apartment (in *The Hours* (2002)), just before Lewis arrives.) Complicating matters is recurrence—even if a song is in the background in one scene, it can become a motif if repeated in other scenes in a way that draws attention to the recurrence (and the association being made to a character, object, venue, or situation). The several diegetic performances in *The Birdcage* (1996) all work differently. The two renditions of "We Are Family" create a powerful frame for the entire film, the recurrence itself being an important factor. The Indian-themed and mambo numbers in the first scene are fragmentary (although we understand clock time to continue) and mostly backgrounded (part of the club's environment), and "Little Dream," although foregrounded, is subverted by narrative as the rehearsal is repeatedly interrupted.

In general, diegetic music as a musical performance by one or more of the main characters serves a restricted range of knowledge in the narration. Exceptions occur when the performance contains ironic elements—a theme or lyrics that refer to a plot or story element of which the performer is unaware—or reveals subconscious aspects of a lead character's personality. Performances by characters other than main characters may be backgrounded (that is, belong to the scene's ambience or to the establishment of period), but they can also serve a more foregrounded role as commentary, as happens notably in *Good Night and Good Luck* (2005). Other diegetic music will probably not be relevant to range of knowledge unless a character specifically draws attention to it—specific pop music genres become tied to characters in *High Fidelity* (2000) in this way, for example.

Finally, because of the influence of music video style over the past two decades, we should heed the comments of music scholar Nicholas Cook, who writes about the music video "Material Girl" that it routinely threatens to invert the normal relation of music and image in a structured performance:

> The closed, seamless nature of the song . . . means that the video necessarily adds to what is already, in essence, a self-sufficient textual and musical structure . . . Under such circumstances . . . we would expect the added medium—the pictures—to create space for itself by, in effect, mounting an assault on the autonomy of the song . . . There is, in effect, a collision between two competing hierarchies, and . . . the result is to destabilize the meaning of the words and, through them, the closure of the song as a whole. The pictures, in short, serve to open the song up to the emergence of new meaning.[2]

Montage or Fantasy Scene

The term montage can be synonymous with continuity editing or simply film editing, but its alternate meaning is more familiar in everyday speech: a short scene with a series of brief shots (often combined with inserts or graphics) that are either related to one another, in the manner of a gallery of images, or that advance the narrative quickly by compressing time (and frequently changing locations, as well). Claudia Gorbman describes one such usage in *Citizen Kane* (1941):

> Montage sequences often use nondiegetic music to bridge gaps of diegetic time. The famed breakfast-table sequence in *Citizen Kane*, for example, showing Kane and his first wife sitting at progressively greater distances from each other as the years pass, visually signaling the emotional distance that grows

between them, has a theme-and-variations music—as well as equally symmetrical shot compositions—to simultaneously bridge and demarcate the temporal discontinuities in the narrative.[3]

This montage technique is sometimes used for dream sequences, as well. In the classical Hollywood cinema, music was always present in such scenes and functioned in much the same way as in action scenes, simultaneously keeping up strong rhythmic movement and giving a sense of cohesion to the series of rapid shot changes.

GONE WITH THE WIND, MONTAGE SEQUENCE IN THE PROLOGUE TO PART 2

The filmic unit of the montage is actually closely related to the prologue, which in its more elaborate versions takes on the character of a montage, as in the prologue to *Casablanca*, for example, which combines voice-over narration with graphics, newsreel footage, and filmed shots. The prologue to Part 2 of *Gone with the Wind* (1939) is a montage in this sense. Part 2 begins with a 90-sec overture (it is titled "Entr'acte" after the instrumental music played between the acts of plays or musical theater pieces). Then the background—a stationary graphic image of a vividly covered early evening sky—disappears in a fade to black (while the music continues), but the colors reappear as lurid clouds and smoke in motion; titles are superimposed and so are moving images, of fire first, then silhouettes of soldiers. With a title mentioning Tara, the O'Hara estate, the montage and prologue end. Thus, the entire campaign of Sherman's March to the Sea is compressed into 1 min. We are given a strong sense of the devastation it caused but we need to know little else than a sense of the passage of time, as none of the lead characters was directly involved in the campaign (at least not after the burning of Atlanta, an episode that occurs near the end of Part 1). The music throughout the Entr'acte is a traditional silent-film "hurry" but with a substantial sense of menace. When the montage begins, the music becomes louder and harsher.

PRIDE & PREJUDICE, THREE MONTAGE SEQUENCES

The recent feature-film remake of *Pride & Prejudice* (2005) includes several "out of time" sequences that can be understood as actualizing something in the heroine Elizabeth's imagination. Of these, one is a traditional montage. Two others might be labeled fantasy montage as they combine irrational, dreamlike elements with the time-distorting devices of montage.

The traditional montage sequence is an attractive variant of the classic "passage-of-time" montage: it shows Elizabeth (Keira Knightley) sitting on a swing and slowly twirling around as the seasons pass, from late November to April. The scene is framed by her friend Charlotte (Claudie Blakley), who challenges Elizabeth for doubting Charlotte's decision to accept a particular suitor. Elizabeth is taken aback, Charlotte leaves, and Elizabeth is left to reflect. She turns slowly in the swing and the camera mimics her point of view as it pans her surroundings in a rapid circular motion. As the fall harvest, winter rains, and early spring renewal pass by her eyes, Elizabeth contemplates the changes in her own life. With spring arrived, the scene ends as she is invited to visit Charlotte's house and she seems grateful for the opportunity. Music in a reflective, contemplative mood accompanies the scene throughout, covering over the all-too obvious gaps in time and the several cuts. Also corresponding to the method of the classic montage, the music overlaps into the first moments of Elizabeth's arrival at Charlotte's home before it fades out under dialogue. The sound track, however, is complicated by another layer: a voice-over of Elizabeth's reading a letter to Charlotte, accepting her invitation to visit and catching up on news. The scene closes with the reconciling embrace of Charlotte and Elizabeth upon her arrival. Thus, the scene includes (and overlaps) three levels of passage of time: the immediate experience of Elizabeth's reverie, the passing seasons in the background, and the narration of the letter.

The first of the two fantasy montage sequences we will discuss occurs earlier in the film, during the extended Netherfield ball scene, after Darcy (Matthew MacFadyen) asks Elizabeth to dance. She surprises herself by accepting (her sharply negative opinion of him had been formed by his boorishly arrogant behavior during an earlier evening of dancing). In the foreground of two lines of dancers, Elizabeth and Darcy converse awkwardly as the dance begins. A series of visual and aural cues in this scene begins very subtly but mounts toward a decisive disruption of physical space and time: the other dancers are (mostly) in the background, they are in soft focus (or slightly out of focus), and none of them is heard or even depicted as speaking (despite the fact that conversation during country dancing was not only common but expected). The isolation of the couple from the remaining dancers is further emphasized when they stop on the dance floor in a tense verbal exchange, and the dance continues behind and around them; this effect is then taken to its extreme as the other dancers are eliminated from the scene, and Elizabeth and Darcy continue to dance in an emptied room.

Instead of the band of musicians who play for dancing elsewhere in the film, we hear a solo violin, a sound that reinforces the idea of the couple in their own time and space, but, as the emotional connection between Darcy and Elizabeth advances, more and more instruments are added until a full string orchestra sound is achieved as they finish the dance alone. The scene closes as the proper diegesis abruptly returns, the pair bow to each other, and the dance ends.

The second fantasy montage scene is essentially a classical passage of time montage, but it is made more complex by layering different levels of time and by superimposing these layers visually. Still visiting Charlotte, Elizabeth reflects on a disastrous first proposal from Darcy and his subsequent letter in which he tries to explain himself. Early in the day Elizabeth is aimless, sitting on her bed, wandering through the hall, glancing at a book; she looks out the window and then stares at herself in a mirror, deep in thought. The light streaming in from the window to her left shifts and changes as day turns to night. The scene becomes dream-like in the dark room: Darcy's voice is heard above a melody in the cello and he appears behind Elizabeth to deposit a letter; she does not react to his presence. Darcy is seen riding away outside, the music continuing as before. Charlotte suddenly appears in daylight and the scene and music end abruptly and unresolved as she speaks to Elizabeth. Four temporal strands overlap here: the compression of passing time in Elizabeth's reverie; the sequence of Darcy's entry, departure and voice; the implicit time of Elizabeth's reading Darcy's letter; and the actual time emphasized by Charlotte's appearance and voice. The music plays to Elizabeth's reverie, rather than Darcy's actions or the diegetic reality, the score both compressing and suspending time.

BRIDGET JONES'S DIARY, "OUT OF REACH" AND "I'M EVERY WOMAN"

In recent decades it has become common to structure a montage as the visual accompaniment to a recorded song (usually nondiegetic and usually very much in the aural foreground, even if on occasion diegetic clues are offered, such as a radio or television at the beginning or just before the montage starts). The consistent beat, voice, and instrumentation, as well as the highly predictable designs and even lengths of popular songs make them excellent devices to structure a montage sequence. In the following examples, the song fades out before it ends, which makes for a smooth transition; a stronger (but possibly more problematic) formal articulation is achieved with a complete song. Using a song performance, as a diegetic performance or as an apparently diegetic music coming from radio or phonograph, to help structure a scene or subscene was already a relatively common device in the classical era. Once popular music began to be used more commonly as nondiegetic music, the function was transferred there as well, making the use for montage both convincing and practical.

In *Bridget Jones's Diary* (2001; also based on Jane Austen's novel *Pride and Prejudice*, although more in the manner of a parody), two montage scenes use this technique. Of these two, the one in the film's last major sequence is the more straightforward and conventional (01:23:19, DVD ch. 16). Bridget (Renée Zellweger) is on a train back to London, having humiliated herself by opening her heart to Mark Darcy (Colin Firth) and then making a foolish and emotional speech in front of everyone at his parents' anniversary party.

The montage begins with the train ride, over which we hear the introduction to the song, "Out of Reach" (written and performed by Gabrielle) (see

Figure 7-7). The scene changes at the verse, as Bridget, still in a deflated mood, arrives at her apartment. The verse continues as we see Darcy's arrival in New York, his face marked with regret and uncertainty, and the music moves into the first part of the chorus. In the middle of this chorus, cut to Bridget taking out her frustrations by writing in her diary. A single line of the second verse overlaps, with its lyrics about despair and drowning, with a cut to Bridget, dejected, eating out of a jar. Just before the last line, "I know I will be ok," she answers the apartment buzzer: her relentlessly cheerful friends come up to the apartment as the song fades out in the middle of the second chorus. Throughout, lyrics and melody match the mood, which is that of Bridget, emotionally spent and resigned.

In an earlier montage (00:46:15, DVD ch. 9), Bridget is devastated upon learning that the man she has been dating, her boss Daniel Cleaver (played by Hugh Grant), is in fact engaged to another woman. The montage begins as Bridget decides to write him off and become her own person. During the introduction of "I'm Every Woman," Bridget downs some vodka, passes out, and goes into a dream-like flashback of her time with Daniel. Then, as the first chorus begins, a series of shots shows her attempts at turning over a new leaf as she throws out her empty liquor bottles and books on how to attract men; she begins exercising, replaces the trashed books with others on empowering women, and looks in the classified ads for a new job.

Through most of the first verse (which follows the chorus here), we see shots of Bridget tumbling off her exercise bike but thereafter walking confidently across a London bridge. The latter part of the montage shifts emphases

Figure 7-7. *Bridget Jones's Diary.* Second montage.

a	b
c	d

in the sound track because the dialogue can be heard over the music. During the final lines of the first verse, music fades considerably, and we see the first of three job interviews; this continues through the repeat of the chorus. The second interview starts with the second verse, and music is still low behind the dialogue. The third interview starts with the last line of the second verse and continues over the chorus, which fades out before finishing.

ADDITIONAL EXAMPLES

Montage scenes are common throughout the historical and contemporary repertoires of feature film. Here are instances in four more films. In *The Godfather* (1972), the 5-min sequence "Baptism and Murder" presents parallel and sharply juxtaposed narrative strands in the manner of a montage, with music running continuously throughout. In *Witness* (1985), the first part of the barn-raising scene (01:10:28–01:15:25) is best understood as an extended montage (the music in this scene is also reused in the end credits). The "Training Montage" in *Million Dollar Baby* (2006) runs 4 min (00:35:00-00:39:00), includes both music and voice-over narration, and contrary to formal expectations makes use of dissolves. Finally, Finnish director Aki Kaurismäki's *Mies Vailla Menneisyyttä* (*The Man Without a Past*, 2002) includes a montage (starting at about 00:20:00) in which Irma (Kati Outinen) plays music on a radio after she gets in bed for the night—the music continues as shots of homeless people in the neighborhood are shown.

Ingmar Bergman's early film, *Smultronstället* (*Wild Strawberries*, 1957), has four substantial scenes that are either dreams or reminiscences with some of the qualities of dream, but these are strikingly different from our earlier examples in that music is either absent or plays a secondary role. All are experienced by the protagonist, Isak Borg (Victor Sjöström), an aging doctor who is provoked to review his life and priorities as he travels to another city to receive an honorary degree from its university. The first of the dreams (also the one most often cited in the film literature) begins immediately after the main-title sequence (at 00:03:45). Borg himself calls it a nightmare. Initially, a shimmering dreamlike music is heard against Borg's speech, and this music overlaps for a few seconds into the dream itself in which Borg finds himself walking through empty city streets. He sees a clock without a face, then a man with a strangely pinched face who falls and bleeds profusely when touched, then a hearse from which the coffin drops and in which he not only sees himself but whose occupant catches hold and pulls him forward (Figure 7-8).

A sinister and insistent music (little more than one high pitch) enters as Borg recognizes his face in the coffin. The majority of the nightmare scene, however, has no music: instead, we hear slightly exaggerated footfalls as Borg walks, a repeated drum beat (against the clock), the man's fall, and the horses' hooves

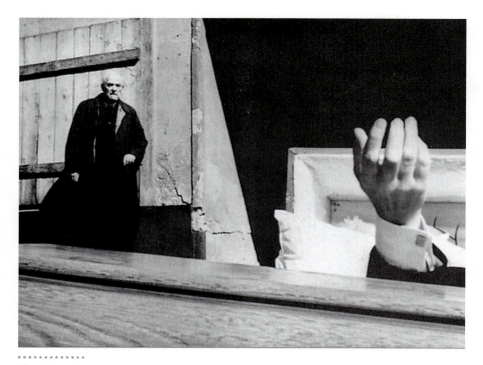

Figure 7-8. *Smultronstället* (*Wild Strawberries*). Professor Borg approaches the coffin.

and creaking noises from the hearse. When there are no other effects and Borg is standing still, the sound track is silent. The absence of music through most of the dream puts the emphasis outside Borg's subjective experience, which becomes all the more disconcerting because we understand the entirety of the dream—including its sounds—as depicting exactly that: Borg's subjective experience. (The same kind of disconcertingly realistic treatment of environmental sound was a cliché of *The Twilight Zone* television series (1959–1964) and can be found in scenes in some horror movies as well.)

By withholding information about the nuances of Borg's emotional reactions—music's particular role in a fantasy scene—the sound track conveys the nightmarish sense of a lack of control over events. In other words, the "objectification" of the sound track—like the simplification of the images—allows us to experience the nightmare ourselves, rather than simply empathize with Borg as he goes through the experience.

The other dream scenes or reminiscences in *Smultronstället* are: a flashback (to one summer when Borg was a young man) (00:20:00–00:31:20), a more complex combination of reminiscence and nightmare (00:53:30–1:11:23), and the final reminiscence (01:29:25–01:31:14).

SUMMARY

Many musical performances, especially those that are carried out onscreen with minimal narrative interruption (from cutaways or panning, with or without superimposed dialogue), are capable of lending the formal properties of the music to the image track, in many cases because the film is in fact edited to the music (this was especially true of performances in film musicals). Although the procedure of editing may be the same and one will normally hear continuous music, the narrative effect of montage or fantasy scenes is quite different: the focus is not so much on the music "as music" as it is on its formal capacities: music is added on top of a diverse, weakly connected collection of images to lend a degree of temporal coherence that the images themselves cannot manage.

Film Style and the Sound Track

Introduction

Narrative conventions for the classical cinema were established by the 1920s and codified in the system of continuity editing that is familiar to all filmgoers today. Similar conventions for sound and music were not established until the late 1930s. Music had already been used in characteristic and predictable ways in silent-film performance practice (after about 1910), especially with respect to dramatic or emotional codes that were themselves inherited from the 19th-century theater, especially melodrama: the hurry for action scenes, the love theme for romantic scenes, the fanfare or overture for the main-title sequence, the "mysterioso" for suspense, etc. In the 1930s, music also became codified with respect to film form—as would be expected, given that music was now composed, recorded for, and closely matched to the film's continuity editing.

In the previous chapters of Part II, we considered this latter topic by exploring music's placement in a film's overall design and its use in characteristic film segments (the establishing and end-credits sequences, performances, and montage fantasy scenes). In this chapter, we look more closely at the way music participates in the characterization of time and place and the representation of individuals through the style topic (conventionally coded types of music) and the recurrent theme (short musical phrases that, through repetition, become linked to important narrative elements, such as individuals, specific locales, and even narrative situations). As we shall see, in many instances the stylistic and thematic properties are combined in a single musical cue.

Neither characterization nor thematic association is entirely new: we have already referred to both categories in previous chapters. In chapter 1, we described the use of stereotyped music for particular characterizations ("Indian" music in the classical western; military marches or national anthems in war films, etc.), and we have mentioned such uses in many of the discussions of films or film scenes since. The device of the recurrent theme (sometimes called "leitmotif") was also discussed in the context of the ways music provides narrative information (and compares with speech and effects in that task); and, of course, musical cues and themes were involved in the descriptions of music in film design in chapter 5—recurring musical elements necessarily contribute to the articulations and associations of film form (as in Martin Marks's score for *Lady Windermere's Fan* (1925), especially with the opening theme of *The Sacrifice* and Marks's own "fan motive"; or, more simply, in *The Birdcage* (1996), where a strong framing effect is achieved by the two chorus performances of "We Are Family"). As we shall see, the deeply rooted historical conventions of music, derived primarily from stage music, remained essential to the practices of sound film, although changing musical styles over the decades of the 20th century complicated and partly broke down the clichéd topical categories.

Style Topics and the Leitmotif

INTRODUCTION: THEME, MOTIF, AND MOTIVE

The word "theme" in literature is a concise general statement about a story or poem that says what it is about. This could be an extremely brief description of action ("*King Kong* is about a great ape who comes to and devastates New York, but dies in the end") but is usually a characterization of what we understand as its essential idea or focus ("*Romeo and Juliet* is about tragic love" or "*Romeo and Juliet* is about the ways culture can interfere with and damage healthy expressions of human love"). In music—especially in purely instrumental music—this essential idea or focus is taken to be the most clearly defined melodies (or "themes") that are "developed" (or altered and commented on) in the other, more figural or dramatic sections of a composition. This distinction is important to us here, because when instrumental music is moved into the realm of the film sound track, the theme really functions like a motif, that is, the theme is no longer the "idea" of a piece but a significant recurring sound element (a narrative motif is usually defined as a significant recurring element; in film, visual motifs are very common, perhaps the most famous instance being the pervasive bird motif in Hitchcock's *Psycho* (1960)). As we see later, the leitmotifs of Richard Wagner's operas are also sound motifs in this sense.

Unfortunately, the term motive is used in music to mean something entirely different than motif, as we noted at the beginning of chapter 5. A motive is the shortest significant musical idea, usually one to two measures long, and it is one of the constituent elements of a phrase, usually (but by no means always) the phrase's most important element. (It was this last property that inspired composer Arnold Schoenberg[1] to coin the term "basic idea" to refer to the motive.)

Because "theme" and "motive" are as deeply embedded in musical discourse as are "theme" and "motifs"—with their meanings—in literary and film-narrative discourse, we will not try to resolve the discrepancies (and certainly not by coining any new terms). We will have to leave it to you to be aware of these discrepancies as you read the literature and write about films yourself.

"LOVE" THEMES

Style topics are conventional musical figures that evoke, represent, or signify a particular mood, place, emotion, or some other character trait in the narrative. When we speak of a "love" theme, for instance, we are dealing with a style topic. The music has a certain quality—a "style"—that allows us to recognize it as a love theme even if we have not heard it in a narrative context (such as a film) that would allow us to specify that meaning. The meaning does not reside just in the melody: love themes, for instance, are typically scored for strings with the melody in the violin, and the texture places a strong emphasis on melody with flowing accompaniment. In addition, the tempo is generally on the slow side of moderate (roughly at or just a bit slower than the average resting heartbeat rate). The overall effect is one of a deeply felt lyricism. Love themes are generally very prominent in films that make use of them, and, as might be expected, they are typically associated with the heroine.

Writing in the "picture palace" era, Erno Rapee described the importance of the love theme as follows:

> The choice of the Love Theme is a very important part of the scoring—it is a constantly recurring theme in the average run of pictures and as a rule will impress your audience more than any other theme. Special care should be taken in choosing the Love Theme from various angles. If you have a Western picture dealing with a farmhand and a country girl you should choose a musically simple and sweet ballad. If your Love Theme is to cover a relationship between society people, usually portrayed as sophisticated and blasé, choose a number of the type represented by the compositions of such composers as Victor Herbert or [Cecile] Chaminade.[2]

The "two-part" model for music in the establishing sequence went so far as to allow the audience to become accustomed to the love theme even before the first scene because the "lyrical" melody in the "part two" position was usually also the film's love theme. In *Meet Me in St. Louis* (1944), recall that the title song is heard first, but at the turn to the lyrical melody we hear "The Boy Next Door," which Judy Garland's character sings early in the film, thus firmly tying the song not only to her but to her desire for a romantic relationship. (At this point, it is the desire itself that is significant, however, as we know little to nothing about the neighbor who is its object.)

Despite the ease with which we can identify love themes, their signification is somewhat ambiguous because they generally refer both to the heroine and the romantic relationship between hero and heroine. The fact that the love theme doubles the signification in this way reinforces the male-dominated point of view that characterizes most narrative film—at least in classical Hollywood. This is especially the case where the male character has a well-defined theme of his own. The love theme defines the heroine in terms of the relationship. In a sense, the music suggests that she *is* essentially identical to that relationship, whereas the theme for the hero establishes a musical identity for him that cannot be reduced in the same way.

We can see something of this process at work in *Captain Blood* (1935). The melody in Figure 8-1c is the love theme associated with Arabella. This one is a bit unusual for a love theme in being relatively short. Compare this to the themes for Peter Blood (Figures 8-1a, b, and d). One thing to note is that Peter has three themes, each representing a somewhat different character. Knowing just this much, we can be fairly certain that Peter will receive the bulk of the musical treatment. Another distinction is that, unlike Arabella's theme, where the characteristic part of the motive is presented in the example, then repeated, all of Peter's themes have typical continuations that extend beyond the initial gesture. Peter's themes, in other words, are all fully formed in a way that Arabella's is not. Moreover, throughout the film, Arabella's theme never seems to go the same place, its

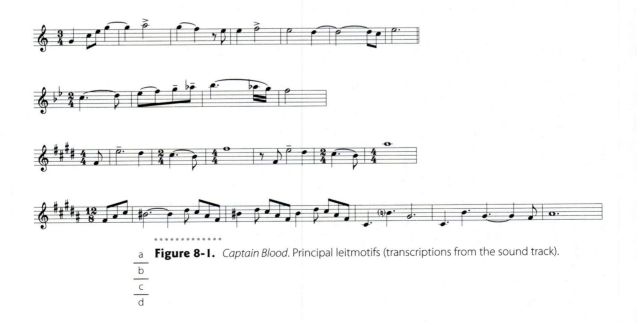

a **Figure 8-1.** *Captain Blood.* Principal leitmotifs (transcriptions from the sound track).
b
c
d

continuation being much more determined by context (it is in fact often linked to the end of Peter's theme "b"). This musical treatment suggests that Arabella will be a rather ill-defined character except in terms of her relationship to Peter. (See Figure 8-2 for an image of the composer, Erich Korngold, working.)

Fig. 8-2. The composer of *Captain Blood*, Erich Wolfgang Korngold, with fellow composer Franz Waxman (standing). *Photo © John W. Waxman Collection. All rights reserved. International copyright secured. Used with permission.*

In *Out of Africa*, the complex character of Isak Dinesen has no theme assigned to her; instead, her romantic relationship with Denys Finch Hatton is represented by a gramophone and Mozart, which, it is made clear, equally represents *him* (because he loves classical music and he gives her the gramophone as a gift). The gramophone, recall, is in the first image of Figure 6-4; we shall encounter it again in chapter 9 in the context of a love scene.

In other words, when a style topic becomes so well established by repeated use in films that it becomes a convention, or even a cliché, it can also be exploited by its absence—that is, the signification shifts if we encounter the heroine in a situation where the statement of a love theme in the underscoring would be expected. As an additional example, consider the fact that Lauren Bacall's character, "Slim," in *To Have and Have Not* (1944), is never associated with music outside of her performance of "Am I Blue?" (and one other short performance) with Hoagy Carmichael, and that tune is never repeated in the nondiegetic music. What this confirms for the audience is the suspicion gathered early on that Slim might represent the "love interest" but if so she is certainly an unconventional heroine.

THE LEITMOTIF

As we noted in chapter 1, a theme used to refer consistently to a character, as in the case of the love theme and the heroine, is called a *leitmotif*, a term that derives from the music dramas of 19th-century German composer Richard Wagner, where it designates musical themes or motifs associated with people, objects, and even ideas. The device is used most consistently in *Der Ring Des Nibelungen* (*The Ring of the Nibelung*), a cycle of four music dramas (or operas) based on Germanic and Scandinavian myths. The Sword, the Ring, and the Rhine River all have their own themes, as do characters such as Loki, Thor, and Wotan. Some of the principal characters, such as Siegfried, have several. The signification is somewhat more complex than is suggested here, however. For instance, the leitmotif that is generally associated with Wotan also designates his spear, which in turn stands for a contract he is bound to uphold. (This contract is the cause of much tragedy in the drama.) Likewise, some of the leitmotifs refer to rather abstract ideas such as the so-called "Redemption through Love" theme. Throughout the cycle, the leitmotifs undergo variation and transformation that reflect the dramatic situation.

Wagner's influence on music for the theater in the decades after this death in 1883 can hardly be overstated, and therefore it should be no surprise that film composers, also, adopted the technique of the leitmotif, albeit generally in a much simplified form (at its most basic, in fact, it is no different than the use of a recurrent theme). Most telling is just the number: whereas Wagner juggles dozens and dozens of motifs across his music dramas, film composers usually restrict themselves to only a handful. Often, they will use only two or three themes: the main title for the hero, a love theme for the heroine, and perhaps recurring music for a place, villain, or something or someone else of particular narrative importance. This is the case in *Captain Blood*, whose principal themes were shown in Figure 8-1. Even such sprawling multi-film epics as *Star Wars* (1977–2005) or *Lord of the Rings* (2001–2003), although in many respects quite close to Wagner's complex usage otherwise, do not attempt abstract signification to the same degree. An essential difference is that characters in music dramas sing whereas on screen they talk: far more information can be conveyed more quickly through normal speech than through texts that are sung.

Leitmotifs in films also tend to be much more direct in signification, the theme appearing only when the character does or, occasionally, when the character signified by the motif is clearly referred to in the dialogue. As music scholar Justin London says, "In filmic contexts the introduction of musical leitmotifs is highly conventionalized. Usually this introduction involves the simultaneous presentation of the character and his or her leitmotif, especially when we are given a striking presentation of both early on in the film."[3]

The leitmotif does not just signify its referent, that is, the character, thing, place or idea. It is also modified to reflect its context. This is done through musical variation. Such variations can be subtle—changing the orchestration, adjusting the tempo or dynamics, or the key—but they can also be quite substantial—altering the meter, rhythm, mode (for example, from major to minor), accompaniment, etc.

A simple example may be found in *Casablanca* (1942): the reunion scene that we analyzed in chapter 4. The scene before this one acts in many respects as a prologue to the reunion scene: the evening after their arrival in the city, Ilsa and Laszlo go to Rick's café; after a while Laszlo walks to the bar to talk with a man who has revealed himself as a resistance fighter, and Ilsa tells a waiter to ask Sam to come over to her table; Sam arrives and she asks him to play "As Time Goes By." From this point, we hear that melody four times in a row: sung (hummed) by Ilsa, then played and sung by Sam; then heard twice in the nondiegetic orchestra, first as the slow-motion reaction music in the oboe, and then as a slightly distorted waltz when Ilsa refers to Paris. Each time the tune is different in some way—not only in orchestration but also in its signification. The first appearance of this now-famous melody in the film is through Ilsa's humming and brief wordless singing: instantly it becomes the love theme as it is literally embodied in her while we see her in close up. Sam's repeating it reluctantly but fluently tells us that this melody has a history, something associated with it in Ilsa's—and Sam's—memory. That suggestion is powerfully realized in the "point of view" music that immediately follows the stinger chord, as we "hear" the sudden encounter register in the minds of Rick and Ilsa. Finally, we learn where this history can be localized—in Paris, as Ilsa makes a reference to the city and we hear "As Time Goes By" in waltz form.

Despite such elegant and effective uses as this, there are certainly dangers in the film manner of thematic treatment. The early film music scholar Frederick Sternfeld described them as follows:

> There are obvious conveniences to [the leitmotif] system that employs the same succession of notes whenever the same character or situation appears. For copyright reasons new tunes must be tagged, and the trick of using the X theme every time X appears on the screen is facile and produces quick results. The proof of the pudding lies, of course, in the eating. If the technique is applied sparingly and thoughtfully, it will seem appropriate—even to the critical observer—besides providing the necessary coherence for the entire fabric. But if used slavishly and mechanically, it will convey a feeling of monotony to the uncritical, while the sensitive listener will be both bored and irritated.[4]

Two other films with Max Steiner scores can provide examples. In *Mildred Pierce* (1945), despite building the nondiegetic music in the leitmotivic manner, on multiple recurrences of just a few themes, the composer usually varies the themes and does not often repeat them in overly obvious situations. Even the "Mildred Pierce" motive (the first three notes of the main theme (recall Figure 5-9a)) is reserved for appropriately dramatic moments (the theme is specifically associated with Mildred, but it is not a love theme; rather, in its often blatant and even harsh presentation, it speaks to the difficult, ultimately tragic circumstances of her life). In *The Big Sleep* (1946), on the other hand, although the love theme is used both sparingly and effectively, and Carmen's theme is so short and indistinct (just two held notes, the second lower than the first) that it is often lost in the texture, the whimsical motive for Marlowe is repeated far too often and in situations where it seems to undermine rather than support his character and threatens to turn the detective story into a comedy.

Style Topics

Like love themes, most leitmotifs are also instances of style topics. This is because style topics are an effective means of musical characterization. In Figure 8.1, for instance, Peter Blood's themes a and d both have a brash character consistent with the heroic side of his personality. Theme b, on the other hand, is gentler, more flowing and lyrical, consistent with his personality as a caring doctor. (It is also similar to a love theme, which is one reason it dovetails so easily with Arabella's theme.) Yet we should note that the musical meaning seems much more specific in the case of the heroic side than the caring side. This is because calls and fanfares, especially those scored for trumpets, have a long history of serving military functions (signals, such as calling to arms) as well as heraldic ones (marking the entrance of nobility). Horns have a similar connection with hunting. These associations were easily imported into theater music—especially opera, operetta, and melodrama—and from there spread to instrumental genres such as program music. In *Captain Blood*, the trumpets give the theme in Figure 8.1a a strong fanfare flavor, despite its somewhat unpredictable rhythmic structure. Played by the horns, Figure 8.1d, by contrast, bears an affinity to hunting calls, perhaps fitting for Peter's new occupation as pirate. "We, the hunted, will now hunt," he declares as he signs the compact with his men (1:03:16). When the bugler plays the theme later in the film, it becomes an explicit call to arms.

Fanfares, military calls, and hunting calls are specific musical topics. Another topic often times associated with these or used in conjunction with them is the march. Being especially linked to the military, marches are ubiquitous as title themes for war films. A good example is *The Great Escape* (1963). The themes to *Star Wars* or *Raiders of the Lost Ark* (1981) are both also marches; as leitmotifs, they serve much the same function of marking the character as heroic as was the case in *Captain Blood*.

The signifying properties of a musical style topic very often affirm our understanding of a scene. Most obviously, national anthems are used in this way. In *Casablanca*, Rick's flashback in the after-hours scene is inaugurated by the opening phrase of the Marseillaise, situating it in Paris. The Germans are likewise characterized through "Deutschland über Alles" in distorted form, which marks them as villains. Songs often work this way as well. "Dixie," for instance, is commonly employed as the musical sign of the Confederacy in Civil War films. It is also used generally for the antebellum South, where it is often coupled with minstrel songs and spirituals; here, music offers a romanticized picture of plantation life, making it seem pastoral and benign. *Gone with the Wind* (1939) is one among many films that draws extensively on such associations. By contrast, the Union in Civil War films is not represented so specifically. Sometimes, "Yankee Doodle" is used or one of the most famous of Civil War songs, "Battle Cry of Freedom," but obviously it would be inappropriate to use songs that represent the entire United States outside the historical period of the Civil War, such as the national anthem or songs like "America" or "Columbia, Gem of the Ocean."

In these cases, the music comes culturally determined, through lyrics and other uses, but signification is similar for other music, even if the meaning will be more difficult to fix than with anthems and other national songs. We have already noted how love and heroic themes have a style that allows us to identify the sort of situations or characters they are associated with. In fact, much film music works this way. For instance, music for battles, storms, deaths, pastoral scenes, and the West—each of these has a relatively distinctive sound that allows us to make a fairly good judgment of the sort of scene a certain type of music will accompany without even seeing the images. The same holds true for mood: mysterious, agitated, grotesque, action—each of these, too, has a characteristic sound. Of course, it is seldom the case that we can make an exact determination—the same music may well be acceptable for both a battle scene and a storm—but a certain type of music has a limited range of scenes for which it will fit comfortably. It would be highly unlikely to hear soft pastoral music accompanying the height of a battle, or battle music accompanying a quiet pastoral scene. Such music would seem utterly inappropriate—unless it seemed plausible that playing against the situation in this way had a narrative purpose.

The Villain ordinarily can easily be represented by any Agitato, of which there are thousands.

—Erno Rapee[5]

Occasionally, lyrical, elegiac music will be used over a battle—especially when all other sound drops out—to emphasize the heroic pathos of the moment. This is one way of underscoring "lost causes," such as near the end of the opening scene of *Gladiator* (2000) where Emperor Marcus Aurelius mournfully surveys the battefield as Maximus and the Romans obliterate the barbarian army in the battle of Germania. Here, the fact that the most conventional use is not observed—we do not hear the music we expect—is precisely what suggests that the film at this moment is about something other than the battle—Marcus Aurelius sees the cost of war and, like Maximus, recognizes the humanity of those he is conquering. Yet the very fact that we can identify such a disjunction tells us that music has a definable range of signification.

MUSICAL STYLES

The musical style of diegetic music is almost always an obvious marker of time and place: a marching band, a gamelan, a jazz combo, a symphony orchestra—such music is an effective means of quickly establishing a milieu. When we hear a string quartet playing at the Christmas party near the beginning of *Die Hard* (1988), we are not at all surprised to learn that those attending it are upper management of the company. Class is hardly an accidental part of the story, whose romantic strand involves a tension between John (Bruce Willis) and Holly (Bonnie Bedelia): their marriage is strained to the breaking point because of the difference in their respective social classes. As Robynn Stilwell notes, classical music is also associated with the villain in this film, giving him an aristocratic air that darkens the associations of the music in general.[6] The opposite effect is achieved by the association of music-like Australian aboriginal sounds with Paul Hogan's character in *Crocodile Dundee* (1986): as a result, Dundee acquires qualities of mystery and deep-historical rootedness.

The same applies to nondiegetic music, although it must be remembered that the symphony orchestra is not marked as such, except in the most general sense. Jazz underscoring was frequently used in the 1950s for gritty, urban films such as *The Man with the Golden Arm* (1955) or *Sweet Smell of Success* (1957). Recordings of popular music frequently began appearing nondiegetically in the 1960s, where it could signify anything from youthful angst, as in *The Graduate* (1967), to social rebellion, as in *Easy Rider* (1969). By the 1980s, romantic comedies would frequently feature "compilation" scores, where the choice of popular music style was used to delineate character and set the terms of the romantic relationship. *Clueless* (1995) offers particularly good examples of this device, with Cher (Alicia Silverstone) being associated with synthpop and Josh (Paul Rudd) with grunge.

The topical associations of music have changed over the decades as well. Film scholar Jeff Smith describes what happened at one critical juncture, the early 1950s: "The [traditional] romantic idiom continued as an option throughout the fifties, but it no longer wielded as strong an influence as Hollywood composers began to broaden the classical score's range of styles. At one end of the spectrum, polyphonic textures, modal writing, and atonality surfaced more regularly in the works of Miklós Rózsa, Alex North, Bernard Herrmann, and Leonard Rosenman. At the other end of the spectrum, various jazz and pop elements appeared in the scores of David Raksin, Elmer Bernstein, and Johnny Mandel."[7] (It should also be noted that the new popular music style of rock and roll found its way very quickly into films and film musicals aimed at a teenage audience, such as beach movies and Elvis Presley musicals.) Some composers, especially starting in the 1980s, became specialists in combining different styles, effectively creating a new "cross-over" style; as film music critic and scholar Royal S. Brown describes it, "Many scores by composers such as Jerry Fielding, Lalo Schifrin, and David Shire bring together sophisticated facets of both jazz and classical scoring."[8]

LOCATION AND STEREOTYPE

Style topics are a particularly good means of marking locale. In *Captain Blood*, for instance, the arrival in Tortuga is accompanied by music with a distinct Spanish flavor, suggesting an exoticism probably meant to evoke the spirit of the Caribbean port. This conflation of place with ethnicity is common in classical cinema. "Chinese" music—inevitably centered around a pentatonic scale—might be used either for a place or a character. The establishing scene for Hong Kong in *The Painted Veil* (1934) contains an excellent example of music of this sort. Such music was also easily adapted to Japanese and other Asian locales. An excellent later example that makes much more subtle use of the stereotypical "Chinese" elements—but has to work around a clichéd Irving Berlin song in the process—is Franz Waxman's music for *Sayonara* (1952).

"Arabian" music—or, as it was usually called in the silent era, "oriental"—likewise has its distinctive figures, typically flowing, ornamented melodies using scales featuring the augmented second or lowered second scale degree, as well as percussion. (Most of the stereotypical elements are evident in this citation from the middle section of Tchaikovsky's "Arabian Dance" (*The Nutcracker* ballet): Figure 8-3.) Such music could be used for a wide range of locations, including North Africa, Egypt, the Middle East, and some places in southeast

Figure 8-3. Tchaikovsky, ballet *The Nutcracker*, Arabian Dance (middle section).

Asia. *Casablanca* employs music of this sort as the "indigenous" music of the city, most notably in scenes in the *Blue Parrot* café (see Figure 8-4). The same is true for the open fifths or beating tom-toms of the "Indians." *Stagecoach* (1939) rather crudely marks cutaways to the Indians with music of this sort (see Figure 8-5a for the contents list of a silent-film era collection and Figure 8-5b for the opening of its "Indian Music" selection). In a different context, such music could be used to signify the "primitive" in general. Indeed, markers of the exotic and primitive are often quite malleable (reflecting a general cultural conflation of the terms)—see Figure 8-6, which assigns the "oriental" to an aboriginal group in an unspecified place in the eastern Indian Ocean.

As these examples make clear, style topics work by means of stereotypes. *Lawrence of Arabia* (1962) features a number of themes that employ the "oriental" topic. The theme for Lawrence (Figure 8-7a) is constructed around two overlapping pentatonic scales, which make prominent use of the augmented second. It is also richly harmonized and lushly scored, producing an exquisite, exotic effect. The theme for the Arabs (Figure 8-7b), on the contrary, is harmonized and scored crudely (often simply monophonic accompanied only with drums) and based on a modal (Phrygian) scale. By contrast, the call to prayer (00:43:32; Figure 8-7c) is rendered by solo voice alone, quasi-diegetic and seemingly "authentic." Here, then, are three distinct registers of the oriental topic. It should be noted that though the last example is an actual Muslim call to prayer, it is no less stereotypical than are the other two in musical function: it serves to make the place exotic. A similar effect is used at the beginning of *Blackhawk Down* (2001), where the use of indigenous sounding music likewise marks the place as exotic and strange, as a place beyond understanding.

Because the style topics familiar from film music at least through the 1970s (and in somewhat altered ways even after that) originated in 19th-century prac-

Figure 8-4. *Casablanca.* Music for the *Blue Parrot* café (transcription from the sound track).

Figure 8-5. (a) An earlier example of music written specifically to accompany silent film. Note the contents are organized along the lines of style topics. (b) The opening of "Indian Music." Note the minor key and stereotypical open fifths in the left hand.

a
b

tices, it will be useful to look at some lists from the silent era that reflect and build on those older historical models. In Figure 8-8, we reproduce the sidebar from Rapee's *Motion Picture Moods* (1924), a collection of music meant to serve as a single anthology for a theater pianist's or organist's use. This particular

Figure 8-6. *King Kong.* "First Contact" sequence. The music accompanying this scene uses the style topic of the "primitive." The music is not unlike the "Indian Music" of the Sam Fox collection shown above.

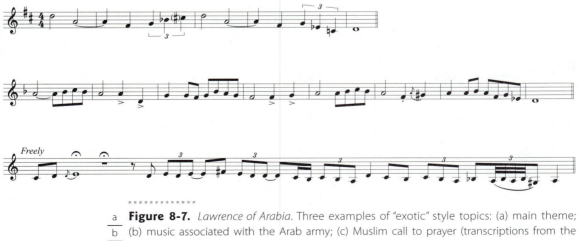

a
—
b   **Figure 8-7.** *Lawrence of Arabia.* Three examples of "exotic" style topics: (a) main theme;
—   (b) music associated with the Arab army; (c) Muslim call to prayer (transcriptions from the
c   sound track).

sidebar is reproduced on every page of music in his book to allow the keyboardist to note pages and flip quickly to an appropriate topical category for a new scene or situation. The headings cover the whole range of categories we have discussed in this chapter, from mood or affect indicators (grotesque, happiness, horror, joyfulness, mysterioso, passion, quietude, sadness, sinister, but also neutral) to characteristic music for objects (aëroplane), groups (children, national, oriental, western) or scenic situations (battle, chase, festival, love-themes, parties, race, sea-storm), to musical sound effects (birds, calls, chatter). Dances are listed separately—whereas some would be strongly marked (*mazurkas* for Poland, eastern Europe, Russia, or gypsies; *minuets* for 18th-century high society; *tangos* for Latin American society, but also for strong sensuality), others could serve a variety of purposes (for example, marches, but also waltzes, which in the silent-film era still were markers of a traditional popular music). Recall in this connection that Martin Marks used gavottes in *Lady Windermere's Fan* not for their pastoral or other historical connotations but because they "speak in accents of wit and romance," qualities that fit "comic images of formal behavior and ritualized social interactions, such as constrain the film's aristocratic characters."[9]

Perhaps because of their necessary brevity, the labels in Figure 8-8 do not reflect the conflation of mood and style topic that was central to musicians' planning and performance for feature films in the silent film era. In the *Carl Fischer Analytical Orchestra Guide*, compiled by Julius S. Seredy and published in 1929, we find clearer indications of these combinations in headings such as "Agitatos—for General Use—see also Furioso, Battle, Storm, Hurries"; "Dramatic—for longer dramatic scenes, trials, etc., see also . . . Anger, Argument, Foreboding, Grief, Passion, Pulsating, Regret, Resignation, Tragic"; "Hurries—General Use—see also Agitatos, Excitement, Furiosos, Chase, Dramatic Pursuit, Exotic and Comic Hurries"; "Love Scenes—see also Love Themes and Dramatic Love Scenes for Lighter Courtship Numbers, see Garden Scenes"; and "Mysteriosos for General Use," with its subcategories "Mysteriosos—Comic (Burlesque)—see also Mystic Suspense in Comedy," "Mysteriosos—Grotesque—Spooky—see also Comic Mysteriosos, Exotics," and "Mysteriosos—Heavy Dramatic."[10] The last of these, "heavy dramatic," is an instance of another level of categorization that was very common throughout the silent era and meant to reflect differences in the intensity of mood in a scene. Several years before Seredy's *Guide*, Rapee also published his own catalogue of works for sale, somewhat pretentiously called the *Encyclopedia*

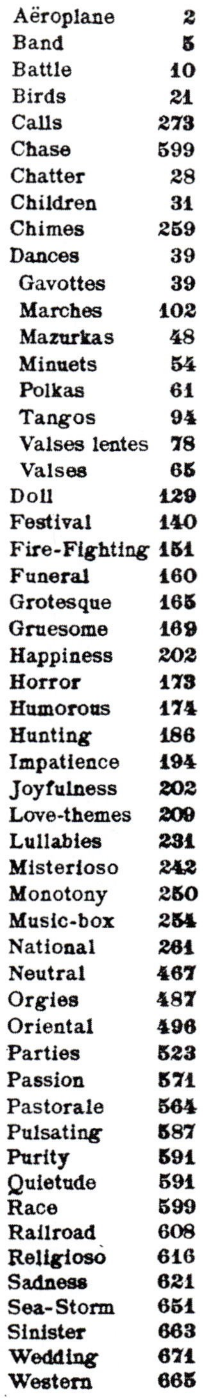

Aëroplane	2
Band	5
Battle	10
Birds	21
Calls	273
Chase	599
Chatter	28
Children	31
Chimes	259
Dances	39
Gavottes	39
Marches	102
Mazurkas	48
Minuets	54
Polkas	61
Tangos	94
Valses lentes	78
Valses	65
Doll	129
Festival	140
Fire-Fighting	151
Funeral	160
Grotesque	165
Gruesome	169
Happiness	202
Horror	173
Humorous	174
Hunting	186
Impatience	194
Joyfulness	202
Love-themes	209
Lullabies	231
Misterioso	242
Monotony	250
Music-box	254
National	261
Neutral	467
Orgies	487
Oriental	496
Parties	523
Passion	571
Pastorale	564
Pulsating	587
Purity	591
Quietude	591
Race	599
Railroad	608
Religioso	616
Sadness	621
Sea-Storm	651
Sinister	663
Wedding	671
Western	665

Figure 8-8. Erno Rapee, *Motion Picture Moods*. This sidebar ran on every page of the book, giving the player a quick index of topic categories.

of Music for Pictures (1925). The excerpt shown in Figure 8-9 highlights the intensity labels: "heavy" for the most serious situations, "light" for those that tend to the comedic, and "medium" (others use the word "neutral") for general accompaniment without a specific emphasis.

STYLE TOPICS IN *REBECCA*

To draw together the several aspects of style topics we have discussed in this chapter, let's look at an extended example from the classical repertoire—the opening 10 min of *Rebecca* (1940).

Like many studio logo cues, the music for the Selznick Studio fits the style topic of the dramatic and perhaps the majestic (dramatic cues in the silent era were sometimes labeled alternatively with the traditional Italian musical term *maestoso*), and the first few seconds of Franz Waxman's main-title cue just as plainly fit the *mysterioso* (alternatively the *agitato mysterioso* or "grotesque"— recall this last is one of the categories in Figure 8-8). With the appearance of the main title, however, a lyrical melody rises in a sumptuous orchestral setting—by convention, we know this is Rebecca's theme and leave open the chance that it is also the love theme, although, as in *Mildred Pierce* (1945), the setting is noticeably too strong, too loud and full, so at the very least we would consider this a "heavy" love theme (in the three level intensity scale of light-medium-heavy). Thus, this film is unlikely to be a straightforward romance; if romance is involved, it will be in the context of drama and perhaps even to a tragic result. (Eventually, we learn that Rebecca is in fact the acousmêtric villain of the story.)

At about 00:01:25, the theme suddenly breaks down and we return briefly to the *mysterioso*, but the tempo slows and another string melody enters over a pulsating accompaniment of repeated chords. We will learn in the prologue that this melody is the theme for Manderley (Maxim De Winter's fabled mansion) and that will secure its associations and function. For the present, the style topic is hard to pin down—it could fit Seredy's category of "resignation" or Rapee's "sadness." Many cues of this type were simply called "andante," after the musical term for a moderately slow, but not too slow, "heartbeat" tempo. We might call this one a "heavy andante" ("dramatic andante" is another common term), given its minor key and melancholy affect. Note, by the way, that Waxman has maintained the two-theme title cue structure; here, however, the dramatic theme belongs to Rebecca and the lyrical theme to an object that signifies the past for Maxim (Laurence Olivier). In both cases, the formal position helps to confirm our judgment about their affective qualities.

As the prologue begins with Joan Fontaine's voice-over (at 00:01:44), the melody slows down even further and is heard in a plaintive solo oboe, but layered against it is an obvious return to the suspenseful *mysterioso* mood: the

AGITATO

(H)	Before Titles — means	"HEAVY"
(L)	" " "	"LIGHT"
(M)	" " "	"MEDIUM"

Title	Composer
(H) AGITATO No. 37 (For Fights and Riots)	Andino
(M) AGITATO ALLEGRO No. 8.	"
(M) DESCRIPTIVE AGITATO..	Boehnlein
(M) AGITATO IN D MINOR	"
(L) RHYTHMIC AGITATO	"
(M) AGITATO No. 20	Borch
(L) LIGHT AGITATO	"
(H) TURBULENCE	"
(M) AGITATO No. 10	"
(H) HEAVY AGITATO No. 12 ..	"
(H) MOURNFUL AGITATO	Hilse
(M) DRAMATIC AGITATO No. 1 (For General Use)	Hough
(L) ALLEGRO AGITATO No. 1 (For General Use)	Kiefert
(M) AGITATO No. 6 (Angry Discussion or Riot)	"
(H) FURIOSO No. 11	"
(M) TREMBLING AGITATO ...	Kilenyi
(H) FURIOSO No. 1	Levy
(L) AGITATO No. 69 (Scenes of Tumult)	Minot
(H) FURIOSO No. 60	Shepherd
(M) AGITATO No. 49 (For General Use)	"
(H) DRAMATIC AGITATO	Ketelbey
(H) AGITATO FURIOSO	"
(H) MOLTO AGITATO	Breil
(A) STORMS—AGITATOS, FIRES—EXPLOSIONS,	
(B) CONSEQUENT MOB EXCITEMENT, followed by	
(C) VICTORY OR RESCUE.	
(H) ALLEGRO AGITATO	"
A—Hurry For Races, Runways, Speeding Trains with	
B—Sudden Crash or Stop...	
C—Consequent Disaster or Quieting of Excitement	"
(M) MOLTO AGITATO	"
(H) MOLTO AGITATO No. 5 ...	"
(L) MISTERIOUS FURIOSO	Langey

Figure 8-9. Erno Rapee, *Encyclopedia of Music for Pictures*. This is an excerpt from the section "Agitato."

result is wholly appropriate to the dream that Fontaine's character is recounting and would probably fit Seredy and Rapee's category of "reverie." With the
entrance of an emotionally more intense version of the Manderley theme on a
solo cello (at 00:02:35) comes a brief turn to a "dramatic andante" again, but
the music soon relapses into reverie.

With the dissolve to the first scene and after the loud intrusion of wave
sounds, a new *agitato mysterioso* starts up, now suspenseful, sinister, "heavy,"
and it continues to the moment that Fontaine's "I" shouts, thereby preventing
Maxim from following through on his plan for suicide. Their brief conversation (Figure 8-10) is treated musically as dialogue underscoring, and consequently the topical associations are offered only in brief passages that shift
as the conversation evolves: first tremolo strings revive the lighter side of the
mysterioso, then a plainly lyrical melody is hinted at (the love theme for the
two of them? Yes, as it turns out). A suddenly soaring version of the Manderley
theme is heard after "I" leaves and Maxim turns to look toward the cliffside he
had almost thrown himself over.

With the dissolve to an establishing shot of Monte Carlo, the music retains
its contemplative mood from the previous cue but with the second establishing shot, an elegant hotel seen from its entrance , we hear the introduction to

Figure 8-10. *Rebecca*. Opening scene. Encounter between "I" and Maxim.

a classical waltz (actually composed by Waxman, as it happens). In the early 21st century, the details of a topical reference like this have been mostly lost: a "Strauss" waltz (like *The Blue Danube* or *Tales from the Vienna Woods*) does connote elegance and upper-class or aristocratic society and thus fits a particular social stereotype, but for an audience in 1940 it would also have specified locale, because the orchestration Waxman uses is that of a hotel orchestra, which would have played similar music at various points through the day in a high class hotel. (In fact, Waxman wrote this waltz for another hotel lobby scene, in *Lady of the Tropics* (1938).)

The music now adopts a formal role as well: the introduction finishes with the second establishing shot, then the waltz proper begins with the first interior shot (a wealthy older woman, Mrs. Van Hopper, and her paid companion, "I"). The waltz ends and a new one begins with the dissolve to the next scene, next morning's breakfast. Waltzes play throughout the breakfast scene and cadence, a bit abruptly, with the dissolve (the Terrace, which follows, is discussed in ch. 9 as a dialogue scene). Through the entire hotel sequence, the order of the waltzes is: Waxman, Hotel Lobby (Waltz) from *Lady of the Tropics*; Joseph Lanner, *Die Pesther*; Johann Strauss, Jr., *Artist's Life* and *Roses From the South*. The waltzes do not start up again with the return to the hotel after the Terrace scene. Contained in the two initial hotel scenes, then, they signify both elegance and wealth as characteristic of the venue. In the process, they suit Maxim's character quite comfortably but play anempathetically against "I," whose social discomfort is only too obvious (especially in the breakfast scene).

A Note on Sound Topics

Many of the musical topics have their correlates in sound. The pastoral, for instance, can be as easily evoked by bleating sheep, lowing cattle, or a cowbell as it can by pastoral music. (If it were not so dense—almost like white noise—the wave sound that starts the first scene of *Rebecca* could have signified "seaside" or "sea cliff" to us without the corresponding image.) The squeal of a tire suggests a chase about to begin. A low rumble, such as the Empire's ships in *Star Wars IV: A New Hope* (1977), is often ominous; whereas a crisp, bright sound, such as the skull crushed by the robot at the opening of *Terminator 2: Judgment Day* (1991), suggests immediate danger. Gary Rydstrom suggests that the distant sound of a train has similar connotations: "Traditionally trains in the backgrounds [have] been used to signify danger or tension. There's a train in *American Graffiti* [1973] when they hook the cop's rear axle. There's a train in *The Godfather* [1972] when Al Pacino gets the gun from the bathroom to shoot the guy. *Bugsy* [1991] has a train when Warren Beatty shoots Elliot Gould. It's a long-standing tradition."[11] At the beginning of chapter 2, we noted the use of echoing footsteps as a sign of existential despair. A loud, resonant clank like the one that frames the title sequence of the *Terminator* films or the fall of Sauron's helmet in the prologue of *Fellowship of the Ring* (2001) portends mythic doom.

Crickets may well be the best established sound topic of all. Although often used to suggest a nocturnal setting in general, in *Close Encounters of the Third Kind* (1977) crickets are one of the means used to heighten the suspense of the aliens. Preceding each encounter, the ambient sound of the crickets' crescendos, only to disappear immediately for the encounter itself. As Frank Warner, Supervising Sound Effects Editor for the film, explains:

> At the end of each [encounter] I imagined that one little cricket would look up over a rock and another one would look up, I keyed them up the scale and then maybe a dog bark, then the wind would come back. It all happened until finally at the end of the scene, everything came back in and settled down. You only had to do it once, twice maybe. Then throughout the picture, when things would go quiet, in your mind you'd go, "Uh oh, something's going to happen."[12]

The associations of crickets with night is so conventional that even their absence from the sound track can be made significant. Sound Designer Mark Mangini explains his minimalist approach to *Kafka* (1991): "Kafka was a bizarre and paranoid man. The sound tends to mimic this in its starkness. You will hear very few sounds of life or living things, not many sounds of other human beings. I shunned the use of crickets for night exteriors and interiors, as I think they give too warm and cozy a feel to scenes. The track is pretty spare and uses disjointed reverberant sounds and odd mechanical activity."[13]

The daytime analogues to crickets are cicadas and their relatives. Generally louder than crickets, their sounds are also more varied, and the quality of the sound differs because they "sing" from trees and bushes, unlike the ground-level sounds of crickets. An unusually prominent—and humorously ironic—use of cicada noises occurs in the cemetery scene of *La Cage aux Folles* (1978), where Renato (Ugo Tognazzi) and Albin (Michel Serrault) talk on a train-station bench. The scene is devoid of action outside of their somewhat subdued conversation and the loud singing of the (unseen) cicadas.

Summary

Style topics are categories of musical types that are familiar to the film's intended viewing audience. Themes (motives or leitmotifs) are short, usually melodic, gestures that become associated with characters, places, or situations in the course of the film. Such conventional musical figures can be used in a variety of ways: to add additional information missing in the image, to "certify" or over-determine what is already available in the image, to provide or qualify emotional qualities in individuals or social situations, to lend humor or make a critique through ironic juxtaposition, or even to deceive with incorrect information.

Chapter 9 provides more detail and several examples for three scene types where style topics and thematic associations routinely play a strong role: dialogue scenes, action scenes, and love scenes.

CHAPTER 9

Music in Character and Action Scenes

Introduction

In chapter 6 we looked at characteristic uses of music in the framing segments at beginning and end of a film (establishing sequence and end credits). In chapter 7, we turned to the special cases of the performance, where music must necessarily be foregrounded, and the montage or fantasy sequence. In this chapter we will look at three instances where music is sometimes—but by no means always—used in segments that commonly appear internally within films, are strongly focused on narrative, and tend (even in modern films) to make substantial use of the kinds of thematic references and style topics we explored in chapter 8: dialogue scenes, action scenes, and love scenes. As in chapters 6 and 7, each of the scene categories and its typical music is described and then illustrated with two or three detailed examples.

Dialogue Scene

Dialogue underscoring (recall that this means nondiegetic instrumental music played "under" speech) is one of the most characteristic features of film music in the 1930s and 1940s and the one least like any other genre of music. Because it was expected to follow the shifting emotions, associations, and references of conversation, a dialogue cue sacrifices musical form for the sake of conforming to the shape of the scene. Max Steiner, who pioneered the practice in the early 1930s, called this "fitting the film like a glove."[1] It has also been referred to pejoratively as "mickey-mousing," from a similar use of close synchronization in cartoons. This style of dialogue underscoring can be compared to "overall scoring," which establishes a mood or tempo for a scene but does not try to follow action closely. In this sense, music acts in a way similar to ambient sound but is not a replacement: one might perhaps say that ambient sound normally establishes or reinforces the "mood" or qualities of a physical space, where a musical cue in the overall scoring manner establishes or reinforces the mood(s) of the characters.

Some of the effects of nondiegetic dialogue underscoring can be achieved using diegetic (or apparently diegetic) music. A song playing in the background of a scene on a phonograph or on a radio can help identify (or intensify) the mood we sense in speakers in a conversation. Neutral or even anempathetic diegetic music played behind conversation, however, is related to but different from overall scoring: a song played by a band or coming from a phonograph in the background is really a third, "negative" style of dialogue underscoring that can contradict or otherwise undermine the speakers, as in *Mildred Pierce* (1945), where a distraught Mildred talks incoherently to Wally while thinking of her spoiled, immoral daughter Veda: behind them and in a corner of the screen, we see a young woman on the lighted club stage singing "You Must Have Been a Beautiful Baby." At lower sound levels—and without the ironic references—neutral diegetic music has many of the functional qualities of ambient sound.

Music in relation to dialogue underscoring has a complex history. In the transition decade (1925–1935), technological limitations and a bias toward realistic depiction at first kept music out of dialogue scenes altogether. By 1932, and increasingly throughout the decade, more and more dialogue was underscored as part of the trend toward covering a very large percentage of a film with music (examples from 1939 include *Gone with the Wind*, *Dark Victory*, and *The Hunchback of Notre Dame*; from 1940, *Rebecca* and—somewhat surprisingly—the espionage film *Foreign Correspondent*). As film sound historian Rick Altman describes the evolving aesthetic priorities in the 1930s: "Like atmospheric effects, the music thus remains continuously present, even when its volume is reduced to assure maximum dialogue comprehension. This system has two functions: to guarantee comprehensible dialogue and to confect a sound track with virtually constant total volume."[2] This is the continuous-volume or integrated sound track that was referred to under Exercise 1 at the end of chapter 2.

At the same time, many B-films were lightly scored (probably in good part because of the music production and sound postproduction costs), and it was common in films dominated by dialogue to have very little music (in some romantic comedies but particularly in stage plays translated to cinema). *His Girl Friday* (1939), for example, has a minute-long opening sequence and 1 min of music for the end credits (it actually sneaks in a few seconds before the final scene ends) in a film that lasts just over 90 min. There is no other music of any kind. *Philadelphia Story* (1940) is very similar, although it does includes a very few scattered, additional minutes of underscoring. Musicals, also, typically did not use dialogue underscoring, as they generally restricted music to the film's framing elements and its performances.

By the mid-1940s, the trend of the previous decade started to reverse, and extensive dialogue underscoring became less and less common (three films from this period that, from a modern perspective, can be said to suffer from overly extensive background scoring are *Double Indemnity* (1944), *Spellbound* (1945), and *The Big Sleep* (1946)). The exception to this trend was the heightened emotional environment of spectacles (especially historical films) and melodramas (two heavily scored examples from these genres are *Ben-Hur* (1959) and *Magnificent Obsession* (1954), respectively) and underscoring became more common in musicals. In general, this bias toward a limited use of dialogue underscoring except in a few film genres has persisted to the present day, with the very important qualification that, from the early 1970s, multitrack sound has allowed effects to take on some of the functions previously ascribed to background music, including close synchronization (recall instances of this from our discussion of scenes from *Good Will Hunting* (1997)).

We will use just one scene to illustrate classical practice for dialogue underscoring. Because love scenes are, in almost all instances, variants on the dialogue scene model, *Out of Africa's* "second dinner" scene analyzed in that section later in the chapter can serve as an additional example.

REBECCA, TERRACE SCENE

The close pairing of music and continuity in a typical classical dialogue scene is well illustrated by the "terrace scene" in *Rebecca*. This scene occurs early in the film, after Joan Fontaine's character, a shy, diffident person (known only as "I" in Daphne DuMaurier's novel) who is the companion to a demanding wealthy woman, meets Maxim DeWinter (Laurence Olivier), a mysterious and wealthy man, bored with Monte Carlo. Through her employer, "I" meets Maxim in the hotel lobby, and they share breakfast the following morning after "I" spills water over the tablecloth at her own table. Maxim offers to drive her to a spot where she intends to sketch, and the scene changes to an unspecified place on the ocean, a stone terrace with a low wall (see Figure 9-1a).

The cut to the establishing shot of the terrace brings a pastoral, pleasant, and relaxed music, which continues through their initial conversation (see Figure 9-2). An abrupt shift to several disconnected, playful little musical gestures accompanies the insert of the sketch and Maxim's comments about it. When "I" puts the sketch down and joins Maxim at the terrace wall, they talk amiably; the music returns to the character of the beginning, but now introduces a theme that the composer, Franz Waxman, identifies in his sketches as "Love."

Figure 9-1. *Rebecca.* Terrace scene, part 1.

a	b
c	d

A sudden but not overly loud chord (labeled a "mild stinger" in Figure 9-2) alerts us to the significance of Manderley, the palatial DeWinter home in Cornwall. As Maxim begins to talk about Manderley, we hear its theme, which has appeared twice earlier in the film and by now is easily associated with the great house. As he continues, Maxim's voice becomes troubled (we hear high tremolo violin chords that bear a suggestion of suspense), and he soon stops speaking. To cover the gap, "I" begins talking about the weather and swimming. Shortly after she mentions drowning, Maxim turns suddenly (to another stinger gesture) and walks away; the music slowly calms down again as we hear him, offscreen, tell "I" that he will take her back to the hotel.

The music changes not according to the conventions and expectations of instrumental music (a musical "logic" that states and develops clearly

Establishing shot of a terrace
overlooking the ocean (Figure 9-1a).
Maxim looks out and "I" sits, sketching.
He teases her about the sketch (Figure 9-1b).

He looks at the sketch, which
distorts his nose (Figures 9-1c, d).

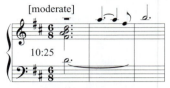

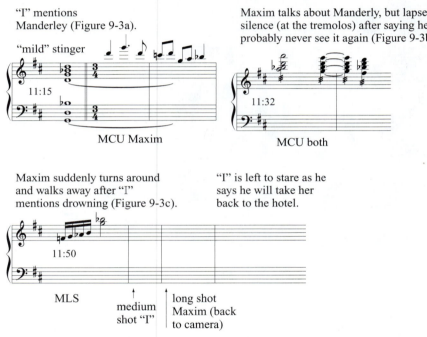

Figure 9-2. *Rebecca.* Terrace scene. Music and action in summary form (transcription from the sound track).

defined themes) but in a manner that makes clear and expressively intensifies the changes in conversational and emotional interactions of the two
characters. Thus, the music guides us carefully in our shifting reactions to the
scene. In this it complements the continuity editing. Note that the "neutral"
establishing shots (extreme long shot of the terrace, and two long shots, from
opposite directions, of the couple) receive pleasant music that is not distinctive; the insert has its own musical "insert"—the brief scherzando (playful)

phrase—after which we return to the mood of the beginning, but with just slightly more intensity, as the camera moves in a bit and the "Love" theme is stated.

We move in further with the cut to a medium close-up of "I" as she mentions a postcard of Manderley (see Figure 9-3)—this, with the mild stinger, brings us to the central point of the scene, which is Max's mysteriously unsettled relation to Manderley, his own home. From this point until Maxim turns and walks away, the music continues in the same tempo (although with varying figures and instrumentation) as shots alternate in three framings: the medium close-ups of "I" and Maxim and a 2-shot of them at the same distance. The final 12 sec of the scene are a confusing visual whirl, as Maxim walks out of the frame, then cut to a medium shot of "I", then a long shot of Maxim with his back turned, and finally back to "I"; here the music gives some order to the series of shots as it begins by mirroring Maxim's sudden physical actions but ends by echoing the deflated mood and disappointment that "I" clearly reveals.

As a final note, the terrace scene might indeed be understood to constitute a scene, but the music in fact continues across several similar scenes. Eventually we realize that each segment is probably better regarded as a scene segment, the larger scene being a slow-moving montage that, altogether, constitutes the courtship and marriage of Maxim and "I". After the marriage, the location shifts to Manderley, and thus the entire segment—from the beginning to the marriage—constitutes the film's first sequence, or "chapter."

ADDITIONAL EXAMPLES

The reunion scene in *Casablanca* (1942) can be understood as a scene consisting of two smaller dialogue scenes, the first between Ilsa and Sam, the second between the four persons sitting at a table. In *Catch Me If You Can* (2002), the Christmas Eve conversation is played out in a mechanically (telephone) aided shot/reverse-shot sequence with backgrounded diegetic music; and the diner scene that follows, by contrast, emphasizes effects (restaurant noises

Figure 9-3. *Rebecca.* Terrace scene, part 2.

and rain) that compete with the conversation between Carl and the young waiter—effects move aside when the nondiegetic music enters. In *Good Will Hunting*, the Boston Common scene is a dialogue scene in which effects take over at least some of the roles of music (helping to maintain a continuous level, punctuating the conversation, and even subtly affecting emotional perception through brittle bird sounds and distant sirens). Here again, effects "duck out" under the nondiegetic music that enters shortly before Sean leaves Will alone on the park bench.

In all the examples cited here, nondiegetic music enters after the scene (and the dialogue) has begun and at an emotional turning point (in all cases, the music then overlaps into the following scene). We do not wish to suggest this as a broad generalization—the classical Hollywood practice of underscoring all of an emotionally significant dialogue scene is at least as common—but in more recent decades it has become much easier to balance the sound track elements, and this "in and over" method (in at the emotional crux, then spilling over into the following scene) is a very common way to deploy music in dialogue scenes.

Action Scene

Music has a long history of association with action scenes in the theater—as early as the 18th century a type of music had evolved for this purpose out of rapid-tempo dances. In the 19th-century melodrama, these pieces became known as "hurries," and they retained that designation throughout the silent-film era, although one frequently finds the musical term *agitato* applied to them as well. Hurries were used for chases, lively crowd scenes, trains, airplanes, and—in their more serious or "heavy" forms—for battles.

In the classical Hollywood cinema, music was almost obligatory for action scenes. Music is still common in such scenes today, although sound effects typically are foregrounded in the sound track, with music frequently struggling for attention or merely providing a bit of additional emotional "edge."

WO HU CANG LONG (CROUCHING TIGER, HIDDEN DRAGON), "THEFT OF THE SWORD"

A scene early in *Wo Hu Cang Long* (*Crouching Tiger, Hidden Dragon*, 2000) deftly combines the classical and contemporary practices. Yu Shu Lien (Michelle Yeoh) is transporting a fabled sword, Green Destiny, to its new owner. As the scene opens, it is night and we see guards walking in the garden of the house where the sword is being kept (see the top of Figure 9-4); music had entered briefly before the scene change when Jen Yu blows out a candle before apparently settling down for bed. The music matches the calm but positive mood of the guards. An ominous note suddenly sounds as we see something

Figure 9-4. *Wo Hu Cang Long* (*Crouching Tiger, Hidden Dragon*). The theft of the sword.

slip quickly over the roof in the background; a brief but loud stinger immediately raises tension and the music quickly turns quiet but stays very tense as the thief (later revealed as Jen Yu [Zhang Ziyi]) takes the sword. The high-pitched drum rhythm of this music suddenly gives way to low-pitched drumming as the thief and a guard fight. From this point on, we hear only these drums—part music, part sound-effect, the drumming permits dialogue and physical noises to continue unimpeded. When Yu Shu and the thief do battle, the volume level rises. The music stops abruptly as the scene ends and the thief escapes.

Music, paradoxically, raises and maintains the level of physical excitement—usually with its rapid rhythms and abrupt shifts, as here—but at the same time it gives structure to the similarly rapid rhythms and abrupt cuts that usually occur in the image track during action scenes. Music makes the design of the theft scene exceptionally clear: the early moment of calm, the theft, the initial battle with ineffective guards, and the much longer, dangerous battle with Yu Shu are all given distinctive music.

THE MATRIX, "TRINITY IN A JAM"

Ultimately, the first scene of *The Matrix* (2000) is better understood as a prologue that ends a long and complex establishing sequence (totaling about 6 min). In fact Trinity's escape from three Mr. Smiths, the Matrix agents, is thoroughly embedded in the sequence, not simply added on in the manner of a traditional prologue. The scene is pushed at the very beginning by music introduced under the two studio logos; the music intensifies (already speeding up to suggest a chase) and overlaps into the main title, whose background green-lit numbers on a computer screen (whose frame is not seen) continue into the first voice-over—a phone conversation between Trinity (Carrie-Anne Moss) and another resistance fighter—and are shaped and distorted in the subsequent short graphics sequence. At 00:01:30, with the appearance of a policeman's face, the apparent first scene begins. Trinity is found in a room of a ramshackle and probably abandoned hotel; she overpowers the policemen, but one Mr. Smith appears in the hallway with more officers; Trinity runs out of the building and over rooftops, finally spiraling across a substantial gap into the window of another abandoned building; but she must get to a pay phone to be pulled out of the Matrix environment and has to race the other two Mr. Smiths to reach it. Their massive garbage truck demolishes the phone booth. Another graphic transition overlaps to an extreme close-up of a computer screen; the camera pulls away and we see Neo (Keanu Reeves) asleep. The establishing sequence is over.

Music plays a prominent role throughout the establishing sequence, but most of the time it is also mixed with—and sometimes indistinguishable from—the sound effects. The scene is essentially an action scene but it stops and starts several times. Each time the action (chase) starts, it does so abruptly, and the music is characteristic: repetitious, rhythmically driving with its accents clearly profiled and frequent quick swells in loudness, and not strongly melodic.

ADDITIONAL EXAMPLES

Music is very often used to accompany action-battle scenes in historical films, and one of the dangers of such treatments is that music will "romanticize" the scenes, valorizing one side, endowing one or more characters with heroic qualities, or "toning down" the brutality of the image track's depictions. Battle scenes in *Glory* (1989), *Dances with Wolves* (1990), *The Last Samurai* (2003), or similar films deserve a critical viewing from this standpoint. (You might also consider how music's rhythms are matched to those observable in the image track or ways in which music's formal designs organize the image track [hint: parts of battle scenes are typically edited as montages].) Where music is not emphasized in battle scenes, the combination and positioning of the other sound track elements normally creates effects like those described earlier for music.

Action music can be played for comedy, too. Silent-film era style topics of the "mysterioso," "the grotesque," or "light agitato" often played to active comedic scenes. Max Steiner sometimes headed similar cues in his scores with terms like "mysterioso—screwy" or "screwyissimo." One such scene in *Mildred Pierce* (1945) involves extended mickey-mousing. The scene is near the beginning of the film. Wally has been locked inside a beach house after he tries (clumsily) to seduce Mildred; she sneaks out, locking him inside (with a dead

Figure 9-5. *Mildred Pierce.* Wally is locked in the beach house.

body, as it turns out). Wally is basically a comic character who has been duped by Mildred, and he now looks a bit of a fool as he crashes about the house trying to find a way out (Figure 9-5). We learn from this episode that Wally, who has been onscreen nearly from the beginning of the film, is actually a minor character, and we also discover that Mildred is a resourceful risk-taker.

Love Scene

Of all the categories we have discussed in the chapters of Part II, the love scene is the most difficult to pin down generically. That may be true in large part because the love scene in its simplest definition—a scene focused on the erotically charged interactions of a couple—is ubiquitous in the movies: overwhelmingly, both classical and modern film narratives serve the basic theme that scholars call "creating the couple," a process that typically works itself out in one or more attraction-repulsion cycles that motivate the twists and turns of the narrative. Even where the main theme of a film is something else—as in war films, westerns, or films about large political events—the progression of an intimate relationship (normally of the lead characters) is typically the most important subplot.

The most basic form of the scenario creates the couple as the conclusion of the film, the moment where all the plot elements converge (the formula is commonly, if crudely (and often incorrectly), referred to as "boy gets girl"). Most of the Astaire-Rogers musicals work this way (for example, *Swing Time* (1936) and *Top Hat* (1935)). More recent examples include *Grease* (1978), *When Harry Met Sally* (1989), *Sleepless in Seattle* (1993), *Le Fabuleux Destin d'Amélie Poulain* (*Amélie*, 2001), and *Pride & Prejudice* (2005). Even one Hitchcock film draws on the formula—*The Trouble with Harry* (1955).

The possible variants, however, are almost endless. The couple may be formed early in the film and the vicissitudes they endure structure the narrative, as in several early Hitchcock films (including *Young and Innocent* (1937), *Rebecca*, *Suspicion* (1941), and *Spellbound*), but also *North by Northwest* (1959) and, in a psychologically twisted way, *Vertigo* (1958). Other films from the classic era include *Made for Each Other* (1939), *The Young in Heart* (1938), *Now, Voyager* (1942), among many others (especially those, like the three named here, that belong to the genre of melodrama or "women's films"). This variant is particularly suited to stories that end in the breakup of the couple, whether through desertion or death, as we see later in *Shadowlands* (1993). Quite often the breakup occurs about midway and the remainder of the film is driven by the consequences, whether it be the two characters trying to establish separate lives (and perhaps new couples) after a breakup (as in *Mildred Pierce*, where Mildred goes through two cycles of divorce), or the surviving person doing the same after a death (as in *Out of Africa* (1985), where Karen tries to maintain her life in Kenya after Denys' death in an airplane crash), or criminal investigation or civil proceedings (as in *Psycho* (1960) after the death of Marion). It is, of course, also common for a separated couple to succeed in (re)establishing a solid relationship at the end of the film (as in *Good Will Hunting* or *His Girl Friday* and its remakes *The Front Page* (1974) and *Switching Channels* (1988)).

Despite the difficulties posed by the genre, we can still make some practical distinctions. When most people think of a love scene, they think of the moment in which two people not only realize they are attracted to one another but accept the consequences of that attraction (if not always completely at first). If the attraction is immediately played out in a physical coupling, then the love scene is foreplay; otherwise, it establishes the emotional bond that influences the characters' further actions. Although many other encounters of couples may be erotically charged (as in flirting or in an established couple's arguing), we use the commonplace idea of the love scene as our definition here.

Because "music itself signifies emotion,"[3] as Claudia Gorbman points out, it is not surprising that music usually plays a role in love scenes, if not necessarily always in the form of the classical cliché of soaring violins. In the following examples, the first relies on diegetic music to accompany a straightforward love scene leading to a physical encounter. The second example (the Laendler from

The Sound of Music (1965) again) charts and endorses, in successive strains of the music, the dawning recognition of physical attraction. The final example is multiple, showing compactly four approaches to different moments in a love relationship.

OUT OF AFRICA, "ON SAFARI: THE SECOND DINNER"

Meryl Streep's character, Karen, the Baroness von Blixen (whose pen name was Isak Dinesen), goes on safari with Denys Finch Hatton (Robert Redford). During their enforced isolation, the hint of a possible attraction slowly evolves into a full-blown sexual relationship. Two extended evening dinner scenes are crucial to this. The first begins shortly before 01:30:00, with a cut from a scene in which he assists her in washing her hair. A scene showing the following day's hunting is succeeded (with a simple cut at 01:37:21) by that evening's dinner. Denys puts the needle down on the gramophone (see the top of Figure 9-6), and we hear the first part of the theme for the first movement of Mozart's Piano Sonata in A major, K. 331, a pleasant pastoral melody. The gramophone itself is a motif with special significance (recall that you can see it in her room at the beginning of the film [Figure 6-4]: it was a gift from Denys [Figure I-6]). The elaborately set dinner table stands apart from its surroundings, as do Karen and Denys with it (the music—traditional European

Figure 9-6. *Out of Africa.* Second safari dinner (love scene).

concert music—only reinforces that separation, marking itself as "music for Europeans in Africa").

The music almost appears to choreograph their actions: she comes out of her tent just as the second short phrase starts, then cut back to him standing up and looking toward her as the third short phrase starts, and at the end of the first part, she sits down. The music is repeated, starting against a cut to the table with him opening wine; and so on. The end of the repeated music overlaps with a sentimental waltz to which they dance and that we are presumably to understand as diegetic (as played on the gramophone), although it is obviously far too loud. They finish the dance, return to the table and start to tell stories; but the waltz only fades slowly under her speaking several seconds later. When finished, she goes to her tent, and he follows after a short interval; they kiss, and we hear a short audio overlap (the film's main-title theme) before a cut to the next day, their third day of safari.

Note that music is used through most of the scene but not for the kiss (or the immediately preceding moment when he unties the strap of her blouse). A stereotypical upswell in the music normally serves a double role as transition or audio overlap if the scene ends, as here, with the kiss. Instead, the roles are kept very distinct: the two pieces on the gramophone (combined with the change from sitting at the table to the physical contact of dancing) gradually raise the emotional level, and the audio overlap is a simple, functional transition played at a low level. The physical contact between Karen and Denys in the tent, then, is separated from its surroundings, the final step in their isolation, as it were: the isolation of a couple making love.

SOUND OF MUSIC, "THE LAENDLER" (AS LOVE SCENE)

We have already looked at the formal aspects of the Laendler scene in ch.7, where we noted that this is the scene in which Maria and Captain von Trapp first realize they are physically attracted to one another. There is no speech during the dance itself, but the narrative is advanced because we are given a number of clues, in their own deportment and facial expressions, in the cutaway to the Baroness, and in the immediate aftermath of the dance (as Maria and the children leave the terrace). All this, of course, is in addition to the cultural convention of erotic potential in a couple dance, particularly when the couple is dancing alone.

The timeline in ch. 7 includes comments on the changes in their facial expressions: these can be summarized as a progression from uncertainty (on Maria's part, due not only to the stiffness of the Captain's character heretofore but also to her discomfort at the idea of dancing with her employer) to the neutral smile of the courteous social dancer to growing discomposure as they begin to look at each other with more emotion. After one rather intimate figure in the dance, the series of hammerlocks, Maria and the Captain come to a halt, trapped in each other's gaze. Maria becomes flustered and backs away during the last moments of the music, claiming implausibly that she has forgotten the rest of the dance.

One visual clue supplied by the editing and one aural clue provide all the additional information we need to confirm that this was no ordinary dance. During strain D (in the midst of the hammerlock series), we cut away from the dance to the Captain's fiancée, Baroness Eberfeld, who walks onto the terrace and sees the two of them. The look on the Baroness' face makes it clear she is uneasy about what she sees. The aural clue comes after Maria stops dancing and backs away from the Captain. One of the children, Brigitte, suddenly appears onscreen and blurts out "Your face is all red"; Maria barely covers her embarrassment with "Is it? I don't suppose I'm used to dancing."

Managed subtly though it is, the Laendler is unmistakably a love scene, in the limited sense we are using that term here: the moment of realization that creates the couple—even if Maria and the Captain are not quite ready to recognize it openly yet (they kiss for the first time in the subsequent Gazebo scene). The Laendler is also, appropriately for a story turning on a love relationship, the narrative crux of the film, because their falling in love is the catalyst for many changes: the Captain realizes he is not in love with the Baroness and breaks the engagement, Maria runs away to the Abbey only to confront the fact that the life of a nun is not for her, then Maria and the Captain marry and begin a new life together.

SHADOWLANDS, FOUR SCENES

This film, released in 1993, is based on a memoir written by the famous British author C. S. Lewis (known as Jack to his family) about his relationship with and marriage to Joy Gresham, a divorcee from the United States. Jack (Anthony Hopkins) has never been married; he lives with his brother and his life has been that of a writer, academic, and gentleman bachelor. He meets Joy (Debra Winger) and as a favor that will allow Joy to remain in the United Kingdom, he marries her in a civil ceremony. It is only afterwards, however, that the two begin to develop a relationship.

The four love scenes show the progression of Jack and Joy's developing love, and more important, Jack's ability to express his love. Jack touches Joy more and becomes physically closer in each scene, starting with holding hands in the first, to a passionate kiss in the fourth. The music mirrors this growth in each scene. Each scene has progressively more music (in terms of total duration in seconds), increased volume, and a lusher quality.

In the first love scene (which starts at 01:20:45), Joy is hospitalized with advanced cancer and Jack visits her. He has come to realize his true feelings for her, and he tells her that he wants to marry her again, "before God and the world"; he proposes as he sits beside her and holds her hand (Figure 9-7). The

Figure 9-7. *Shadowlands.* First love scene.

music is very quiet and occurs only in the last 15 sec. It begins extremely quietly during Jack's words, increasing in volume only after Joy's closing words.

The second scene (01:24:54) is their second wedding, as Jack and Joy are
married in a religious ceremony in the hospital (Figure 9-8). Jack sits next to
Joy's bed, leaning in toward her and gazing seriously and lovingly throughout.
They kiss (for the first time in the film), Jack's hand brushing Joy's cheek, at
the close of the ceremony. Here, music (strings) plays throughout, but it is very
subdued and even, except for a slight swell as Jack begins his vows.

In the third love scene (01:32:40), Jack has brought Joy home from the
hospital. The first night he helps her up the stairs and into his bedroom. He
plainly feels awkward (Figure 9-9), but he is finally put at ease as he tells Joy
his bedtime routine, at the end of which she tells him it will be the same, ex-

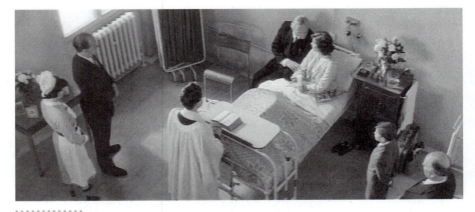

Figure 9-8. *Shadowlands.* Wedding (second love scene).

Figure 9-9. *Shadowlands.* Third love scene.

cept that she will be there with him at the end of the bedtime ritual. She asks him to show her how he goes to sleep, he climbs next to her on the bed, and they kiss and embrace. In this scene, the music begins only halfway through, after Jack begins to explain his routine, again very subdued. As Jack explains and then shows how he goes to bed and sleeps, the music is very tender, with piano, harp, then clarinet over strings. It swells considerably as they embrace and kiss at the end.

In the final love scene (01:44:57), Jack and Joy have taken a "belated honey-moon trip" in the countryside. Having found shelter from a rain shower while on a walk, Jack tells Joy how happy he is and he never wants time to move forward again. Joy reminds him that she is dying and says that the pain is part of their happiness, too (Figure 9-10). She tells him, "That's the deal" and he

Figure 9-10. *Shadowlands.* Fourth love scene.

Figure 9-11. *Shadowlands.* Fourth love scene.

reaches out to touch her. He takes her in his arms and raises her up to him, the music swelling and increasing in volume. Their kiss and the embrace are the most passionate and intimate in the film (Figure 9-11), as though Jack has truly felt the depth of his love and passion for Joy. Music, lush and full, is heard from the beginning until Joy speaks about her death—for about 1 min we hear only rain sounds and thunder behind their dialogue. As Jack walks toward Joy, music re-enters softly, steadily rising in volume until their embrace and kiss.

Summary

As with the formal framing segments of the main-title sequence and end credits, music early on acquired conventional functions for scenes within the narrative proper, in particular for dialogue scenes (to underscore speech), action scenes (to provide both momentum and unity), and love scenes (usually to provide an additional element of emotion). Music is by no means obligatory in any of these types—practices vary widely, even within recognized national schools, studios, over decades, and in the work of individual directors—but, when music is used, a relatively restricted set of style topics and sound track treatments does prevail.

In chapters 6 and 7, and in this chapter as well, we have described a number of scene types that typically involve music in significant ways. These types were illustrated with detailed examples. What should emerge from those descriptions, covering about fifty years, is the strength of the scene types as categories, or frameworks within which we expect to position music and interpret its functions in film narrative. That is to say, historically, music has played an important role in film exhibition, whether in silent-film performance practice(s) or in the sound track of sound films. Although the variety possible within the framework of the traditional narrative feature film is great, a relatively small number of scene types commonly predominates. Apart from the formal functions of the establishing sequence and end credits, those scenes where music by convention has a place vary considerably in whether music is indeed present (and if so how prominently it figures) and whether the scene has an important place in the narrative unfolding.

Writing About Film Music: Interpretation

Introduction

In the interlude that concluded Part I, we explored the writing of scene analyses and short response papers. These exercises were concerned mainly with describing how the sound track of a film works. The descriptive language was for the most part put to analytical use to show how the elements of the sound track interact with one another and with the image track to produce particular filmic effects. The goal of the writing was to draw attention to the basic materials of the sound track and to the ways a particular film organizes and uses its materials.

In this interlude, we are concerned with developing an interpretive essay. This type of writing seeks to put observations about a film to a critical end—that is, to uncover how a film organizes its meanings and to what purpose. The goal is to draw the sound track and music firmly into a thematic reading of a film, showing how these elements support or resist the dominant directions or emphases of the narrative. Like the response paper, the more extended interpretive essay relies primarily on research information gathered by watching a film and making notes on the action, characters, sound track, and music (exactly the same kind of information that formed the core of the analysis report). In its most basic form, the interpretive essay resembles a "long" or more detailed response paper that will typically run to 2,000 or 3,000 words (or eight to twelve typed, double-spaced pages). A closer focus on argumentation is necessary, however, because the interpretive essay will be making a case for a particular way of "reading" or understanding a film.

Developing a Reading (1): Finding a Thesis

THESIS OPTIONS FOR *CATCH ME IF YOU CAN*

From the tables and notes in the interlude to Part I, we have all the material we need to begin an interpretive essay on *Catch Me If You Can* (2002). What we lack is a thesis—an idea that we want our reader to find true, correct, or plausible thanks to the examples and arguments that we provide in the body of the paper. To arrive at a thesis, ask yourself questions related to your own interest in the film: "What do I find intriguing or disturbing about the film? What broad narrative theme(s) does the film explore? What makes the film noteworthy, in my opinion? Does it illustrate some aspect of filmmaking with special clarity? Does it have an unusual effect on the viewer?"[1] To this list, we can add questions that are directed specifically to film sound, "Are sound track and image track balanced in their effects? How does music and sound influence narrative (through styles, leitmotifs, or empathetic/anempathetic cueing)? Does music—or sound in general—have any subversive effects on narrative?"

In general, the thesis of an interpretive essay needs to relate to a narrative theme of the film. In the case of *Catch Me If You Can*, one of the primary themes of the film concerns counterfeiting—Frank's talent for passing not only bad checks but for presenting himself as having professional credentials he did not actually earn. A strong interpretative thesis would link the sound track to this theme. For instance, you might explore how Frank's uncertain professional status relates to the frequently uncertain diegetic status of the music. Another tack might be to consider how, if at all, the sound track differentiates between Frank's reality and his deceptions and what that might tell us about Frank's level of self-understanding. The body of the essay, then, marshals evidence and arguments in favor of the chosen thesis. It is customary to end an essay with a confirming restatement of the thesis.

Leitmotifs and, more generally, sound motifs also offer good entry points for interpreting a sound track. In the Introduction to Part I, we discussed the scene where Carl receives a call from Frank on Christmas Eve. We noted that at the end of this scene, nondiegetic music appears that was originally associated with Frank's feelings for his father. The recurrence of this music suggests a transference of affection from father to Carl—at the end of the film Carl will assume this father function overtly when he sponsors Frank's social rehabilitation. This connection is strengthened by Bing Crosby's "Mele Kalikimaka" heard on the radio at the beginning of the scene. As we pointed out in our earlier discussion, Christmas music is an important aural motif in the film. Carl and Frank tend to be in contact around Christmas, so this music serves as a temporal marker emphasizing this fact. Yet the motif also plays on the notion that Christmas is a time for family. When Frank, having escaped one last time from the FBI, stands outside his mother's house to the sounds of Nat King Cole's "The Christmas Song," he seems to recognize that he has no place in this family; he asks Carl to put him in the car before his mother has a chance to see him. The parallel use of the Christmas music in these two scenes helps support an interpretation that Carl's function in the narrative is not so much to be Frank's adversary as to be his surrogate family.

Another useful entry point for interpretation is lyric analysis. For instance, "Mele Kalikimaka" and "The Christmas Song" are obviously Christmas music, but we might ask what makes these particularly good (or not so good) choices for this film. First of all, the two are linked by the fact that each ends with the line "Merry Christmas to you." They are addressed like Christmas cards. This point of commonality also allows us to draw distinctions (in the manner of compare and contrast). The sentiment of "Mele Kalikimaka" is rather abstract and impersonal. Clearly evocative of exoticism and travel, the song emphasizes beauties of the place ("the land where palm trees sway") rather than any kind of personal, familial connection. "The Christmas Song," by contrast, dwells on the figure of the child—"tiny tots," "every mother's child" and "kids from one to ninety-two." The cutting in the sequence underscores these particular lines, drawing out the song's nostalgic portrait of a family Christmas. As intimated in our discussion of this scene in chapter 3, the song seems particularly poignant here because it underscores the familial relationship that Frank wants but does not have. A fuller interpretation might link this idea to the theme of counterfeiting: outside his mother's house, Frank finally recognizes the relationship that he wants for himself but at the same time the fact that his deceptive life has made that relationship impossible.

EXAMPLES FROM THE PUBLISHED LITERATURE

The academic and tradebook critical literature on film, film music, and film sound has many examples of interpretive essays that you might use as models for your own work. For that reason, we will not present a completed essay here but instead will comment on one from the published literature and then point to thesis statements in several others.

In chapter 5, we quoted from Claudia Gorbman's essay on the music for *Mildred Pierce* (1945). That essay appears at the end of a book chapter that delineates "seven rules" for nondiegetic music in the classical Hollywood sound film, and as such it is not surprising that the initial thesis statement announces a descriptive and analytical paper: "I will now emphasize the 'unity' principle [that is, her "rule" 6] by exploring the film's use of musical themes in the context of its narrative." Gorbman adds another sentence, however, with another thesis, one that is clearly interpretive: "I will also suggest ways in which Steiner's compositional style, above and beyond its adequacy to the classical Hollywood model, is paradigmatic for melodrama in particular."[2] In other words, she is making a stylistic claim: that the specific way in which Steiner deploys nondiegetic music is especially appropriate to a genre of films, the melodrama or women's film of the 1930s and 1940s. Granted, a generalization like this relies on external knowledge—familiarity with other films in that genre—but Gorbman stays very close to *Mildred Pierce* in working her argument out.

The essay runs just under 2500 words. After some introductory background information on Steiner, Gorbman asserts that "only in actively deciding to listen for the music will we realize how structured and repetitive it is, and how central to our emotional reception of the narrated events,"[3] and the bulk of the essay then marshalls evidence of the presentation, recurrence, and variation of five melodies (leitmotifs, on ch. 8's terms). At the end, she ties Steiner's mickey-mousing and other ways of closely "coordinating [music] with diegetic action" to the "'melodramatic spirit'—a desire to externalize and explicate all inflections of action, from emotional values in a scene to the very rhythms of physical movement. . . . On several levels, . . . the musical score exhibits a pronounced tendency toward hyperexplication. . . . Just as melodrama displays a tendency to use the close-up on the female star's face . . . Steiner's music has a similar effect." Finally, then "the background score has a key function of guiding the spectator-auditor unambiguously into [a] particularly compelling [emotional] identification."[4] Because such emotional identification is fundamental to the film melodrama, a repetitious, "hyperexplicative" music is especially effective and meaningful. (By implication, such music will not be so effective in all genres—but that is another thesis and another essay.)

Here are some thesis statements for other recent articles and book chapters that focus on music. The first three link music to characterization. Robynn Stilwell argues for music's contributions in *Die Hard* (1988):

> Action films tend to be based on simple juxtapositions of hero and villain. As in musicals, so much of the film's running time is taken up with set pieces—songs and dances, chases and demolitions—that a fairly schematic plot, individualized only by local detail, is essential for narrative clarity. But while the identities of the key players in *Die Hard* are clear, just who is antagonist and who protagonist is not so clear, and music is one of the primary elements undercutting the nominal hero and elevating the "villain" to anti-hero.[5]

Similarly, Miguel Mera, writing about *The Ice Storm* (1997), asserts that the film maintains clear boundaries between diegetic and nondiegetic music and that the former seems to be guided by the characters themselves:

> As it is theoretically owned by the characters, the source music acts primarily as a historical and sociocultural locator, particularly in scenes such as the Carvers' dinner party in reel 1 or the three different "party" locations of reel 4. If

"nothing more infallibly classifies than tastes in music," then the choices the characters have made about the music they wish to hear tells the audience how those characters should be perceived.[6]

Julie Brown applies the idea to the television series *Ally McBeal* (1997–2002), which she says

revels in sound track games. Formally, it flaunts its awareness of the inclusive nature of the sound track as a phenomenon while playing around with several types of musical multimedia: film, music video and staged performance. A musical "sound track" of sorts also invades the diegesis: through various subplots and dramatic conceits music, especially a particular type of pop music, is elevated to the role of central plot and series metaphor, above all in relation to Ally's character.[7]

Discussing the role of music in fairy-tale musicals, Rick Altman inventories the musical styles used in one sequence from *Love Me Tonight* (1932) and then extrapolates from that to the thesis that "[The film] is built around an opposition between the idle rich and the working poor—yet paradoxically this very first sequence assures us that contact is possible between penniless Maurice [Chevalier] and loveless Jeanette [MacDonald], but only through the magical continuity provided by music and song."[8]

Finally, in a negative formulation, William Darby and Jack du Bois discuss the music of *Scarface* (1932), a film that, according to them

exhibits some . . . musical sophistication when it presents Tony Camonte (Paul Muni) as a gangland killer who whistles [music by Italian opera composer] Verdi before committing murder. While Camonte's allegiance to Italian opera might well be passed off as simply a national passion, his choice of the "Slaves' Chorus" from *Nabucco* may well offer a discreet comment on his life of violence. Except for this character touch, the musical effects in *Scarface* are obvious, underdeveloped, and schmaltzy.[9]

Developing a Reading (2): Reading against the Grain

Thus far we have focused on developing interpretive strategies that uncover the way the sound track subtly augments the general narrative theme of the film. We have isolated elements of the sound track that seem more or less harmonious with that theme; the paired Christmas songs in *Catch Me If You Can*, for instance, certainly seem to add a fine aesthetic texture to the narrative of the film, and as such the songs form part of the general class of subsidiary filmic motifs that structure, support, and enable the central narrative.

An interpretation need not, however, engage in such direct fashion with the central narrative theme as it does here. Indeed, analytical attention toward aspects of the sound track that run counter to even subvert, the dominant narrative theme often produces interpretive readings that reveal important uncon-scious or at least implicit social assumptions that enable that theme. In other words, an interpretation might avoid taking the film at its word, so to speak, and instead interrogate it for meanings that it does not highlight or that it even seems actively to suppress. This is a common strategy in professional academic writing. An essay in cultural analysis, for instance, might go beyond Gorbman's interpretation of *Mildred Pierce* to question the role of melodrama as a genre in mid-1940s American films, or the ways music is used to characterize (and support or undermine) gender categories and class hierarchies. One could also interrogate the ways the film is used to enforce class and value clusters for mu-sic (for example, popular music is heard in a seaside dive at the beginning of the film; the proprietor [Wally] even refers to "slumming").

Interpretive strategies such as those described above use analysis to ap-proach the film from an angle other than that encouraged or explicitly au-thorized by the film's narrative. These alternate angles are generally social in nature, and each can be considered to embody a mode of critical theory; com-mon ones are based around gender, race, class, and cultural hegemony (for example, colonialism).

Obviously, each mode of critical reading will attend to different social themes of the film and so also to the elements of the sound track that support those themes. Similarly, most films explore more than one important narrative theme, and critical emphasis on one of these themes or the other will draw out somewhat different thematic correspondences in the sound track. It is a mis-take, however, to think of the resulting multiplicity of interpretations as a sign of an unwillingness (or inability) to make evaluations, or what is sometimes called "cultural relativism." Although it is true that a particular reading is the product of a certain thematic attention, not everything goes. Some readings are more plausible than others. In all cases, details of the sound track must sup-port the interpretation if the reading is to be convincing; and it is the power to deliver a convincing insight into a film that allows a reading to seem produc-tive rather than forced or even absurd. (In fact, these criteria are no different than those that apply to the kinds of readings we discussed in the previous section—those looking for correspondences to explicit narrative themes.) It is the power to convince and deliver insight that is most important. As a rule of thumb, interesting critical readings will be neither forced nor too obvious.

EXAMPLE: *CASABLANCA* AGAINST THE GRAIN

The aim of a critical reading is to uncover something about the film that is not obvious on the surface. Let's take *Casablanca* (1942) as an example. We can be-gin by noting that the character of Sam is a typical role for African Americans in Hollywood of the period. He is an entertainer and properly deferential toward his "boss," Rick. Although not a surprising representation for the 1940s, such a relationship, needless to say, seems problematic from our standpoint today. If we explored this critical direction further we might point out the manner in which Rick, as he prepares to leave Casablanca, "sells" Sam's contract to Ferrari, who agrees to Rick's inflated terms because "it wouldn't be Rick's without Sam." This somewhat inadvertent slip "exposes" the exploitive nature of the relationship between Rick and Sam: Ferrari apparently believes that Rick's can survive without Rick but not without Sam—and that Rick had been underpaying him.

The sound track supports this interpretation. Sam appears primarily in the first half of the film, almost exclusively in his role as a singer. He performs a series of upbeat American popular songs, which serve to distract the patrons from the harsh realities of the world. (It is interesting to note that the one song that departs from the generally optimistic tone of the music, "Tango Delle Rose," is also the only one Sam does not sing.) Sam sings so others may forget—not just the patrons but also Rick. This theme of forgetting is underscored by the taboo Rick places on "As Time Goes By," a song he associates with his lost love Ilsa. For Rick, Sam is both a reminder of Ilsa (because he was in Paris with them) and, through the taboo, a means of forgetting her.

When Ilsa returns and Sam breaks the taboo, playing the song first for Ilsa and then for Rick, Sam's work is done and he is, as it were, discarded by the narrative, a move underscored by the nondiegetic orchestra replacing Sam's diegetic song. No longer an instrument of forgetting, Sam is forgotten, his song silenced. He reappears substantively only once more during the film, during Rick's negotiation with Ferrari, where he sanctions the sale and expresses his willingness to play for less than he's worth: "I don't have time to spend what I make now." Sam, unlike Rick or even Renault, is incapable of personal growth; of the major characters, only Sam's status remains what it was and where he was at the beginning of the film—an entertainer; and the black entertainer has no other role to play in this war.

In many respects, this sketch of the underlying work that race does in *Casablanca* is not unlike that of the analysis of *Catch Me If You Can* offered earlier. The difference is primarily one of thematic attention. In the case of *Catch Me If You Can*, the analysis used the central narrative to look for thematic correspondences to that narrative in the details of the sound track. We might think of the theme percolating through the details. In *Casablanca*, on the contrary, the theme of race does not correspond to—or at least seems peripheral to—the central narrative and so can appear coincidental or at most subordinate. As the analysis suggests, however, this racial theme runs under the main narrative, articulating it and in many respects enabling it in a substantive way. Here, details have absorbed a theme otherwise repressed by the narrative, and our analysis of the sound track was used to show that this repressed theme appeared not only peripherally in the narrative itself but also that the details of the sound track supported this theme.

Readings that focus on repressed themes such as race, class, gender, and cultural hegemony are sometimes called "symptomatic readings," and collectively such themes are sometimes referred to as the "political unconscious," with an analogy being drawn from psychoanalysis. One premise shared by most psychological and cognitive theory is that individuals do not react to all stimuli on a conscious level. The concept of the "political unconscious" applies that premise to culture at large: beyond its overt values (such as freedom, justice, diversity, liberty, etc.), cultures are organized by covert values and assumptions (unrecognized or only dimly recognized by individuals) that enable the appearance of those values, that mask the contradictions in the particular social appearance of such values, and that sustain the status quo as the "natural" manifestation of them.

Collectively such overt and covert values are known as "ideology." Understood this way, then, critical readings of a film offer a means of exposing these implicit values and underscoring the contradictions in their appearance. Although such readings are often used in the context of advocacy, it is important to recognize that the adoption of a particular mode of critical reading need not necessarily imply a corresponding political view. For instance, when the late Reverend Jerry Falwell interpreted Tinky Winky of *Teletubbies* (1997–2001) as a homosexual figure, he was tacitly accepting the fundamental validity of the queer interpretive mode—because he required that mode to make the interpretation at all. (Queer reading is the academic term given to the interpretive mode of critical theory attentive to themes of homosexuality.) Similarly, the cultural critic who argues against entrenched political structures acknowledges the power of those structures through the very attention given to their analysis; and so on—the "political unconscious" is simply that, an unconscious that structures society; and identifying symptoms point to the location of a social disturbance but do not prescribe a particular "treatment."

Interrogating gender in *Casablanca*, we might point to how Ilsa displaces Sam only to be likewise displaced by Louis at the end. On the sound track this is represented by the replacement of "As Time Goes By" with the "Marseillaise." Ilsa, too, is merely an instrument of Rick's psychological journey from cynicism to idealism. The place of Sam and Ilsa in the narrative may seem to be primarily a result of the fact that this is Rick's story, but one can argue that this is misleading, in the sense that it ignores the way race and gender are terms against which Rick's journey is defined.

Another interpretation might give a queer reading to the one earlier. This reading might suggest that Ilsa is in fact an otherwise superfluous figure who blocks "proper" homosocial camaraderie of the "beautiful friendship" from expressing a latent "improper" homosexuality. In this reading, Rick's affections pass over the course of the film from the eunuch-like Sam to the sexually potent Louis by way of an alluring but obstructing Ilsa, just as cynical and impotent diegetic music turns into an apotheosis of the Marseillaise by way of a seductive "As Time Goes By" that can find no end. At the end of the film, both Rick and Louis find a "properly" homosocial bond under the sweet string strains of the Marseillaise.

A reading emphasizing cultural hegemony, on the other hand, might concentrate on the way the ruling class—Rick, Ferrari, Major Strasser, and especially Louis—are all foreigners, and the way indigenous culture is reflected only in colonialist representations of it. Throughout, Casablanca is portrayed as a characteristic oriental city of danger and illicit love, nowhere more so than in the opening sequence. Musically, this takes form most obviously in the stereotyped melodic arabesques, which are used to give an exotic atmosphere to Ferrari's club, the *Blue Parrot*, every bit as much as Sam's songs give *Rick's Café Américain* its equally exotic, if culturally intrusive, musical accent. In both cases, music represents; it projects a characteristic image.

In terms of class, we might point to the way Rick's benevolent management allows a solidarity to form among his workers despite their otherwise divergent backgrounds. Clearly, this idealized representation is determined by the needs of war-time propaganda, a point that is emphasized by the contrast between Rick and Ferrari. Such benevolent management extends only so far as Rick, which is acknowledged obliquely by his need to negotiate with the profit-minded (and ethnically marked) Ferrari on behalf of his staff when he sells the café. Music marks the difference between Rick and Ferrari in a subtle way: only in the *Blue Parrot* do we hear the stereotypically exotic—"Arabian" or oriental—music of 19th-century theater and of silent film.

On a somewhat more abstract plane, we might look at the propaganda work of the sound track. If the basic trajectory of the story is Rick's journey from cynicism to idealism, a path that also traces his growing commitment to the war effort, music in particular helps underscore a progressive shift to melodrama that determines the ideological force of that idealism. As the gray ambiguities of cynicism become the black and white certainties of good and evil, music becomes an agent of demonization and veneration. Music already plays a melodramatic role in the prologue, and the first moment of melodramatic demonization occurs shortly after the return of nondiegetic music, when Ilsa mentions the entry of the German army into Paris and the music responds with a distorted version of "Deutschland über Alles." Over the course of the film, such gestures, especially of demonization, occur more and more frequently marking the growing clarity of Rick's understanding. (One of the unacknowledged ironies of the film is that, although it associates Rick's trauma with the German arrival in Paris, his relationship with Ilsa is in fact conditioned by Laszlo's absence that was produced by the war.)

Although we have tried to be neutral in our presentation of each previous mode of critical analysis, it is important to recognize that these readings are not uniformly convincing. Whereas each draws our attention to a particular facet of the film, some seem more forced or tangential than others to the larger concerns of the film. Some also find better support in the sound track (and other elements of the film). Nevertheless, even readings unconvincing in themselves might prove useful in projects uncovering, say, unrecognized or repressed cultural assumptions pervading a particular set of films.

Summary

This interlude offered strategies for developing and writing an interpretation of a film in terms of its sound track. We presented two different models, one that built an interpretation directly on the overt thematic concerns of the film, the other that worked against the grain of those concerns. In both cases, we stressed the importance of finding suitable evidence because the interpretation will seem convincing only if the evidence does not seem forced.

Although it is possible to produce an excellent interpretive essay based solely on the evidence of the film itself, you should never be reluctant to use any specialized knowledge you have or can find. Information about film history, music history, cultural history, the production process, or biography all present potential entry points for interpretation, as do, in a somewhat different way, other interpretations of the film.

PART THREE

The Sound Track:
A Technological History

In Part III we direct attention to the history of music in film sound, specifically as that history is organized around technological innovations and their role in film production and exhibition. The heterogeneous venues and practices of the early cinema (ch. 10) give way to a rapid series of technological changes in the first few years of sound film (ch. 11) and an aesthetic "follow up" in the standardization of studio practices for sound film by the later 1930s (ch. 12). Beginning about 1950, shifts in aesthetics occur (especially with respect to the range of musical styles) but the treatment of sound technology in the two subsequent decades remains surprisingly conservative (ch. 13). In the early 1970s, however, the introduction of **Dolby** stereo marked a major advance in sound technology, quickly stimulating practices we recognize as modern sound design (ch. 14) and leading eventually to the characteristics of contemporary digital sound production and postproduction (including music; ch. 15).

This historical account of sound within film production and exhibition adds context to the descriptive terms and analytical tasks of Part I and to the formal and stylistic conventions for music that we delineated and illustrated in Part II. Beyond that, both the descriptive and interpretive modes of writing about film sound and music—including the critical mode—that were outlined in the two Interludes will benefit from a grounding in physical and technological aspects of film production and exhibition (or, in more recent years, other modes of consumption).

Music and Sound in the Silent Era (1895–1929)

Introduction

Irving Thalberg's remarks in the sidebar reflect a very common viewpoint: it has often been asserted that silent film was never truly silent. Presentations from the earliest days typically included some form of musical accompaniment, although the manner of that accompaniment varied widely, depending especially on place of performance and time of day. For example, a **vaudeville** theater, the dominant venue for exhibiting motion pictures before the rise of the nickelodeon, would be more likely to have musical accompaniment than would a tent show, which might have only an automated drum for ballyhoo—if that; but even in theaters dedicated to motion picture exhibition, the first show of the day and the dinner show would occasionally be run without accompaniment even as late as the 1920s. As another example, early sound practice was more likely to include substantial sound effects than was later practice, which tended to restrict effects to key narrative moments (thunderclaps, the fateful knock on the door, etc.). Finally, it was common for certain films, such as the popular travel documentaries, to be accompanied by live narration, a mode of presentation that did not disappear until as late as the 1960s; and, although we usually think of 1927 as the initiating moment of the sound film, successful, if commercially unviable, attempts to synchronize film and recorded sound go back to the earliest days of film.

The sound practice of the silent era divides itself into roughly three phases: (1) early cinema, 1895–1905, where the sound practice was extremely heterogeneous, almost wholly determined locally and by venue; (2) the nickelodeon, 1905–1915, a transitional phase when sound was first institutionalized as a specifically cinematic practice and determined more and more by the institutions of cinema exhibition; and (3) the picture palace, 1915–1929, the mature period

There never was a silent film. We'd finish a picture, show it in one of our projection rooms and come out shattered. It would be awful. We'd have high hopes for the picture, work our heads off on it, and the result would always be the same. Then we'd show it in a theater, with a girl pounding away at a piano, and there would be all the difference in the world. Without that music, there wouldn't have been a movie industry at all.

—Irving Thalberg (producer)[1]

of the silent film, when relatively homogeneous performance was expected, as determined by the multireel feature film and a sound practice weighted heavily toward music; also in this period the theaters were highly stratified into various levels of performance, for each of which specific kinds of musical performances were required.

The Early Years

In early cinema, sound practice was mediated by venue, which is another way of saying that the cultural and commercial institutions of cinema did not yet exist to regulate its own sound practice. Consequently, music and sound were used in a manner in keeping with the place where an individual film was shown. A vaudeville theater, for instance, would treat a film as an "act," and, insofar as we can tell, the music was generally chosen to accord with similar, live vaudeville acts (see Figure 10-1; here the picture is a dance act). A speaker

Figure 10-1. This ad is for a vaudeville exhibition of the Vitagraph in 1896. The conductor is watching the screen, the orchestra is clearly playing, and it seems likely they would have been playing music appropriate for the dance act depicted. As such acts would have been usual vaudeville entertainment, this scene does not tell us how, or whether, a vaudeville orchestra would have accompanied a scenic—say, a film of a train or pictures of the sea shore.

in a lecture hall, by contrast, might use film as a substitute for magic lantern slides, and music would be adapted to this situation; most probably it would be used in the familiar manner of the popular stage melodrama—for introductions, entr'actes, exit music, and so forth. Traveling lecturers such as Lyman Howe, on the other hand, placed great emphasis on the realistic use of sound effects. So did the Hale's Tours, an early, dedicated film exhibition venue introduced at the St. Louis World's Fair in 1904 and made up to look like a train car. Effects included hydraulic lifts to simulate motion, realistic train sounds, and in some cases even a short run of track to help create the illusion of actual train travel. With this conceit of a train ride, the Hale's tour obviously left little room for musical practice. This attraction, which was generally positioned in amusement parks and theatrical districts, proved quite popular until the rise of narrative films. The nickelodeons, which quickly eclipsed other venues for cinema, were cheaper to build and more adaptable to the narrative film, whereas the Hale's Tour seemed best suited to the exhibition of travelogues, especially, of course, those shot from trains.

The Nickelodeon

The nickelodeon's origin was the storefront theater; these first began appearing in appreciable numbers around 1905 and were often located, as were the vaudeville theaters, near transportation hubs at the edges of major retail areas. Indeed, in the early days the shows were often known as "mechanical vaudeville." Figure 10-2 shows a basic floor plan for a small nickelodeon. The typical

a | b **Figure 10-2.** Nickelodeon theaters. (a) Plan for a typical storefront theater, c. 1911. (b) Photograph of a storefront theater as seen from the back of the room. Note that the piano in the corner is not well positioned to see the screen.

theater held between two and three hundred spectators (the plan shown in Figure 10-2 accommodates 192), and a characteristic program consisted of two or three reels of film (each reel was 1,000 feet long and might take anywhere from 10 to 18 min to run, depending on the projectionist, the size of the crowd outside, and the policy of the theater); the intervals between reels were usually filled with some form of live entertainment, such as a brief illustrated lecture or an illustrated song.

Illustrated songs were a particularly common part of the program. Film historian Richard Abel notes that many theaters featured their live singers as prominently as films in advertising for their shows.[2] As the name implies, illustrated songs were popular songs accompanied by a set of lantern slides, which were often richly colored. The singer would sing two verses and two choruses, and then the audience would be encouraged to join in on a final chorus (see Figure 10-3). Frequently criticized as shoddy and indecent, the illustrated song nevertheless maintained a strong presence on the program until the mid-1910s, when the emergence of the multireel feature encouraged most theaters to invest in a second projector. The added equipment facilitated the film showing by eliminating the interval for changing reels but therefore also eliminated the performance niche for illustrated songs.

In addition to the singer, the musical forces were usually a pianist, occasionally a small orchestra in larger theaters, or sometimes just a phonograph in smaller ones. Many theaters featured large phonographs or mechanical pianos

Verse I

Young Johnnie Steele has an Oldsmobile

She is the queen of his gas machine.

She tries to learn the auto.

He lets her steer while he gets her ear

Chorus

Verse 2

Chorus

"Tag"

Figure 10-3. These images are from paper proofs of an illustrated song slide set for "In My Merry Oldsmobile" (1905) sent to the U.S. Copyright Office in 1907. The actual lantern slides used for exhibition would likely have been hand colored, and a slide with the full chorus would have been included at the end. Many theaters would sell sheet music of the day's songs, and song publishers would pay for the singer in larger theaters as a means of plugging the song.

at the entrance specifically to hail passersby (ballyhoo); in the smallest theaters this might be the only music. Besides the illustrated song, music within the theater was also used as entrance and exit music to distract the audience as it filtered in and out of the crowded theater before and after the films, and as an attraction in its own right. Music was also commonly—but not always—played while the film was screened (see Figure 10-4). Initially, then, music was not understood so much as an accompaniment to the film as an "added attraction." In most theaters the music would have consisted of a series of popular hits in ragtime style; but other theaters used classical music as a way of attracting a particular class of patronage. In either case, music was considered foremost a diversion for the ear that complemented the screen's entertainment for the eye. The musicians sought to engage the audience by offering variety to the program. Consequently, except when music was used as a sound effect, such as to accompany a scene of a dance, coordinating music to the film was not a high priority.

Sound effects, which had already been used to accompany films in vaudeville houses and on lecture programs such as those of Lyman Howe, became

Figure 10-4. *Those Awful Hats* (1909). Notice the piano player in the lower right corner. This film is a humorous short reminding women to remove their hats. It is akin to contemporary trailers reminding us to turn off our cell phones.

more common in theaters specializing in motion picture exhibition as the size of these theaters and their number began to increase around 1908. In a period when demand for films far outstripped supply, theaters across the street from one another might easily end up with the same film on their programs. Along with special musical offerings, the illusion of synchronized sound effects was one way for a theater to distinguish its shows from those of other nearby theaters (see Figure 10-5).

"PLAYING THE PICTURE"

Although nickelodeons included all sorts of pictures of their programs, narrative film was the mainstay. Over the period, these films grew both longer and more complex in their story telling. In 1905, stories rarely filled a single reel; by 1915, the production of feature films of modern length was already becoming standardized. As the films became more ambitious, theater owners realized that audiences seemed more engaged when music and sound seemed attuned to the story. (Another way to put this might be that film viewers were intuitively recognizing—or being encouraged to recognize—the validity and force of Chion's notion of an audiovisual contract.) Although it was admitted that the audience might prefer the sounds of ragtime music in general, this amusement now became something of a problem if it served to distract the audience from the story and made the musician seem indifferent (anempathetic) to the plight of the characters. Simply put, music that did not support the narrative often made it difficult to follow the story, and, consequently, musicians were increasingly urged to "play the picture."

This radical aesthetic change shifted priority from entertaining the audience to accompanying the film: conceptually, music now played to the screen rather than the audience. Previously, attracting notice (drawing the audience in) had been one of the primary goals, but now, to keep that audience, the music could not be allowed to become an obstacle by distracting attention away from the pictures. Over and over again, trade papers criticized musicians for giving concerts rather than "fitting" or "synchronizing" music to the film. As the poem on pp. 255–256 illustrates, the trade papers were merciless in ridiculing those who seemed indifferent to the film, especially those who played nothing but ragtime. Whereas ragtime and popular song had dominated in the early nickelodeon years, light classical and melodramatic mood music were now seen as the creative solution to **playing the pictures**, especially for the multireel dramatic features that became the main attraction by the mid-1910s. This is not to say that popular music disappeared from the program; its use was widespread in comedies, for instance, where musicians frequently drew on the frenetic pace of popular dance music to match the action. Any scene featuring contemporary dancing would almost certainly require popular music, and films set in a modern urban environment were amenable to such treatment as well. Thus, that

Figure 10-5. Ad for Yerkes Sound effects. The three sound effects operators (they were usually called "drummers") are working behind the screen, where their equipment would be out of sight. This was the recommended placement for sound effects. The musicians, by contrast, were almost always placed in the theater, where they would remain, to some extent, visible to the audience. In the 1920s, the bigger theaters placed the musicians on hydraulic lifts that could lower the orchestra into the pit below the sightline for screening the film but also raise them to stage level for highlighted performance opportunities such as the overture.

variety of musical expression that we characterized early on in this book with the assertion that "film music is any music used in a film" can be seen to have been a characteristic trait of commercial film exhibition from the beginning.

Lizzie plays at the nickelo—
Plays for the moving picture show,
All the time her fingers go
With an endless whirl and a rhythmic flow
And a ceaseless flitting to and fro;
She fakes and vamps till her hands get cramps
And there is no tune that she does not know;

With a tum-te-tum and an aching thumb
She keeps the time with her chewing gum,
She chews and chaws without a pause,
With a ragtime twist to her busy jaws,
And her fingers fly as the hours go by;
She pounds the keys with a languid ease
Till the folks go home and the pictures cease;

She never halts, it is march and waltz
While her aching thumb to the bass keys vaults;
And the two-step, too, and the song that's new—
The tinkling tune of the summer moon
And the lazy croon of the loving coon
And the air of the song of the throbbing heart
That will tell of two that the world can't part
And is wholly free of the taint of art;

But Lizzie plays like a grim machine,
And she never thinks what the measures mean,
For she's played them oft and the notes don't waft
Any thought to her that is sweet and soft;
There's a wrangling chime as her fingers climb
Up the yellowed keys as she beats the time,
For the show that costs but half-a-dime.
And she chaws and chews as she seems to muse
On the flying film and the flitting views,

And her hands jump here and her hands jump there,
While betimes with one she will fix her hair,
But she keeps right on with the other hand
In a ragtime tune that is simply grand
With its rum-ti-tum as her fingers drum.
And a burst of bass when she whacks her thumb
On the lower keys, and a sudden frown
As she jabs the loud, loud pedal down.

But she wears no smile, for all the while
She chews and chaws in a solemn style—
And at night in sleep all her fingers keep
An unchanging flight as they rise and leap
O'er the counterpane in a wild refrain
Of the tunes she has played with might and main.
And her aching thumb beats a bass tum-tum
While she chaws and chews in her hard-won snooze.
In her dreams her task she still pursues—

Lizzie plays in the nickelo—
Plays for the moving picture show.
                —Wilbur D. Nesbit, "Lizzie Plays for the Pictures" (1911)[3]

Coordinating music and story was by no means a simple task. Some style topics were obvious—soldiers suggested a march, a dance scene suggested a waltz, tango, or one-step—but it was not always so clear what to play in other, less strongly profiled situations, especially as most theaters continued to favor a repertory of popular song where possible. Three methods were tried—using song titles as "links" to film content, classical music for drama, and musical topics and moods borrowed from stage melodrama. As we shall shortly see, the last of these proved most effective—although all three continued as practices into the sound era.

One method was to select music on the basis of appropriate titles. For the film, *Statue Dog* (1910), for example, one writer made the following musical suggestions: "When the title 'A Rah Rah Boy' comes on you play 'He's a College Boy' or 'College Boys,' then comes a title '2 A. M.,' you can play 'We Won't Go Home Until Morning,' and when the title 'Kelly' comes on you can play 'Has Anybody Here Seen Kelly?'"[4] This remained a standard approach to accompany comedies throughout the silent era. It was a different matter with dramas, where such choices often had the unfortunate effect of parody. One trade paper, reasonably enough, was very critical of a pianist's decision to play "No Wedding Bells for Me" to accompany a scene where a man mourned his wife's death.[5] This parodic practice was known as "funning" or "guying" a film and, although common, was generally reproved, because it ran contrary to the intention of the film. More often, however, the problem was that the title in the song seemed irrelevant to the event on screen: playing "Where the Shannon River Flows" when a character named Molly Shannon appeared on screen, for example, made little sense even for those who know the lyrics, because the character and the river have nothing in common. The result of that choice might be confusion because attention would be focused on unimportant details.

Dramas, especially tragedies, and historical pictures posed even more of a challenge to song title accompaniment. In the case of tragedy, the bright, up-tempo sound of ragtime was inappropriate if not outright callous to the sentiment of the sorrowful stories; in the case of a historical setting, the contemporary sound contradicted the image in a way that many found bothersome. Some observers, including musicians, saw such films as opportunities for "bettering" the musical taste of the audience and therefore urged the use of classical music. Generally speaking, then, the music for main features was typically heavier (more classical), as was felt appropriate for dramatic action, but it was also more disjointed because of the increased responsibility to synchronize with the unfolding action.

Besides classical music, stage music based in the melodrama tradition offered another obvious alternative to song titles as a guide to accompaniment choices, and in fact that repertoire would ultimately prove the basis for the dominant practice (or what we referred to as the principle of synchronization in ch. 4). The number of musicians with requisite experience was quite limited in the early 1900s, however, and the exceedingly rapid expansion of the nickelodeons thus insured that the vast majority of theaters would be staffed by musicians with little or no training in theater music. This deficiency was addressed in a number of ways. Beginning in 1909, the Edison company began releasing "musical suggestions" to help pianists and musicians with the difficult job of finding suitable music. Each film was broken down into scenes, with appropriate music listed for each. Table 10-1 gives an example of the Edison *Kinetogram*'s suggestions for *Frankenstein* from March 1910.

Table 10-1 *Frankenstein* (1910). Musical Suggestion from The Edison *Kinetogram*, 15 March 1910 (vol. 2, no. 4). Note in particular how the cue sheet associates music from Weber's *Der Freischutz* with the monster. "Annie Laurie" is likewise connected with the heroine. The way these two themes are used suggests a rudimentary leitmotivic conception. Stage melodramas often followed a similar strategy, and such simple associations of themes with characters remained a common means of devising accompaniments throughout the silent era.

At opening.	Andante ([Balfe] "Then You'll Remember Me")
Till Frankenstein's laboratory.	Moderato ([Rubenstein] "Melody in F")
The monster is forming.	Increasing agitato
Till monster appears over bed.	Dramatic music from [Weber] *Der Freischutz*
Till father and girl in sitting room.	Moderato.
Till Frankenstein returns home.	Andante ([Scott] "Annie Laurie")
Till monster enters Frankenstein's sitting room.	Dramatic (*Der Freischutz*)
Till girl enters with teapot.	Andante ("Annie Laurie")
Till monster comes from behind curtain.	Dramatic (*Der Freischutz*)
Till wedding guests are leaving.	Bridal Chorus from [Wagner] *Lohengrin*
Till monster appears.	Dramatic (*Der Freischutz*)
Till Frankenstein enters.	Agitato
Till monster appears.	Dramatic (*Der Freischutz*)
Till monster vanishes in mirror.	Diminishing Agitato

When trade papers began adding columns on music soon after, cue sheets of this sort featured prominently there as well. Although programs on the whole changed too frequently during the nickelodeon period for cue sheets to have practical value on a large scale, they proved pedagogically useful in that they taught players how to think of music in terms of dramatic classification, that is, in terms of the style topics or musical "moods" that we discussed at some length in chapter 8. In particular, these cue sheets frequently used terms such as *hurry, lively, plaintive,* and so forth, which alerted musicians not trained in the stage tradition to the existence of this sort of functional music, and by extension how to recognize these functions in music not specifically written for the stage. Regular tempo indications likewise carried melodramatic conventions. In the *Frankenstein* cue sheet, for instance, "moderato" and "andante" suggest functions of "neutral" music and "heroine" (or "love theme") respectively; as we have seen, these are common tempo designations for these functions. So among other things the cue sheet for the 1910 *Frankenstein* tells us that Rubinstein's Melody in F can be construed as a species of neutral music. Similarly, many allegros could be substituted for a hurry—indeed, sometimes a hurry was simply listed as an allegro on a cue sheet.

By necessity, the musical suggestions tended to be rather general, focusing on broad functional categories, or naming extremely well-known exemplars (Liszt's "Liebestraum," for instance). The point of these suggestions was not to insist that other musicians follow them slavishly; rather the idea was that the individual musician could use them as a general guide, substituting suitable numbers from his or her own library for the sake of variety, taste, or accessibility. Clearly, this system required that players have a well-rounded library catalogued by dramatic function. Around 1910, one writer offered the following advice for compiling such a library:

> A few marches and waltzes, though these are indispensable, are not sufficient. Long *andantes* such as [Schumann's] "Traumerei," [Lange's] "Flower Song," [Braga's] "Angel's Serenade" and the like are useful. The intermezzo, valse lento and gavottes make convenient "fill-ins" where the scene is neutral yet the general character of the picture is subdued or pathetic. Religious music, national airs (of different countries), Oriental music and dances are frequently called for. Popular songs are useful, especially in sentimental pictures and comedies. . . . Your library should also include some melodramatic music, such as mysterious, *agitato*, "Hurrys" for combats, storms, fire scenes, etc.[6]

The size and refinement of an adequate library grew quickly. About this same time, music written specifically for use in movie theaters began appearing, as did catalogues of pre-existing music, much of it from the standard classical repertory, organized according to dramatic function (we saw examples of such anthologies and catalogues from the 1920s in ch. 8).

Playing the picture usually meant using a compilation of pieces. Musicians favored music that was sectional, with frequent cadence articulations, and amenable to repetition of sections. This form was preferred because it allowed the music to be adapted more easily to the varying length of film sequences. Most music composed for silent film was structured in this way. Figure 10-6 is an example of a hurry from 1913. By referring again to chapter 5, you will note that the music chosen by Martin Marks to accompany *Lady Windermere's Fan* (1925) has these design properties, as well.

Some players favored improvisation to playing from score, in part because it offered obvious advantages in terms of matching music to the scene. At the same time, improvisational skills were not easily acquired. Some theaters also preferred performances of classical music because it helped to draw a particular kind of audience; improvisation, by contrast, lacked the same force of cultural prestige. Most players had a repertory of memorized music they could draw on—and more easily modify—when they needed careful coordination with the picture. In practice, improvisers frequently quoted folk tunes, national airs, and similar familiar works, whereas those playing from score limited themselves to improvising transitions from one piece to the next.

The job of "playing the picture" was a strenuous one. Programs rarely stayed longer than a week. In smaller theaters, the entire program was commonly changed daily to encourage—and reap the profits of—habitual patronage. The standard program during the period was three reels of film, an illustrated song or two, and perhaps a vaudeville act, which required music to cover entrance and exit even in those cases where the act itself did not need support from the theater musician(s). The piano player was expected to play as necessary for the film, the songs, and the acts, to provide entrance and exit music between the shows, and even to have music ready to dissipate audience panic in case of an incident (fires were a common occurrence in theaters at the time, and nickelodeons were particularly susceptible to panics because of highly flammable nitrate film stock as well as narrow aisles and inadequate exits).

Throughout this era, musicians complained bitterly that they did not have sufficient time to prepare the shows, that they would only infrequently have an opportunity to screen the program before they had to play it, and that consequently requiring them to play the picture in anything but the most rudimentary fashion was simply demanding the impossible. The following account from 1914 illustrates how a typical small-town program was put together.

> We try to "play to the picture" so far as we are able and manage to play a pretty fair class of music as well. But it is a pretty hard matter sometimes to fit the picture as we know it should be done, for the reason that there is so little time. Our house gives evening shows only. Four reels—usually three shows nightly. Change the bill every day. The first show we "dope out" the

Figure 10-6. J. S. Zamecnik, "Hurry Music." This is a typical piece of cinema music from 1913. Note that the music is modular, which gives it great flexibility in terms of how it might be performed. It not only contains an opening repeat and reprise (*D. C.* means "go back to the beginning") but also a number of other internal stopping points (cadences), which are indicated by the arrows. These are places a pianist might easily use to jump to a different piece when a scene changed—or the pianist might play through the piece (or one of its sections) more than once for added length. Most music written for the silent cinema was composed with this sort of modular structure to allow for easier synchronization with the action.

music—roughly of course, that is more in the nature of a rehearsal than any-thing else. The second show is played just about as we first laid it out. The third show we smooth up the rough spots—and then it is time to go home. Just about the time we are ready to play the picture the way we think it ought to be played, it is time to quit.[7]

As film companies began shifting toward the long multireel feature, the situation grew worse, as the practice of a daily change remained in place in most small theaters but the film program seemed to grow ever longer. Depending on the venue, the singer was displaced by extra reels of film, by vaudeville, or by intricate stage shows, and the whole program grew steadily in length toward the 2- to 2½-hr standard of the picture palace era.

SPECIAL SCORES

Throughout the period when the nickelodeon dominated film exhibition, decisions about music and sound were in the hands of the theater owners and staff, rather than the studios. Nevertheless, the studios recognized the importance of the accompaniment, and the dissemination of cue sheets was one way they attempted to influence how their films were presented. Some film companies went a step further and even tried distributing music along with the films. In 1908, Camille Saint-Saëns composed an intricate score to Societé Film d'Art's *L'Assassinat du duc de Guise*. Its premiere in Paris anticipated the careful, fully worked out scores of the 1920s, and the original performance itself followed Wagner's custom in concealing the orchestra from view, a device that deluxe picture palaces would attempt to imitate in the 1920s. The precedent of the Saint-Saëns score had no direct impact on American exhibition practice, however, as, for unknown reasons, the film circulated without the score in the United States. More typical was the Kalem studio's experiments, beginning in 1911, with the regular release of what came to be known as "**special scores**" composed for its major films. These were modest piano scores of discrete pieces; the effect was similar in many respects to an accompaniment based on a cue sheet.

Special scores never became the dominant means of providing films with music during the silent era, as they posed a number of difficulties to theaters. Three sorts of challenges were particularly significant. First, the musical ensembles of nickelodeons were by no means standard. Even in those places dedicated to playing the picture, one theater might have only a pianist, whereas another had an orchestra—and the music would have to be quickly adaptable to any group. Second, censorship was not uniform across the nation, meaning that scenes might have to be omitted in some locales. Scores would have to be modified accordingly. Finally, as mentioned earlier, rehearsal time was practically non-existent during the nickelodeon period. It was far easier for musicians to work with pieces in their own library than to learn music that they

Figure 10-7. Sheet music for Joseph Carl Breil's "Perfect Song." This is the leitmotif Breil composed as the love the theme for Elsie and Ben. It proved to be a significant hit and is an early example of music being used as a source of ancillary income (note that the music is copyright by David W. Griffith Corporation). As the cover indicates, the piece was available in six separate arrangements: song, piano solo, cello and piano, small orchestra and piano, large orchestra and piano and band. The song would later be resurrected to serve as the theme for the immensely popular *Amos 'n' Andy* show in the late 1920s.

would be able to use only for a single film; this would particularly be the case for any theater working with a daily change of program.

Toward the end of the nickelodeon period, long, multireel features began to appear regularly. These films were for the most part not distributed through nickelodeons, however: they were more likely to be treated as road shows to be played in legitimate or standard theaters with larger orchestras, special scores, and prices scaled according to the venue. This was the case, for instance, with *The Birth of a Nation* (1915). Unlike the intense pressure on musicians in the nickelodeons, the road show offered, from the musicians' point of view, a more familiar and amenable mode of work, very similar to a theatrical show or opera. Joseph Carl Breil's score for *The Birth of a Nation* set the standard for this sort of production. The music is partly original and partly compiled, and the whole is carefully coordinated with the film. Breil borrowed traditional songs and marches but also such orchestral excerpts as Weber's *Freischütz* Overture and Wagner's "Ride of the Valkyries." Breil himself considered the score Wagnerian because he composed a number of themes that he used as leitmotifs for many of the characters. The musical roots of Breil's themes, however, often lay closer to popular song than classical music or melodrama. Indeed, as Figure 10-7 shows, his love theme was close enough to a sentimental ballad that it was fit with lyrics and became a hit as "The Perfect Song." A number of the other cues in Breil's score were also drawn from such popular song genres as waltzes and tangos.

The Picture Palace

STRATIFICATION OF EXHIBITION

When most of us think of silent-film exhibition, we probably have in mind the picture palace—a large well-appointed theater with a large orchestra and "mighty Wurlitzer." In fact, these venues dominated exhibition only in major metropolitan areas, and many of the largest and most famous theaters did not appear until the very end of the silent era, when most were built, paradoxically enough, already wired for sound. Although by the late 1920s picture palaces were responsible for capturing the majority of the revenues for film exhibition, the absolute number of deluxe theaters was quite small compared to the vast number of smaller, more modest theaters located in outlying neighborhoods and small towns. In these venues many of the exhibition practices of the nickelodeon, with at best a small "orchestra" of a handful of players or perhaps nothing more than a phonograph, continued well into the 1920s. Something along the line of deluxe performance was achieved by the occasional employment of small-time vaudeville acts, in addition. The relatively small size (and modest revenues) of such theaters, however, made actual deluxe performance prohibitively expensive. The result was that neighborhood and, even more so, rural theaters were hardly able to compete effectively with large downtown theaters for the middle-class audience that was the key to leveraging large profits.

Exhibition practices thus became more and more stratified as the size of the theater—and so also the expenses that it could support—increased rapidly through the 1920s. This trend toward increasing largess of the deluxe theaters culminated in the 5,920 seat Roxy Theatre in New York, run by its namesake, Samuel L. Rothafel; this included among its musical features fourteen grand pianos spread throughout the building and three separate organs: a massive theater organ and two smaller organs to provide music in the lobbies and foyers. The main theater organ had three separate consoles, which would appear to rise spectacularly out of the abyss of the orchestra pit on hydraulic lifts. Radio City Music Hall, another theater built to the specifications of Rothafel, was in many respects the swansong of the picture palace era, as the conversion to mechanical sound and the upheaval of the Great Depression made the economics of live acts in large movie theaters less and less tenable.

THE SHOW

Modeled on high-class vaudeville houses, the picture palace began emerging around 1910, at the same time that "playing the pictures" gained ascendancy. During the first half of the 1910s, theaters routinely changed back and forth between featuring vaudeville and film exhibition as the primary attraction; and it was out of this intersection that the picture palace aesthetic, which combined film and live performance, was born.

If the illustrated song had largely disappeared as an expected part of exhibition practice with the arrival of the multireel feature and a second projector, live performance—really an extension of the vaudeville aesthetic—continued to dominate in that the "show" was often considered more important than the picture. The firm of Balaban and Katz, which would grow from a modest set of theaters in 1916 into a widely imitated large chain of picture palaces that formed the basis of Paramount Publix in 1925, established the high reputation of its theaters through the production of elaborate shows. Prior to its merger with Lasky-Famous Players (Paramount), Balaban and Katz was unaffiliated with any of the major film production companies, and because it could not guarantee the quality of the pictures in its theaters, the firm devised an exhibition strategy that minimized the importance of any particular film. In a Balaban and Katz theater, it was not the picture per se, but the distinctiveness of the "show"—which included the picture only as a part in the whole. The audience attended for the entire experience—in addition to the performances, the look of the façade and marquee, the appointments of the lobby and auditorium, and the smart discipline of the ushers and other theater personnel were all crucial components of the "show." (Table 10-2 is a section of the Publix Theaters training manual applying to the music department.)

Table 10-2 The rules of conduct for orchestra members from the *Manual of Instructions and Information for Publix Theatres Employees* (1926).

Music Department

Orchestra

Members of the orchestra are under the direct supervision of the Orchestra Contractor who is held responsible for the conduct of the personnel. In most cases the Conductor or Orchestra manager is the Contractor.

1. All conversation in the orchestra pit is forbidden.
2. No musician is expected to be looking at the stage or screen at any time while the orchestra is playing.
3. Members of the orchestra are expected to refrain from all noise-making during the performance.
4. The chewing of gum, tobacco, or smoking while in the pit will not be tolerated.
5. No pencil other than a soft black lead pencil will be used for marking music.
6. A prompt response to the bell for rehearsals or performance is expected from each member of the orchestra.
7. When the tuning bell is struck, get the pitch immediately, preluding or improvising is absolutely forbidden.
8. Every member of the orchestra must be ready to play when the performance or rehearsal is called. All tuning or fixing of instruments must be done before this period. This applies especially to wcod wind players and to string players.
9. No one is to leave the orchestra pit or rehearsal room during a performance or rehearsal without obtaining the permission of the Conductor.
10. In entering and leaving the pit be exceptionally careful to prevent the creating of any noise or unnecessary disturbance.

The model for Balaban and Katz's success was Samuel L. Rothafel (Figure 10-8), better known simply as "Roxy," who had in many respects pioneered this approach while managing a series of theaters in New York during the 1910s, most notably The Strand, the Rivoli, and Rialti. Among other things, Roxy emphasized lush interior decoration of both theater and lobby space, a trained, uniformed, and courteous staff, and many amenities, all of which were specifically designed to make the spectator feel pampered. Already in 1910, even before moving to New York, he had declared:

> The secret of the successful motion picture theatre of the future will be the ability of the management to make the people forget that they are witnessing a motion picture, to make them forget that they only paid you five or ten cents to witness the performance.[8]

Roxy believed that a proper musical atmosphere was the key to such "forgetting," and thus to the success of any show. He therefore continually improved

Figure 10-8. Samuel L. Rothafel, better known as "Roxy."

his theaters by investing first and foremost in music, adding elaborate theater organs, hiring top-flight musicians, and increasing the size of the orchestra to the limits of what theater attendance could support. (Both the Roxy Theatre and Radio City Music Hall were his.) The idea was to be able to present a musical program that could serve as a feature in its own right. Roxy was known particularly for his staging of spectacular finales, what became known as the "Roxy finish."

Although, strictly speaking, the central piece of such exhibition remained the long feature, the "show" was based around a program where that feature was balanced by live performance and shorter films. The basic aesthetic of the program was variety, consistent with the idea of the elaborate and popular revues of impresarios such as Florenz Ziegfeld. The programs often, although not always, followed a theme drawn from the feature (see Figure 10-9). A typical program would consist of an overture, the feature, several short films (usually including a comedy and a newsreel), and a variety of live performances.

MUSIC AND SOUND PRODUCTION IN THE PICTURE PALACE

Music was fundamental to the picture palace, perhaps more so than even the film itself. For music was present not only for the film: it also accompanied most of the live acts and often served as an act in its own right. The importance of music can be measured in its cost to the theater: in the late 1920s theaters expected expenses for musicians' salaries alone to equal that of the film service.

Music featured prominently in the architecture of the theaters as well. The pit was a major architectural consideration, and by the 1920s the pits were generally placed on hydraulic lifts, which would allow the orchestra to be raised or lowered depending on the portion of the program—stage level for the overture, below eye level for the film, and so forth. Organ consoles—often there were multiple consoles—were treated similarly. One common theatrical trick was to have the "Mighty Wurlitzer" emerge from the depths of the pit, with lighting effects adding to the spectacle. These organs were often exceptionally large and were equipped not only with standard organ stops but a whole battery of sound effects as well. Beyond the music in the auditorium, some theaters had pianos or occasionally even a small organ installed in the lobby to provide music for patrons as they waited to be seated.

Because of the importance of music to the show, the position of music director was a powerful one in the picture palace, perhaps more powerful than any other than the general manager. Indeed, music directors frequently served as managers. Hugo Riesenfeld, for instance, was in charge not only of the music but also of general operations of the Rialto, the Rivoli, and the Criterion in New York. Often, the conductor had final authority over projection speed—the podium was usually equipped with a signal to the booth that allowed the conductor to call for a change in projection speed—and could even mandate editing of the film to insure proper synchronization between music and film.

The music director oversaw the range of musical activities in the theater. These activities included: rehearsing, acquiring and cataloguing music, fitting music to the film, laying out the musical portion of the program in consultation with the general manager, hiring musicians, assistant conductors, and librarians. The size of the music staff was dependent on the size and nature of the theater. In the most prestigious theaters, the staff consisted of multiple assistant conductors, arrangers, organists, librarians, and the musicians of a large symphony orchestra.

FITTING THE PICTURE

Much as was the case in the nickelodeon period, compilations and improvisation were by far more common than original scores, and these different approaches often shared the same program, depending on whether the orchestra or the organist was playing. In general, an organist would play the lunch, dinner, and late night show. Even during the regular shows, the organist would assume duties during the union-mandated break times. Not only would the orchestra and organist split duty over the various shorts (comedy, newsreels, etc.), but quite often they would share responsibility for scoring the feature as well. One common division of labor was having the orchestra begin and end the film but take a 30-min break in the middle where the organ would assume the duties of accompanying.

The basic principles of accompanying films with compilations or improvisation did not change markedly from the nickelodeon era. Compilations continued to enjoy the advantages of cultural prestige, a more predictable accompaniment not dependent on immediate inspiration, and a wider range of coloristic possibilities (although large theater organs could by the 1920s rival and in some ways even surpass the orchestra in this respect). Improvisation, by contrast, promised the ability to match action far more precisely than an orchestra playing a compiled score could.

Quite apart from differences in the precision of synchronization, the compilation and improvisation methods addressed the film with somewhat different aesthetic emphases. Because a compilation score was assembled from pre-existing music, the chance of consistently matching action at a close level of detail was remote; consequently, pieces were chosen primarily on the basis of the appropriateness of the mood for that particular sequence. Following the fluctuation of these moods was the aesthetic foundation of the compilation score; matching action, especially using thematic variations to underscore changes in the situation of the main character, was the foundation of improvisation. Nevertheless, in practice, improvisation and compilation did not lead to radically different results. The musical language of both was derived from

a | b

Figure 10-9. (a) Program for the Egyptian Theatre's presentation of *The Big Parade* (1925). Although the film had a special score prepared by William Axt and David Mendoza, Sid Grauman, like many silent-film impresarios, preferred to have a score put together by his theater's musical staff. Grauman, like Roxy, was renowned for his elaborate programs, and Grauman was especially known for his extended prologues. This one, as was usually the case for Grauman, was linked topically to the film. The two attached ticket stubs indicate the theater used reserved seating much like live theater. (b) Program for Loew's State Theatre in Eureka, California. The program here is much more modest than the Egyptian's, and there is a far greater proportion of film on the program—two newsreels and a short (two-reel) comedy in addition to the feature. Fanchon and Marco was a production company that supplied dance acts to vaudeville and movie theaters, particularly on the West Coast.

popular song, waltzes, marches, melodramatic, and other incidental music. In the case of the compilation score, the choice of mood was most often based on considerations of character; and, in the case of improvisation, one of the major considerations in working out a variation was fitting the theme to the proper mood.

By the 1920s, compilation had become a fine art, and a whole industry had developed around the practice. An ever increasing amount of "photoplay" music was commissioned and published in appropriately catalogued collections and series (see Figure 10-10; also recall the facsimile from Rapee's *Encyclopedia* in ch. 8). The major music publishers produced catalogues of their music—not just "photoplay" music—organized by appropriate moods.

In conjunction with the studios, those same publishers offered cue sheets, which suggested appropriate music from that particular publisher's catalogue. These cue sheets would be distributed with the picture or published in various trade papers and were the primary way studios attempted to assert some control over the musical accompaniment. Figure 10-11 is the first page of a cue sheet for *Coney Island* (1928). In this case, the film's distributor, FBO, which sent films mainly to unaffiliated theaters in the midwestern United States, was responsible for the cue sheet. Note the mix of popular songs and characteristic pieces: a new foxtrot by Irving Berlin (1), a "galop" (an old dance) that could

THE SYNCHRONIZER
By M. L. Lake

SIX SYNCHRONIZING SUITES FOR MOTION PICTURE SETTINGS IN LOOSE LEAF FORM
A complete library of Incidental Music in six volumes. Each Suite provides all the necessary material for any given picture. Individual movements of any Suite may be used independently for any motion picture situation.

THE PLAN OF THE SYNCHRONIZER

Suite No. 1. General Use	Suite No. 4. Spanish-Mexican	**EACH OF WHICH CONTAIN**
Suite No. 2. General Use	Suite No. 5. General Use	**FIVE MOTIFS AS FOLLOWS:**
Suite No. 3. Oriental-Indian	Suite No. 6. General Use	

MAJOR LOVE MOTIF
To announce the entrance of the Heroine or Hero; also to predominate in normal (or joyous) scenes wherein these characters appear.

MINOR LOVE MOTIF
To announce the entrance of the Heroine or Hero; to predominate in pathetic scenes wherein these characters appear.

SINISTER MOTIF
To announce the entrance of the "Heavy" (Villain).

AGITATO (based on Sinister Motif)
To predominate in scenes wherein the Heavy appears.

HURRY OR FURIOSO (based on Love and Sinister Motif)
To predominate in scenes wherein the Heavy and the Heroine or Hero appear.

PRICE OF EACH SUITE: Piano Part, 40c; All Other Parts, 20c Each; Piano Solo, 75c

Figure 10-10. Ad (from the 1920s) for music especially composed to be used in silent-film performances. Each suite not only presented the basic motifs as themes but also developed them into a hurries, agitatos, and pieces of other melodramatic function. This would allow the music director to create a score that seemed better integrated musically. The music for any one of these suites would be sufficient to accommodate the needs of most feature films of its type.

have been called a hurry or comic hurry (2), an agitato (3), a one-step (a more rapid late 19th-century dance that could also be a hurry), a "grotesque" or mysterioso also marked as a theme (5), a schottische (old-fashioned dance that could be "comic") (6), the love theme, a waltz and also a recently copyrighted song (7), and another light comic cue (8).

The *Coney Island* cue sheet is more complex than most, but with its recently copyrighted Irving Berlin numbers, it does participate in one of the music promotion practices common in this period: the "theme song," an early attempt to realize synergies between the film and music industries. In this practice, the compiler of the cue sheet suggested a theme, sometimes something classical, sometimes an original theme written specifically for the film. If a theme proved popular, it might be fitted with lyrics and sold as sheet music that made an explicit tie-in to the film.

Tensions between the music and film industries in the late 1910s and 1920s prevented full exploitation of the potential synergies. The American Society of Composers, Authors and Publishers (ASCAP) had won a ruling in 1917 that required theaters to pay a "music tax" if they wanted to use music by any of its members—and these included the best known song composers of the day, such as Irving Berlin and Victor Herbert. Theaters could avoid the tax by using music that was out of copyright or by buying music from publishers who sold music with performance rights included. The ASCAP "tax" therefore prevented many theaters from using music specifically associated with the film. Nevertheless, the financial success of the title song to *Mickey* in 1918 suggested that linking film and popular music systematically could be very profitable, and many songs from the time featured covers with pictures of stars or a scene from the film as a selling point (see Figure 10-12). In the 1920s, most film studios purchased chains of theaters to serve as guaranteed exhibition outlets for their films, and one way they managed the risk of this so-called "vertical integration" of their business was to acquire music publishers so that they would have better control of the music as well. It was at this point, toward the end of the silent era, that theme songs proved immensely profitable. Erno Rapee's "Charmaine" from *What Price Glory?* (1926) sold well over a million copies, as did his theme for *Seventh Heaven* (1927).

Cue sheets were often less than optimal: compilers usually worked for music publishers and their suggestions reflected this fact. Many complained that the cue sheets often were nothing but a form of advertisement (the *Coney Island* cue sheet raises that suspicion). Also, especially in the early years, compilers sometimes worked without having had a chance to see the film, meaning they had to rely on timings and a synopsis provided by the studio. Given that the interest of the compiler was not always making the best accompaniment for the film, it is hardly surprising that many theaters simply disregarded the suggestions, although the music directors probably found the timings useful as a starting point.

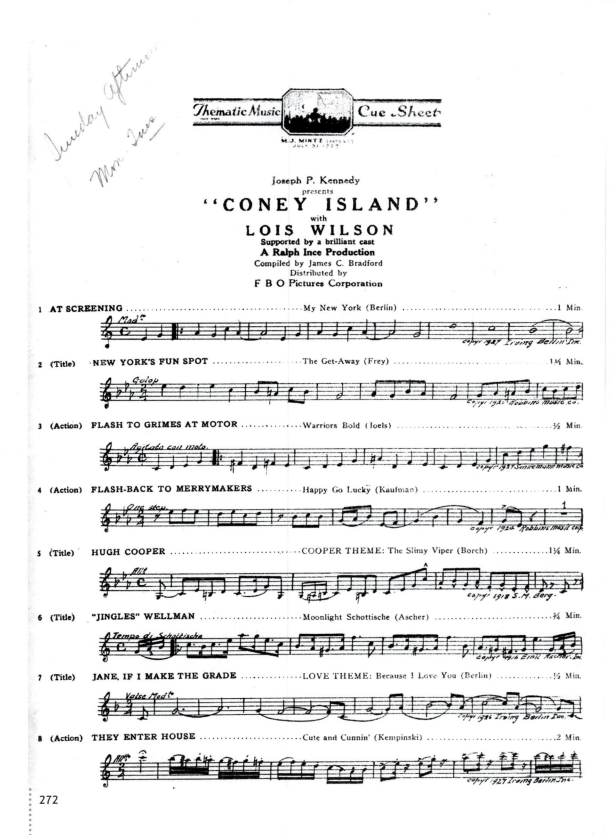

In the larger theaters, the music staff took great pride in assembling accompaniments. This was an arduous task. Rapee was Rothafel's music director at the Capitol, the Roxy, and at Radio City Music Hall, and he proposed that creating an accompaniment should begin with a simple analysis. "Firstly—determine the geographic and national atmosphere of your picture,—secondly—embody everyone of your important characters with a theme. Undoubtedly there will be a Love Theme and most likely there will be a theme for the Villain."[9] (Recall that this was exactly the case in the *Coney Island* cue sheet.) The staff would then go painstakingly through the film with the timings. For each sequence, among other things they would consider the mood, the length, what appropriate music the theater had in its library, and how recently that music had been used. Riesenfeld made the following observation about choosing music.

> There are millions of ways of selecting music to serve as accompaniment for a picture, but there are only two ways that a good musician would choose. One is to select beautiful music that is appropriate for the scenes of the picture, and the good musician, inexperienced in motion picture presentation would undoubtedly follow this course. The second course, and the one that requires the hardest work, is to select music such as would be chosen in the first mentioned way, but with an ear to its subjugation. There may be half a hundred waltzes that would go prettily with certain scenes, but the experienced scorer of motion pictures will, after listening to the piece, know whether it is too striking—or even too beautiful.[10]

Once selected, the pieces would be run against the film, the speed of which could be increased or decreased to make the musical selection fit better. In some circumstances, the film might even be re-cut to better fit the musical selection. Someone from the staff would be assigned to write short transitional passages where needed; occasionally new music might be composed if nothing appropriate could be found in the library. All of this was then collated into a "score" that could easily exceed one hundred pieces for a feature film.

SPECIAL SCORES IN THE 1920s

By the 1920s, any film with ambition—one where an extended run was expected or the film was to be distributed through a road show—would likely have a commissioned score of some sort. Fully original scores were relatively rare until the coming of sound. Some notable examples of original scores include Victor Herbert's *The Fall of a Nation* (1916), Mortimer Wilson's *Thief of*

Figure 10-11. The first page of a studio-issued cue sheet for *Coney Island*. Note that someone (music director, pianist, or organist) has marked dates of performance in pencil at the upper left.

Figure 10-12. Hugo Riesenfeld was hired by Rothafel to conduct the Rialto orchestra. When Rothafel left to take over the Capitol Theatre, Riesenfeld assumed Rothafel's role as general manager of the theater as well as the Rivoli. Later he added the Criterion. Riesenfeld provided scores, usually a combination of compilation and original composition, for a number of major films, including *The Covered Wagon* (1923) and *Sunrise* (1927). His score for *Covered Wagon* was recorded and distributed using the Phonofilm process; his score for *Sunrise* was the first synchronized score released using the Fox Movietone process. With the coming of sound, Riesenfeld went to Hollywood as music director of United Artists.

Bagdad (1924), Edmund Meisel's *Battleship Potemkin* (1925), William Axt's *La Boheme* (1926). Most scores, however, continued to be at least partially compiled. This was true even of such spectacles as *The Big Parade, Ben-Hur: A Tale of the Christ* (1925), and *Wings* (1927). The special scores were used when the film was exhibited in a road show, and they were available to those theaters who wanted to rent them through syndication. In addition, individual chains often circulated scores through their theaters. All of this is to say that, although studios may have gone to the expense of commissioning a special score, the existence of that score in itself could not guarantee anything like a standardized exhibition of the film.

ROAD SHOWS

Only films that were distributed exclusively through road show engagements that reproduced all aspects of a production, as was the case with *The Big Parade* (which followed the New York City Astor Theatre production) and *Ben-Hur* (the Embassy), could be sure of having a relatively uniform exhibition. Road shows had been used regularly for film exhibition since the mid-1910s, when the enormous success of *The Birth of a Nation* had ensured that the musical score became a fixed part of the production. Only a handful of pictures per year went on the road, however, in large part because a successful road show required a large theater where the film could remain for an extended run. That is to say, rather than the common movie theater practice of continuous performance and general admission, road shows ran by the principles of regular theater with reserved seating and typically two shows per day. The prices were on par with, and often exceeded those of, legitimate theater. This meant that road shows were geographically restricted to large urban centers. Moreover, each urban center had only a small number of theaters appropriate for producing such shows, a fact that placed an absolute limit on the number of films that could be exhibited through road shows at any one time. If theaters were not available when a film was ready for distribution, the film would either have to wait or go immediately into regular release. Even films exhibited first through road shows would eventually go through a regular release, and at that time they were unlikely to be accompanied by their original score.

MUSIC ON THE SET

Music was often used as part of film production during the silent era. Many actors and directors felt that performance before the camera improved with music that set a proper mood. The practice has a long history. Already in 1907, one trade paper reported

> In order to add to the reality of the moving pictures, music is always played while the actors pose. A very fine phonograph is one of the important

properties of the factory. When there is a picture where quick motion is needed, a lively record is played by the phonograph; where pathos or emotion is to be expressed, some of the plaintive music from [Bizet's] Carmen or [Grieg's] Peer Gynt is used; and where there is a dream scene mysterious music is played. It is wonderful help to the actors in throwing themselves into the part.[11]

The use of music on the set grew more and more common over the course of the silent era, and by the 1920s it was standard practice. The phonograph recordings were replaced by live musicians, who played more or less the same sort of mood music that patrons would hear in the theater. Generally, these ensembles were small, consisting of a violinist or pianist, say, but for large-budget pictures it was not unheard of to have a much larger ensemble; Cecil B. DeMille, for instance, reportedly hired a thirty-piece orchestra to provide military music during the filming of the Exodus scene in *The Ten Commandments* (1923). Although miniscule in comparison to music expenses at theaters, the cost for studio music was not small. In 1927, MGM spent more than $50,000 for musicians on the set; by way of comparison, this was roughly equivalent to the yearly cost of a modest sized orchestra (16 players) or the Roxy's live entertainment budget for one week (which included the orchestra, organists, corps de ballet, and Roxyettes, as well as other contract soloists and headliners).

Summary

In this chapter we offered a historical narrative for sound and music in the early decades of cinema, roughly 1890 to 1930, tracing a path from the earliest stages through the **nickelodeon** to standardization of exhibition practices in the 1920s. Early on, the exhibition venues varied widely and sound practices varied with them. After about 1905, the nickelodeons—storefront film theaters—came to dominate exhibition, and with them a gradual process began that tended toward a common sound practice for feature film presentation. (This common practice was only achieved in the sound-film era.) Films were part of a program that featured considerable amounts of live musical performance as well. Once feature films expanded to four reels or more (about 1915), the demand for music that was appropriate to the picture's character and mood became stronger. Feature films and theaters expanded dramatically thereafter, and in larger cities theaters became "picture palaces" that could often marshall considerable resources to music (as well as effects).

The music played during a film showing varied widely, from popular songs and ragtime early on, to a complex mixture of classical music, popular and traditional song, and dance music.

A Note on the Music for Silent-Film Releases to VHS and DVD

At least as long ago as Morodor's 1984 electronic score for *Metropolis* (1927), silent films have been released in VHS or DVD with newly composed accompaniments. Some of these have been sensitive to historical styles and practices of silent-film exhibition, but many have not. In principle there is nothing wrong with a newly composed score that uses musical styles not typical of the first quarter of the 20th century, but for the purposes of a course based on this textbook, it will be more useful to study films with scores that were actually composed for the film or that are newly composed and fit the era. We highly recommend the series *Treasures from American Film Archives* (2000–2009), which now has four multi-DVD volumes: "Treasures from American Film Archives" (2000), "More Treasures from American Film Archives: 50 Films, 1894–1931" (2004), "Treasures III: Social Issues in American Film, 1900–1934" (2007), and the recently released "Treasures from American Film Archives, Avant Garde" (2009). All accompaniments in the first volume are by pianist Martin Marks, who is also the music curator for the other volumes, which make use of a wider range of instrumental groups. (*Lady Windermere's Fan* (1925) is on "More Treasures.") In the 1980s and early 1990s, Carl Davis also composed a series of orchestral scores for well-known silent films. Where they are still available, we recommend *A Woman of Affairs* (1928), *The Crowd* (1928), *Napoléon* (1927), *Ben-Hur: A Tale of the Christ*, *The Phantom of the Opera* (1925), *Greed* (1924), *The Thief of Bagdad*, and *Intolerance* (1916).

The Transition to Sound Film (1926–1932)

Introduction

As we have seen, sound and music were both very much involved in the performance practices of the silent-film era. By the early 1930s, however, the program of an American movie theater was dominated by film projection, not by performances, and almost all of those films—and certainly all features—included a recorded and edited optical sound track. The path from one film exhibition culture to another was a long one, and it started as soon as the moving picture was invented. This chapter traces that history but focuses on the final segment, the transition to the sound film, a period that ends in 1932 as the basic procedures for sound film began to codify after the development of a reliable method of rerecording, an advance that allowed much work on the sound track to be moved out of production and into the postproduction phase of filmmaking.

Issues of Technology and Economics

Sound synchronization was attempted almost from the time Thomas Edison invented the apparatus for taking moving pictures. Indeed, Edison's guiding idea from the start was to combine film with the phonograph—he conceived his Kinetograph as doing for the eye what the phonograph did for the ear. He wanted to bring great performers and artistic works to those who could not afford to attend concerts or who lived too far away from urban centers. His specific stated goal—to distribute grand opera to the masses—very much embodied the American ethos of cultural uplift of one's class position through education and the arts. William K. L. Dickson, Edison's assistant on the **kinetoscope**, did in fact manage to produce a number of short experimental films with synchronized sound as early as 1895. A screen grab of one of these films is shown in Figure 11-1. Some models of Edison's original peepshow-style Kinetoscope were also outfitted with headphones, although these pictures were not shot as synchronized sound films: they were coupled with a cylinder having more or less appropriate music (Figure 11-2).

Over the years a number of schemes were proposed to provide what was portrayed at the time as "the missing voice" of the picture. Devices such as the Cameraphone, the Picturephone, the Cameragraph, the Faceagraph, the Auxetophone, the Theatrephone, the Biographon, the Synchronoscope, the Cinephone, and so forth, all promised a means of synchronizing film and phonograph. The first really serviceable system of mechanically synchronized sound was the **Gaumont Chronophone**, introduced in 1902 and frequently exhibited as a novelty in vaudeville houses beginning around 1905 before it moved into

Figure 11-1. *Dickson Experimental Sound Film* (c. 1894). W. K. L. Dickson, Edison's main assistant in developing the motion picture camera, plays a selection from Jean Robert Planquette's opera, *The Chimes at Midnight*, on the violin while two lab assistants dance. The need to have the recording horn close to the sound source was one of the obstacles to synchronized sound film. One common solution was to prerecord the sound and then perform the action for the camera to playback. The horn is visible in this film because it was never intended for commercial release. The film was restored by Walter Murch and Richard Schmidlin.

Figure 11-2. The Edison Kinetophone was a Kinetoscope outfitted with a phonograph and headphones.

the nickelodeons around 1908. The Chronophone had limited success in the United States but had a longer run in European countries, especially in France.

As with most early sound synchronization schemes, the Chronophone's most serious defect was not in the synchronization, which a capable operator could master reasonably well, but in amplification. The volume of standard commercial phonographs was insufficient for a theater any larger than the most modest nickelodeon, and the use of compressed air as a device for amplification tended to make the sound excessively tinny. In addition, the frequency response of phonographs of the time was limited, especially in the upper range (sibilants [s-sounds] were a particular problem), which negatively affected the intelligibility of dialogue. Theater acoustics were usually optimized for live musical performance rather than reproduced sound, and this tended to muddy dialogue even further. Still worse, the length of a sound disk (or the cylinder in Edison films) could not be pushed much past 4 min, which meant that a system of dual phonographs needed to be employed for longer films. These, of course, were also susceptible to both mechanical failure and operator error. Finally, it was virtually impossible to edit sound recordings. Invariably recordings were made first and the action was then lip-synced to the recording, a technique that would be rediscovered when the industry turned to sound film on a large scale after 1927, especially for the production numbers of musicals. Therefore it is hardly surprising that most of the sound films in these early years were short musical performances; in the United States, singers from the musical and vaudeville stage predominated.

The failure of the Chronophone in America nevertheless seems to have come about not because of these very real technological limitations, but rather primarily for economic reasons. Apparently, the cost of the special equipment was simply too dear for most theaters, the great majority of which were run on very tight budgets. The sound films ran about twice the price of regular films but the demand for the former was still relatively low. The cost of keeping the films in good repair, which was absolutely essential to effective performance, was also much higher than for regular films. Ultimately, costs were simply too high to make sound synchronization a going proposition for theaters that were small enough for the phonographic sound to be adequate for the space.

Perhaps the most successful early scheme for providing films with speech, especially in the larger theaters, was the so-called "talking picture." This involved placing a troupe of three or four actors behind the screen to speak lines of dialogue and provide sound effects. The sidebar provides one account of how this was done. This method, although popular with audiences at first, suffered from high production, labor and transportation costs because a film would need to be specially edited, the actors rehearsed, and both film and company moved from theater to theater on a circuit. The novelty soon wore off, and the costs, as with the contemporary systems of mechanical synchronization, proved too high to remain viable.

Another major push toward synchronized dialogue occurred in 1913, when Edison introduced a new system of mechanical synchronization that included a number of innovations, such as longer and larger cylinders and improvements in microphone technology that allowed the recording of dialogue and filming at the same time (Figure 11-3). This system was not a success, however, due to inadequate amplification and difficulty in maintaining synchronization, problems that were only compounded by the increasing popularity of multireel features.

SOUND RESEARCH IN THE 1920s

The amplification problem was finally solved by developments in radio, or, specifically, by the technology of the radio tube. Electronic public address systems based on the radio tube were introduced in 1919, but it wasn't until the later 1920s when some further improvements to amplification and loudspeaker technology, along with the public's growing familiarity with amplified sound through radio, set the stage for a successful introduction of sound film. In addition, better sound recording was enabled in the electrical pick-up as the record-

If details and effects are to be brought out in talking pictures, the actors and actresses must use judgment in regard to placing the voices of the character in speaking from the center of the drop. The line should be read directly behind the character that he or she is impersonating. This will apply either to the right or the left of the center. At all times, in talking from behind a drop, try to keep as near to where the character is standing as possible. All letters and titles, before scenes, should be taken out, so that the story will not be told before the actors and actresses have read their lines, as this will have a tendency to kill the dramatic climax. The operator must also be drilled carefully and thoroughly in regard to the running speed of films, of struggles, horses galloping, battles scenes, which must be run very fast, while scenes in offices and homes must be run at a certain speed to bring
(continued)

Figure 11-3. *Nursery Favorites* (1913) was one of the films Edison made using the second version of the Kinetophone. This new effort at sound pictures proved no more profitable than the first. The films suffered from the familiar problems of amplification and synchronization, but the introduction of the long, multireel feature pushed down the demand for other sorts of film-based novelties. When a fire destroyed the studio equipped for making sound pictures in December 1914, Edison chose not to rebuild it. For more than a decade, Edison's failure with the Kinetophone made filmmakers very skeptical about the potential of sound film.

ing industry shifted from the recording horn to the microphone for commercial releases in 1925. Finally, theaters found an incentive for a change-over to sound synchronization in the devastating effect that commercial radio quickly was having on the size of theatrical audiences (the Keith and Orpheum circuit of vaudeville went so far as to ban its performers from appearing on radio for a period in the mid-1920s, a tactic the company would repeat briefly with sound film a few years later). In the mid-1920s, RCA (a subsidiary of General Electric), which owned a number of useful amplification patents from its radio technology, and AT&T, with its work in public address systems, phonograph recording and radio, competed to develop a workable solution to amplification and synchronization. In 1926, the two companies agreed to cross-license their patents for use in amplification. This allowed rapid development of sound-film recording and exhibition technology without fear of a major lawsuit.

Industrial research pursued two basic approaches to sound film: (a) **sound-on-disk** and (b) **sound-on-film**; and it focused in three areas: (a) so-called "nonsynchronous sound" for adding recorded musical accompaniments to features, (b) short features of music and vaudeville, and (c) newsreels. Each of these placed somewhat different demands on technology, but all three required the development of a suitable means of amplifying sound in the large theaters.

Work on nonsynchronous sound centered on increasing the time length available in the recording medium to equal a reel of film and on improving the fidelity of recording and reproducing equipment, particularly with respect to the sound of a full orchestra. Most research on sound film prior to the 1920s had used a sound-on-disk (or, in the case of Edison, sound-on-cylinder) method, but the longest standard commercial phonograph recording format at the time was only about 5 min—less than half the length of the usual 1,000 foot reel of film. This did not prevent theaters from using phonograph records as a substitute for live musicians; many small theaters employed phonographs when musicians were either unavailable (such as on dinner break) or too expensive. The short duration of the recording, however, meant that the records would have to be changed independent of the reels, which made coordination with the image both labor intensive and unreliable. To distribute a recorded score efficiently with a film would require a recording format that matched a reel of film. Although variable in the silent era, average projection speed increased over time and, by the late 1920s, 90 feet per minute (24 frames per second) was considered about normal. At that rate—which became the standard in the sound-film era—a reel of film ran about 11 min. Any sound-on-disk method would need to increase the length of the record accordingly. This could be done by increasing the size of the disk (or cylinder), by increasing the density of the grooves, or by reducing the speed of rotation; each of these posed distinct technological challenges in preserving the quality of the recording.

out the desired effect of the character, and to give the necessary illusion. But many will ask, How can this be brought about? The answer is in rehearsing and drilling the people, not alone by explanation, but by having everyone act the character thoroughly, as if he were appearing on the stage, without being hidden by the drop. As an example, take a woman in tears. She should go through the same action that she would if it were happening to her in real life, using the handkerchief and hands and all gestures that accompany it. Struggles should be gone through in the same manner. To make the effect more complete, the breaking of a glass or the shooting of a revolver or a gun, or slapping the hand on a table to bring out a convincing point in an argument should always be done by the person speaking the line.

—James Clancy
(impresario) (1909)[1]

Sound-on-film, by contrast, was limited in terms of time only by the length of the reel. A sound-on-film technology had been developed around 1905 by Eugene Lauste (a former Edison employee), although it proved infeasible for commercial exploitation at that time. Nevertheless, the minimal restriction on length was attractive especially to those working in radio who were looking for a reliable way to record longer material for broadcast. This was one of the important reasons that Lee de Forest, an early radio pioneer, began working with sound film, but he quickly realized that he could also use his improvements in recording sound on film to make synchronized sound pictures. Developed in conjunction with Theodore Case, de Forest's Phonofilm system (Figure 11-4) was demonstrated in 1923 and placed in limited circulation thereafter. Hugo Riesenfeld was a principal sponsor of de Forest's research and featured Phonofilm frequently at his Rivoli Theatre. Although Phonofilm specialized in short films, de Forest also recorded scores for features such as *The Covered Wagon* (1923) and *Siegfried* (1924), both (not coincidentally) with scores by Riesenfeld. Although de Forest made significant improvements on the sound-on-film process, he never adequately solved the amplification problem. Phonofilm reportedly also suffered from pronounced "wow and flutter," which reflects a basic incompatibility in sound-on-film: whereas projecting the image requires an intermittent action, where the film must start and stop at the projecting head, reproducing sound requires a continuous action, where the film moves past the projecting head at a constant rate.

a | b   **Figure 11-4.** Phonofilm produced primarily short films of such musical and vaudeville acts as (a) Sissle and Blake but also included films of famous people such as this one of (b) President Coolidge (1924). This latter film, the first sound picture of a U.S. President, was heavily promoted, but de Forest neglected to credit Case's contribution to the device. Case consequently withdrew from the partnership and worked with William Fox to develop Movietone.

Western Electric, a subsidiary of AT&T, was responsible for the **Vitaphone**, a sound-on-disk system developed for Warners that would prove to be the first commercially viable system for synchronized sound. Although Western Electric had also considered sound-on-film—like de Forest, Western Electric was heavily involved with radio research—the company opted eventually to work on a disk-based system. Because they had been largely responsible for developing electrical recording for the phonograph, they knew that disk recording, unlike sound film, was a mature technology, relatively inexpensive with a very reliable manufacturing procedure. Sound-on-film, by contrast, remained experimental, with uneven quality and much higher production costs throughout the 1920s.

The Vitaphone system consisted of a special phonograph mechanically coupled to a projector. The real advantage that it enjoyed over Phonofilm and other earlier attempts at sound film lay not in the medium, however, but in the amplification. Indeed, as amplification systems improved in general in the later 1920s, many theaters turned to phonographs as a means of supplementing (or replacing) their live musicians. Nonsynchronous scores did not require the special synchronizing equipment that sound films did, and theaters that could not afford the installation by AT&T or RCA or were judged to be of insufficient importance to have synchronized sound systems installed immediately often turned to regional theater sound companies, which installed an amplification system connected to a phonograph that allowed for effective but nonsynchronous sound. Collections of records catalogued by mood could then be used to construct a full orchestra score for a film, in the already familiar manner of the compiled score for live performance (although, of course, without the finesse that was possible in a synchronized live performance).

Short features of musical and vaudeville acts were another area of sound research, and Vitaphone proved particularly appropriate for such use (Figure 11-5). Just as the recording of the nonsynchronous score could substitute for the musicians, so too these recorded musical and vaudeville shorts could replace live stage acts and prologues. These films were shot as performances in a theater; they required a method to present a theatrical act from the perspective of a good seat from the orchestra section (the main floor) of the theater. In a sense, such films could be considered visualized sound recordings as much as they were sound motion pictures. In any case, the important thing was that the performance was staged for the camera and microphone in a highly controlled environment, and the phonograph was perfectly suited to exhibition of such films.

Newsreels were the final area for sound research, and these posed a completely different set of challenges to sound than did a vaudeville or musical act, which were filmed in a studio, theater, or some similar acoustically controlled environment. Newsreels had to capture news where it happened, on location. Consequently, they required a production system that was highly

Figure 11-5. *The Voice From the Screen* (1926). This was a film made to demonstrate the technical aspects of the Vitaphone. The camera records from the soundproof booth; here with the side removed for the purposes of illustration. The recording engineer is visible at the left; again the sides of the recording booth have been removed for illustration.

At 16 inches, the Vitaphone disk was far larger than the largest commercial records (12″) and it rotated at 33 ⅓ rather than 78 rpm. This allowed for sufficient recording time to accompany a standard reel of film. For improved playback, the material used in the production of the Vitaphone disk was softer than commercial disks, which meant that each disk could be used only twenty times before it needed to be replaced.

efficient, relatively mobile, and with a robust recording mechanism rather than one focused on capturing the highest possible fidelity of sound. Intelligibility of speech was far more important than the fidelity of the recording for the needs of the newsreel. Because a newsreel was made by splicing together a variety of short strips of film so that a series of events could be shown in short vignettes, the ability to edit the footage was another crucial factor to creating a sound newsreel.

Sound-on-disc and sound-on-film each held distinct advantages during the period of development. The sound-on-disc process, based on the phonograph, initially had a higher (or at least more reliable) level of sound fidelity than did the sound-on-film process, and therefore it is not surprising that Western Electric's Vitaphone, which pursued the idea of recording performances, should have developed a sound-on-disc method. Vitaphone was well-adapted to use for nonsynchronous scores and short films of performances. It was not, however, well adapted to location work. **Movietone**, a sound-on-film process Theodore Case perfected for Fox after he broke with de Forest, was by contrast extremely portable (Figure 11-6). Although Fox dabbled a bit in recorded vaudeville as well, he saw a much greater opportunity in recording newsworthy events, thus capturing for the cinema some of the radio-like immediacy of events as they happen. The early Movietone newsreels thus emphasized synchronized sound through the presentation of short speeches and other public activities that might feature sound. The recording apparatus for Movietone was much less bulky and, because it did not involve a delicate needle cutting grooves, was less affected by the rough handling that was an inevitable part of recording on location (Figure 11-7).

Figure 11-6. *The King of Spain* (1927). Frame enlargement of a Movietone sound film release print. The variable density sound strip runs along the left side between the sprockets and the image. Note that the area available on the film strip for the image was necessarily reduced, and the resulting picture has a squarer aspect ratio (roughly 1.19:1). Many filmmakers disliked the square format, and in 1932 the Academy of Motion Picture Arts and Sciences stepped in and established the standard 1.37:1 (known as the Academy ratio). (Because the sound track of the Vitaphone was on a record, the full filmstrip was available for the image and its aspect ratio was the standard 4:3 (1.33:1) of silent film.)

Figure 11-7. The commercial potential of sound newsreels was made particularly evident with the recording of Charles A. Lindbergh's departure for his historic Atlantic flight on 20 May 1927. The Movietone footage and sound of the take-off created a sensation at the Roxy Theatre when it was shown that same evening.

SOUND FILM AND THE STANDARDIZATION OF EXHIBITION

In all of these cases, the sound film was a "short" meant to supplement the feature on a theater's program. The primary impetus for the development of the sound film in the 1920s was in fact the standardization of exhibition, not the development of a feature-length talking picture (with synchronized dialogue).

As we noted in the previous chapter, the business of movie exhibition became more and more stratified in the 1920s. The deluxe theaters in large urban areas presented films with lush orchestral accompaniment and improvisation played on majestic organs, and they featured entr'acte performances such as vaudeville headliners, chorus lines, singers, and so forth. From the standpoint of the movie studios, which by the end of the 1920s owned large theater chains, the deluxe theaters, although profitable, were also expensive.

At the same time, the smaller neighborhood theaters and, even more so, the rural theaters could not afford to compete on anything like the same scale.

At best, such theaters might have an "orchestra" with five or six players, and they could support some small-time vaudeville. At their worst, small theaters used only a mechanical piano (with piano rolls) or a phonograph. A lack of standardization in accompaniment therefore made it difficult for the studios to calculate accurately how a film might play. A good accompaniment could make an otherwise indifferent film seem remarkable; whereas an indifferent accompaniment could make an otherwise fine film seem flat and unremarkable. Recorded sound therefore offered a way to standardize exhibition that would control both labor costs (at the large theaters) and quality (at the small theaters). The studios could offer a standardized product to be distributed nationally, thus giving all spectators a more or less uniform film experience that could be calculated in advance by the studios. The patrons of smaller theaters would enjoy access to the same sort of deluxe show available in the downtown picture palaces; and the studios would gain huge economies of scale in their fast expanding theater chains, economies of scale that would allow them to put intense competitive pressure on the independents.

The gala program Warner Bros. used to premiere Vitaphone gives a good indication of how the company initially understood the technology. The program, shown in Figure 11-8, contained an introductory film of Will Hays talking, a series of short musical films, and, after an intermission, *Don Juan* (1926), a big-budget John Barrymore feature. Although *Don Juan* had been produced as a regular silent-film feature, Warners decided to add some synchronized sound effects and a complete synchronized orchestral score by composers David Mendoza, conductor of Loew's Capitol Theatre in New York and William Axt, who had written a number of special scores including one for *The Big Parade* (1925). The score was even recorded by a prestigious classical symphony orchestra, the New York Philharmonic. Although it was the Vitaphone shorts that received the bulk of the attention in the press, the program overall remained a traditional one: a series of presentation acts and a long silent feature. Fox's approach was similar: the first Movietone feature was *Sunrise* (1927), a silent film with a synchronized score by Riesenfeld.

SOUND AND THE FEATURE FILM, 1927: *THE JAZZ SINGER*

By the beginning of 1927, both Warners and Fox had established regular production of sound pictures, Warners specializing in short musical and vaudeville acts with an occasional silent feature with synchronized music and effects and Fox in newsreels. The other studios followed Warners' and Fox's experiments but were not ready to commit themselves to production because sound film was by no means on solid economic footing. As often happens, the problem was circular: there were not yet a sufficient number of wired theaters to absorb the cost of production, and therefore no possibility of enough high-quality productions to fill the need for weekly, or even biweekly, program changes. These issues

VITAPHONE PRELUDE

Will H. Hays (President of Motion Picture Producers and Distributors of America)
  Welcome

New York Philharmonic Orchestra, Henry Hadley Conducting
  Wagner, *Tannhäuser* Overture

Marion Talley
  Verdi, "Caro Nome," from *Rigoletto*

Roy Smeck
  "His Pastimes"

Anna Case
  "La Fiesta"

Mischa Elman, violin, accompanied by Josef Bonime
  Dvorak, "Humoresque"

Giovanni Martinelli
  Leoncavallo, "Vesti la guibba," from I *Pagliacci*

INTERMISSION

Don Juan, starring John Barrymore
  Musical score by Major Edward Bowes, David Mendoza and Dr. William Axt.
  Played by the New York Philharmonic Orchestra, Herman Heller, conducting.

Figure 11-8. Inaugural Vitaphone Program. John Barrymore starred in *Don Juan* (1926), the first feature-length Vitaphone film. With a recorded orchestra score, occasional hard synced sound effects, but no sync dialogue, it was what would later be called a "synchronized" film.

were addressed to some extent when Warners and Fox both made agreements with Western Electric so that films from either company could be shown at any theater having a Western Electric sound installation; previously, the company would wire theaters for one system or the other (Figure 11-9). Despite the agreement, the rate of installation remained painfully slow.

Moreover, already by spring 1927 interest in the Vitaphone had begun to flag—a number of recently wired theaters canceled their service. In a bid to maintain or rebuild public interest, Warners announced they were making a feature film with Al Jolson that would have some synchronized sound sequences. The success of this film, *The Jazz Singer*, proved to be a turning point in the history of the sound film, as it demonstrated that synchronized sound could be effectively incorporated into a feature presentation, offering an entertainment that was

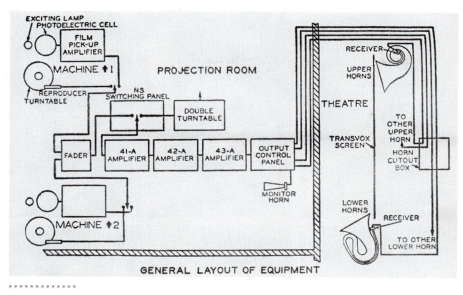

GENERAL LAYOUT OF EQUIPMENT

Figure 11-9. Schematic for Western Electric sound installation. The projection room is equipped for both sound-on-film and sound-on-record reproduction, giving theaters the ability to play films either format.

something more than simply a canned vaudeville act or a silent film with synchronized score and sound effects. Apart from this, the film did not mark a definitive break with silent-film practice, however, although it is often portrayed that way. Indeed, even a casual look will show that *The Jazz Singer* was conceived as a silent with a few synchronized sound sequences added. In fact, it was received by many in its contemporary audience as a series of Vitaphone shorts inserted into what remained a silent film (like *Don Juan*, *The Jazz Singer* has a complete synchronized orchestral score in addition to the performances). The sound sequences, in other words, were supplementary rather than essential: that the film was perfectly intelligible without them is attested by the fact that a purely silent print of the film also circulated and did a reasonable boxoffice business.

The sound sequences were, however, chosen to reinforce the general rhetorical thrust of the film, which aligns the new technology of synchronized sound with the youthful hero and the hip urban life (and secondarily with canting in the synagogue), whereas the silent sequences are used primarily for old-fashioned family melodrama. The initial synchronized sequence shows the young Jakie illicitly singing in a saloon (Figure 11-10a). The extremely loose synchronization of this sequence serves to emphasize the placement and regulation of the voice. When we next see Jack, he is singing at Coffee Dan's (Figure 11-10b), now to perfect synchronization. Between these two scenes, there is a synchronized sequence of Jack's father canting

a | b
c | d
e

Figure 11-10. *The Jazz Singer.* (a) Young Jakie sings "My Gal Sal" at the saloon. Even in long shots, the synchronization is poor. (b) Jack sings "Dirty Hands, Dirty Faces" at Coffee Dan's. After finishing this song, Jack banters with his audience, using Jolson's famous tag line: "You ain't heard nothing yet." (c) Jack's father says "stop." This is in fact the only actual piece of spoken dialogue in the entire film. The other spoken lines consist of Jack addressing the audience at *Coffee Dan's* and his odd monologue to his mother (including Jack sitting at the piano vamping) that immediately precedes this scene. (d) Jack and his father argue over singing "jazz." This sequence is accompanied by an orchestral score (Tchaikovsky's *Romeo and Juliet Overture*). (e) Jack sings the Kol Nidre as the spirit of his father hovers behind him. According to production records, Jolson lip synced the scene to an edited playback recording of Cantor Josef Rosenblatt. As Donald Crafton[2] notes, this proves that rerecording and filming to playback were already in use in 1927.

in the synagogue. In this way, the film seems to ask: is the proper place for Jack's voice on the stage or the synagogue and who has the right to determine it? The one exception to the basic pattern is also the only speech outside of the context of a performance: when Jack's father shouts "stop" as he finds Jack singing Irving Berlin's "Blue Skies" to his mother (Figure 11-10c). Strikingly, the father's word (00:46:53) brings Jack's synchronized singing to an abrupt halt and plunges the sound track into more than 20 sec worth of pure silence. When sound returns, it is in the form of a synchronized orchestra music, which is used to underscore the subsequent argument between Jack and his father over tradition, the theme of the family melodrama (Figure 11-10d). In this way, the score seems to follow Jack's father in rejecting the sound of Jack's (synchronized) singing, and the old-fashioned values of the melodrama also seem to accrue to the sound of the silent-film orchestral score. Even here, however, the film hedges its bets because the two synagogue scenes (as well as a performance by cantor Josef Rosenblatt)—moments that should rightly be classed with the melodrama—are also given with synchronized sound (Figure 11-10e).

The commercial success of *The Jazz Singer* encouraged other studios to think seriously about the possibility of the sound picture as a "talking picture," but we should be wary about attributing too much influence in such matters to any one film. MGM in particular remained cautious, even after *The Jazz Singer* was held over for extended runs. After all, three earlier films, *Four Horsemen of the Apocalypse* (1921), *The Big Parade*, and *Ben-Hur* (1925), all had runs that exceeded the box-office performance of *The Jazz Singer*. It was actually the huge success of the decidedly mediocre *The Lights of New York* (1928), the first all-talking film, and *The Singing Fool* (1928), Jolson's follow-up to *The Jazz Singer*, that finally convinced Hollywood to the convert to sound (Fig. 11-11). Seeing the returns from these films, the studios changed course and committed to the production of sound film.

THE TRANSITION FROM SILENT TO SOUND FILM

The passage from silent film to sound film took roughly five years, from 1926 through 1930; but many of the technical and aesthetic issues were still not satisfactorily settled until 1933, some even later than that. The studios themselves did not complete the changeover in production until the fall of 1929. The theaters would not be completely wired until the early 1930s: by the end of 1927 only 157 theaters in the United States had been wired for sound (although these included most of the important urban venues); by the end of 1928, after RCA began competing with Western Electric to wire theaters, roughly 4000 theaters (including most of the studio-owned theaters) had installed sound and one year later more than 8,000 theaters were so equipped (although this was still only about 40% of the total).

Figure 11-11. Al Jolson and Davey Lee in *The Singing Fool*. Although less well-known today than *The Jazz Singer*, *The Singing Fool* enjoyed greater commercial success—it would remain the highest grossing film until the release of *Gone with the Wind* (1939)—and carried more weight in the other studios' decisions to invest in feature sound-film production.

Partly because of cost, partly because equipment was in short supply, many smaller rural and neighborhood theaters were not converted to sound even in 1931. Although production of silent films had ceased in 1929, new films were released in two prints, sound and silent with intertitles as late as the end of 1930, by which time a sufficient number of theaters had converted to sound to make the market for sound film viable—but even then nearly a quarter of the theaters in the United States remained unwired. (Many of these theaters would never convert to sound.) Not surprisingly, theaters owned by studios were among the first to be converted, and this placed them at a distinct competitive advantage. Their profits were positively affected in two ways. First, because of the novelty factor, theaters with sound did proportionally better in ticket sales. Second, theaters with sound were considerably more cost efficient than theaters without sound because they saved on musicians' salaries.

Although much has been written about the devastating effect the change-over to sound had on Hollywood stars, the effect was even more acute for musicians. As theaters were wired for sound, they had less need for live musicians, and large numbers of musicians were laid off. The elimination of orchestras and organists occurred quickly (musicians' salaries typically totaled $3,000 per week in the largest theaters), and the union ran an ad campaign designed to win continued support for live music (Figure 11-12), but without notable success. In Minneapolis and St. Paul, for instance, only a single theater retained an orchestra by the end of 1929. National unemployment in the musicians union was about 50% in the 1930–31 season. A number of the deluxe theaters kept their musical programs for a period after the coming of sound, but the challenges of the Depression made it more and more difficult for even these theaters to attract sufficient patronage to meet expenses. Wiring costs became a problem once the Depression hit because wiring for sound was typically financed, and the declining audience after 1931 made it more and more difficult for theaters to meet the debt payments. Soon, the deluxe theaters, too, lost their musicians or at least reduced the number on the payroll. In addition, many of the prominent musical directors, as well as the best musicians, had relocated to Hollywood or moved to radio, so that the programs lost some of their luster and prestige. Riesenfeld, for example, left his post as director of the Rivoli, Rialto, and Criterion theaters in New York to become musical director of United Artists in Hollywood. When the music library of the Capitol Theater was transferred to the New York studio to form the basis of the MGM music library, it became absolutely clear that the time of musicians in the movie theater was short.

TYPES OF EARLY SOUND FILM

In 1929, sound film was understood to fall into one of three types: "synchronized" (recorded orchestral accompaniment and sound effects); "**part-talkie**" ("synchronized" recorded orchestral accompaniment interspersed with talking sequences); and the "**100% talkie**." This terminology can be confusing because a "**synchronized**" **film** in this typology is what we would now call a silent film; "synchronization" here refers to the fact that the *music* has been fit to the action. (Recall that in contemporary usage the term refers to a general principle of sound and image coordination—"playing with the film"—and is opposed to counterpoint, or "playing against the film"; see ch. 4.)

"Synchronized" films often make use of sound effects, both hard and loosely synchronized as was the case in "live" performances. A fateful knock on the door, for instance, was likely to be closely synchronized in live performance either by the drummer or by a supernumerary backstage—and so such synchronization in *Don Juan* was fully typical. Swordplay and other more atmospheric noises, on the contrary, were treated more casually (as they would continue to be in later sound film), and this was also the case in *Don Juan*. The loosely synchronized opening sequence of MGM's *Wild Orchids* (1929) is likewise fully in keeping with silent-film practice (see Figure 11-13a). *Wings* (1927)

CANNED MUSIC ON TRIAL

OYEZ! OYEZ! OYEZ!

THIS is the case of Art vs. Mechanical Music in Theatres. The defendant stands accused before the American people of attempted corruption of musical appreciation and discouragement of musical education.

Theatres in many cities are offering synchronized mechanical music as a substitute for Real Music. If the theatre-going public accepts this vitiation of its entertainment program a deplorable decline in the Art of Music is inevitable.

Musical authorities know that the soul of the Art is lost in mechanization. It cannot be otherwise because the quality of music is dependent upon the present mood of the artist, upon the human contact, without which the essence of intellectual stimulation and emotional rapture is lost.

Is Music Worth Saving?

No great volume of evidence is required to answer this question. Music is a well-nigh universally beloved art. From the beginning of history men have turned to musical expression to lighten the burdens of life, to make them happier. Aborigines, lowest in the scale of savagery, chant their song to tribal Gods and play upon pipes and shark-skin drums. Musical development has kept pace with good taste and ethics throughout the ages, and has influenced the gentler nature of man more powerfully perhaps than any other factor.

Has it remained for the Great Age of Science to snub the Art by setting up in its place a pale and feeble shadow of itself?

THE AMERICAN FEDERATION OF MUSICIANS

(Comprising 140,000 professional musicians in the United States and Canada)

JOSEPH N. WEBER, President, 1440 Broadway, New York City

Figure 11-12. "Canned Music on Trial" was part of an ad campaign in 1929 against wired theaters. The collapse of the vaudeville circuit around the same time only exacerbated the problem for musicians. Some were able to find work in Hollywood and radio stations; and the large number of idle musicians undoubtedly contributed to the proliferation of big bands, since the economic conditions and general oversupply of musicians helped hold down the labor cost of running a touring band with a large number of musicians.

Figure 11-13. *Wild Orchids.* (a) The opening sequence contains a flurry of sound effects, a | b most prominently the blaring horns on the wild car ride to the ship and the crowd noises on the dock. Yet these sounds are atmospheric: they are not closely synchronized to the image but rather suggest a basic soundscape. Indeed, they seem to float uncannily above the scene. This fact is heightened by the continuation of the sound over the intertitles. Compare the treatment of sound here with the hard synchronization of the exotic, "native" dance sequence later in the same film. (b)This latter scene is pure sonic spectacle, with numerous crisp claps used to show off the precision of the synchronization. There is nothing in this synchronized sequence necessary to understand the narrative, however, so it was easily adaptable to exhibition in those theaters not wired for sound (a different music might be used or the scene might be deleted).

supplemented its live orchestra and sound effects personnel with a synchronized disk sound track of airplane and machine gun noises to heighten the spectacle of the battle sequences; this arrangement also made for efficient road show exhibition (although the technology was anything but flawless). In all of these cases, sound effects were used as an element of spectacle, much as was color during the silent era; the "synchronized" sound film was simply a means of mechanizing these effects, just as the recorded score mechanized the orchestra.

A fully synchronized sequence would, in these terms, simply be a way of *heightening* the spectacle. Ideally, such scenes could add to the experience of the film without being absolutely necessary to understand it, so that the films could play at those theaters that had sound installed as well as those that did not. *The Jazz Singer* followed this strategy, which seems to have been the motivation for the part-talkies. In fact, audiences soon proved resistant to the part-talkie, at least when presented as such, preferring either the all-talkie or the "pure" silent film. A film like *Wild Orchids*, however, which was essentially a "synchronized" film, could still effectively contain a number of sequences with hard sync, perhaps because (like those in *The Jazz Singer*) they were framed as performances (Figure 11-13b).

The 100% talking film, by contrast, could be shown only in a theater equipped for sound. The first such feature film was *Lights of New York*, which Warner Bros. released in 1928, but only one year later, when MGM, which had long been the holdout on the talking picture, won the Academy Award

Figure 11-14. *City Lights* (1931). Charlie Chaplin took an extreme position with respect to sound film, remaining almost fully committed to the silent-film aesthetic. He composed and closely supervised the placement of the music, which was "synchronized" and ubiquitous in silent-film fashion. Yet he drew on the resources of recorded sound to give the muteness characteristic of the silent film a new, albeit financially untenable, eloquence in the sound era; that is, he was able to use the control that synchronized sound allowed and even demanded but in some degree to turn it against the realistic aesthetic of sound film.

Moments in his films that gesture toward synchronized speech tend to emphasize the monological quality of the discourse, especially the political power that comes along with the control of speech. This happens, for instance, early in *City Lights*, where the voices of the public officials are presented as voices, but represented as noise: their speech is unintelligible. The effect is wonderfully deflating of the pretensions of public speech even as it illustrates, in its miscarriage, the way that such speech carries the voice of authority. *Modern Times*, released in 1936 and Chaplin's last film featuring his trademark figure of the Tramp, likewise remains almost entirely silent. Many sound effects are hard synced, as are snippets of dialogue (even some nonsensical bits of the Tramp's and the Tramp's climactic song performance that concludes the film). Here, too, the power of speech is associated with abusive, arbitrary authority.

for Best Picture for *The Broadway Melody*, it was clear that talking film was quickly becoming synonymous with sound film. By 1930 in Hollywood, production of silent film had, with a few notable exceptions such as Charlie Chaplin, essentially ceased (Figure 11-14). Europe took somewhat longer to make the transition, and a film such as *Le Million* (1931) resembles a part-talkie in the way it plays talking and silent sequences off one another. Even outside the United States, however, going to the movies was quickly coming to mean going to the talkies.

MUSICALS IN EARLY SOUND FILM

Early sound films were predominantly musicals—"all singing, all dancing, all talking" was standard advertising copy. The reasons are several. First, musicals offered an easy means of exploiting popular music. Much of the vaudeville recorded in Vitaphone shorts was based in popular song, and, as mentioned earlier, *The Jazz Singer* was understood initially at least as a silent film with added Vitaphone shorts of Al Jolson singing popular songs. These songs were a commodity in their own right, and Warners had invested in acquiring music publishing firms around the same time the studio was developing Vitaphone. Clearly, Vitaphone and the music publishing concerns were intended to be mutually reinforcing from the standpoint of producing profits. Although hardly a film lacked a theme song in the late 1920s, musicals exploited popular music in a highly efficient manner. In any case, the preponderance of musicals in the early sound film meant that popular music was at first *the* music of the sound film.

Musicals offered a further advantage: the narrative was understood as being punctuated by the spectacle of musical performances. In that respect, the production process of a sound musical differed little conceptually from that of *The Jazz Singer*, which could therefore serve as a model (much as that film also served as the model for the part-talkie). The difference was mainly that the narrative was carried by recorded dialogue rather than by intertitles. All-talking dialogue films ("talkers") were another entity altogether, as it was not clear where or even whether music should be introduced in such films, an aesthetic problem that simply points to another advantage of musicals: they gave a diegetic motivation for the presence of music and offered opportunity for staged spectacle—many musicals included at least one production number filmed in two-color Technicolor, usually a final production number.

Confining music to performance had the further benefit of minimizing the need for rerecording. Although it had been technically possible to dub sound tracks since at least 1927 (*The Jazz Singer* used some rerecording), the process was risky due to the significant loss of fidelity in the process. Consequently, rerecording did not become standard until after 1930. Even filming to playback—that is, recording the sound and playing it back as the scene was acted out—was seldom done (Figure 11-15). Any voice doubling that did occur—in musical numbers at least—occurred on the set, with the voice double positioned outside the frame but in proximity to the actor. In general practice, then, sound tracks were recorded live, along with the film. In terms of the musical practice this meant that scenes with dialogue and music required that the musicians be assembled on the same soundstage as the scene being shot. The musicians would then play for every take of the scene. (As mentioned in the previous chapter, the practice of musicians on the set to help actors catch the pace and mood of a scene went back to the silent-film days, but, of course, the stakes of this music-making became much higher when the music became part of the film.)

Obviously, such an arrangement was inefficient from the standpoint of labor time. Moreover, watching the balances in this real-time recording was a

Figure 11-15. *The Broadway Melody*. The production number, "Dance of the Painted Doll," was initially recorded and filmed at the same time. After it was decided that the scene needed to be reshot, Douglas Shearer, who would become the longtime head of the sound department at MGM, suggested they keep the audio, which was excellent, shoot to playback, and resynchronize in postproduction. Although this was not the first instance of shooting to playback, its success helped make the practice standard for production numbers.

challenge for the sound personnel. Because the early microphones were weak in sensitivity, fidelity, dynamic range, and directionality, music often had a detrimental effect on the intelligibility of dialogue, which was understood then as now as the primary consideration in making an effective sound film. Many of these problems could be mitigated when music was treated as a performance—as, again, would be the case with musicals. Thus, until technology advanced sufficiently that it was possible to rerecord—that is, to record dialogue, music, and effects separately and then mix them down later—music tended to be used only when it was deemed indispensable.

Mastering the Sound Track and Elements of Style

The arrival of the sound film brought with it a number of basic questions. First among them is that the three components of the sound track—dialogue, sound effects, and music—must contend for aural space. As Rick Altman puts it, sound film is governed by an "intermittent" rather than a continuous system.[3] Sound film contrasts markedly with silent film in this respect. In the latter, music is ubiquitous, the determining sound element of the performance. In the mature silent cinema, for instance, verbal narration might occasionally be used, although by all accounts infrequently in the United States and Europe (the practice of using a narrator continued longer in the Japanese cinema), whereas sound effects often appeared to mark narratively pertinent details or to add to aural spectacle in a particularly pitched scene (such as a battle). Once exhibition practices stabilized around the long feature in the mid-teens, sound effects became supplementary to the music, much as sound effects from the stage are understood as supplementary to the music in opera. Even in comedy, which permitted a more raucous style of accompaniment with extensive use of humorous effects, sound effects never really eclipsed music.

In the sound picture, by contrast, sound effects and dialogue became tied very strongly to image; and unlike the silent period, where the decision on whether to render a sound effect could be overridden for musical purposes, in the sound era it became extremely rare that a noticeable visual event, such as moving lips or, say, a glass being placed on a table, was not rendered with synchronized sound. Indeed, any moments of non-synchronization under those circumstances would be fraught with significance in the sound era.

Another particular challenge for early sound design was how to understand nonsynchronous sound. Synchronized sound clearly belonged to the image. Synchronized dialogue, for instance, had its (obvious) source in the figure depicted speaking. By contrast, the source of nonsynchronous sound and so also its relation to the image was unspecified. In particular, it was not clear whether such sound should be considered as coming from offscreen space or from somewhere else, and if it was coming from somewhere else, where that place was located.

In general, early sound film managed this ambiguity by approaching the filming as though it were a recording of a performance. Nonsynchronous sound, unless it was a mistake—such as ambient set noise or perhaps the sound of the camera itself—was then simply conceived as the sound of offscreen space. Offscreen dialogue, for instance, would be simply dialogue where the speaking character was not visible but still presumed present in the scene. The conception of nonsynchronous sound in this case presumes an identity between nonsynchronous sound and offscreen diegetic space. This identity made it easy to rationalize nonsynchronous sound, but it left little room for music. Recorded silent-film music accompaniment was certainly not diegetic; but neither was it music of the theater in the way that live orchestral music would be. It seemed to belong nowhere. Finding a place for such music therefore required breaking down the identity between nonsynchronous sound and offscreen space. In short, it required conceptual work: the division of nonsynchronous sound into diegetic and nondiegetic spheres.

The identity between nonsynchronous sound and offscreen space obtained its interpretive stability by reducing film to a species of recorded theater. This worked so long as sound film remained a novelty, but when audiences complained of "staginess" filmmakers spent considerable time pondering the status and potential of nonsynchronous sound, realizing that its non-redundancy with the image offered sound film possibilities not present with the stage. Nonsynchronous sound, in other words, was a trait of sound film that was particular to it, that potentially distinguished it from the stage but also from the silent screen.

At the same time, intimate scenes, especially love scenes featuring close-ups, were making audiences feel uncomfortable in a way that a similar scene in a silent film would not. In 1928, one reviewer wrote, "Having so much smoldering sexiness, [*The River*] is occasionally liable to laughter. . . . Coming from the women mostly there may have been a factor of overflowing tension expressing itself as tittering."[4] A similar sentiment was expressed the next year: "Some of the love scenes [in the talkies] aren't so effective when the actors are putting their emotions in words. This is especially true when the hero pleads with the heroine for her love. While she is deciding what the answer will be, we hear nothing but the whispering, coughing audience and the suspense is terrible."[5] In 1930, a reviewer went so far as to call for a return to playing such scenes as silent film: "An old observation has it that nothing seems so silly to a man as another man's love letters. But there is something sillier, it would seem; not only public, but audible, love making. It appears to be the consensus of opinion that all love scenes should be silent—unless comedy is intended."[6]

Figure 11-16 shows love scenes from four films, two of which use music, two of which do not. A comparison of these scenes suggests that music apparently helped authorize the physical proximity by seeming to give the audience emotional proximity to the characters' feelings, thus illuminating the intention of a scene. This suggests that the construction of nondiegetic space offered a means of improving narrative clarity by giving filmmakers an additional dimension for presenting information.

Figure 11-16. The love scenes from (a) *Dance, Fools, Dance* (1931) and (b) *Queen Christina* (1933) both minimize dialogue and feature stylized, pantomimic acting to prominent background music. The effect in each case is highly reminiscent of silent film. Two similar scenes from (c) *Behind Office Doors* (1931) and (d) *Red Dust* (1932) are both driven by dialogue and neither uses music. (*Red Dust* features a constant background sound of rain here as in much of the film.) These two scenes share an ambiguity with respect to how receptive a character is to a sexual advance. As a comparison of these four scenes demonstrates, music was particularly effective at unobtrusively resolving such ambiguity.

Production

PRODUCTION PHASES

During the early sound era most of the work on the sound track needed to be accomplished during the production phase—indeed, getting a good recording became just as important as getting film footage. In any case, the introduction of sound directly affected the visual sphere. Before effective sound insulation was devised for the cameras, scenes would typically be shot with multiple cameras, each enclosed in a sound-proof booth, so as to allow for cutting while ensuring that the sound would remain in sync. Because each of the cameras was required to remain out of the visual field of the others, this arrangement severely limited the number of possible set-ups for each scene. With fewer shots to choose from, directors and editors tended to use longer takes, often in medium and long shot. The need for a controlled acoustic environment also meant that most shooting was done on soundproofed soundstages rather than on location or even in the back lot (Figure 11-17).

By 1932 engineers had devised solutions to most of the pressing technological problems: better microphones with increased sensitivity, fidelity, dynamic range, and directionality; improved film stock and development timing for sound film; the microphone boom; improvements in lighting to make the apparatus quieter; effective sound insulation for the camera; and so forth. Most important, these improvements made it feasible for rerecording to become a

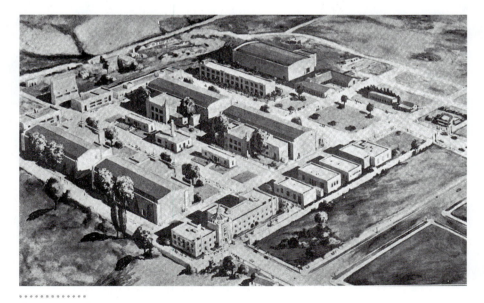

Figure 11-17. Fox Movietone Studio, Los Angeles, c. 1929. Increasingly, sound stages took the place of the back lot.

normal part of postproduction. This meant that music and effects no longer needed to be recorded during principal shooting, and the recording engineer would thereafter only have to be concerned with capturing dialogue. Music and effects, if needed, could be recorded separately and added later; the three components—dialogue, music, and effects—could then be mixed together before the final sound track was printed to the release print.

This change greatly simplified the making of sound film, both saving money and giving filmmakers much more flexibility. It also greatly facilitated dialogue replacement or looping, the rerecording of dialogue to an existing segment of film, a technique that could be used to fix flubbed lines but, more important, to dub dialogue in foreign languages, the key to Hollywood maintaining its dominance of the world film market. Prior to rerecording, films would need to be re-shot completely in a foreign language—a procedure that was normal practice in the early years of the sound era.

MUSIC DEPARTMENT

The music personnel for the early sound pictures was drawn from two primary sources: the large deluxe theaters and the popular music industry, especially the part associated with musical theater. Their duties were divided along predictable lines. The deluxe theater musicians (many of whom also began in music theater), primarily well-known musical directors such as Riesenfeld, Rapee, or Mendoza, were at first assigned to provide scores for the "synchronized" silent films. These scores would be prepared much like any other silent feature. The main difference lay in distribution. Rather than scores being available to theaters for live performance, the music would be recorded by an orchestra with sound effects added (when appropriate). It is worth pointing out that for these synchronized silents, music and effects were thus added in the postproduction phase—exactly as they would be for regular sound film once rerecording became standard.

Because the films with dialogue were primarily musicals, music for these films was provided by those who worked in the music theater industry. Songwriters were an obvious necessity, and studios quickly placed large numbers of them under contract. Songs of a musical were essentially part of the script, and they needed to be composed in the preproduction phase, that is, prior to the filming. Beyond that, they needed to be arranged and orchestrated in a fashion suitable for recording prior to the filming as well. Arrangement and orchestration were considered specialized skills in the music industry at the time (and arranging for microphone was an even more specialized skill), so it is hardly surprising that musicals also drew many experienced professional arrangers and orchestrators to Hollywood.

Especially after 1929, songs were generally prerecorded and then the scene was shot silent to playback—a practice that remains dominant in filming musical numbers to this day. Such prerecording gave the cinematography of these numbers, nowhere more than in production numbers (many of which were originally also in color), a vividness and liveliness lacking in dramatic scenes dominated by dialogue.

Many of the music professionals who started on film musicals would in fact make the jump to feature film scoring. Louis Silvers, for instance, received initial acclaim for his Broadway work on Gus Edwards' revues in the 1910s and early 1920s. His best known piece was "April Showers," which he wrote for Al Jolson's appearance in the 1921 show. This number was included in Jolson's first Vitaphone short, *A Plantation Act* (1926), and Silvers' work on that film led to his being assigned the score for *The Jazz Singer*. He went on to supervise, arrange, and compose numerous feature films in 1930s and served as music director at Columbia and 20th Century Fox. Alfred Newman, who would succeed Silvers at 20th Century Fox, likewise began on Broadway; he came to Hollywood in 1930 at the bidding of Irving Berlin. Max Steiner also worked on Broadway for a decade before coming to Hollywood in 1929 to score an adaptation of Florenz Ziegfield's *Rio Rita*. In Germany, Franz Waxman began his career in a jazz band, where he arranged some numbers for Frederick Hollander, a highly regarded and exceptionally well-connected German cabaret and music theater composer. When Hollander was asked to write the music for Josef von Sternberg's *Der blaue Engel* (*The Blue Angel*, 1930), Waxman was called to orchestrate and conduct the score. That in turn led to work on a score for *Liliom* (1934) and then to arranging Jerome Kern's music for *Music in the Air* (1934).

During the transitional period, music departments tended to be organized on a somewhat ad hoc basis. This was simply a reflection of the fact that the nature of sound film was in constant flux. The standardization that would allow the formation of a regular music department would come only after rerecording had developed to the point that most music work could be moved into postproduction.

SOUND DEPARTMENT

Early on, most of the personnel working on sound were technical specialists, drawn primarily from the telephone and radio industries, because Western Electric and RCA were the two primary companies involved. Those working on sound, unlike those in music, understood their tasks as more technical than artistic in nature, and in the early years at least both progress and accomplishment were measured mostly by advances in technology: noise reduction, increased dynamic and frequency response, better directionality, and so forth. Because almost all of the sound that would end up on the sound track of a talking picture was at first recorded on the set, there was not much need for sound postproduction. (Figure 11-18 shows some of the jobs on a sound stage.) The sound track was cut along with the picture (or, more often, the picture was cut to the sound track). Only toward the end of the period, when rerecording became common, did dialogue editing begin to emerge from picture editing as a separate job with its own particular set of responsibilities.

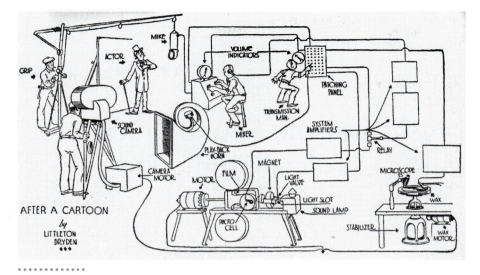

Figure 11-18. This cartoon diagram of the Western Electric System (1929) shows distinct duties for the grip, mixer and transmission man. Note the presence of the playback horn, suggesting that music was occasionally prescored. A disk recording was often made even when primary recording was sound-on-film for the purpose of checking the sound on the set. The wax masters would be replaced by acetate transcription disks in the 1930s.

In terms of sound, the situation with synchronized silent films was, like music, somewhat different in that the work was from the beginning done in postproduction. The synchronized silent features would in that sense become important models (and the training ground) for the postproduction of sound in general.

Summary

In this chapter we continued the historical narrative for sound and music that was started in chapter 10, beginning with early experiments in sound reproduction and leading up to the role of radio technology (and competition from commercial radio broadcasts) in the 1920s. By the late 1920s, the transition from silent-film performance practices to the film with a reproduced sound track was well underway, but a range of problems occupied both the technicians and film artists. The crucial technical issues were synchronization, fidelity of sound in recording and theater reproduction, and the effective mixing of the sound track elements. To these were added aesthetic issues: how to manage the "intermittent" sound track (and the hierarchy of sound track elements), how to understand nonsynchronous sound, and how to manage sound in relation to the physical space depicted in the image track.

Music and the Sound Track in the Classical Studio Era

Introduction

The late 1920s were a period of extensive experimentation and a wide variation in practices, but by the mid-1930s studios settled into a regular production system, dominated by genre films, and along with that model necessarily came a rapid codification of the sound track. As in earlier decades, however, both economics and technology were drivers of change. Economically, the Great Depression adversely affected movie attendance, giving film producers every incentive to find formulas to streamline costs. Technologically, the development of an effective system of rerecording was key, as it greatly simplified shooting by allowing a large number of tasks to be shifted to the postproduction phase, where they could be handled not only in more systematic fashion but also with greater finesse. Without question the most important impact of rerecording on the sound track was that production sound could now concentrate on dialogue.

Issues of Technology and Economics

IMPROVEMENTS IN RECORDING TECHNOLOGY

By 1930, sound-on-film (optical sound) had become the accepted standard for both production and distribution. By 1932, the available technologies had improved remarkably in nearly every area: among the most notable advances were better microphones and speakers, quieter cameras and lights, and several significant refinements in the sound-on-film process.

Two optical sound formats, variable area and variable density, would compete with one another for more than two decades. Not only were they compatible from the standpoint of exhibition, meaning there was little incentive for the studios to standardize, but the competition in fact worked to the studios's advantage. RCA controlled one method and Western Electric the other, and maintaining both formats helped to ward off legal complaints of monopoly while encouraging both companies to invest in further research. Sound-on-film had always been easier to edit and easier to use in location shooting, but enhancements in film stock, the adoption of the double system of recording (separate cameras and film strips for image and sound), the "noiseless" film preparation, and a reduction in the wow and flutter of optical sound projection had increased the fidelity of sound-on-film to the point that it equaled or exceeded that of the disk system. Sound-on-film also had the advantage of being physically attached to the release print and of being more durable, so that the cost advantage of sound-on-disk soon disappeared (see Figure 12-1). By 1930, even Warners, the last studio to insist on distributing its sound tracks via disk, had begun offering optical prints as well. Disk recording continued to have a presence on the movie set, however, as it was a far more efficient means

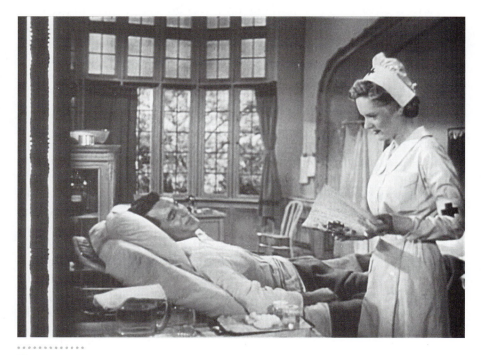

Figure 12-1. *Okay for Sound* (1946). A scene from *Night and Day* (1946) with variable area sound track exposed. Note the two sound tracks, 180° out of phase: originally a means of noise reduction, these were later exploited for stereo reproduction. In the 1970s, Dolby managed to matrix these two tracks in order to encode four channels of stereo sound on them.

of double checking a scene than developing and printing a proof copy of the optical sound track.

The development of directional microphones was another important technological innovation that eliminated much of the extraneous set and camera noise. Introduced in 1931, the ribbon microphone, for instance, was bidirectional, meaning that it could be placed between actors, but it was insensitive to sounds coming from the sides (such as camera and crew). In 1936, RCA developed the unidirectional microphone, which allowed for an even narrower focus. This, along with additional soundproofing measures taken on the set and in the camera apparatus, allowed for a much more fluid use of the camera and a return to the standard single camera setup that had been common in the silent era.

The improved fidelity of the recording technology had a direct bearing on music, especially with respect to instrumentation. In the early sound era, much consideration had to be given to scoring that suited the microphones available, but by the mid-1930s the accommodations to the microphone had become minimal. Studio orchestras tended to be smaller than the live orchestras they emulated; they also had fewer strings relative to the other instrumental groups compared to what a live group would need. This imbalance was compensated for by microphone placement, mixing and "sweetening"—the string section, for instance, sometimes played a cue a second time and that recording was mixed with the original take to give a fuller sound. Physical placement also aided microphone setup as much as the musicians: Figure 12-2 shows two common seating arrangements for a studio orchestra.

RERECORDING

The consistent use of rerecording allowed sound work on the set to focus on capturing dialogue because the other sounds—effects and music—could be added during postproduction.

Although rerecording had been possible earlier, the process, as we saw in chapter 11, was difficult, expensive, and the results were often unsatisfactory. The loss of fidelity was such that, in the first few years of sound-film exhibition, the sound track could not even be rerecorded to the release print. Instead, each shot would simply be reproduced at whatever level the mixer had set and a cue sheet with instructions on volume adjustment would be sent out with the film. The projectionist was expected to make these changes while the film was shown. As can be expected, the results varied widely depending on the skill and attention of the operator, and complaints about sound levels in theaters were frequent. The problem disappeared once postproduction mixing became standard and the sound track could be set to a master level.

Studios established rerecording as a normal part of postproduction during 1932, and it was at this point that the sound track was divided into its three familiar components—dialogue, music, and effects. Each of these was assigned its own crew of personnel. Dialogue was captured primarily during produc-

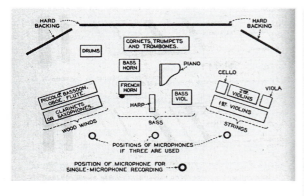
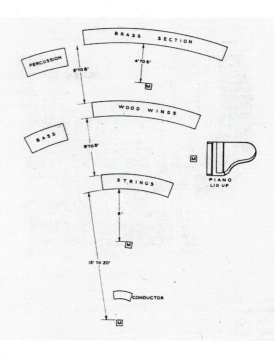

• • • • • • • • • • • • •

Figure 12-2. Two common studio set-ups for recording an orchestra in the 1940s. The signals from the multiple microphones were either mixed live at the recording session or recorded separately and mixed later.

tion, and the sets, microphone placement, and actor positioning and movement were all designed with the idea of capturing dialogue clearly. During postproduction, the editing of dialogue closely paralleled the picture editing and was in many respects simply an adjunct to it. Although some sound effects would also naturally be recorded as part of the production sound, most effects were dubbed in during postproduction. Indeed, filmmakers tried to avoid non-dialogue sounds as much as possible during production, not just because they could easily obscure dialogue, but also because they limited editing possibilities when they were mingled in with the dialogue. Nondiegetic music was almost always recorded after the fact, and onscreen music, more often than not, was prerecorded so that the actors could concentrate on the visual parts of presentation during filming. Once the dialogue, music, and effects tracks were created, they could be combined through rerecording into a final sound track mix, where the elements were placed in (narrative) balance. Through rerecording, the filming of sound film was greatly simplified, giving filmmakers more flexibility and making the whole process more economical.

SOUND IN THE THEATERS OF THE 1930s AND 1940s

Mechanical sound reproduction for films in the 1930s was limited in two important respects: frequency response and volume response. In addition, sound reproduction was forced to contend with the overly reverberant acoustics of most theaters, many of which had been converted from previous uses. The live performance media of silent film, vaudeville, and legitimate stage all demanded a warmer hall, one with a significant amount of reflected sound, but that acoustic property muddied reproduced sound.

The typical theater of the 1930s wired for monaural sound had anywhere from two to six speaker horn placements, depending on the size and configuration of the theater. Once a sonically permeable screen was developed in the late 1920s, the speakers were generally moved behind the screen to reinforce the illusion that the sound emanated from the film world (Figure 12-3). As engineers improved frequency response they discovered that volume needed to be increased to match, because otherwise the sounds seemed too distant from their apparent sources on the screen. Increased volume could also be used as a means of masking flaws in the auditorium, a strategy that resulted in complaints of excessive volume in theaters, especially after the introduction of the so-called "wide-range" sound systems of the mid-1940s. These wide-range systems shifted from a two-speaker design introduced in the mid-1930s, based on separating low frequency and high frequency sound, to a three-speaker design that separates out a mid-range of 300-3000 cps (this setup would also become the standard in home stereos by the early 1960s).

Besides matching increased frequency response and masking flaws in auditoria, a third reason motivating the increased volume was undoubtedly the sonic spectacle that the new systems made possible. The increased fidelity permitted theaters to produce louder sounds without distortion, and this ability became a spectacle in its own right; that is, theaters with the latest sound equipment could distinguish themselves from lesser theaters on the basis of sound reproduction, a fact that led some to emphasize the difference by turning up the volume. Suddenly every word, every note, even a whisper, could boom forth with unmistakable clarity and volume to every corner of the theater. (A similar strategy seems evident today, when theaters seem intent on displaying the power and fidelity of their sound systems by blasting spectators from their seats.)

Yet the larger dynamic range also allowed for a more effective dramatic use of sound, as the obtainable contrast between soft and loud sounds expanded. Loud sounds may have been the most immediately spectacular elements on the new sound systems, but these systems also permitted much more sonic detail at low volume as well; even silences were more effective as the hiss from the apparatus was greatly reduced in the 1940s. (Recall Robynn Stilwell's comment cited in this book's Introduction: "In the film industry, sound seems to be of greatest concern to those who produce big movies; we have come to expect teeth-rattling explosions and bombastic scores in modern blockbusters. However, sound can be even more intensely felt in intimate, quiet films, where the slightest whisper or silence can have a marked effect."[1]

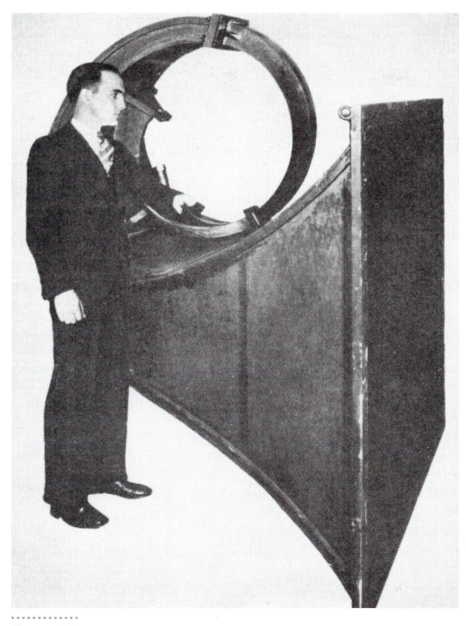

Figure 12-3. Speaker horn designed for placement behind the screen.

In general, however, the recording technology available exceeded the reproducing capabilities of even the best theaters. By 1940, film could be recorded at upwards of 8000 cps and through 60 dB of dynamic range. The weak point remained the amplifying equipment, which required constant maintenance:

The rerecording Mixer, when rerecording a picture, should limit the volume range to 30 DB; that is, the difference in level between the lowest signal and the loudest signal should be no more than 30 DB, which means the loudest signal will be thirty-two times greater than the lowest. . . . When a picture having more than a 30 DB volume range is shown in a the-ater, one of two things happen—both of which are detrimental to the picture. If the projection-ist adjusts the volume so that the high level signals are [toned down, the low level signals are] completely lost and, consequently, the sound becomes unintelligible. If the projectionist adjusts the volume so that the low level signals are intelligible, then the high level signals will—in many cases—be badly distorted due to the overloading of the sound reproducing system. If distortion does not occur, then the loud signals will become very annoying to the audience and distract greatly from the picture.
—James Cameron,
Sound Motion Pictures
(1947)[2]

theaters, economically squeezed during much of the 1930s, were often neg-ligent in replacing radio tubes, with the result that amplifiers would hum or buzz. Even the best equipment in good repair, however, was rarely capable of exploiting the signal captured, and studios wisely adopted protective measures to ensure that sound would remain acceptable in theaters with less than opti-mal equipment. As the quotation in the sidebar demonstrates, dynamic range in particular was often compressed to no more than 30 dB. Dialogue, of course, was favored in the mix; and an automated balance regulator was developed to keep it well above music and effects (this was the "up-and-downer" that we mentioned in ch. 2).

THE GREAT DEPRESSION AND THE CONSOLIDATION OF GENRES

Attendance, which had reached 80 million per week in 1930, tumbled to 55 million only two years later. The revenues from foreign markets were also de-clining, not only because of the general economic downturn but also because most of the foreign theaters had been wired for sound by this time and natu-rally were demanding pictures with dialogue in their own languages. With the cost of producing a sound picture running about double that of a silent, it became difficult for studios to turn a profit. One of the ways that American studios responded was to distribute films with dubbed dialogue (and often different music tracks)—films dubbed in Spanish in particular were impor-tant income sources for studios throughout the 1930s. Even more important, the studios turned to genre films, which helped to regularize production and create more predictable attendance numbers. Genres were standardized in as many dimensions as possible, including the use of music and sound.

The Sound Track in the Studio Era and Elements of Style

THE CLASSICAL SYSTEM

During the late 1910s and 1920s, Hollywood had developed a filmmaking sys-tem that was dominated by editing, whose fundamental commitment there-fore was to a narrative assembled from various shots in postproduction. The transition to the sound film briefly challenged this commitment inasmuch as it offered the alternative of recorded performance. Then, too, early sound film often needed to be staged for the microphone, which took precedence in choosing camera angles, blocking, lighting, vocal delivery and so forth. As Hollywood developed its recording technology, however, it did so in directions that reasserted its commitment to the narrative built through editing. In partic-ular, the technology was pushed to facilitate the expression of narrative clarity (a priority that we discussed early in ch. 1). Microphone techniques ensured a preponderance of direct sound, and the basic mixing strategy heavily favored dialogue, but the key innovation was the development of a reliable system of rerecording, as it permitted a conception of the sound track not as a simple reproduction but as an entity to be built in postproduction through editing.

What emerged from this was a clear separation and functional differentiation in the sound track components. Sound film became a talking film, that is, a film centered on dialogue. This made sense from the standpoint of story centered on character because dialogue is, like the visual close up, the most overt aural expression of character. Dialogue was usually further emphasized by being presented in synchronization, departures from which were generally motivated by an appeal to narrative hierarchy—for instance, reaction shots or use of offscreen sound to motivate a cut. Filmmakers went to great lengths to make sure that nothing on the sound track interfered with the intelligibility of dialogue. When it came to making decisions about what should be rendered on the sound track, comprehension almost always trumped realism. When this principle was violated, the inversion generally served a clear narrative function. For instance, a loud background such as a raging fire might overpower a character shouting, making the words somewhat inaudible. This heightened the realism of the sequence, to be sure, but more important, the apparent elevation of the sound of the fire served the narrative function of emphasizing its power: the fire threatened to consume the voice and by analogy the character. In this sense, the sound of the fire would be treated almost as a voice, one that transformed the fire, if only for a moment, into something like a character. (See Figure 12-4 for an example and commentary). The point to be taken from this is that the exception was validated by an appeal back to the story.

FOREGROUND AND BACKGROUND

The sound film of the studio era maintained a consistent distinction between audible foreground and background with dialogue most commonly occupying the foreground. As David Bordwell notes, "classical sound technique articulates foreground (principal voice) and background (silence, 'background' noise, music 'under' the action) with the same precision that camera and staging distinguish visual planes."[3] As with the image track, such hierarchy was effective in rendering a clear narrative representation. The sidebar refers to an attempt from the time to draw a theoretical analogy between the sound and image track: where the image used lighting and contrast to create depth and narrative focus, the sound track attempted the same thing with volume and reverberation (reflected sound). All things being equal, something relatively loud with a high degree of direct sound will be taken as foreground. Not surprisingly, in classical Hollywood film the foreground usually consisted of dialogue, and it was usually synchronized to a visible body.

With the two-dimensional camera, which bears the same psychological relation to the eye as the monaural sound does to the ear, the illusion of depth can be achieved by the proper use of lighting and contrast, just as by the manipulation of loudness and reverberation with the microphone. And just as the eye can be drawn to particular persons or objects by the adjustment of focal length, so can the ear be arrested by the intensification of important sounds and the rejection of unimportant ones.
—Leon S. Becker (1944)[4]

Figure 12-4. *You Can't Take It with You* (1938). The Kirbys, a well-to-do family, make an unexpected visit to the Vanderhofs, the eccentric family of their son's fiancée, Alice. When the visit is interrupted by a police raid, the entire group is hauled off to jail, leading to a courtroom scene that opposes the Kirbys and their lawyers to the Vanderhofs and the larger community that has packed the court in their support. During the proceedings, the crowd grows unruly, all but drowning out the attempts by Mr. Kirby, his lawyers, and even the somewhat bemused judge to impose order. In the shot above, Tony Kirby, the son (played by James Stewart), attempts to reason with Alice (Jean Arthur), but his words are obscured by the crowd noise. In the scene, the crowd itself briefly becomes the dominant character, reflecting the narrative theme that the community of friendship has far more power than wealth in producing happiness.

The system of regulating sound is functionally defined, meaning that different components of the sound track—dialogue, music, or effects—can serve different functions intermittently. The background, for instance, can be formed by any of the components, although dialogue only rarely is placed there, and, when it is, it is most often construed as a sound effect such as crowd noise. Music, sound effects, or dialogue can all occupy the foreground position, which will be determined by narrative salience. When Lola Lola (Marlene Dietrich) sings a song in *Der blaue Engel* (*The Blue Angel*, 1930), music is obviously treated as a foreground event. When she is talking to Professor Rath in her dressing room with the door open, dialogue occupies the foreground, and music, in the background, is understood as ambient sound, as emanating from the diegetic world beyond the door.

The hierarchical stratification of the sound track is correlated with but not determined by volume. Foreground events, especially dialogue, are generally closely miked with a high degree of direct sound and mixed at higher levels than background sound when both occupy the sound track simultaneously. On the other hand, background sound is typically mixed at a higher level in the absence of foreground events; thus, nondiegetic music, for instance, can become very prominent at moments when foreground sound is largely suspended, as in establishing shots, for example, or when the film brackets off the unfolding of "normal" diegetic time and sound, as in montage sequences. It is also noteworthy that both establishing shots and montage sequences often appear mute, without diegetic sound, and thus offer a throwback, as it were, to the silent film. More important, such scenes also tend to be associated with filmic spectacle.

At any moment any of the three sound track components may or may not be present as well. This intermittent quality offered filmmakers useful flexibility and choice: music or sound might be used for ambience; dialogue or music might express character feeling; offscreen dialogue ("hello") or effect (knock at the door) might serve to motivate a cut; and so forth.

The presence of a strong hierarchy between foreground and background was almost as important to establishing narrative clarity as making a clean recording of the dialogue. Filmmakers controlled the hierarchy of the sound track in various ways. First of all, the foreground was louder, generally with low reverberation. Background sound, by contrast, was usually treated nonsynchronously, and one of the important functions of that lack of synchronization was to allow foreground events—dialogue and sound effects—to emerge as important and narratively marked by virtue of their synchronization. Synchronized bodies are narratively important bodies: this was a fundamental premise of classical Hollywood sound design (and remains fundamental to all cinema to the present day). The audience came to know that a character was important because the sounds that his or her body (dialogue, sound effects) made as it moved through the diegetic world seemed to demand synchronization. Many crowd scenes were shot silent and fit with non-synchronized sound later, not just to save money but also because a lack of close synchronization encouraged spectators to read the noise as background. When synchronization did occur in such scenes, it served generally as a figure of individuation: focus fell on the bodies that the sound track granted individuated representation through synchronization.

In early sound film, the audio background consisted primarily of silence, undoubtedly due to the conceptual and technological challenges of mixing (Figure 12-5). Conceptually, silence was the simplest background: through mere presence, foreground sounds stood out against a background of silence. In such a "monophonic" context, whatever was heard would occupy the foreground by

Figure 12-5. *Das Testament Des Dr. Mabuse* (1933). A conversation between Prof. Dr. Kramm (Theodor Loos) and Prof. Dr. Baum (Oscar Beregi, Sr.): The silent background allows for better intelligibility of dialogue but it can neither distinguish one place from another nor can it distract from the prominent hiss of the sound track.

default. Because this basic hierarchy of presence and absence was simple, it was often used, particularly early in the era. Although effective, this hierarchy was also drastic. Because silence established no basic sound level against which narrative pertinence could be measured, every sound was fraught with significance; and it was only with great difficulty that the relative importance of sounds could be established against a background of silence. Therefore other sounds had to be carefully managed. Silence was also wholly undifferentiated and thus ineffective at marking place (room, outdoors, etc.) as characteristic. Consequently, it could not be used to distinguish one sequence from another or to set up a hierarchy among the shots on the basis of the unity of place.

A silent background was also extremely difficult to cut dialogue against. Subtle changes between shots and takes, variation in microphone placement and so forth were accentuated when the only background was silence. Indeed, negotiating the cut with a simple background of silence proved a particular aesthetic and technological challenge. The most obvious solution to managing the relation of sound and image across a cut in this situation—matching a cut in image with a cut in sound—has the effect, as film sound historian James Lastra points out, of emphasizing the autonomy of the shot at the expense of the coherence of the sequence.[5] The commentary for Figure 12-6 discusses this issue with respect to the opening sequence of *The Broadway Melody* (1929). The prohibition against cutting sound and image at the same point within a sequence was one way of forcing filmmakers to conceptualize sound in terms of narrative sequence rather than image, to conceive background sound vis-à-vis foreground, and, ultimately, to think about sonic continuity across the cut.

Another factor that discouraged using silence as the primary background was that it could not mask the hiss of the sound reproducing apparatus, a hiss that with optical sound became progressively more audible with wear. Critical complaints about the early talkies, especially dramas, spoke not just to the stilted dialogue that was a product of theatrical projection and the technological shortcomings of early microphones but also to the audibility of the silence between the lines, as opposed to the live situation of the theater: in other words, the hiss revealed talking film as nothing other than recorded drama. So long as the background remained conceived in terms of silence, filmmakers could only conceal the hiss by filling the sound track with diegetically motivated sound, often to cacophonous and narratively disorienting results.

The invention of the concept of audio background—a ground other than mere silence—was therefore crucial to constituting sound film; and this concept required in turn the availability of rerecording to make its realization feasible. However much clarity of dialogue may have seemed to drive the construction of the sound track, it was the underlying continuity of audible background sound across cuts that encouraged spectators to bind a series of individual disparate shots into longer spans—scenes and sequences. The audio background thus became the constructive equivalent to the early practice of the visual master shot, a medium to long shot of a sequence, filmed uninterrupted from beginning to end, which was used to ensure synchronization and continuity of action and sound across the sequence. Sound would be recorded along with the master shot, and then closer shots, whether taken simultaneously with or separately from the master shot, could be cut in on the basis of that continuity. In the finished film, the visual master shot was generally used at the beginning of the sequence and other points of spatial and narrative redefinition in the sequence, and it established the geography of the place and orients the figures in relation to a visual background that maintained visual continuity across cuts. Similarly, the audio background served to unify the sequence by means of what might be termed sonic ambience, that is, the characteristic sound of the place. (In moving to a audio background, film was moving from a monophonic conceptualization of the sound track to one characterized more

a	b	c
d	e	f
g	h	i

Figure 12-6. *The Broadway Melody.* In the opening sequence, each cut in image is matched by a cut in sound; the sound exactly matches the image. The opening shot (a) presents the exterior of the building and we hear the blending of several musical performances. The second shot (b) moves to the interior, and we hear some distant lines of dialogue spoken by Eddie (Charles King, left, at the piano) amidst the general musical din. Shot 3 (c) moves inside one of the practice rooms shot, the sound of the woman's singing voice now treated clearly and without disruption of the noisy musical background. Shot 4 (d) returns to the outer room, the background just as noisy as before despite the closer framing. The fifth shot (e) and seventh (g) are treated analogously to (c); whereas the sixth (f) likewise goes back to (d). Finally, shot 8 (h) starts again with the loud background, which is mitigated slightly for the move to a medium shot (i), during which Eddie's dialogue is somewhat elevated with respect to the general noise of the background. With no background but silence to mediate the cuts between shots—and with the background silence masked by the extensive foreground sounds—the sound here is guided by what is happening immediately in the shot rather than by the coherence of the overall sequence. Although this might seem like a perfectly natural way of proceeding—the sound of each shot is "realistic"—the effect in fact is narratively quite disorienting and runs counter to what became codified as classical Hollywood sound practice, which insists on a structured relationship between foreground and a generally audible background.

akin to melody and accompaniment, with dialogue usually understood to occupy to the place of "melody.") This sonic ambience was generally added in
postproduction, where filmmakers could select realistic ambient sound (crowd
noises, crickets, water, and so forth) or take the more stylized route of music, a
choice that became increasingly common after 1933.

BACKGROUND(ED) MUSIC AND THE SOUND TRACK

Given the limited fidelity of the early optical tracks and the constant concern about the intelligibility of dialogue, music generally turned out to be
a more effective medium for the background than did ambient sound itself.
The primary reason was that, with the exception of a few characteristic "white
noise" sounds, such as crowds, waterfalls, engine sounds, and so forth, it was
difficult to construct a consistent and continuous background of ambient
sound that did not distract from the intelligibility of the dialogue. Although
somewhat more common by the 1940s, ambient sound only began to used
as a background regularly in the 1950s, thanks in part to the advent of stereo,
which allowed a spatial separation of ambient sound from dialogue, in part
to the higher fidelity of magnetic tape recording, which likewise increased
the intelligibility of dialogue. Earlier, ambient sound tended to be employed
in highly conventionalized contexts; it also tended to be restricted to establishing shots, as in Figure 12-7, because it would not then interfere with

Figure 12-7. *The Big Sleep* (1946). In the casino scene, the choice of ambient sound rather   a | b | c
than music pertains to the exterior setting of the casino itself, which is marked sonically by
the sound of music (heard in counterpoint to the crickets). Understood in terms of sound, the
sequence as a whole is structured as a sort of palindrome, moving from (a) sounds of nature in
the exterior to (b) diegetic music and performance on the interior and then (c) into the private
meeting with casino owner Eddie Mars (John Ridgely), which serves as the central moment of
the sequence. The process then reverses, as Marlow (Humphrey Bogart) returns to the casino
and watches Mrs. Routledge (Lauren Bacall) win at roulette before leaving, at which point the
sound track returns to the footsteps and ambient sound of crickets. The sound in the sequence
thus tracks an underlying thematic thread of the narrative: crickets are opposed to music, as
exterior is opposed to interior, the innocence but loneliness of nature to the decadence but
community of culture.

dialogue. Music, by contrast, had the advantage of being composed, and a skilled composer could work it in and around dialogue to a degree that ambient sound could not match. This was an important consideration in the relatively low fidelity environment of early optical sound. Another consideration was that the underscoring, unlike ambient sound, was understood to be fully nondiegetic; that is, it was a representation of ambience rather than making any pretenses toward being a depiction of ambient sound itself. Consequently, the dynamic level of music could be more freely manipulated in the mix without threatening to dissolve the rendering of reality in which the diegetic sound track otherwise engages. These later two situations are discussed in the commentary for Figure 12-8.

SCORING PRACTICES

Composers adopted a variety of approaches to sound film. Two basic methods had been inherited from the silent era: playing the overall mood of a scene, which had been associated especially with the orchestral practice of the picture palace, and playing to the details, which had been associated with improvising keyboard players. Both methods continued in the sound era, with overall mood being favored for establishing, spectacle, and montage sequences and playing to details being favored for underscoring dialogue, especially in melodramatic scenes.

a | b **Figure 12-8.** *The Adventures of Robin Hood* (1938). Two early scenes provide a good example of the interplay between dialogue and music. (a) The dubbing volume of Erich Korngold's rousing score is routinely raised and lowered in the first tax collection scene and the meeting of Robin Hood (Errol Flynn) with Sir Guy (Basil Rathbone). (b) The varied orchestration throughout the following court scene allows the score to be played at a consistent level throughout the dialogue between Prince John (Claude Rains) and Maid Marian (Olivia De Havilland).

Playing to details had an advantage in dialogue sequences in that the music was carefully composed to fit between and around the lines dialogue, whereas playing to the overall mood—say a love theme—necessarily simply went on as written. The conductor might be able to coax the music around the dialogue somewhat by judiciously pushing the performance forward or holding it back, and proper orchestration could mitigate masking, allowing the music to sound somewhat louder without affecting the intelligibility of the dialogue. The balance with the dialogue, however, would have to be accomplished primarily through mixing.

Playing the overall mood remained a common solution, however, because it held the important advantage of continuity, of presenting well-rounded musical themes and ideas, rather than constantly breaking off into a series of seemingly musically incoherent fragments, fermatas and stingers, however well motivated they might be dramatically. Musical continuity could also bind a series of otherwise disparate shots together, thereby reinforcing the principle of the sequence. This was the basis for its use covering establishing and especially montage sequences, but it could also be used to emphasize the central idea of a sequence. A love scene, for instance, was often scored through the simple device of playing a love theme under the dialogue. Doing so had the effect of cueing the basic mood of the scene rather than the individual words, which in and of themselves could be trite, mundane, or even ridiculous and, as mentioned in the previous chapter, often caused audiences discomfort. Music in such cases could productively divert attention away from those words to the particular sentiment of the scene (Figure 12-9).

In practice, most composers drew on both methods, and the cues themselves were often as not hybrids: based in thematic material, the music would nevertheless follow the dramatic course of a scene and mark especially important turning points with changes in its own direction.

Composers also followed silent-film practice in favoring the leitmotif as a principle in constructing their scores. Indeed, the device was probably more common in the sound film if for no other reason than the score was specifically composed for the film. (Special scores of the silent era also tended to be leitmotivic.) As in the silent era, leitmotifs tended to be conceived as well-rounded themes, and composers would usually restrict themselves only to a handful, usually associated with the principal characters (main theme for the hero, love theme for the heroine) but sometimes referring to more abstract ideas. The recurring music Miklós Rózsa used to initiate the flashbacks in *Double Indemnity* (1944) is a good example of this more abstract use.

What we have described here, of course, is the classical practice that was the focus of most of our discussion and analyses in the chapters of Parts I and II. Although it certainly dominated cinema by the later 1930s, this classical

Figure 12-9. *Yankee Doodle Dandy* (1942). After singing "Mary," a song George (James Cagney) has written for his fiancée (Joan Leslie), the couple engages in a brief, intimate conversation, which is underscored by the song in a light orchestral arrangement. This practice is typical of musicals, where the transfer of the song from diegetic performance to nondiegetic orchestra serves to underscore the ideal of romance. (It resembles an audio dissolve.) But love scenes in dramatic films are often treated analogously, with the love theme being played without musical interruption. (In this case, the song has been shortened but the continuity is unaffected.)

practice was not, however, the only possibility. Mainly outside Hollywood, debates on the proper relation of sound and image raged almost from the moment sound feature films were first exhibited. Some critics thought synchronized dialogue was overly redundant and urged using the sound track more imaginatively. Sergei Eisenstein thought sound could best be most effective when considered in counterpoint to (rather than synchronization with) the image and proposed that music be treated similarly. In this way Eisenstein thought sound (and music) could take on the character of montage.[6] (Eisenstein found a sympathetic ear of many composers because in working with Sergei Prokofiev he had brought the composer in early in the production process and even reversed the usual procedure by cutting some scenes to music.) Since the silent era, "synchronization" had always been taken as the goal of film music; that is, music was understood as a reflection of, or reaction to, the drama. Counterpoint suggested other relations: Music might, for instance, play against the image or remain indifferent to it. In any case, music might be more proactive.

Production

PRODUCTION PHASES

The sound film became codified with the establishment of the postproduction phase of sound; with the ability to rerecord, studios created three major departments devoted to sound— production, music, and sound (effects). Each department had clearly defined responsibilities. Production sound (all sound on the set) was devoted almost entirely to capturing dialogue. In general, rerecording dialogue was, with the exception of dubbing into foreign languages, avoided until the late 1930s because it was difficult to match microphone perspective in rerecording dialogue. Production sound therefore had to do everything possible to ensure a clear recording of the dialogue. Dialogue might be touched up during postproduction, but initially at least many of the dialogue editing chores were handled by the picture editor, who cut the picture to the sound track during the early years of multicamera shooting and would often follow the master shot for continuity after the return to single-camera filming. Sound edits would be cut in and joined using a bloop so as to avoid pops on the sound track at edit points (Figure 12-10).

Sounds other than dialogue (footsteps, clothing noises, etc.) were minimized on the set because they could inadvertently obscure lines of dialogue or cause continuity problems when shots from different takes were joined. Instead, like music, the vast majority of effects would be added during postproduction where the levels could be careful balanced to ensure the clarity of dialogue and, even more important, the proper narrative focus of a scene. Footsteps, for instance, could be introduced or not, depending on the perceived needs of the scene. Inevitably, however, the fact that music and effects were added in postproduction reinforced the sense that they were to be considered something added, supplementary rather than primary.

Although optical sound meant that the sound track was physically attached to the image track for purposes of exhibition, this was not the case until the final print was made. Each department produced its own sound strip (indeed often more one) and only at the end of postproduction would these be mixed down into a single track, properly balanced for narration and modulated for distribution. This combined track would then be placed beside the image on the exhibition print (see Figure 12-11).

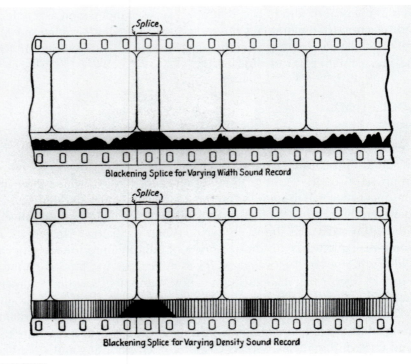

Splice

Blackening Splice for Varying Width Sound Record

Splice

Blackening Splice for Varying Density Sound Record

Figure 12-10. Blooping. Each edit of the sound track needed to be blooped to avoid a "pop" where the wave forms did not perfectly match up. Blooping involved placing an opaque elliptical or trapezoidal mark across the edit point. This produces the effect of a quick fade out and fade in. A semicircular stroke of a pen would also do the trick.

MUSIC DEPARTMENT

The music department was run by a director, who was responsible for such administrative tasks as budget, scheduling, and assigning composers (and other musical personnel such as orchestrators and music editors); the director might occasionally also perform other tasks such as conducting when the composer was unavailable to do so. Unlike the music director of the silent era picture house, the job in the studio was generally more managerial than creative in scope. Nevertheless, most music directors were also working composers. Indeed, often they were top-notch composers (for example, Herbert Stothart at MGM, Alfred Newman at 20th Century Fox, and Victor Young at Paramount).

Once the task of scoring a film became an accepted part of postproduction in the early 1930s, the basic job of the film composer was to write the underscore and to oversee its performance and recording. (Although the methods and constraints have evolved greatly over the past eighty-five years, the duties

\multicolumn{4}{c}{RERECORDING CUE SHEET}			
PICTURE TITLE Dangerous Speed		REEL #4	
EFFECTS A	EFFECTS B	MUSIC	SYNC MARKS DIALOGUE
			CAR IN AND STOP
ILLING MOTOR			DIALOGUE
↓			↓
CAR START OUT		MUSIC	
CONTINUED THROUGH DISSOLVE			
PASSING CAR		↓	
	MOTOR NOISE		DIALOGUE
APPROACHING CAR		MUSIC	
	PASSING CAR		
TIRE SKID			
	PASSING CAR		
TIRE SKID			
	PASSING CAR	↓	
MOTOR NOISE			DIALOGUE
CAR HITS FENCE	WOOD BREAKING		SCREAMS
GLASS CRASHING	WRECK CRASH		

Figure 12-11. Rerecording cue sheet for a final mix. These instructions for the rerecording mixers would typically be prepared by the picture editor in consultation with the music and sound department. In this case there are four sound strips, two for effects, and one each for music and dialogue. Note that the initial car sound effect and screams are contained on the "dialogue" strip. Because the dialogue track accompanies the picture during editing, significant sounds would often be placed on this track at moments dialogue was absent.

of the composer remain largely the same today). During the studio era, most composers worked full-time in the music department of the studio that hired them (although, like stars, directors, and other personnel they were sometimes "lent" to other studios to work on individual projects). The composer was the central creative agent in the music department. Once a picture assignment was made, the composer would meet with the director in a "spotting session," compose the music, and usually record the score with orchestra—all within the confines of the studio lot itself. During the spotting session, the composer and director would discuss the general concepts of the entire score as well as specific requirements of certain scenes. This was quite similar to the sorts of discussions music directors and their staffs would have had over how to fit music to the picture in the silent era. (See the commentary for Figure 12-12 for a discussion of structural spotting in *King Kong* (1933).) Although the composer's life during the studio era had a great amount of stability (one could work without worrying where the next job would come from), it also lacked flexibility: generally speaking, composers had limited control over their film assignments, and only the most prominent had much negotiating power in terms of compensation because composers (like almost everyone else, including actors) worked on a salary basis for the studios. Composers typically did not even own the rights to their music, as everything was done on a work-for-hire basis (a practice that became less common in the 1950s but has persisted to a surprising degree even into the present day).

During the studio era, the actual labor of composing film music was always broken down into writing the music and scoring it, or composition proper and orchestration. These were considered two separate occupations, and jobs were most commonly, although not always, filled by separate people. Although this division of labor has struck many—even those in the industry—as illogical, it had a precedent in the theater (where many of the film composers started). In any case, it did increase the speed at which music could be composed because the composer did not have to worry about writing out music for all of the parts. The orchestrator could also serve as a kind of musical copy editor, catching incorrect clefs, accidentals, and other sorts of errors before they found their way into the parts and disrupted the recording session. (A good copyist—the person responsible for creating the parts for the orchestral musicians—could serve a similar function.) Moreover, particularly early in the sound era, the microphone posed scoring issues that benefited from specialized knowledge that an experienced orchestrator could provide. In any case, the division of labor between composition and orchestration has proved resilient in the film industry, and it continues to this day.

Typically, the orchestrator was assigned to take the composer's sketch score of each cue (usually written on four to eight musical staff lines) and separate out the individual instrument parts onto a full score (which contained as many as thirty to forty staff lines, each for a different instrument). The sketch score could vary in detail, but it would usually contain at minimum a melodic line and indications for harmonic treatment; often these sketch scores were more or less reductions of the full score, with countermelodies, accompaniment patterns and instrumentation all present in the sketch. In the latter cases, the orchestrator was responsible for determining the final balance and making sure the music sounded as good as possible given the orchestra that was budgeted. In the former case the orchestrator could play a much more substantive compositional role—for instance, assigning the melody to the violins, clarinets, and horns, devising a countermelody for the violas and English horn, or working out an ostinato accompaniment pattern in the cellos, basses, percussion, and piano parts. When time was short, trusted orchestrators often became what might be considered assistant composers, writing cues within the guidelines specified by the actual credited composer. (The practice of "uncredited" music was common—and in fact remains so to this day; especially in B-films, one might find that several staff composers wrote cues for a film, whose music was more often than not credited to the music department director.)

Besides the orchestrator, the composer also worked closely with the music editor. One of the most important initial duties of the music editor was to compile a cue sheet for each scene that would require music. The composer would consult this in working out the score. The cue sheet included a list of exact timings, a detailed description of the action, the type of camera framing and angles used, and every word in the dialogue track. Hugo Friedhofer described the process as Max Steiner used it in the 1930s and 1940s:

> Steiner, after running the picture once—at the most twice—would depend entirely on the cue sheets which were supplied to him by his music editor—who was really not a music editor, in that there were some union restrictions at that time that specified that nobody except a film editor could touch a foot of film at any time. So what he did was simply to time the stuff on the movieola [an editing machine] and make up the cue sheets.[7]

Once the music had been composed and scored, the music editor was responsible for preparing a click track (if needed) and a marked-up, working print of the film itself. The click track was essentially a metronome track that would be played back to the musicians through headphones. It was created by punching holes in the sound track of blank leader and was commonly used in cartoons and those scenes that needed precise timings (such as chases or comedy scenes with "hits" on action). Those scenes not requiring a click track (the majority) would be conducted "to picture": the film was actually shown without sound on a screen positioned behind the orchestra (see Figure 12-13). The music editor would have prepared this print to aid the conductor by marking the various segments with streamers (a diagonal line drawn on the film used to indicate beginnings and endings of sections) or punches (holes punched on the film at regular intervals used to indicate tempo).

The actual recording process obviously required the presence of musicians—conductors and players. The conductor was usually the composer or the head of the music department at the studio. The composer was generally preferred because he—in the studio era composers were almost always men—

Figure 12-12. *King Kong* shows how effective the systematic use of spotting can be. The film breaks down into three large segments determined by locale: New York City, Skull Island, and a return to New York City. The sound is treated in a characteristically different fashion in each segment. In the original sequence in the city (a-b), the sound is very "efficient": Dialogue drives almost every sequence, there is no music and little ambient sound. Effects are confined to only most obvious sounds. Essentially, we hear exactly what we see. This appears as a rationally organized sonic space: Everything in its proper space, but a dearth of sound makes the city feel lifeless (a). The lack of music means that we are as unsure of Denham's intentions as is Anne during their meeting (b).

a	b
c	d
e	f
g	h
i	j

The scene on the ship begins, like the initial New York City sequence, with no music. When the ship enters the fog around Skull Island (c), however, music enters, and music continues to be present for almost the entirety of the Island sequence (d-h). Moreover, the music often hovers in an uncertain state—drums are confused with "breakers," the images of the native drummers do not coincide with full orchestra we hear (d), and sound effects are sweetened with music. When the leader descends the stairs (e), for instance, each footstep is rendered by the orchestra. The overall impression of this treatment is that the island is a fundamentally musical place, and that the island is therefore an enchanted space. The power of dialogue, by contrast, is subverted on Skull Island. It is still present, to be sure, but over the course of the sequence it tends to devolve into the barking of orders, which are nearly always ineffectual, or screams, which places human speech on the same plane as the sounds of the animals encountered (f). Music is present for the entire sequence on the island except the battle between Kong and the tyrannosaurus rex (g); the exclusive use of effects here is in line with the representation of a regression to pure animality. Music and effects dominate the sound track on Skull Island, then, which leaves the impression that the island is a primitive, pre-rational (because pre-linguistic) aural space. Skull Island is not lifeless like the city, but it lacks any sense of rational control of its sound. In any case, it is significant that dialogue reasserts control over the sound track once Kong has been captured at the end of the sequence (h).

At this point, music is transformed into theater music, which leads to a dissolve back to the city and crowds entering to see an exhibition featuring Kong. With this theater music playing in the background, the impression of the city is quite different from the lifeless image of the opening sequence, but the musical treatment is also distinct from the island, an impression that is furthered during the show when Denham's theatrical speech calls up fanfares and marches on cue: the music here is functional, contained, bound to the image. Music appears diegetically shackled here just as Kong is shackled. This changes when Kong escapes (i): the music breaks free of its theatrical trappings and becomes completely nondiegetic the exact moment Kong bursts his bonds, and the sound track regresses to the effects, screams and music that had been characteristic of Skull Island. As with the island, music is ubiquitous in the remainder of the sequence, disappearing only for the final battle between Kong and the airplanes (j), which recalls the fight with the tyrannosaurus rex and suggests a basic inhumanity to the human actions in the scene. This effect is emphasized by the music, which returns empathetically scoring Kong's pain just as he is mortally wounded. Dialogue takes over again only after Kong is dead, with the music, however, continuing in empathetic mourning.

The spotting of the film for music and sound makes for a clear tripartite, dialectical scheme: The city is initially presented as rational, but mundane and lifeless. The island, by contrast, is presented as teeming with life, but it is irrational and uncivilized. The return to the city seeks to reconcile the lifeless city with the irrational island but an actual "synthesis" of a city rationally organized and alive comes only at the expense of the sacrifice of Kong.

Figure 12-13. *Okay for Sound.* This is a music recording session for *Night and Day.* The music recording mixer (in the foreground) adjusts the mixing panel according to notations in the score.

knew the music best, had the best sense as to how the music was to fit with the film, and could ensure that the (expensive) time in the studio was minimized. Even if not up to the dimensions of a full symphony orchestra, the number of musicians in a studio orchestra was considerable, and they were paid by the hour, so any delays in the studio could prove costly. The job of film studio musician was (and remains) one of the most demanding jobs in the industry. These players have legendary reputations. During the studio era, Hollywood attracted many of the best orchestral musicians in the world. They were certainly the best sight readers: they were called upon daily to play anything a composer had written with little rehearsal and no mistakes.

Although most work on music was done in postproduction once rerecording became the norm, an exception was source music (either in drama or in musicals), which required "prescoring." (Animation often used prescoring as well, although music and image production could also proceed in parallel, both composers and animators working off of detailed cue sheets.) As the term suggests, prescoring involved writing music prior to the shooting. Filming could then be done silent to playback. In the previous chapter, we mentioned that shooting to playback was common in the early sound era (because it gave the cameras more freedom), and it remained the norm for onscreen musical performance throughout the studio era because it continued to give film makers more flexibility in terms of editing. By the late 1930s, prescoring usually involved multichannel recording for vocal music. The singer would be aurally isolated from the other musicians, which allowed for much better balance control and permitted the editing of the vocal track. (See Figure 12-14 for an exceptional use of this technique.)

Prescoring involved many of the same personnel that would work on the actual scoring—at least the job descriptions were similar. Stylistically, music that was prescored was often in popular style, which required a different ensemble from the studio orchestra. It also often needed to be arranged for a vocalist (or choral ensemble) and choreography. In musicals, the credited

Figure 12-14. *One Hundred Men and a Girl* (1937). This film pioneered massive multitrack recording of music. Eight separate channels were used—six for individual sections of the orchestra, one for the orchestra as a whole and one for Deanna Durbin's voice. This process allowed the performances themselves to be assembled through editing and with precise control of balance. Durbin was also able to rerecord portions of her numbers, especially some high notes, which were then combined with other takes to produce the edited version of her performances in the film.

composer was frequently well-known—someone like Irving Berlin, Jerome Kern, or George Gershwin—and not under long-term contract to the studio. In this case, the composer was commissioned only to write the songs. The songs would then be dispersed to arrangers, who would work out arrangements suitable to the actors' voices and to any choreography for the scene. These arrangements would in turn be given to orchestrators, who scored the music for the appropriate ensemble. Sometimes, but not always, one person served as both arranger and orchestrator of the song. Orchestrators for prescoring and scoring were no more interchangeable than were song composers and composers who wrote the background score. Some were accomplished at both, but orchestrating popular song was considered its own specialty and most of these specialists had backgrounds in dance band arrangement (Figure 12-15).

Figure 12-15. *Casablanca* (1942). During Rick's flashback, Rick and Ilsa go dancing at a night club. The dance band music for the scene, an arrangement of the song "Perfidia," segues smoothly out of the preceding orchestral score and will move without a break back into the orchestra at the end of the brief scene. Whereas Max Steiner composed the orchestral score, another Warner Brothers staff member, Frank Perkins, was responsible for arranging the song, which had also been used earlier that same year in *Now, Voyager* (1942), another film Steiner had scored. Perkins wrote many of the diegetic music arrangements for Steiner's films in the 1940s, including a number of other band arrangements for *Casablanca*.

SOUND DEPARTMENT

Sound was usually divided into two departments, one devoted to production sound, the other to postproduction. In the studio era, the production sound department was organized to capture dialogue and its principal workers—boom operators, mixers, and recordists—reflected that fact: everything they did was predicated on ensuring a technically clean dialogue recording. In postproduction, dialogue continued to be treated separately from other sound, and its editing was closely allied with the picture editing.

Sound effects, by contrast, came under the full jurisdiction of the sound department. Although effects might also be taken from production sound, they were far more likely to come out of libraries. Because most sound effects were physically cut in, simultaneous sounds required a separate sound strip for each sound. It was common to have a half dozen sound strips in use at any one time—even more than a dozen was not all that unusual. Although in principle, the number of simultaneous (or near simultaneous) sounds was unlimited, in practice the difficulty of working with large numbers of sound strips was another limiting factor on density.

In general, the sound department was less elaborately organized than the music department in the 1930s; before the rise of sound design in the 1970s, it was understood more as a technical department than an artistic one. This valuation can be seen in the types of screen credit given and the academy awards, both of which centered on departments (or department heads) rather than individuals.

Summary

The sound track of the studio era was codified around developments in the techniques of rerecording. Rerecording allowed studios to cut the cost of sound-film production by making it possible to return to single camera shooting and by simplifying the work of the production sound team, which could thereby focus on dialogue. Adding music and effects in postproduction offered the filmmakers much needed flexibility as they could build their story through editing the sound track just as they could with editing of the picture.

CHAPTER 13

The Stereo Sound Track and the Post-Classical Era (1950–1975)

Introduction

Experimental work on stereo sound had begun already in the 1920s, when research was pursued, primarily by AT&T and RCA, as a means of improving the fidelity of recorded and transmitted sound. The collapse of the recording industry at the outset of the Great Depression combined with the limited bandwidth for transmitting radio broadcasts to discourage the immediate commercial exploitation of stereo sound. Film, on the other hand, was in a better position to exploit stereo than either the recording industry or radio, and studios experimented with widescreen film and larger area for sound tracks (which offered both higher fidelity and a wider dynamic range) during the early sound era, culminating in the Fox Grandeur system (see Figure 13-1). The film industry, however, was also financially stressed by the Depression, and the studios collectively decided it was in their best interest to consolidate and standardize sound-film production rather than expending money to rewire and re-equip their theaters and production facilities. Although stereo sound was commercially feasible by 1940—Disney deployed such a system for *Fantasia* (see Figure 13-2)—it would not be systematically exploited by the industry until the introduction of **Cinemascope** in the early 1950s.

Issues of High Fidelity and Stereo Sound

LEGAL AND ECONOMIC CHALLENGES TO THE INDUSTRY

In a relatively short span of time following WWII, changes in technology, law, and social conditions prompted a move toward stereo sound. Technologically, the development of the long-playing record with a greater frequency response

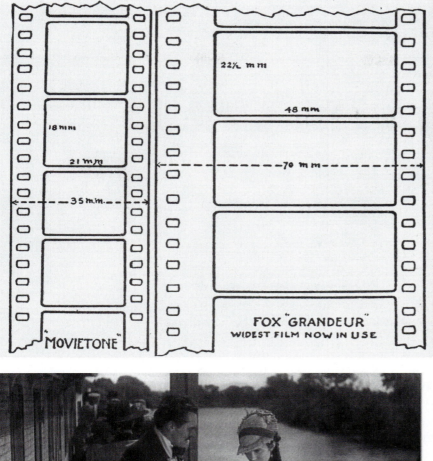

Figure 13-1. (a) A comparison of Movietone and Grandeur formats. Note, in particular, the larger space (between the left sprocket holes and the image) available for the sound track in the Grandeur format. (b) A frame from the Grandeur version of *The Big Trail* (1930), which was also shot in a regular 35 mm version. The Grandeur format was abandoned in the early 1930s due to cost and the limited number of theaters capable of exhibiting films in the format.

a
b

Figure 13-2. Sound mixers making a multitrack recording of the Philadelphia Orchestra for use in *Fantasia*. Eight channels were used, and a mixer was required to monitor each channel.

brought vast improvement to music in the home. The introduction of magnetic tape likewise allowed an efficient and relatively inexpensive way to record and mix sound into a number of channels. This also provided an efficient way to provide a variety of mixes, which proved expedient when many theaters decided against installing stereo sound.

The 1948 United States Supreme Court's decision on the Paramount consent decree (1940), which prohibited studios from owning theaters, completely transformed the economics of the film industry. The traditional studio system dissolved over the 1950s. As the studios moved out of the business of exhibition, they also withdrew from production, focusing instead on financing and distribution, which was more profitable and seemingly less risky. Production grew increasingly independent, which placed a stronger burden on each film to be profitable because losses on one film could no longer be covered by gains on another. The emphasis on profit also led to a production strategy favoring fewer but more spectacular films because the latter films were more likely to generate a substantial profit. This strategy represented a change from the studio era. Formerly, vertical integration, where studios were heavily invested in producing, distributing and exhibiting films, had ensured that films made by a studio always found an exhibition outlet. This meant that during the studio era, regularity of production was as important to the industry as was turning out films that were considered "events." Over the course of the 1950s, however, more and more films emphasized spectacle and grandeur, and the introduction of the widescreen format and stereo sound furthered this goal. Smaller (and less expensive) films would continue to be made, but there were fewer of them, and production as a whole bifurcated into expensive, spectacular epics for general audiences on the one hand and inexpensive films made for niche audiences (especially the burgeoning youth market) on the other. (This distinction was mirrored in the sound track, where big films would be outfit with a full symphony orchestra and stereo sound, but smaller films would make do with a small ensemble—if any original music was used at all—and monaural sound.)

Finally, the demographic shift to the suburbs after the war moved the American movie audience farther from the central city theaters. Because of the Supreme Court decision, studios were not able to build theaters in the suburbs; but movie attendance was also declining, so the independent theaters did not rush in to service the suburbs either. The result was that the growing suburban population was often located far from theaters. At the same time, the extraordinarily fast dissemination of television meant that film needed to offer something more than was available on the small screen. Television was already having a devastating effect on film attendance. Even the most conservative estimates suggested that attendance by those with televisions had decreased by more than 20% in 1950. One study determined that television had caused a 3 to 4% fall in overall attendance. The erosion of the audience increased over the decade as ownership of televisions rapidly grew. In these circumstances, the only types of films that could reliably draw large audiences into the city were those that could be marketed as events worthy of making a special trip, and large spectacles fit the bill.

Ironically, the consent decree insulated the studios from the full effects of the audience decline. The studios could adjust their production to the changes in audience, decreasing production as attendance fell. The theaters, on the other hand, had a fixed number of seats to sell. Moreover, the falling production of film titles generally gave the studios an upper hand in negotiating favorable terms with the theater owners. By the end of the decade, many theater owners had concluded that the consent decree had in fact benefited the studios. The thin to almost nonexistent profits of exhibition meant that only those top theaters specializing in the spectacles could afford to invest in maintaining, much less upgrading, the sound systems. The other theaters—prominently among them the new drive-ins—serviced (smaller) niche markets and cut costs by retaining monaural sound.

WIDESCREEN AND STEREO FORMATS

Beyond the issue of financial risk, the lack of a standard for stereo hampered its adoption. Widescreen formats suffered from a similar lack of a clear standard, but the investment required for the larger screen, a different sprocket gauge on the projector, and special lenses was relatively modest compared to installing new sound systems, especially because those already available sounded far superior to the small speakers of the television (or radio and phonograph, for that matter). In terms of cost, it is significant that exhibiters were resistant not only to the requirements for stereo but also for the so-called "Miracle Mirror" screen, which produced a brighter, better defined image without the reflections common to other screens. When 20th Century Fox introduced Cinemascope, the studio initially demanded that theaters exhibiting films in the format install not only systems for reproducing sound in magnetic stereo but also the special screen. The importance of stereo to the original conception of Cinemascope can be seen in the fact that 20th Century Fox continued to insist on stereo installation a full six months after the company allowed the exhibition of Cinemascope films without the Miracle Mirror screen. When Fox finally relented on stereo as well, its release prints contained three sound track formats: four-track magnetic, four-track optical, and monaural optical (Figure 13-3).

In terms of sound, **Cinerama** offered a more advanced system, with seven-channel (five front, two rear) magnetic sound tracks, but the system required specially equipped theaters and highly trained projectionists (Figure 13-4). It was also costly, often requiring investments upward of $100,000 for the projection and sound equipment. Labor costs were also high, requiring about half of the revenues to cover operating expenses. Although it was an attraction in its own right for a number of years—the Cinerama corporation acquired its own theaters for exhibition—it never proved viable for large-scale studio production. (In this respect it played a role in film exhibition similar to the one IMAX theaters play today.)

Cinemascope was developed by 20th Century Fox on the model of Cinerama and turned out to be as close to an industry standard as would be possible once the studios decided that the move to widescreen was inevitable. Later in the decade the only two aspect ratios in use were 1.85:1 (the familiar 16:9 ratio developed by **VistaVision** and now the standard for HDTV) and 2.35:1 (the wider ratio of Cinemascope). Like Cinerama, Cinemascope used multitrack sound, with four channels arranged as in the Fantasound system Disney developed for *Fantasia*: center, right, left and rear (surround; Figure 13-5). VistaVision used an optical track. "Perspecta" sound likewise used an optical track, with encoding to allow some—but not full—stereo separation.

Still another system, Todd-AO, used six tracks, five front speakers, and one surround channel; this setup as a whole had a frequency response of 40–12,000 cps (Figure 13-6). Although it was adopted only by a small group

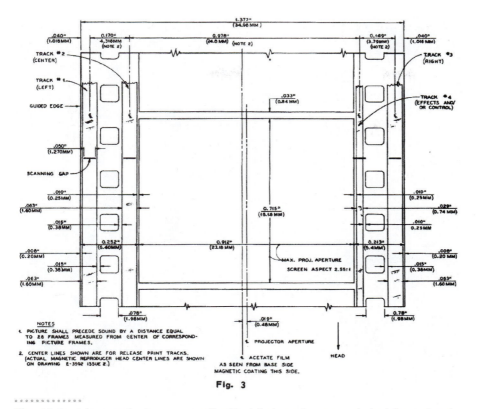

Fig. 3

Fig. 13-3. Schematic for Cinemascope film. The left channel runs outside the left sprocket, the center channel inside the left sprocket, the right channel outside the right sprocket. The track inside the right sprocket was used for the rear effects. Note that the aspect ratio of the image frame (about 1.27:1) is close to the academy ratio of traditional sound film (1.37:1). The film would be projected into widescreen format (here, 2.55:1) through the use of anamorphic lenses. Later, the format would be changed, allowing space on the print for both optical stereo and a regular monaural optical track, a change that required downsizing the image slightly (2.35:1).

of elite first-run houses, Todd-AO was generally agreed to be an improvement on the sound of Cinemascope because the increased number of speakers reduced the effect of "channeling," the impression that the sound is issuing from a particular set of speakers rather than from the screen. Nevertheless, Todd-AO was employed almost exclusively for films planned for special road-show exhibition and even then seldom used because it required a special camera to take full advantage of the system.

The adoption of widescreen and the (limited) move to stereo sound along with tentative attempts at 3D film all point to a change in aesthetic sensibilities that were responses to changing consumption patterns of movie audiences

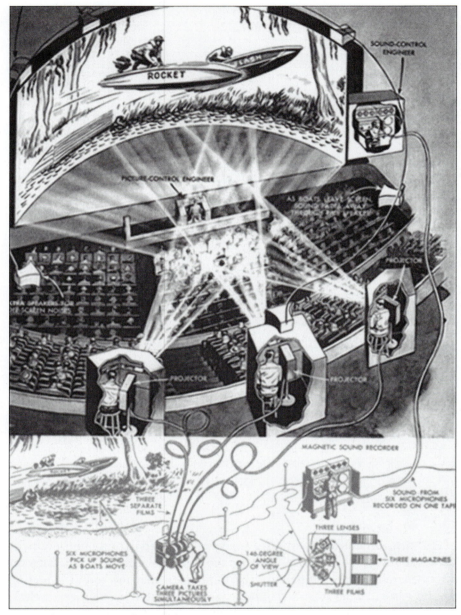

Figure 13-4. Schematic of Cinerama installation. The bottom shows the three-camera-in-one filming process, the top the projection system. The need to abut the images of the three projectors inevitably led to perceptible lines on the screen where the images joined. Consequently directors avoided placing action at the seams, and indeed often staged the shot in three parts. Many of the shots in the Cinerama version of *How the West Was Won* (1962) are

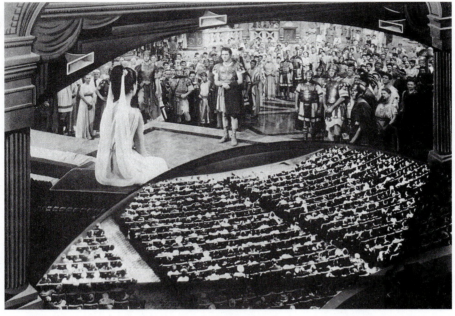

Figure 13-5. Ad for Cinemascope showing a scene from *The Robe* (1953), the first Cinema-scope feature. The huge curved screen was important to the effect of the spectacle, but so was the four channel stereo. Note the three speaker horns positioned above the screen: left, center, right. Unlike typical theater installations, which hid speakers behind the screen, here the front speakers are clearly visible, like the curved screen, a display of technology. The fourth speaker was located in the rear of the auditorium.

in the wake of television and suburbanization. In what one critic calls the "aesthetics of sensation," audio and visual spectacle rose in importance in these films, vying with and sometimes even displacing the narrative needs for dialogue.[1] Such films became "events," precursors to the more standardized blockbuster production that dominates Hollywood filmmaking to this day. The 1960s and early 1970s saw a brief shift away from this sort of production—at least the kinds of films that could succeed on the basis of spectacle changed markedly. The extraordinarily expensive *Cleopatra* (1963), the last

done this way. The system used a seven-track sound system, with five channels across the front and two in the rear. A Sound-Control Engineer (shown in the upper right) would mix the sound live to the theater according to a script, where, among other things, the two rear channels would be addressed to the proper configuration of rear speakers: right-left, right-center, or center-left.

Fig. 13-6. This artist's rendition of an installation of Todd-AO (displaying a scene from *Oklahoma!* (1955)) shows five speakers in front and two on the side. The presence of the horns serves as a display of technology. Experiencing that technology was one of the draws of these shows.

of the gigantic "sword and sandal" epics until their recent resurrection (most notably in *Gladiator* (2000)) was a monumental flop, as were 20th Century Fox's follow ups to the enormous success of *The Sound of Music* (1965), *Doctor Dolittle* (1967), and *Star!* (1968). The huge losses on these two musicals (more than $25 million) contributed significantly to a marked turn away from the genre. Smaller films with faster editing patterns and music that appealed to youth audiences proved far more profitable. In this environment, the narrower VistaVision aspect ratio came to dominate, especially outside Hollywood where Panavision, which retained the wider aspect ratio of Cinemascope, was still favored, because filmmakers found that the wider aspect ratio encouraged slower editing patterns. Nevertheless some films aimed at younger audiences, such as *The Graduate* (1967), continued to be released in the wider screen format (in that case Panavision) and with multichannel sound. The aesthetic of sensation and the widescreen would return with a vengeance in the 1970s, with the series of big disaster films, such as *Airport* (1970), *Earthquake* (1974), and *The Towering Inferno* (1974), as well as the New Hollywood "high-concept" blockbusters, such as *Jaws* (1975), *Star Wars* (1977), and *Close Encounters of the Third Kind* (1977). All of these films except *Jaws* were released in widescreen 70mm, and only *Jaws* was released with just a monaural sound track.

MAGNETIC TAPE IN PRODUCTION AND POSTPRODUCTION

Technologically, the biggest changes in the 1950s and 1960s concerned the introduction of magnetic recording and stereo reproduction, which affected production and postproduction phases in both music and sound departments. Magnetic sound was the more basic: it was quickly adopted because it offered many advantages over optical sound in production and postproduction. Notably, it was more portable, offered superior fidelity, allowed many generations of rerecording, permitted filmmakers to exploit more dynamic range, especially on the soft end, and did not require further technical development. Its disadvantages arose only in distribution: optical sound was more robust in exhibition (the magnetic striping wore out more quickly than optical tracks) and it was cheaper (magnetic sound required a new sound head for the projector along with rewiring of the theaters because all magnetic striping on film was stereo).

The portability of magnetic tape facilitated location shooting, which became increasingly common over the 1950s and 1960s. Labor costs in particular were much higher in Hollywood, and foreign governments offered filmmakers generous financial incentives to move production overseas. Filmmakers found the foreign settings attractive along with the incentives, but taking full advantage of those settings meant moving the production outside and shooting on location rather than on a sound stage. In the U.S., location shooting became far more common as well.

All of this location shooting altered the routine practice of relying on production sound almost exclusively for the capturing of dialogue. This in turn changed the nature of postproduction, especially with respect to the handling of dialogue. Although location shooting was common enough in the studio era, most dialogue continued to be shot on the controlled acoustic environment of the sound stage. On a sound stage, little was left to chance. The sets and lights were soundproofed, the crew was trained to remain silent, and things were arranged to get good microphone coverage. Obviously, an external environment could not be controlled to the same extent. A plane overhead, a police siren, a subway rumbling, a car driving by—these so-called "wild" sounds were captured by the microphone (even a fairly directional microphone) along with the actors' voices. In and of themselves, such wild sounds could increase the "realism" of the scene, because they placed the scene within an appropriate environment—although an airplane sound for a Western scene, say, would be a problem. Even when appropriate to the film, however, such wild sounds nevertheless severely handicapped the ability to edit a sequence because the sound present in one take would not be present in another.

This is an artifact of the way films were (and are) normally shot. Most dialogue scenes used a single camera with changing set-ups. After a master shot of a sequence was filmed, closer shots were taken, especially over-the-shoulder ones designed for shot/reverse-shot editing: first all the lines for one actor, then all the shots for another, and so forth. Note how this arrangement had the potential to pose difficulties for location sound. One actor's lines might have had a siren or subway in the background, whereas the second had an airplane going overhead or a car driving by. The final edit therefore might have to go something like: line 1 (siren in background), line 2 (plane overhead), line 3 (subway rumbles), line 4 (car goes zooming by), and so forth. Moreover, the sound of the siren, plane, subway, or car was unlikely to begin exactly when a line started and ended, so there would be an audible break of that environmental sound on the edit. To control for such problems, recordists usually used a second mike positioned solely for the purpose of capturing wild sounds so they could be added as needed behind other dialogue in editing. The recording of wild sounds thus allowed the impression of continuity in the background, and such continuity would in turn ensure the unity of the action.

Location sound was difficult to control in other ways as well. For example, the environmental noises might simply prove too loud for effective dialogue recording, or the nature of the shot might allow no way to keep a microphone out of sight. (The increasingly common use of wideangle shots would help speed the development of effective body mikes.) Such issues would need to be addressed in postproduction either through manipulation of the audio by dialogue and sound editors or through looping (recall our discussion of this method, also known as ADR, in ch. 4; see Figure 13-7.)

In this way, sound work was moved more and more into postproduction, and the production sound—especially the wild environmental sound—simply became a layer to add to the mix. Mixing was often done to make the sound "big," both through compression and by the addition of layers. In general, the result was thinking more in terms of "building" a sound track, where sounds were mixed as much on the basis of inherent aesthetic effect as "naturalism"

Figure 13-7. *The Good, the Bad, and the Ugly* (1966). Automated dialogue replacement (ADR) became increasingly common during the 1960s. Indeed, the so-called "spaghetti westerns" of Sergio Leone relied exclusively on the technique. Each actor in the international cast would speak lines in his or her own language and the lines would be dubbed in the appropriate language during postproduction.

or even for narrative clarity. In this sense the paradoxically constructed realism of location shooting ran to an extent against the more artificial manipulation of the sound track. As the shooting went outside, the recording moved into the studio.

ISSUES OF STEREO

Stereo faced two substantial obstacles: Its slow adoption by the theaters prevented it from affecting filmmaking to the same extent as magnetic sound; and it required significant conceptual adjustments. For stereo changed the terms of representation, destabilizing the narrative hierarchy in the process. In classical sound practice, film makers had allied perspective with narrative hierarchy. With monaural sound, the placement of microphones on the basis of shot scale was a relatively subtle technique that principally affected the amount of reflected sound recorded (due to the directionality of the microphone). Such fine gradations of distance did not threaten to overwhelm our sense of the continuity of background, which could be maintained across fairly large shifts in shot scale. Due to the aural perspective permitted by stereo imaging, however, sounds recorded in stereo are much more sensitive to microphone distance; that is, shot scale becomes much more audible. Producer Darryl Zanuck, the head of 20th Century Fox studios, advocated image composition and blocking that maximized stereo perspective. "Stereophonic sound," he argued, "is not effective when two people are face to face, unless of course they are in big close-ups or a big 2-shot. The full value of stereophonic sound comes from the distance between the two people who are talking. If one person is planted at one end of the set and the other person is on the other side of the set then the sound has an opportunity to add to the illusion of depth."[2]

One effect of this "illusion of depth" was the so-called "traveling dialogue." As characters moved across the screen—especially across the distances of a wide-screen—stereo miking rendered the movement audible: dialogue and other sounds appeared to travel with the moving body. Stereo miking, particularly when coupled with shot scale, was also generally more sensitive to reflected sound, to the "presence" or ambience of the space, which increased with distance and was especially noticeable in reverberant spaces. In such spaces, cuts between shots markedly different in scale seemed audibly jarring to the extent that the audio backgrounds of the two shots were too distinct, threatening the continuity that subjugated the individual shots to the logic of the sequence.

Analysis: *The Robe*

In *The Robe*, the first feature film shot in Cinemascope, the audio background shifts, sometimes markedly, with the scale of each shot (Figure 13-8). In the trial of Marcellus before Caligula that concludes the film, the disjunctions in audio background continuity are especially acute, emphasized by the relative silence behind the dialogue, despite the presence of a crowd that might have been tapped as a source of ambient sound. The audio background in this scene is therefore carried primarily by room resonance, which varies quite strikingly with shot scale, even within individual speeches (listen, for instance, to

Figure 13-8. *The Robe.* Caligula and Gallio exchange dialogue in widescreen space. Each voice is reproduced by a more or less spatially correct speaker. Although filmmakers at the time thought such effects should produce greater "realism," in fact many in the audience found the effect distracting, since it violated the cinematic norms established by monaural sound. The disruption was even more noticeable with changes in shot scale: not only was the reverberation altered, but the voice would jump from one speaker to another.

Caligula's speech that begins "Senators, Romans" [02:02:57]). Throughout the sequence, crowd sounds appear only intermittently, generally in reaction to a particularly charged bit of dialogue, and music appears only in a quasi-diegetic mode of heralding entrances (brass fanfare representing the power and majesty for Caligula; drums alone representing the fateful march to judgment for Marcellus). The crowd sounds and music therefore only add to the disjunctive quality of the sound design in the sequence in that they punctuate dialogue. They do not function as background continuity but as foreground sound effects, which, like dialogue, simply fill in the silence that dominates the conception of background.

Although not as pronounced as the opening of *The Broadway Melody* (1929), shifts in sound here nevertheless assert, at least on the surface, the autonomy of the shot in the face of the narrative pressure and need of the sequence. Only at the very end of the sequence, in response to Caligula's judgment on Marcellus and Diana, does nondiegetic music displace silence as the figure of background continuity. The music appears here, first of all, to mark the gravity of the verdict, the muted brass sounding as a transformation of Caligula's fanfare, indicative of the world awry, an abuse of worldly power. Against the muted brass, a wordless chorus, which had been introduced over the opening credits and throughout the film associated with the figure of Christ (particularly with the entrance into Jerusalem on Palm Sunday), rises up and comes to dominate the orchestration. As Marcellus and Diana recede from Caligula's throne, the seat of worldly power, toward their execution, the music swells, marking sonically the passage from the rule of Rome to the rule of God. The symbolism here is emphasized by the way the music is mixed to dominate Caligula's desperately sarcastic line, "They're going into a better kingdom" (02:12:06) and by the shift to offscreen sound for Caligula's final line, "They're going to meet their King," which renders him completely impotent: His voice, although it speaks the truth despite itself, simply becomes irrelevant—the music remains wholly indifferent to his interjections—in the absence of his body, the site of his power as Caesar.

In this respect, it is interesting to compare the treatment of Diana's final line as she delivers the robe to a Christian in the crowd. Here the music seems to listen to her dialogue, to make way for her line, "for the big fisherman," suggesting that she, unlike Caligula, has the ear of God. If God thus becomes an audible presence through the mixing of the sound track, the deployment of sound, especially music, at the end of the sequence allows a somewhat different interpretation of the seemingly incoherent sound design in the earlier part of the sequence: what is represented there is the rule of Caligula as godforsaken. The bodily presence of Caligula, even his speech, is unable to hold the sound together in a coherent way. The regal music, which serves to mark his presence and underscore his power especially in contrast to Marcellus, only works to further the incoherence of the sound design in the early part of the sequence. Music and sound only come to serve coherence when they represent divine rather than worldly power.

STEREO AND SPACE

Although stereo sound is used effectively in the final sequence of *The Robe* because its disjunctions were mined for symbolic value, it proved difficult to control the directionality of dialogue recorded in stereo, with the result that many viewers found traveling dialogue distracting. Audiences were acclimated to monaural sound, and, however "realistic" it might be, having dialogue move with the characters seemed representationally uncanny and unnatural. The shifts in perspective also tended to underscore the autonomy of the shot at the expense of the integration of the shot into the sequence. These shifts were undermining narrative hierarchy of foreground and background, and therefore the challenge was, as with the coming of sound, how to construct a consistent aural background against which the foreground sound events could be interpreted.

The solution ultimately adopted was to channel sound according to function. Onscreen dialogue and most foreground sound effects were recorded in monaural sound and played on the center channel (or perhaps slightly panned to location), thus mimicking the standard optical sound track, whereas background (underscoring and ambient sound) was rendered in stereo in the side speakers; offscreen sound would be highly channeled to the appropriate side speaker as well. The rear speaker, little used, was reserved for special "surround" effects such as offscreen cannons in *Battle Cry* (1955), which Darryl Zanuck reported as "a tremendous and realistic thrill when you hear the roar of the cannon coming from behind you and then it seems to pass over your head and land on the screen in the distance."[3]

Stereo Sound, Magnetic Tape, and Elements of Style

ISSUES OF AESTHETICS

Stereo allowed for a number of changes to the sound track, the most important of which was a shift away from thinking of it in terms of stems (dialogue, music and effects) arranged hierarchically in foreground and background toward a concept of graduated layers. Among other things, this change allowed for an increased role for ambient sound and a more nuanced and textured sound track. When a dialogue scene needed ambience in the studio era, music had generally been the preferred choice because it was easier to control. With the increased fidelity of magnetic sound and stereo separation, however, ambient sounds could be used much more freely and at much greater volume, and thus it became possible for ambient sound to absorb some of the functions that had traditionally been reserved for music. Music might still perform these functions on a stereo sound track, of course, but the tinkling of offscreen cowbells and the twittering of birds in the side channels could evoke the rural pastoral just as easily as music. The decision as to whether to render the ambience of a sequence through music or sound was now precisely that: a decision (Figure 13-9).

SCORING PRACTICES

Music scoring practices in this era did not change markedly with the improvements in technology. Or, to put it another way, the methods of scoring films developed in the studio era remained common choices, especially for the most prestigious pictures. The romantic and post-romantic idiom based on the tradition of the symphony orchestra dominated epic films, such as *Ben-Hur* (1959), *The Ten Commandments* (1956), and the ill-fated *Cleopatra*; and, allowing for differences in genre, the orchestra remained the preferred ensemble in war films (*The Bridge on the River Kwai* (1957), *The Great Escape* (1963), and *Patton* (1970), horror (*Creature from the Black Lagoon* (1954), *Psycho* (1960), and *The Devils* (1971), and science fiction (*Fahrenheit 451* (1966), *Planet of the Apes* (1968), *THX 1138* (1971). The musical language was expanded somewhat with the appropriation of advanced compositional techniques and popular idioms, especially jazz, but even in those cases scoring film remained grounded in the orchestra and the approach to narrative remained mostly classical in orientation.

Figure 13-9. *2001: A Space Odyssey* (1968). The low noise of magnetic recording allowed a much greater role for silence—or rather the low level ambient sound characteristic of quiet spaces. The soft wind and nature sounds in the "Dawn of Man" sequence, for instance, serve to underscore the serenity of the landscape, whereas disruptions of this basic quietude serve as figures of violence (but also of life).

If it did not bring a marked change in approach, the new technologies of magnetic tape and stereo reproduction did yield subtle coloristic shifts. Stereo and the higher fidelity of the magnetic sound track made the traditional studio orchestra of twenty-five to thirty players sound anemic—especially compared to the full frequency recordings of orchestras then becoming commercially available for home consumption. The result was a move toward larger orchestras, especially for grand biblical epics such as *The Robe* or *Ben-Hur* or for sweeping westerns such as *The Big Country* (1958). The sound of the orchestra became an attraction in and of itself, as for instance in the long symphonic prologue to *How to Marry a Millionaire* (1953), which seems to exist only to show off the quality of the musical reproduction. The stereo separation also allowed the music to be mixed at much higher levels, and for the scoring to be somewhat heavier without affecting the intelligibility of dialogue. Musicals, too, drew on the resources of an expanded orchestra and stereo separation for the orchestral backing to give the scores a more luxuriant sound (Figure 13-10).

The shift away from integrated studio production and exhibition to independent film production also brought with it a strong interest in developing ancillary product, and it was this focus on ancillary production that had the

Fig. 13-10. *Silk Stockings* (1957). The exaggeration of widescreen space and stereo separation is used to humorous effect in Cole Porter's "Stereophonic Sound." The film was, of course, shot in Cinemascope and released with pseudo-stereo Perspecta sound. Perspecta sound, it should be noted, does not possess the wide field of other stereo processes and in that respect is somewhat closer to monaural sound.

The recording of songs in musicals generally followed the division of the sound track into foreground and background based on channeling: the singer was recorded and reproduced like dialogue—normally closely miked, resulting in a high degree of direct sound, and placed in the center speaker; the orchestral accompaniment was treated as background—recorded in stereo with some degree of reflected sound for warmth and presence and placed in the side speakers.

farthest reaching consequences for scoring films. Filmmakers became far more interested in revenue recordings could generate (and the recording industry in general), and particular recordings, rather than simply songs, increasingly began to be featured in films. Musical tie-ins to films had been long recognized and exploited, and with the need for each film to maximize its profitability music was quickly put to work. Thus, although the basic approach to scoring a film remained relatively unchanged with the dissolution of the studio system, writing music that could be excerpted and marketed as a product in its own right became another part of the composer's task. This practice was in fact already common enough in the studio era, although it was not done consistently for any genre other than the musical, and there was a special emphasis now on producing commercial recordings rather than saleable sheet music.

According to Ted Wick, music had been used occasionally as a pre-release promotional device since at least 1944, when portions of Max Steiner's score to *Since You Went Away* were sent to radio stations one month prior to the release.[4] Moreover, lyrical instrumental themes, particularly love themes, had often enough resembled popular song sufficiently that they could cross over and become hit songs themselves. Essentially these were instrumental themes that would be turned into popular songs through the addition of lyrics after the fact. Joseph Carl Breil's "The Perfect Song" (Figure 10-7) is an early example of this (also recall Erno Rapee's "Charmaine," also mentioned in ch. 10). David Raksin's theme from *Laura* (1944) is a particularly well-known later example, as is Victor Young's "Stella by Starlight" from *The Uninvited* (1944). Indeed, Victor Young, who also contributed to several Broadway shows, was extremely adept at turning out such tunes: "When I Fall in Love" from *One Minute to Zero* (1952) and the title song of *Love Letters* (1945) are two further examples. As might be expected, such themes generally featured prominently in main titles and, like the theme songs of the silent era, appeared frequently in the score. Often, such a theme recurred repeatedly, leaving the impression that the score was essentially monothematic. "Lara's Theme (Somewhere My Love)" from *Doctor Zhivago* (1965) works similarly; indeed, the filmmakers felt sufficiently confident of the appeal of the tune that they replaced many of the cues originally written for the film with repetitions of this theme.

Main Theme from *High Noon*

From the beginning, the producers of *High Noon* (1952) had planned to exploit its theme both to generate ancillary income and as a means of promoting the film. Given this motivation, it is not surprising that the theme is a vocal number sung by Tex Ritter over the main credits. Yet it is interesting to note that in terms of this promotion Ritter's version was only one of six recorded and released at or near the time of the film's premiere. By releasing it in different versions, the thought was that the song would sell more copies and garner more radio airplay because it would appeal to different audience tastes. As film scholar Jeff Smith notes, United Artists (UA) "had no specific expectation for a particular rendition, but Max Youngstein [UA's vice president of marketing] was confident that one of them would reach the Hit Parade's Top Ten within two months of the film's release."[5] Like "Laura" or "Stella by Star-light," the song is conceived as sheet music, and Ritter's performance, although belonging to the film, is understood as only a particular rendition (see Figure 13-11). There is no sense that his will be the only recording of the song.

Like the instrumental theme song used monothematically, "High Noon (Do Not Forsake Me, Oh My Darlin')" served as the primary musical material for the score, but Tex Ritter's vocal rendition of it appeared seven times in ad-dition to the beginning and end of the film. Film music scholar Neil Lerner points to the narrative significance of the title song:

> Since the title song suggests Kane's point of view, and since the film revolves mostly around Kane [played by Gary Cooper], it comes as no surprise to find a score dominated by melodies attached to Kane: monothematic as analogue to mono-protagonistic. While Kane's character unquestionably received the most screen time and development, other important characters, namely Helen Ramirez and Frank Miller, actually receive their own melodic motives that are independent from "Do Not Forsake Me." . . . The visual narrative, and the music that synchronously tells the same story, begins with Kane but gradually introduces other characters; musically, the score opens with Kane's ballad but soon adds other character motives, alternating with Kane's music as the film progresses; only at the end of the film does Kane's title ballad reassert itself as the dominant and unchallenged center of the narrative.[6]

It is therefore Ritter's vocal performance of the song that is decisive, and its fragmented appearance at key junctures of the film, according to Lerner's analysis, parallels Kane's situation.

The way *High Noon* challenges the traditional scoring model, then, has to do not only with the use of popular music but also with the use of a particular recording in the course of the film. Although the song also appears in other guises in the score, Ritter's version is always charged with particular narrative significance. The fact that it is a recording is important, as the song often en-ters and exits mid-phrase, sometimes with a jarring effect, such as when Amy (Grace Kelly) hastily leaves Kane's office.

POPULAR SONG AND THE UNDERSCORE

In *High Noon*, the song is treated rather traditionally as a musical theme, and it is the intermingling of the score and recording that represents the strongest departure from classical practice in the film. The score overall, however, is not reconceived in a popular idiom.

The underscoring in musicals was, by contrast, much more invested in the popular idiom. General stylistic traits as well as the specific material from

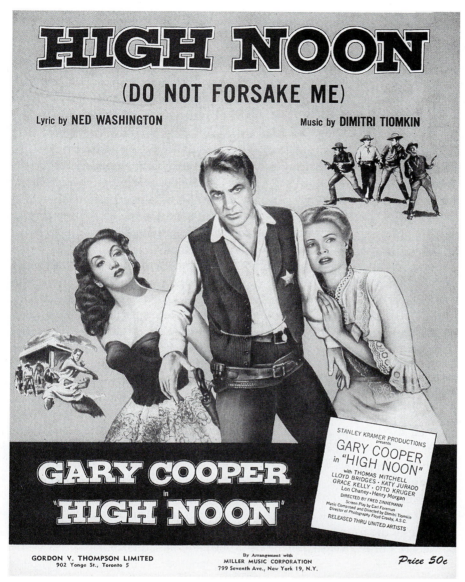

Fig. 13-11.   Sheet Music, "High Noon." Notice that Tex Ritter's name is nowhere to be found in the advertising copy, indicating the primacy of the song over the performance.

a romantic ballad, say, would be continued behind dialogue of a subsequent love scene and its presentation (recall the discussion of *Yankee Doodle Dandy* (1942) in the commentary to Figure 12-9), although breaking up, developing, and even moving away from the song's basic material, would remain within the style of the song's accompaniment (generally scored like an orchestra for musical theater) rather than being converted over into the traditional film music symphonic idiom.

Through the 1950s, dramatic scores sometimes followed suit. Jazz in particular became an important stylistic possibility, although it was at first restricted to films where the music could be motivated by setting. Film biographies (also known as biopics) of important big-band leaders naturally used this sort of score. Examples include *The Fabulous Dorseys* (1947), *The Glenn Miller Story* (1954), *The Benny Goodman Story* (1956), and *The Gene Krupa Story* (1959). Much the same can be said of biopics of popular song composers. *Rhapsody in Blue* (George Gershwin, 1945), *Night and Day* (Cole Porter, 1946), *Till the Clouds Roll By* (Jerome Kern, 1946), *Words and Music* (Rodgers and Hart, 1948) are examples of these films. Not only were big-band swing and the closely related popular song necessary elements of the story; such films were also structured closely around the conceits of musical comedy.

Jazz was also frequently used for crime dramas and other films with seedy urban settings, and it was in this capacity that jazz had a decisive impact on scoring practice. *A Streetcar Named Desire* (1951), *The Man with the Golden Arm* (1955), and *Anatomy of a Murder* (1959) are all important examples. Perhaps even more influential was Henry Mancini's work on the television series *Peter Gunn*. (Mancini wrote the theme for the series and scored 38 episodes from 1958–1960.) These jazz scores adopted a whole set of stylistic markers. Characteristics such as blue notes, instrumentalization, swinging syncopated rhythms, and improvisatory-like textures set the basic sound of the score. Although elements of jazz extended beyond the theme in such films, jazz hardly attained the level of a neutral style the way the postromantic idiom of the classic film score had earlier. Instead, jazz was mainly used as a style topic to signify the dangerous world of crime. (This association led to complaints from jazz musicians; see the sidebar) In this respect, jazz style was appropriated in a way similar to concert composer Aaron Copland's distinctive style was in the 1950s to signify American nostalgia and, later, the American West. (A good example of the former can be found in *The Best Years of Our Lives* (1946), and of the latter in *The Magnificent Seven* (1960) and its sequels.)

Ironically, contemporary romantic comedy proved almost as amenable to scoring with a jazz influenced idiom as did the crime drama, probably because its plots resembled those of musicals (where "jazziness" often signified urban hipness rather than seediness), and so it was relatively simple to transfer the scoring style from the musical to the romantic comedy. More important, such scores could also be composed to resemble the big-band and jazz-influenced orchestral arrangements of popular song—for instance, the instrumental backings characteristic of recordings by Frank Sinatra, Nat King Cole, and Bing Crosby in the 1950s and 1960s.

I think it may kill jazz. All these [T.V.] crime programs with jazz in the background are setting up in people's mind an association between jazz and crime and slick, cheap women.
—Anonymous jazz pianist, quoted in *Variety*[7]

Soundtrack Albums

Along with the rising importance of theme songs, the **soundtrack album** also became an increasingly important format during the 1950s. Although portions of scores had occasionally been released to radio stations on transcription disks and suites had been arranged for orchestral performance at pops concerts or for piano for home consumption, it was the introduction of the LP record after WWII that made possible the large-scale commercial exploitation of the sound track. Although at first these albums consisted of cues taken directly from the recording sessions for the film, by the 1960s they were often crafted as albums, with themes extracted from the score and then arranged as songs appropriate for play on commercial radio.

Jeff Smith argues that Mancini was particularly influential in developing a model for film scoring that could result in a soundtrack album with the potential to produce substantial ancillary revenue.[18] (In the following, we will use the compound "soundtrack" to refer specifically to music destined for albums to distinguish it from music in the sound track of the film.) This soundtrack model would persist through the 1970s. First of all, Mancini conceived the album as a musical (and commercial) entity separate from the film. The soundtrack album might not in fact be all that representative of the film: Audrey Hepburn's performance of "Moon River" in *Breakfast at Tiffany's* (1961), for instance, was not included on the soundtrack album (nor was it released commercially at the time; see Figure 13-12). The soundtrack album might also take the musical material in completely different directions than it served in the film. Whereas cues in a film necessarily broke the continuity of musical themes to satisfy the needs of the narrative, a soundtrack album need not follow the film in this respect. The album could present fully worked-out themes. Moreover, the most commercially exploitable themes could be arranged to fit into the 3-min slot favored by radio stations and have lyrics added to them. (Other artists would also be encouraged to record these songs to maximize exposure in as many markets as possible.)

Second, one of the priorities in spotting a film would be to find places where different themes could be introduced unobtrusively since multiple songs—usually about a dozen—would be needed to fill out the album. Because the underscore still needed to work dramatically, much of the soundtrack album material would consist of diegetic music, even if the cues were sometimes used only very briefly in short snippets. In other words, the tunes would be heard at some point in the film—perhaps coming out of a radio in the background. By carefully spotting a film this way, Mancini would have the music he needed for the album.

Besides the additional airplay and sale of singles that went with commercial exploitation in general, Mancini's practice of focusing on creating saleable soundtracks was also to the advantage of the record companies, as LPs returned a

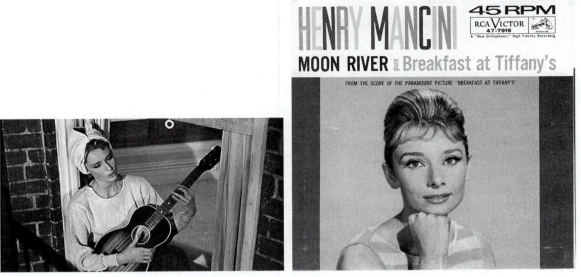

a | b **Figure 13-12.** *Breakfast at Tiffany's.* According to Jeff Smith, twenty-seven recordings of "Moon River" were released within a year of the film's premiere.[9] (a) Although Audrey Hepburn's performance of "Moon River" features prominently in the film, her recording of the number was not one of those released. (b) A single featured Hepburn's picture on the cover, but it actually contained Mancini's instrumental version. It was the song itself rather than the performance that was understood as the principal tie-in to the film.

greater profit than did singles. This was particularly significant inasmuch as film companies had large holdings in the recording industry, and the sale of soundtrack rights played an increasingly important role in financing film production.

Mancini was criticized for the way in which he sometimes seemed to go out of his way to introduce tunes unnecessary for the narrative but useful for the profitable soundtrack albums. Nevertheless, his actual scoring practice tended to be quite subtle. In particular, he only rarely respected the structure of the song form when composing for the sound track. When needed, he was fully willing to stretch, compress, break off and develop material provided by his songs to underscore in a rather traditional way. Indeed, Mancini's handling of "Moon River" in *Breakfast at Tiffany's* was not so different from how Max Steiner approached "As Time Goes By" in *Casablanca* (1942) twenty years earlier.

IMPORTANCE OF RECORDINGS

The crafting of soundtrack albums for sale as recordings is a manifestation of a larger sociological and economic trend. Recording had long been the dominant form by which songs were distributed. By the 1960s, however, recording had significantly eclipsed sheet music as the conceptual basis of the song. As we mentioned earlier, "High Noon" was still understood as sheet music. The same can be said for a number of film songs from the 1960s including "Moon River," "Midnight Lace," "Born Free," and numbers from most musicals.

The same cannot be said of Simon and Garfunkel's contribution to *The Graduate* or the various songs used in *Easy Rider* (1969), *The Last Picture Show* (1971), and *American Graffiti* (1973), to mention only a few films that drew on recorded popular music. In these cases, the recording of the song has become all but synonymous with the song itself, in the sense that any other rendition of, say, Simon and Garfunkel's "The Sounds of Silence" is now understood as a "cover," that is, as a derivative of the original recording.

The use of Tex Ritter's recording in *High Noon* reveals an important facet of scoring with recorded popular music: it is a fixed performance that cannot be altered; any edits will generally be "audible," and therefore it is extremely difficult to sneak the music in or out. Consequently, to be effective, its jarring, fragmented appearance must form part of the idea of the film (as is arguably the case with *High Noon*), the music must be motivated diegetically (so that any disruption of the song seems a product of the narrative editing), or, as is commonly the case, the film must be cut to the recording. This last option resembles shooting to playback in musicals, where the music is all prerecorded and so fixed before the scene is filmed and edited.

Relation to the Musical

Given this resemblance to the musical, it is probably not surprising that songs synonymous with their recording first began to take root in musicals. This trend had begun already in the 1950s, where such films as the Elvis Presley musicals that aimed at a youth audience were tied to the release of recordings from the film. A good example of this is *Jailhouse Rock* (1957), where the title song was released two weeks before the film and also served as the basis of a major production number in the film. The low-budget, "jukebox musicals" that Sam Katzman produced for Columbia, the best known of which are *Rock Around the Clock* (1956) and *Don't Knock the Twist* (1962), likewise appealed to the youth audience drawn to the newly emerging genre of rock and roll. (These Katzman films are the prototype for many later day musical teenpics such as *Footloose* (1984), *Fast Times at Ridgemont High* (1982), and "Brat Pack" films like *Sixteen Candles* (1984) and *Pretty in Pink* (1986).) Defined particularly by its electric guitar driven sound, rock and roll—under the shortened rubric "rock"—would prove to be the dominant form of popular music until the commercial success of hip-hop in the second half of the 1980s. The skewing of the audience toward younger viewers in the 1950s and especially 1960s resulted in the production of more films directed specifically at an adolescent audience; and as the success of the Katzman musicals demonstrates, music was an important component in attracting this audience.

The Beatles' *A Hard Day's Night* (1964), *Help!* (1965), and *Yellow Submarine* (1968) are familiar, somewhat later examples that tied films directly with recordings. All of these are, like the Elvis films, transitional cases, however, in that the recording continued to be anchored by the presence of the performer(s) in the film. This presence makes the song seem more like a traditional production number in a musical. Yet The Beatles' films often play with—and against—this conceit. The "I Should Have Known Better" sequence from *A Hard Day's Night*, for instance, begins with the band playing cards with Paul's grandfather. The music at first accompanies shots of the game, and the sequence plays silent—we hear only music and no diegetic sound. In a kind of reverse audio dissolve, the music gradually becomes diegetic: Paul mouths a couple of lyrics, John plays the harmonica and suddenly the entire band is playing. Just prior to the song fading out, the scene then reverts back to the card game as though nothing had happened. In a later set of sequences, "I Wanna Be Your Man," "Don't Bother Me," and "All My Loving" serve as recordings at a dance party. "If I Fell," "And I Love Her," "I'm Happy Just to Dance with You," "Tell Me Why," and the signature "She Loves You" are all played in the TV studio. "Can't Buy Me Love," on the other hand, is entirely nondiegetic the first time it is heard, and treated similarly in the reprise (although one of the instrumental breaks is used under dialogue). Like the card game, the first of these sequences is shot silent (including the use of the fast motion characteristic of silent-film comedy), but here there is no attempt to ground it in performance. Overall, it comes off as a montage reminiscent of music video. The instrumental "This Boy (Ringo's Theme)" serves more or less as underscoring.

The Beatles' music thus functions in several distinct ways in the film: it is used as performance, as recording, as music backing montage, and as underscore. Although *A Hard Day's Night* is related to the backstage musical, none of its songs serve as the basis of a traditional production number of the sort that the "Jailhouse Rock" sequence does in the Elvis movie.

Although music is not simply the product of onscreen performance in *A Hard Day's Night*, the presence of the Beatles clearly motivates and so also contains the music. If "Can't Buy Me Love" offers a kind of nondiegetic commentary on the scene, it nevertheless seems that the band is commenting on itself, much like a character's voice-over narration might in a dramatic film. There is in that sense little separation of the music from the character(s). One consequence of this is that, although *A Hard Day's Night* goes further than *Jailhouse Rock* in scoring with popular music, it remains a special (limited) case. This is because the appearance of the music is rooted in performance (Figure 13-13).

Figure 13-13. *A Hard Day's Night*. The film ends with an extended performance sequence a | b
(a), and the final song before the credits, "She Loves You," is almost drowned out by screams
of the fans (b). The lack of fidelity offers a clear sign of "authentic" performance, rather than a
recording, since we expect crowd noise in a live performance but not on a recording.

Scoring with Recordings

Particularly with respect to underscoring, *A Hard Day's Night* exemplifies important extensions of scoring with rock-based popular music. Because it remains grounded in the presence of the performers, however, its representational capabilities are somewhat limited. A pronounced loosening of these constraints became increasingly common in the later 1960s. *The Graduate*, for instance, makes no attempt to ground the Simon and Garfunkel songs diegetically (Figure 13-14). Instead, they serve to express Benjamin's inner psychological state: because they are used mainly in meditative sequences, the images

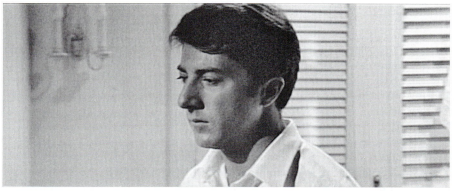

Figure 13-14. *The Graduate*. Like underscoring, Simon and Garfunkel's "The Sounds of Silence" represents Benjamin's (Dustin Hoffman) emotional state.

can be readily edited to the music. This option avoids those problems mentioned earlier with respect to editing music conceptualized as a recording.

The songs in *Easy Rider* function in a similarly meditative way, and the images are likewise edited to the music. The music of both *The Graduate* and *Easy Rider* functions with respect to character or setting the mood of the scene. The use of popular music, however, differs in at least three ways. First, *Easy Rider* uses more songs, which allows the songs to offer more extensive commentary than is the case in *The Graduate*. Second, the music in *Easy Rider* seems to emphasize general mood rather than being restricted to basic inner psychology. Finally, *Easy Rider* has no traditional underscore, which gives its songs a particular prominence.

Another way of conceptualizing the use of rock-based music on the sound track crystallized in the unexpected success of *American Graffiti*, whose score consisted entirely of period songs that served to mark not mood or psychology of character, but rather the time and place of the film's setting. This is not to claim that the use of popular music this way, even recordings, was entirely new. *Blackboard Jungle* (1955), to name just one well-known example, had used Bill Haley and His Comets' "Rock Around the Clock" over its opening titles to situate the urban locale of the film and quickly establish an adolescent culture. That same song was used over the credits of *American Graffiti* as well. This connection is hardly coincidental inasmuch as the use of the song in *Blackboard Jungle* has often been credited with launching the rock and roll era. *American Graffiti* did draw on a set of associations similar to those in *Blackboard Jungle*, the difference being that *American Graffiti* used over forty songs in addition to "Rock Around the Clock" and the songs were employed to evoke not the present, but a particular past era.

As film music scholar Julie Hubbert notes in her discussion of *The Last Picture Show*, the use of recordings in this way was consistent with the values of traditional, studio era scoring:

> In carefully engineering specific song texts to elide with specific events in [*The Last Picture Show*], [director Peter] Bogdanovich also drew on musical sensibilities more closely affiliated with 1950s filmmaking practices. As several historians have observed, throughout the film Bogdanovich clearly uses song lyrics to both parallel and counterpoint the emotions, actions, and relationships of the character on the screen. . . . At the same time that Bogdanovich displays a stylistic allegiance to the music of the 1950s, however, he also displays an adherence to a more contemporary or [*cinema*] *vérité* conceptualization of musical realism. In addition to recreating "what" music would have been heard in 1951, Bogdanovich also carefully documents "how" it would have been heard, and in doing so he faithfully imports the *verité* mandate of "source music only." All the music in the film spills out of visualized sources—radios, jukeboxes, record players, and even live performing ensembles. All of the music in the film is given careful visual representation on the screen.[10]

The visual representation on screen is a sleight of hand that makes narrative underscoring appear as a function of the diegesis (rather than as an external narrative agent).

Production

PRODUCTION PHASES

Despite the technological changes, the job descriptions in both sound and music departments were largely unchanged from the studio era, although work was done more and more on a freelance basis. In other words, workers were hired by the production company rather than the studio, which was now focused on finance and distribution. This change reduced job security but increased flexibility in that organizational charts, chains of command, and job descriptions could differ markedly from film to film. Increased location shooting paradoxically meant that even more sound track work was moved into postproduction.

MUSIC DEPARTMENT

The dissolution of the studio system had a direct impact on the music department, which had all but disappeared by 1960. In 1958, the studios did not renew their standing contracts with the studio musicians, making all but a few music workers into freelancers. Only the heads of the music departments and a few other managerial personnel were retained. Even the role of the music director was diminished inasmuch as the music personnel were now hired by the production company rather than by the studio.

Aside from the fact that employment was less secure, the basic work of the music department on a film remained much as it had during the studio era. Composers were still the head of the creative team, and they still worked with music editors and orchestrators (Figure 13-15). With all the freelance work that needed to be organized, the music contractor played an increasingly visible supporting role. (The contractor was responsible for hiring the musicians for recording. A similar position had existed in the studio days, but the position assumed new importance when the orchestra had to be assembled from scratch for each production.) Much work was moved out of Hollywood to save money, and more and more existing symphony orchestras would be hired to record scores. (The London Symphony Orchestra was a particular favorite.)

The importance of the soundtrack album as an ancillary product meant that composers (and orchestrators and arrangers) needed to devote time to crafting and recording it in addition to their work on the score for the film. Because the soundtrack album was part of the promotional materials for the film, it also needed to be completed during the postproduction phase—indeed often

Figure 13-15. Franz Waxman and orchestrator Edward B. Powell during a recording session for *The Virgin Queen* (1955). By the end of the decade, the studio system would have dissolved and composers, orchestrators, and musicians would be working as independent contractors. Waxman himself was among the first composers to make this move from studio staff to freelance. Photo © John W. Waxman Collection. All rights reserved. International copyright secured. Used with permission.

in advance of the closing of postproduction. The soundtrack album added considerably to the workload of the music department as in many respects it was an entirely separate entity from the film score.

SOUND DEPARTMENT

The trend toward location shooting increased the amount of work done in postproduction, as production sound could no longer be relied on for a clean dialogue recording. Dialogue editing became more complex, as a good deal of dialogue was now rerecorded. ADR (looping) became a regular part of postproduction. The increased fidelity of magnetic tape allowed the regular use of multitrack mixing, which increased the complexity of the sound tracks, even those designed for monaural release. With the ability to make a number of preliminary mixes, sound editors could juggle more sounds at the same time, resulting in livelier sound tracks.

As with magnetic tape, stereo sound required the development of new techniques and new equipment but it did not substantively affect the nature of the job.

Summary

Like film sound in general, stereo began with laboratory research in the 1920s but had to wait several decades before its widespread commercial exploitation. The move to stereo coincided with major changes in the venues of film exhibition, as the maturing of the television industry and legal challenges forced the studios to find new modes of film exhibition. The adoption of widescreen format and stereo sound was the answer. The introduction of the stereo LP record in the later 1950s also gave a kickstart to a practice that had always lingered in the background of film studios' and artists' commercial interests: tie-ins between music for a feature film and sound track LP records.

The New Hollywood, Dolby Stereo, and the Emergence of Sound Design (1975–2000)

Introduction

Although a working commercial system of stereo had been introduced in 1940 and stereo sound had been a significant component of the various wide-screen systems introduced in the 1950s, most theaters did not upgrade their sound systems. Because filmmakers could not be sure that their films would be screened with stereo sound, the result was a decidedly conservative employment of the stereo sound track in film production, a situation that film sound scholar John Belton refers to as a "frozen revolution."[1] Stereo could be used for special effects—and it was—but the sound track also had to be successful in monaural presentation, and therefore the stereo field could contain nothing essential to understanding the film. In other words, the sound track could not be reconceived in stereo (the way, for instance, the almost universal adoption of color film transformed the image track in the 1960s).

Indeed, up through the end of the 1970s, magnetic tape, which significantly reduced the loss of definition in subsequent generations of dubbing, was far more important to changing the nature of sound design in film than was stereo, which would not become an essential component of filmmaking until the wide distribution of Dolby stereo sound around 1980. Such films as *M*A*S*H* (1970), *The Godfather* (1972), *American Graffiti* (1973), *The Exorcist* (1973), and *Jaws* (1975), had strikingly innovative (and award winning) sound designs, but all were originally released with monaural sound. The striking sound of Godard's *Prénom Carmen* (*First Name: Carmen*, 1983) was likewise executed in mono.

This situation began to change rapidly in the second half of the 1970s, thanks to the introduction of Dolby stereo and to falling prices for audio

Figure 14-1. *Star Wars* proved a much better attraction in theaters equipped for stereo sound. The success of the film was key to convincing theaters to make the transition to Dolby stereo.

equipment. Both had the effect of markedly decreasing the cost of installing stereo sound in a theater. In addition, the emergence of the so-called New Hollywood brought with it a strong shift to blockbuster production. Like the widescreen spectacles of the 1950s and 1960s, these films were marketed as "events," and many of them focused on special effects. These effects were aural as well as visual, and theaters that had invested in better sound systems soon found that their revenues were significantly outpacing those that had not. The decisive film in this respect was *Star Wars* (1977), where theaters equipped with Dolby Stereo or 70 mm, 6-track sound had much higher revenues than monaural ones (Figure 14-1).

Issues of Technology and Economics

THE NEW HOLLYWOOD AND SATURATION BOOKING

By the end of the 1960s, the studio system had ceased to exist. The studios had moved into financing and distributing films (and television programming), and they had diversified into other leisure and entertainment fields including book, magazine, and music publishing, as well as amusement parks and hotels. This diversification gave studios strong incentives to find further streams of ancillary income, especially if they could be located within the diversified holdings of the larger corporation.

The result was the emergence of the "New Hollywood," a term that some scholars restrict to the decade between 1965 to 1975, or roughly from the dissolution of the old studio system to the rise of the summer blockbuster. Here, we will use the term more broadly to encompass the industrial reorganization into large multinational entertainment conglomerates, a system that remains mostly intact today.[2] The "New Hollywood" was characterized by a marked shift to production centering on what Justin Wyatt calls "high concept" film-making.[3] The high concept film banked on the synergy of its concept, which each member of the creative team worked to realize. Generally, a high concept film involved a simple premise that made it easy to market, facilitated ancillary product tie-ins, and offered potential to be turned into a series franchise. The budgets were usually large, and the proliferation of ancillary products (and potential for series exploitation) helped increase profits or at least spread risk.

Like the widescreen spectacles of the 1950s and 1960s, the New Hollywood blockbusters were marketed as events. Unlike the earlier spectacles, however, they were not exhibited first as road shows before moving into the regular theater distribution system. During the studio era and through the 1960s, a film was usually released first to major, downtown theaters, then to the suburbs and finally into rural areas. The film was restricted to a certain class of theater within a zone for a prescribed period of time, and it could take more than six months to work its way through the system. Under this system, relatively few theaters would be showing the same film at any one time. The blockbusters, on the other hand, followed the strategy of saturation booking, a distribution strategy that involved opening a film simultaneously on a large number of screens. This strategy had developed for so-called exploitation films (lower budget films aimed at niche audiences), where films would be released simultaneously on a large number of screens to maximize the effects of closely targeted advertising while minimizing any negative word of mouth. *Jaws*, generally acknowledged as the first mainstream film to use this distribution strategy, opened on just over 400 screens (Figure 14-2); by the 1980s, films would appear on as many as 2000 screen at the same time. One consequence of this distribution strategy, however, was that these films would necessarily open in theaters that were not accustomed to showing first run films and that often had antiquated sound systems. Unlike the lower budget exploitation films, moreover, these films placed far greater demands on the sound systems. With saturation booking making cross comparisons among theaters relatively easy, it became all the more evident that the sound of many theaters was very poor indeed.

Director Robert Altman complained in the late 1970s that "sound in the theaters—the overwhelming majority of theaters—is just terrible. The acoustics, the speakers, everything."[4] Not only did the sound in most theaters not match the performance of a decent home stereo, but even when it did the sound insulation between auditoria in the large **multiplex**es that became dominant in the 1970s was often inadequate and louder sound from one film would often "bleed" over into the room next door.

Figure 14-2. *Jaws* used a national campaign of television advertising and saturation book-ing in summer release to set a new precedent for how to market a mainstream film. John Williams' short motif for the shark figured prominently in the ads.

SOUND IN THE MULTIPLEX

During the 1960s and 1970s, a new type of theater, the multiplex, began rap-idly appearing in the suburbs. The multiplex differed quite significantly from the earlier generation of theaters, which had taken the fantasy of the urban picture palace as their ideal. The architecture of the multiplex was by contrast primarily utilitarian, designed above all with an eye to reducing labor and building maintenance costs. For instance, they contained multiple auditoria and centralized projection booths, a set up that allowed a single projection-ist to service multiple auditoria simultaneously—although at the expense of pronounced distortion (*keystoning*) of the image (Figure 14-3). The multiplex also displayed few ornaments either within or outside the theater. The most prominent architectural feature was generally the concession stand. In this re-spect, the multiplex was also a direct descendant of the drive-in, where pro-ceeds from paid admissions took a backseat to the profits of the concession stand. Like drive-ins, multiplexes were constructed around the idea that the primary commodity was not the film—most of the box office flowed back to the studio—but the concessions. Multiplexes also followed drive-ins in being located primarily in suburban areas, where land was cheap, potential audi-ences large (with sufficient parking), and theaters relatively scarce (due to the 1948 Supreme Court decision, which prevented the existing major chains as-sociated with the studios from following the population shift and building theaters away from city centers). Indeed, many of the firms that first developed multiplexes began in the business of drive-ins.

What drive-ins taught exhibitors, besides the importance of concessions, was that theaters could operate profitably with sound of minimal fidelity. The

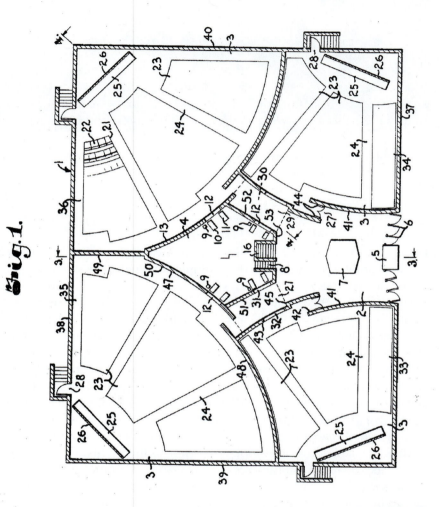

INVENTOR.
ROBERT J. SCHUMANN
BY
Fishburn, Gold & Litman
ATTORNEYS

Figure 14-3. Patent for a multiplex filed by Robert J. Schumann, who worked for American Multi-Cinema. Note the central projection booth that would service all four auditoria as well as the location of the projectors toward the side walls of the two smaller auditoria, which would result in pronounced keystoning.

speakers at drive-ins were small, producing a tinny sound hardly even up to the low audio standards of television at the time. So long as the dialogue was minimally intelligible, however, films, even second- and third-rate films, proved sufficient to lure an audience, and, most important, the low cost of admission—drive-ins frequently charged admission by the car rather than by the individual—encouraged group and family attendance with frequent trips to the concession stand.

With the example of the drive-in, it is hardly surprising that the multiplexes, too, would be constructed with little thought to the sound of the theaters. In general, the multiplex offered what film historian Douglas Gomery calls "minimalist moviegoing."[5] Gone were the many amenities of the first-run theater—the grand lobbies, the troop of ushers, the fanciful architectural details, 70 mm projection, stereo sound. Gone, too, was attention to the finer details of exhibition—the centralized and mechanized booths were often manned by a single employee with little training. Refinements such as minute adjustments to sound and focus as the film unwound, a task that projectionists had always taken to be part of their job, were no longer possible under these conditions. (The multiplex, in fact, devastated the ranks of professional projectionists much as the coming to sound in the late 1920s had wreaked havoc on the employment of theater musicians.) Finally, gone too were the balanced programs—the cartoons, shorts, newsreels, and so forth, that had always accompanied the feature. In the multiplex, the program was reduced to the bare minimum: coming attractions followed by the feature. The whole point was to efficiently turn over audiences with the aim of maximizing revenue at the concession stand.

Unlike the drive-in, however, where the low admission cost allowed it to draw sufficient audiences with indifferent films, the multiplex followed a strategy that placed a high premium on the feature. Audiences did not attend the multiplex primarily to go to the cinema; audiences went to see a particular film, which the multiplex catered to by offering choices. (Originally, multiple screens of the multiplex were intended to provide patrons a choice of films to attend; today, the multiple screens exist as much to give patrons a choice of time.) This emphasis on the feature conformed to the nature of the blockbuster and saturation booking, which necessarily treated cinema as an event structured around a particular film. If the multiplex could not compete effectively with the 70mm projection and stereo sound of larger first-run theaters, and if its keystoned image on a wide but small screen and its low fidelity monaural sound were less than impressive, it did at least offer convenient locations and a semblance of choice. Stanley Durwood, head of American Multi-Cinema, an early innovator in multiplexing, argued in 1972 that multiple screens "enable us to provide a variety of entertainment in one location. We can present films for children, general audience, and adults, all at the same time."[6] In this respect, the multiplexes resembled the shopping malls near which they were usually located. Perhaps more important, multiple screens allowed the multiplex to hedge its bets on successful films while reaping profits from economies of scale: with the low service model of the multiplex, the labor costs for running one screen or four were by and large the same.

As the number of screens multiplied, the architecture of the multiplex reflected a particular strategy of exhibition: one large main theater with five hundred seats or more was surrounded by several smaller ones of one to two hundred seats. The main screen would show the most popular feature, and the others would be used to service films aimed at smaller but dedicated audiences or to test out new films to see which would have the best drawing power for the main screen. Because as many as half the seats in the multiplex might be in the main auditoria, keeping this theater as full as possible was obviously important to the financial success of the entire operation. As long as most films were released in relatively low fidelity monaural sound and so long as stereo sound was limited to a few select films, the multiplex could get away with showing its films, even its feature on the main screen, in monaural sound. The multiplexes increasingly faced uncomfortable choices, however, as Hollywood shifted more and more toward blockbuster production, and as these films placed greater demands on sound systems to differentiate the cinematic experience from television. The climactic sequence of *Earthquake* (1974), for instance, employed Sensurround, a massive subwoofer used to produce a low frequency rumble that could literally shake the seats in a theater (Figure 14-4). Although technically impressive—Sensurround won several awards, including a Scientific and Technical Award from the Academy of Motion Picture Arts and Sciences—and despite being extremely popular with audiences, Sensurround proved almost unusable in multiplexes because the rumble in the main auditorium disrupted the screenings in all the other auditoria of the complex. The multiplex owners faced the choice of showing the film with Sensurround but alienating their small-theater audiences or forgoing it and risking the loss of audiences to theaters where they could experience the effect.

DOLBY STEREO IN THE THEATERS

Although not as disruptive as Sensurround, the increased dynamic and frequency range of Dolby stereo posed similar challenges to multiplexes. These challenges were in some respects more severe than those of Sensurround. Dolby, with its banks of six-foot speakers, became standard equipment in the main auditorium of the multiplex, but the buildings lacked sufficient acoustical insulation to keep the sound from bleeding into adjacent auditoria, and the cost of retrofitting the buildings to address the issue was often prohibitive. This problem, a source of frequent complaint from audiences throughout the 1980s and 1990s, would remain mostly unaddressed until the building

Figure 14-4 A promotional poster for *Earthquake*. The film was marketed literally as "an event," and a large part of its attraction was the Sensurround system. Promotional material for Sensurround ominously warned: "Please be aware that you will *feel* as well as see and hear realistic effects such as might be experienced in an actual earthquake. The management assumes no responsibility for the physical or emotional reactions of the individual viewer." In some newspaper ads, this warning was incorporated into the poster for the film.

boom of the late 1990s replaced older multiplexes with auditoria specifically designed to handle digital sound.

Dolby had its origin in noise reduction, in suppressing the hiss and increasing the response of magnetic tape. In the 1970s, Dolby Labs began developing products for the film industry, first for use in postproduction, then to increase the frequency and dynamic response of the optical sound track on the release print. Dolby-encoded sound tracks began appearing in feature films in 1974, first in mono (*Callan*) and then the following year in stereo (*Tommy*). Stereo had of course been generally available with Cinemascope and Todd-AO, but these systems restricted stereo to magnetic playback. Although the magnetic sound track offered sound that was superior to an optical track, the striping raised the cost of the print by as much as 50%, and magnetic striping was also subject to greater wear than optical sound. Dolby stereo therefore offered one great advantage over earlier sound systems: it used optical sound. The original Dolby stereo required two optical tracks on which were encoded four channels worth of information: right, center, left, and surround. In the theater, then, sound was distributed similarly to Cinemascope stereo. This method also offered better definition than traditional optical sound, especially in the high frequencies (above 12,000 cps), and a wider (but still somewhat limited) dynamic response.

The first films distributed with Dolby stereo were primarily musicals, and prior to 1977 the theaters capable of presenting films in Dolby stereo were few. Consequently, most films continued to be released with only monaural sound tracks, even for first-run theaters. The success of *Close Encounters of the Third Kind* (1977)—and, even more so, *Star Wars*—and markedly higher attendance at theaters equipped with Dolby stereo finally convinced studios and exhibitors to invest in this technology of improved sound reproduction. *Star Wars* has been called "Dolby's *The Jazz Singer*,"[7] precisely for the way in which the film served as an impetus for rapid technological change in both production and exhibition.

The rapid dissemination of Dolby stereo into theaters was aided by the modest cost of installation—around $5,000, if the wiring and speakers of the theater were more or less up to date, $20,000 if the theater needed to be completely rewired. By the end of 1977, more than 200 theaters had been equipped with the system. A year later the number was around 800 rising to over 1,200 by the beginning of 1980. By the mid-1980s about a quarter of the screens in the United States—generally the main auditoria in multiplexes—had Dolby, and the vast majority of all films were being released in stereo. Today, it is rare for even the smallest auditorium of a multiplex to lack some form of stereo sound, and re-releases of older films (such as *The Godfather* in 1997 and *The Exorcist* in 2000) almost always involve remixing the sound tracks in digital stereo.

HOME VIDEO AND THE LIMITATIONS OF TELEVISION
Even as blockbusters became the driving force of Hollywood production, pushing toward a more expansive use of the technological resources of the cinema, the small screen of television was a countervailing drag on their full exploitation. Television rights became a large part of the studios' economic thinking

in the 1960s, and even with the large revenues produced in a theatrical run, projected television revenue remained fundamental to the financing of films. The rapid development of the market for film on videotape in the 1980s only intensified the incentive to make films television-friendly.

Indeed, it can be argued that, of all the technological transformations over cinema history none was more significant than the advent of videotape, because it changed fundamentally the way audiences interacted with, and so also understood, film. No longer did audiences have to go to the theater to see a film or wait several years after an initial release for it to appear on broadcast television. By making it possible for the general population to play a movie at one's convenience, videotape opened the way to transform films into commodities and film audiences into consumers.

In fact, the studios had recognized the transformative effects of videotape in the early 1970s, yet they were resistant to change because that required rethinking the status of their product. They had always treated their film libraries as rental property, receiving payment for use of a film rather than selling it outright. The studios were especially concerned over the recording capabilities of the VCR, which was the most appealing feature of the machine for consumers as it allowed time shifting of broadcast TV. Because they feared that recordings would allow copies of a film to circulate freely, the studios at first resisted the video market, going so far as to sue Sony over the recording capabilities of Betamax. Even before the 1984 Supreme Court decision finding in favor of Sony, however, the film industry had begun to see the economic potential of the format and had decided to enter the videotape market.

Videotape thus turned movies into a commodity, very similar to a music recording, especially after studios recognized the profits that could be extracted by bypassing video rental shops and "selling through" to consumers directly (Figure 14-5). Once the "sell-through" market was established, the studios found it lucrative to sell video transfers of their films, encouraging customers to buy films rather than renting them. The income from video sales was immense, and video (rather than broadcast television) became the dominant way audiences watched films. Videotape also made the movie seem more tangible and offered something of an archival function for viewers—people could collect favorite TV shows and movies and watch them again and again, at least until the tape degraded from overuse.

As a result of the income generated from video and television, studios were required to calculate both the lack of stereo and the 4:3 ratio of the television screen into their decisions about how to make a film. In general studios solved the problem in a way parallel to the late 1920s, when they had made both silent and sound versions of many titles: now they opted to produce two versions of each film—one for the theaters, one for television.

Figure 14-5. The release of *Raiders of the Lost Ark* (1981) on videotape in 1983 helped establish the viability of the sell-through market for VHS tapes. It grossed $30 million in its first month on the market.

The so-called pan-and-scan technique allowed the widescreen image to be broken down through cuts and pans to fit the smaller television format. This option did not always produce satisfactory results—the more the film was conceived compositionally as widescreen, the more difficult it was to transfer the film to television. Eventually the priorities were reversed, however, and filmmakers necessarily began to shoot with the knowledge that viewers of the film on video would be missing at least a third of the picture available in the theaters. Consequently, this third became largely superfluous in terms of containing essential narrative information. The sound track was similarly affected: the movie had to be intelligible not only in monaural sound but also coming from the small speakers with limited frequency and volume response characteristic of televisions at the time. It would not be until stereo television became ubiquitous in the early 1990s that sound tracks would consistently exploit the resources of stereo—yet another historical delay for stereo sound in film.

Sound Design and Elements of Style

ISSUES OF AESTHETICS: SOUND DESIGN

Dolby stereo (and later digital sound) represented less a definitive break with earlier stereo sound than a continuation or "thawing" of the frozen revolution that the original introduction of stereo had promised. The advantages of working with the increased frequency response and stereo sound of Dolby came not just from improved definition and fidelity but from the density of sounds it permitted in the mix. Unlike the earlier generation of magnetic stereo for Cinemascope and Todd A-O, where the surround channel in particular was rarely used, the much wider dispersion of Dolby permitted more extensive employment—especially after the success of *Star Wars*. (The surround fields could also be collapsed or eliminated relatively easily when remixing into mono for television.) As Michael Cimino noted in 1978 during work on *The Deer Hunter*, Dolby has "the ability to create a density of detail of sound—a richness so you can demolish the wall separating the viewer from the film."[8]

This density of detail led directly to more careful construction of the sound track. Before Dolby, the sound track remained of secondary concern. Most sound effects, for instance, were not produced specifically for the film, but instead selected from a stock sound library. This basic indifference to the sound track is perhaps best illustrated by the fact that foley artists—specialists in producing synchronized sound effects—were not regularized as part of postproduction until the 1970s. By one account, there were fewer than ten foley artists regularly working in the early 1970s.

The situation began to change with the emergence of the sound designer, who was employed to give significant attention to the overall sound of the film. The rise of the sound designer is correlated with the rise of a generation of filmmakers formally trained at film schools rather than through informal mentoring. In film schools, the students received training that was as much intellectual as practical. This situation fit with the emergence of the New Hollywood and "high concept" production. Each member of the creative team worked in concert with the director (but also the producer) to realize this concept. (A clear definition of the concept itself through the film was a major concern inasmuch as the clarity of the concept facilitated the ancillary tie-ins.) As the guardian of the concept, the director, who already enjoyed a fairly large level of prestige, became an even more important figure, but other members of the creative team gained as well. Because the "look" of the film played a significant role in clearly articulating the concept, the cinematographer enjoyed a particular elevated level of prestige, becoming an "auteur" of sorts as well. Although lagging somewhat behind the trend in cinematography, sound design increasingly also became recognized as a crucial aesthetic component of filmmaking. Composers continued to occupy an important place, as they had for decades, but sound designers now began to be recognized in a similar way for their contribution. Ben Burtt's work on *Star Wars* and Walter Murch's on *Apocalypse Now* (1979) led the way (Figure 14-6), although the importance of sound in terms of the concept did not realize its full potential until the rise of video games, where sound (as opposed to music) could feed directly into ancillary products.

AESTHETICS AND THE STEREO FIELD

Due no doubt to the experience of Cinemascope and Todd-AO stereo, the implementation of Dolby stereo was understood as an incremental rather than a revolutionary shift in the sound track. As with earlier stereo, Dolby touted its directionality, but now the emphasis really fell on creating a sense of sonic continuity with motion and location rather than on registering motion and location accurately. As Robert Warren, a Dolby engineer, explained: "if a sound moves from left to right, the sound field in front is consistent. You simply observe the motion of it moving; you don't hear it changing color or changing timbre as it shifts."[10] The surround channels on the contrary functioned as background, that is, as ambient sound. An impression of directionality and location was in fact avoided. Instead, the idea is

> to flood the auditorium with sound from everywhere but the screen, so that you have a very wide natural sound field that really doesn't have any direction or motion to it. Since the surround channel is primarily used from ambiences . . . room tone, and special effects, fly-ins and fly-outs, you don't want the surround channel to detract or to pull your attention away from the story on the screen. . . . Probably the best way to observe sound that's

Figure 14-6. *Apocalypse Now*. The "Helicopter Attack" carefully mixes a recording of Wagner's "Ride of the Valkyries" with wind, bombs, guns and various helicopter noises. The overall density of noise is controlled by constantly raising the levels of some sounds while lowering those of others. Indeed, Murch says that he rarely if ever used "more than three thematic groupings of sound at the same time" in the film. He continues:

> If I had played the helicopters and the Valkyries *and* the artillery *and* the background voices at full volume at the same time, it would just collapse into a big mush of sound. . . . You wouldn't hear any detail in it. . . . It wouldn't *sound* loud. If you want something to sound loud you have to have a detail in it—especially for a prolonged sequence—and to have detail you have to limit the information to just less than three conceptual levels. . . . What I was doing in the mix was constantly shifting, only keeping two sounds up at any one moment and a third either on the way up or on the way out, depending on the point of view or what you were looking at. My goal throughout the film was to combine density and clarity. If something is clear but isn't dense enough, if it doesn't have any heft to it, I try to find something to make it have heft. If something is as dense as you want it but you can't understand anything in it, what do I have to take out to make it clear? So I'm always looking for that balance point between density and clarity.[9]

coming from the surround channel is to turn it off. If you can hear the difference, then it's probably loud enough for ambiences and room tones.[11]

Ambient sound has proven an especially effective way to differentiate intercut story lines. Most of *Sleepless in Seattle* (1993) presents action involving Annie (Meg Ryan) and Sam (Tom Hanks) separately. These scenes, however, are often presented together through parallel editing. Subtle shifts in ambient sound underscore the cuts from Annie to Sam and back. The parallel editing illustrates the connection between the two—although they do not know each other. The difference in ambient sound marks the distance that still remains to be overcome. (For another example with commentary, see Figure 14-7.)

If Robert Warren's description defines the normative functions of the front and surround speakers, more inventive use of sound has tended to devolve from blurring the interpretive clarity that such normative functionality provides. Indeed, one of the hallmarks of filmmaking in the era of Dolby sound has been a willingness to push against the limits set by the classical style, to risk, for instance, clarity of dialogue to capture the spectacle of a particular sonic effect (overlapping dialogue, colliding effects and dialogue, etc.). Stereo certainly raised the potential for blurring interpretive clarity if only because it permitted an increased density of sound. A willingness to risk an erosion of clarity, however, is ultimately an issue of aesthetic commitment. Overlapping dialogue, for instance, had already been used effectively in screwball comedies of the 1930s to give a sense of a disordered world. Prior to multitrack recording, overlapping dialogue proved somewhat troublesome because it was difficult to fix mistakes in performance and recording. Multitrack recording addressed these problems by recording each actor on a separate track, allowing the voices to be mixed in postproduction.

a | b   **Figure 14-7.** *The Princess Bride* (1987) is based on the conceit of a grandfather (Peter Falk) reading a story to his sick grandson (Fred Savage). As he reads, the story of "The Princess Bride" comes alive, which then serves as the basis of most of the film. Throughout, however, the story is interrupted occasionally by abrupt returns to the bedroom (a), where the grandson expresses reactions and increasing investment in the story. Background sound here is used to separate the bedroom scenes from the world of the story. The bedroom scenes play with silence as a background, giving this site the feeling of being a relatively antiseptic space. The story space (b), on the contrary, is marked with a rich mix of ambient sound and non-diegetic music, making the story world come alive with sound. Each shift back to the bedroom registers as a sonic disappointment, making the story world seem ever more enchanting by comparison.

This procedure gave much more control to the filmmakers. Although released in monaural sound, *M*A*S*H* made effective and extensive use of overlapping dialogue (recall Figure 2-9). Indeed, the character of Radar is in many respects defined through his exchanges in overlapping dialogue, as he seems to anticipate the needs of Colonel Blake.

Overlapping dialogue achieved its disorienting effect by treating speech contrapuntally, that is, by putting dialogue into conflict with itself, making it difficult to follow both strands of conversation. In this sense, overlapping dialogue was a particular strategy for increasing the density of sound, but its weakness was that the actors' words frequently became unintelligible in monaural sound. Stereo separation allowed for an increase in density without necessarily imperiling intelligibility, and films produced since 1990 have become increasingly complex in this respect. *The Fellowship of the Ring* (2001), for instance, opens with an impressive mix of sounds. The New Line Cinema logo is accompanied by a synthesized soundscape that moves around the stereo field without settling into a specific place. This synthesized sound then gives way to held string tones positioned traditionally in stereo, and a small choir then begins to chant over the instruments. In this short span, the opening of the film marks out a progression of enchantment: the artificial sounds of the synthesizer give way to the natural tones of the strings, which finally turn into support for the sung voice. Over this music, a voice then begins to whisper in Elvish followed by another voice, in the front of the mix narrating in English. The overall effect is one of disorientation, but one that seems to evoke the idea of epic narration: the world of Middle Earth seems to emerge from the almost magical presence of this voice.

The dense sonic texture made possible by the stereo sound track has allowed sound to take on a number of expository functions once reserved for the image track. Establishment is now as likely to be handled aurally as visually. Rich ambient sound allows location to be effectively conveyed without visuals. Rather than showing a shot of a crashing surf and then cutting to a specific location on the beach, filmmakers today are as likely to place the sound of the waves over the end of the previous sequence (as a sound advance) and then use that as a cue to cut straight to the scene on the beach. The idea of using sound to bridge sequences certainly does not require stereo. In the era of monaural sound, music in particular would often overlap changes in location, either heralding the narrative shift with music serving a bridging function or completing a musical thought from the previous sequence as the new sequence is established. As Figure 14-8 suggests, sound bridges today are used much as music bridges were in the monaural period. The main difference is that music bridges typically involve non-diegetic music whereas sound bridges typically use diegetic sound.

Figure 14-8. *O Brother Where Art Thou?* (2000). The film opens with ambient insect sounds, bird calls, and the rhythmic fall of pick axes, all this over the Universal logo. Although the opening black and white shot has characteristics of establishment—a wide-angle shot of a field and then a slow pan—the falling pick axes and the singing leaves the shot uncertain. Indeed, the sound here entirely transforms the signification of the pan, which seems motivated by a need to solve the enigma of the sound source. The camera movement serves not to reveal landscape, as is the typical function of such pans, but to reveal a sound source.

SCORING PRACTICES

After falling somewhat out of disfavor during the 1960s, the orchestral score re-emerged as a usual component of the New Hollywood blockbuster. Credit for revitalizing the orchestral score is often given to John Williams, especially for his work on *Jaws*, *Star Wars* and *Close Encounters of the Third Kind*. Without discounting Williams' real contributions—among other things, he developed a musical approach capable of integrating smoothly with a richly textured, and often extremely loud, sound design—the return of the orchestral score probably had as much to do with the types of films that New Hollywood favored, many of which consciously reworked genres from the studio era and so drew on attributes, including music, appropriate to those types of films. The use of Dolby stereo was also an important factor, as orchestral music sounded particularly rich on it. (In that sense, much as in the 1950s, the orchestral score was a means of advertising the capabilities of sound technology.)

As we mentioned in the previous chapter, popular music became more prominent in films during the 1950s and 1960s, and increasingly the score consisted of a compilation of recordings, usually by more than one artist. *Easy Rider* (1969), *The Last Picture Show* (1971), and *American Graffiti* (1973) are early examples of such compilation scores. This trend continued in the 1970s and became even more prominent in the 1980s, when the emergence of MTV opened a new outlet for **cross-marketing** film and music.

AESTHETIC ISSUES OF CROSS-MARKETING AND PROMOTION

Compilation scores have sometimes come under attack as being motivated solely by the ancillary income they can bring in. Although it is certainly the case that ancillary income is a major consideration in determining scoring decisions, compilation scores can be successful at performing certain narrative functions. Indeed, in many situations the compilation score is a better option than traditional scoring, especially now that most audience members have been raised on recorded popular music. Compilations, for instance, are an extremely effective and efficient means to establish time and place, and it is not surprising that they were frequently used for this purpose: *The Big Chill* (1983), *Dirty Dancing* (1987), and *Forrest Gump* (1994) are three films from the 1980s and 1990s that employed compilation scores (Figure 14-9).

The complaint against compilation scores—or against the presence of popular music in general—acquires more force when the presence of songs seems arbitrary. In these cases, the popular music seems to be unmotivated, filling no particular narrative function. Even more egregious to advocates of traditional scoring is the fact that popular music is employed where the narrative functions might be handled as well or better by more traditional scoring methods. In these cases it seems that the scoring decisions are arbitrary because they are being made wholly on the basis of economics. Composer Elmer Bernstein, for instance, offers this assessment:

> Like many things, the business is money-driven, not art-driven. In the past, the function of music was to serve the film. The concerns now have shifted to, "will this music sell outside the film?" At the moment, film scores are mostly song-driven—by pop songs. People are greedy. Everybody hopes some song will jump out and make them a lot of money.[12]

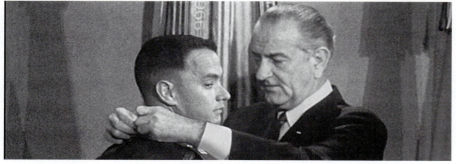

Figure 14-9. *Forrest Gump.* Music serves as an important temporal marker for the film's flash-backs to various periods in the character's life. The compilation score is in some sense simply an expression of the ubiquitous presence of recorded popular music in our life. Like Forrest Gump, many of us measure our personal history by popular music.

As we noted in the previous chapter, criticism of the economic (rather than artistic) basis of determining the placement of music in a film is nearly as old as the history of cinema itself. We also noted that the situation is not quite so simple as the criticism makes it seem: economic decisions entered into traditional scoring (even in the silent era) for the purpose of trying to make a hit. As only one example of many, additional repetitions of "Lara's Theme" were added to the orchestral sound track of *Doctor Zhivago* (1965). Undoubtedly, the changing economics of film production placed increasing financial pressures on the sound track to render hit songs. One response to this pressure was to have songs designed for promotion be motivated either diegetically or thematically. "The Morning After" from *The Poseidon Adventure* (1972) is an example of the former; the title songs for the James Bond films are examples of the latter. The need to have a hit could, however, trump narrative considerations, leading to the presence of a sequence out of joint with the narrative (or at least given undue prominence). "Raindrops Keep Falling on My Head" from *Butch Cassidy and the Sundance Kid* (1969) is one well-known example (for a discussion, see Figure 14-10.)

Saturday Night Fever (1977) set a new standard for promotion and cross-marketing. Four of the songs were released prior to the film's opening. The success of these singles proved very helpful in promoting the film. Indeed, the success of this promotion can be measured by the fact that the film was

Figure 14-10. *Butch Cassidy and the Sundance Kid.* The relationship of the song, "Raindrops Keep Fallin' on My Head," to the narrative is quite tenuous, and it comes across as a relatively unintegrated musical insert (much like a musical video). This leaves the impression that the song was added to the film primarily for the ancillary income it might produce. The song did in fact enjoy great commercial success, spending four weeks atop the Billboard Hot 100 chart in 1970; it also won an Academy Award for Best Original Song.

re-cut so that it could be re-released with a PG rating suitable for the Bee Gees' new adolescent audience. The success of the film in turn increased demand for the soundtrack album (rather than just the singles) (Figure 14.11). The effectiveness of this strategy can be seen by the sales figures. The initial release of the film grossed in the neighborhood of $100 million, a huge return at the time. The album sold more than 850,000 copies prior to the film and then averaged some 500,000 copies per week during the film's run to become by far the best-selling sound track album up to that time. Although *Saturday Night Fever* became the standard by which cross-marketing was measured, it proved a difficult formula to follow. Indeed, the sales of its sound track album have been surpassed since only by the album for *The Bodyguard* (1992).

In practice, a compilation sound track proved a more effective model. *Saturday Night Fever* placed a large bet on the success of the Bee Gees. (Although

Figure 14-11. *Saturday Night Fever*. The film and the album enjoyed great success in cross-promotion. The film was well-timed to take advantage of the wide popularity of disco at the time.

one of the songs—"If I Can't Have You"—released prior to the film's premiere was not performed by the group, it was written by them.) If the Bee Gees had not been sufficiently popular, the soundtrack album would certainly have been a flop and it is likely that the film would have suffered as well. In any case, the film would not have received the advance publicity that the extensive airplay of the singles provided. The strategy adopted by *Saturday Night Fever* was in this respect inherently risky. (It also offered high rewards. It is worth noting that *The Bodyguard* featured Whitney Houston to a similar degree and *Purple Rain* (1984), the third highest selling sound track album, likewise featured Prince.)

The usual compilation album, by contrast, minimized risk by offering a variety of artists. This strategy, similar to the exploitation of theme songs in the 1950s, attempts to appeal to a wide range of tastes. At the same time, when the studio commissions an artist (rather than buying a song from a back catalog), the song can still be used to promote a film. As Geoff King explains,

> Hit records are an ideal form of marketing for films. Radio play and record sales in advance of the release of the film provide what is effectively hours of advertising that is not only free, but for which the company gets paid. Associations with a major blockbuster film and film star, in return, help to sell the music. The sum total is likely to be greater than the parts.[13]

Often the songs bear only a tangential relation to the narrative (as diegetic background, for instance), however, and in such cases the value of the song to the promotion of the film may be minimal no matter how well the song sells on its own. Having such songs on the soundtrack album may, on the other hand, increase the sales of the album. In such cases, the film's use of the song seems to serve as a form of product placement for the sound track album because the album will perhaps receive increased sales from the song but the film will not.

This situation was mitigated somewhat by the development of the promotional music video, which coupled shots of the artist with footage from the film, often edited to form a loose narrative suggestive of (although not always identical to) that of the film. Playing on MTV, such videos proved an immensely successful means of promoting films. In this respect promotional videos turned out to be a way to realize some of the promised synergies of cross-marketing.

MUSIC VIDEO STYLE

Movie + sound track + video = $$$
—R. Serge Denisoff and George Plasketes[14]

Music video did not just serve as a promotional tool. The style of the music video also affected film style. Given that the MTV audience was one of the most important market segments for film in the 1980s (MTV began broadcasting in 1981), it should hardly be surprising that filmmakers would turn to the music video for inspiration. Some of the particularly influential traits of music video style were fast, rhythmic editing patterns and the use of music as an underlying continuity to narratively elliptical editing. Films strongly influenced by music video style include *Flashdance* (1983) and *Top Gun* (1986), both high concept films produced by Jerry Bruckheimer and Don Simpson. Bruckheimer produced films continue to use this style of editing extensively, especially in action sequences.

Indeed, music video style has now become one of the standard ways of assembling action sequences, which are particularly suitable for the style because such sequences are where spectacle, narrative dislocation, and sensory overload are the rule. This is the case in *Top Gun*, where the flight sequences in particular use this style. (See Figure 14-12) The extent to which this strategy has become ubiquitous can be seen in a film such as *The Matrix* (1999), where the fight sequences (for example, the Lobby Shootout) also follow this style. In both these cases, the editing in the action sequences differs from that elsewhere in the film, which gives these sequences a kind of narrative autonomy: they resemble production numbers in musicals that can be easily excerpted as sequences and, to a certain degree, rearranged within the narrative without materially damaging it. In other words, such sequences are "modular" in the sense that Justin Wyatt defines as a characteristic trait of high concept,[15] New Hollywood cinema. Such modularity is one reason that sequences like these can feel like proto-videogames: indeed, the pounding music, loose narrative integration and frenetic visuals of the action sequences often serve as the basis for game transfers from film narratives. (*Lola Rennt* (*Run Lola Run*, 1998) is an example of a film that uses music video style in somewhat less modular fashion—see Figure 14-13.)

Figure 14-12. *Top Gun.* The flight sequences draw extensively on frenetic and rhythmic editing to music. The promotional music videos return the favor by making extensive use of the flight sequences. Kenny Loggins'"Danger Zone" was one of four videos released to help market the film. Typical of these crosspromotional videos, it intercuts (a) shots of the singer or group with (b) flashes of narrative and (c) action from the film.   a | b | c

Figure 14-13. *Lola rennt* (*Run, Lola, Run*). Rather than the modular style of *Top Gun* or *The Matrix*, almost the entirety of *Lola rennt* is conceived in music video style. The narrative premise is that Lola (Franka Potente) has twenty minutes to find 100,000 Deutschmarks and save her boyfriend, Manni (Moritz Bleibtreu). The film goes through the scenario three times. A slight difference at the beginning of each iteration mushrooms through the course of the twenty minutes, leading to remarkably different outcomes, only one of which is happy. Each iteration is underscored by its own song, which controls the sound track through the end of the iteration. Each of these sequences is also dominated by images of Lola running. The editing in all sequences makes frequent use of jump cuts, extremely short shot lengths, and other means of narrative dislocation, all of which serve to emphasize by contrast the brief narrative stability of certain recurring events that allow us to measure the slight differences among the iterations on the one hand and to isolate the act of running itself on the other. The music ensures an underlying continuity to each sequence while also expressing Lola's relentless drive that manifests itself in her run.

Production

PRODUCTION PHASES

Although technological change meant that some job descriptions changed, the work of the sound and music departments retained the outlines that had been established in the studio era. The main addition to the music end was the role of the music supervisor, who managed the placement and licensing of popular music. Indeed, this position would by the 1990s become a dominant player who would frequently be hired during preproduction. With the rapid adoption of stereo, first by theaters, then by television, the sound department adjusted to the regular production of stereo sound tracks. It also evolved during this period from being primarily a technical department to a fully creative one. This shift is marked by the advent of the title of sound designer.

MUSIC DEPARTMENT

By the 1970s, all remnants of the studio system had disappeared. Nevertheless, the basic duties of the composer, orchestrator and music editor remained much as they had always been. The emergence of the New Hollywood and its emphasis on blockbuster production, however, brought with it a stratification of the film music production. John Williams' score to the original *Star Wars* was important in demonstrating that what amounted to an orchestral suite based on the score could sell well as a soundtrack album. The enormous success of the orchestral main title on the singles chart and the album as a whole surprised many in the film industry. Moreover, the themes from the score became fixed properties of the film—the orchestral music seemed to merge with the sound design—in a way that was seldom possible with popular music, so the music from the original film became part of the pre-sold package of any sequel. All of this elevated a successful composer such as Williams into an important source of revenue for a film, and because most studios release the scores on recording labels owned by the studio's parent company, income from these recordings eventually comes back to the studio. As a result, an unofficial "A-list" of composers gradually emerged, with membership shifting and changing depending on the popularity of a composer's recent soundtrack albums. Whereas A-list composers had more work than they could handle—indeed, A-list composers frequently ended up overcommitted and had to hand off some of the compositional work to their orchestrators—other composers found work difficult to come by.

With the loss of centralization that studio production offered, the temp track played an increasingly important part in postproduction. A temp track is a temporary score made by the music editor from recordings. These recordings can be older film scores or albums in classical, jazz, rock or any other musical style the filmmakers requires. Although the idea of the temp track was not new—the practice dates back to the studio era—its use did grow more prevalent, and it began to have a direct bearing on film composition, where composers would often be expected to write pastiches of the temp track.

The temp track served three major uses. First of all, the filmmakers often wanted to test how editing flowed with music. Already in the 1960s, many editors preferred to work with temp tracks to establish a rhythm to the editing (*A Thousand Clowns* (1965) is one example of a film edited to a temp track). Looking for such a rhythm goes hand and hand with the notion that editing by the 1960s was no longer simply a task of establishing and maintaining narrative continuity but had developed a strong aesthetic component in and of itself, one that may at times even cut against the narrative flow. Music was one way

It takes a very confident director to set aside the temp track and allow the composer to create something new. And a very assertive composer.
—Daniel Schweiger (music editor)[16]

to validate this autonomy of editing because its continuity is not necessarily that of the images (or narrative). Second, a temp track could serve as a good starting point when the director and composer spotted a film. James Horner, for instance, finds the temp track productive for this reason:

> Very often when I see the film, the director will ask me if I mind seeing it with temporary music. Temporary music is music he has taken from other movies or whatever and he stuck it in the movie in places to give a sense of flow to the film. I like to see it with that. I must say it gives me a very good starting point with the director from which to either agree and say, "Yeah, I understand what you're doing, that's great," or disagree, be able to say to him, "I don't know why you put that piece of music there, that piece of music does this to me, and the sequence doesn't do that to me. I think you're saying two things, one with the music, and one with the sequence, is that really what you want me to do?" So it gives a good point of departure when the composer sees the film with temporary music.[17]

Finally, near the end of postproduction (but before the music was completed) filmmakers often previewed their films before test audiences so they could learn how audiences reacted. Because music affects how an audience responds, this preview version of the film required a temp track to get reliable response from the audience.

As mentioned earlier, one new position emerged in the music department in the early 1980s, the role of music supervisor. The primary responsibility of the music supervisor was placing popular music recordings. By the 1980s, the pressure to incorporate songs into films was high enough to necessitate hiring a specialist to assist the filmmakers in choosing the songs and negotiating the legal and financial contracts. (These specialists were first called "Music Consultants"—not to be confused with ethnic or historic music consultants that are also used in films from time to time—but the nomenclature soon settled on "Music Supervisor.") As studios and their recording affiliates realized the income possibilities that came along with soundtrack compilation recordings (*Saturday Night Fever, The Big Chill, When Harry Met Sally* (1989)), experienced music supervisors such as Budd Carr (longtime Oliver Stone collaborator), Bonnie Greenberg (*How the Grinch Stole Christmas* (2000), *Something's Gotta Give* (2003)), Peter Afterman (*The Passion of the Christ* (2004)), Sharon Boyle (*Silence of the Lambs* (1991)), and Karyn Rachtman (longtime Quentin Tarantino collaborator) soon became essential as conduits between filmmakers, bands, and recording and film executives. At first, music supervisors were hired, like the rest of the music department, to assist during postproduction because that was the point at which decisions on music had traditionally been made. Recently, however, music supervisors have been hired much earlier in the process, often in preproduction, and have been given much broader responsibilities, from supervising the overall musical content of the film to assisting the director and producers in the selection of composers. These latest shifts in the role of the music supervisor may sound like a throwback to the music department heads of the studio system, but because most music supervisors are hired specifically for their expertise and knowledge in popular song recordings and legal negotiations, it is unclear how this might affect the other work of the music department.

SOUND DEPARTMENT

The shift to Dolby stereo (and digital sound in the 1990s) brought new prominence to the sound department. One indication of this was the appearance of the creative role of the sound designer (or supervising sound editor), responsible for imagining and coordinating the production of the sound track (aside from music) much as the cinematographer does the image. Although the sound design for a film must obviously be made in consultation with the director, the sound designer is the person responsible for making decisions to realize such ideas. As film sound grows in importance, the role of the "sound designer"—a title Murch imported from traditional theater—has become crucial. (The title itself is less common in Hollywood, where the traditional division between mixing and editing remains relatively strict.)

Summary

Technological, commercial, and cultural changes significantly affected the sound of the feature film in the period from the 1950s into the 1990s: the use of magnetic tape in postproduction, the introduction and gradual adoption of stereo sound reproduction and Dolby stereo, the move to multiplex theaters as the dominant mode of film exhibition, and the emergence of the sound designer, coupled with a greater complexity in the treatment of different musical styles (especially the use of popular music as background scoring), all contributed to changes that mark off older films and their exhibition practices as "classic" and that, if anything, have been intensified and exaggerated into the present day.

CHAPTER 15

Music and Film Sound Today

Introduction: the Digital Era

Magnetic tape and Dolby noise reduction were introduced in postproduction well before they were used on release prints. In the same way, digital sound had long held a secure place in postproduction by the time it also became standard for prints distributed to theaters. As early as 1979, *Star Trek: The Motion Picture* used digital signal processing for mixing special sonic effects. By the early 1980s, digital recording and rerecording had become common, though not yet standard. Digital sound had definite advantages: it expanded the dynamic range, it improved the frequency response, especially in the high frequencies crucial to definition, and it all but eliminated noise and signal degradation from multiple dubs. The use of digital sound in postproduction rerecording thus played much the same role that magnetic tape had in the 1950s and 1960s: It was a means of retaining greater fidelity throughout the process of making multiple dubs during postproduction and, as a result, permitted unprecedented flexibility and new aesthetic options for designing a film's sound track.

Issues of Technology and Economics

DIGITAL SOUND

Broadly speaking, digital sound did not alter the fundamental layout and functional differentiation of the sound track. Nevertheless, significant changes resulted in practice because the ease of producing certain kinds of effects greatly expanded their use. Digital sound also offered unique possibilities through signal processing, including extending a sound, changing its pitch, or adding effects with Doppler shifts and digital filters. Perhaps the most significant trait of digital sound, however, was that it permitted random access. Prior to such non-linear systems as AVID, all editing had to be done in sequence within a reel, but digital sound, combined with the easy and relatively inexpensive capability to digitize the image, enabled non-linear editing, or the ability to access and edit any point of the film. In terms of sound, the most important aspect of this shift was a newfound ease in layering sound and shaping the sound track over the course of the whole film. It was actually possible to do such sound design and sound editing prior to non-linear systems, but the work was considerably more time consuming and therefore much more expensive. Now, rather than dividing sound editing duties according to reels, sound department personnel could be assigned tasks according to sound layer and narrative function. The result was much more consistent treatment of sound across the span of the film, which in turn permitted the sound track to be more thoroughly planned or "designed" from the outset.

DIGITAL SOUND FORMATS

The rapidly improving home stereo systems of the late 1960s and 1970s had made the performance of sound systems in the multiplex seem inadequate, and in the 1980s and 1990s the increased frequency and dynamic response of the CD put similar pressure on theaters to continue upgrading their sound. Although it was a substantial improvement on traditional optical sound, Dolby stereo was at a disadvantage in noise, frequency, and dynamic response when compared to the CD, and in the second half of the 1980s the CD quickly became the primary form by which music was commercially distributed. In feature films, due to the properties of the optical sound track, Dolby stereo had difficulty distinguishing low frequency sounds from background hiss, and the restricted space on the optical tracks set an absolute limit to volume control. To remedy these problems, Dolby Labs introduced digital sound for the release of *Batman Returns* in 1992. Ingeniously locating the digital information in the space between the sprocket holes on the film (Figure 15-1), the original 5.1 **Dolby digital** carried six channels—left, center, right, two surround channels, and a separate channel for low frequencies. A year later, in *Jurassic Park*, DTS (Digital Theater System) introduced a competing system, which used a CD synchronized to the film (a distant echo of Warner Bros' Vitaphone system from the 1920s). The last of the digital formats to appear was SDDS (Sony Dynamic Digital Sound), which, like Dolby, was physically encoded on the film. *Last Action Hero* (1993) was the first film released coded with SDDS.

Even so, it was difficult for filmmakers to take full advantage of the improvements offered by digital sound for theatrical releases. As had been the case with stereo, theaters were slow to adopt the technology, generally opting to convert only their largest auditorium in order to handle the blockbuster releases. This reluctance on the part of theater owners, along with the continued dominance

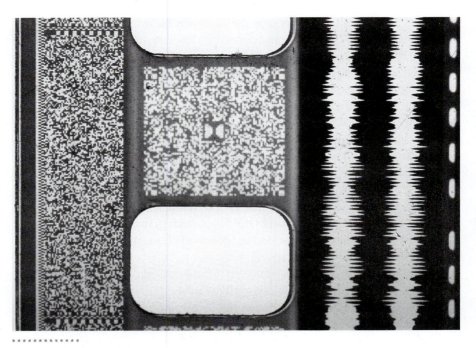

Figure 15-1. Placement of sound track formats on exhibition prints. The space outside the sprocket holes carries part of the SDDS encoding. The rest of the SDDS encoding is placed outside the right hand sprocket holes (not shown). The space between the sprockets is occupied by the Dolby digital encoding (note the Dolby trademark symbol in the middle of the data field). The two analog optical tracks (variable area) are encoded in Dolby surround, and are used primarily for backup. The dashed line along the right edge is the DTS time-code, which ensures synchronization with the special accompanying CD.

of the VHS cassette as a primary consumer market for film purchase and rental, placed filmmakers in a bind. As rerecorder mixer Tom Fleischman notes:

> One of the problems we've had in making technological advances in sound is that there's a catch-22 that exists. For us to be able to use something new technologically, it has to be able to be delivered to the public. Dolby Stereo came out in the early seventies and really wasn't widely used until the late seventies because there was an expense involved in converting the theater to be able to play the track. The same thing happened when they went to Dolby SR. They had converted all the theaters to Dolby Stereo, and again there was a cost involved in upgrading to Dolby SR. Until the owners are willing to make that expense to convert their theaters, there's nowhere to play the track. If there's nowhere to play the track, the producer won't want to use that format. The studio that's got the facility doesn't want to make the investment in new equipment that's needed to provide it. It's like the chicken and the egg—what's going to trigger this cycle to begin?[1]

The rapid replacement of older multiplexes by the newer megaplex palaces with raked seating since the late 1990s broke the logjam that Fleischman describes, so that today most theaters in the U.S. market are equipped with digital sound. The same cannot be said internationally: in France, for instance, many theaters may have one or two auditoria outfit for digital sound, but the others continue to use Dolby optical stereo or in some cases even monaural sound.

VIDEO, DVD, AND TELEVISION TECHNOLOGIES

We made the observation in the previous chapter that stereo could only be fully exploited in the "design" of the sound track when stereo televisions and VCRs became ubiquitous in the early 1990s: the sound track still had to be adequate when heard through the speakers of a television set. Even today, when television sound has vastly improved, filmmakers cannot generally count on more than two-channel stereo with simulated surround in the home setting. Sound tracks therefore cannot take full advantage of the resources of the modern theater—excepting perhaps volume—without risking loss of intelligibility for home viewers, by far the largest audience for any film.

The situation is especially acute with respect to the center channel, which leaves a slight "hole" in the stereo field right where the voice is typically placed. This channel is missing in two-channel stereo, which is why dialogue can seem oddly decentered when listening to television, especially in the wide stereo field of simulated surround. To compensate for this negative result, dialogue is inevitably mixed at a higher level and the music and ambient sound reduced. In point of fact, the same holds true, although to a lesser extent, for 5.1 mixes released on DVD, where dialogue is also boosted under the assumption that the conditions and distractions of home viewing tend to impair intelligibility. The situation with television is rapidly changing, however. The federal government's mandate to change to digital broadcast by mid-2009, along with HDTV channel broadcasts in 5.1, make it likely that the basic DVD (or Blu-Ray) mix will gradually move closer to those heard in the cinema. Nevertheless, the sheer number of formats and viewing conditions will continue to place a limit on standardization of release mixes. Given various-sized multiplexes, DVDs, in-flight films, etc., it is simply impossible to prefigure an ideal mix.

Although the DVD did not (at first) have the capacity to record, its relatively quick consumer acceptance was made possible by the fact that it offered far superior sound and picture compared to videotape (although some cineastes complained that it failed to meet the standards of the laserdisc). The DVD also offered digital encoding, which meant that the image and sound were not subject to the same degradation over time as was the case with videotape. The large data capacity of the DVD permitted higher fidelity sound with more audio channels and a richer set of mixes, so that it has become standard for films to be released encoded in 5.1 sound whenever appropriate (and sometimes

even when not—see Figure 15-2 for a discussion). Finally, the relative perma-
nence and low cost of DVDs strongly encouraged DVD purchases and, with
that, the creation of personal film libraries, a trend that VHS tapes had already
started to a lesser degree.

Until very recently, filmmakers have not fully utilized the greatly enhanced
sound capabilities of the DVD format, but the full frequency sound and wide
field spatiality of the surround channels nevertheless played a crucial role in

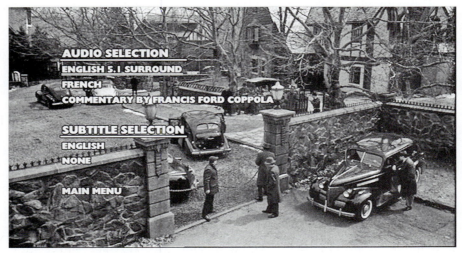

Figure 15-2. Encoding of DVDs in 5.1 surround has become something of a fetish, with
the sound tracks of many older monaural films being remixed often with exaggerated stereo effects. The 5.1 mix of *The Manchurian Candidate* (1962), for instance, contains a significant
amount of overtly panned point of location sound. Sometimes the remix is presented as having been done under the supervision of the director. The collector's edition of M*A*S*H (1970)
advertises: "Director Robert Altman personally oversaw the film restoration for this DVD. The
painstaking process included the re-creation of the film negative and a reengineering of the
film's original sound track." In this case, the disk includes the original mono sound track as well,
but this is not always the case.

The audio menu from the version of *The Godfather* (1972) contained in *The Godfather DVD
Collection* is shown above. Note that it contains only the 5.1 surround mix, despite the fact that
it was originally released in mono and was nominated for an Academy Award in sound.

Finally, the sound tracks of many older films with monaural optical tracks have often been
digitally processed to reduce the background hiss that was present in the original recordings
and prints. This processing has allowed these films to sound better than they ever did at the
time they were exhibited. The DVD of *The Broadway Melody* (1929), for instance, has not only
reduced the characteristic hiss of sound tracks at the time, but has also dulled the sharp audio
pops between shots in the opening scene.

Clearly we need to be extremely cautious about drawing historical inferences from the
sound tracks of DVDs.

what might be called the "cinematization" of television. To put it bluntly, DVD sound made even a 32" screen look puny by comparison with the sound—the sound engulfed the viewer, while the screen merely contained the picture. Even larger televisions suffered because letterboxing effectively reduces the size of the screen: the wider the aspect ratio of the theatrical release, the smaller the image on the television. The point of the widescreen format is to fill the spectators' peripheral vision, producing the illusion that they are in the midst of the film itself, yet the small image of the letterboxed version had just the opposite effect. Even as television screens became larger, the lack of a commensurate improvement in resolution meant the images lost much of their cinematic sharpness. It would not be too much of a stretch to say that cinematic sound contributed significantly to the obsolescence of analogue television.

THE MULTIPLEX PALACE

In the United States, the indifferent architecture of the multiplex has been largely replaced by a new theater aesthetic, leveraged at least in part by the needs of digital sound. These theaters often have ambitious architecture reminiscent of the old picture palaces, and they often boast as many as fifteen to twenty screens (allowing showings of popular titles to start as close together as every 15 minutes), digital sound and projection, and heavily raked (or stadium) seating. If the exterior is reminiscent of the picture palace, however, the basic structure of the multiplex—especially the concession stand dominating the lobby—remains in place. Although raked seating has made the film going experience more comfortable for patrons, the needs of sound insulation, especially heavy curtains along the walls to keep reflected sound in the theater to a minimum, have generally kept the architecture of the auditoria themselves more or less nondescript.

A number of factors have driven the building of these new theaters. The most important of these is that the production rate of Hollywood in the past decade or so has increased to the extent that more screens (if not necessarily more seats) are needed. During the summer months especially, prospective blockbusters often open the same weekend. This can result in a severe shortage of screens, not only pushing other films out of the theater but also constraining the gross receipts of the blockbusters themselves (because the gross is limited by the number of available seats). Increasing the number of seats for an individual film maximizes the effects of the saturation advertising used to promote blockbusters (and, increasingly, smaller films as well); the larger number of screens gives exhibitors much greater flexibility in adjusting the number of seats to demand for particular films.

Having been built to exhibit with digital sound, the auditoria of the newer multiplexes, generally speaking, have vastly superior sound characteristics compared to the older generation of theaters. The acoustic insulation between theaters has also been improved. The bleeding over of low frequency sound from

Figure 15-3. THX is a theater certification standard developed by Tomlinson Holman for Lucasfilm. Unlike, Dolby, SDDS, and DTS, THX is not a format for sound reproduction but a technical standard that ensures that all certified theaters (and mixing rooms) will sound alike.

a blockbuster in one auditorium to the romantic comedy next door has been largely mitigated, if not entirely eliminated. And many theaters now undergo THX certification (see Figure 15-3), which guarantees that the auditoria meet certain technical specifications for image projection and sound reproduction. The weak point in this system remains the lack of a dedicated professional staff for projection and sound, because the volume level in particular needs to be adjusted according to the size of the audience.

Digital Sound and Elements of Style

ISSUES OF AESTHETICS

Although nearly all films designed for commercial release today are produced to be screened with digital sound, the consciousness with which the sound track is given emphasis varies considerably by genre. Part of this has to do with the historical legacy of filmmaking. Spectacular, big budget films tend to deploy their sound more overtly, seeking to wow their audiences with a sound equal to the budget. As we have noted in previous chapters, superior sound reproduction has gone hand in hand with filmic spectacle, a situation that continues, ironically, to make rich, full, highly textured sound a signifier of artifice. Stereo, although not deployed overtly in smaller-scale films such as romantic comedies, nevertheless has fundamentally altered the treatment of sound. In the scene from *Sleepless in Seattle* (1993) analyzed in Chapter 1 (recall Figures 1.8-12), for instance, most of the treatment of sound is made more effective by the presence of stereo. The density of sounds on the road, for instance, would be difficult to convey in monaural sound. Consequently, the magical intimacy of the exchange of "hellos" across the road would be difficult, if not impossible, to render in the absence of stereo sound. It is indeed the reduction of the ambience in the stereo field, the displacement of the street sounds in favor of the dialogue, that gives us this strong sense of a private connection between Sam and Annie. Although it would certainly have been possible to render the "hellos" without stereo sound, it would have been more difficult to achieve the effect of strong contrast, the juxtaposition of this moment with the surrounding noise. In a sense, the disappearance of the rich sonic detail makes the "hellos" sound enchanted, as although the special intimacy between the two characters is able to shut out the world, here symbolized by the ambient field. For a quite different example, where music and ambient sound are set in conflict with one another, see Figure 15-4 and its commentary.

A wide dynamic range is one of the most striking characteristics of modern theatrical sound, but this example from *Sleepless in Seattle* illustrates that it is the ability to control dynamic range precisely that is perhaps of greatest value—the artful use of dynamic contrast is far more effective than absolute volume. Digital sound in particular has offered a new take on silence: rather than background hiss, films can make effective use of extremely quiet sounds such as room ambience just above the threshold of hearing. In addition to their use to create varied sonic backgrounds, such silences can prepare explosions of sound. Many of the terrifying "sonic assaults" in David Lynch's films—for example, the ax blow to the television that ends the opening-credits sequence of

Figure 15-4. *Shakespeare in Love* (1998). Will (Joseph Fiennes) chases Viola through the streets. In this sequence music and the ambient sound of the street are both mixed at fairly high levels. Stereo separation mitigates the conflict to a degree, but the sound track retains a sense of competition between these elements, reinforcing the crowd's function as an obstacle in his pursuit.

Twin Peaks: Fire Walk with Me (2002)—are achieved through the use of startling and completely gripping dynamic contrasts; it is the unexpected contrast rather than absolute volume that achieves the effect.

Although Dolby stereo greatly increased the definition of sound, digital sound has offered particular opportunities in low and high frequencies. Most of us can easily recall hearing the cinematic crashes and explosions that rumble from the subwoofer in depths unknown on television or even most home stereos, but the use of high-frequency sound has perhaps been even more substantive in changing the way films sound because high-frequency definition promises proximity and intimacy. It is therefore somewhat ironic that high-frequency sound has become a hallmark of the rendering of violence. Metallic clangs ring out with high-frequency definition and have become a favorite device for displaying the power of digital sound. In *Gladiator* (2000), for instance, sword clashes punctuate the battle sequences, carefully marking the moments of synchronization despite manipulations of film speed. One effect of the relation between sound and image is to make Maximus (Russell Crowe) seem charmed, almost superhuman.

Occasionally a sudden blast of high-frequency sound is used to startle, as when the terminator crushes a human skull with its foot at the opening of *Terminator 2: Judgment Day* (1991). If the sound tracks of recent films seem particularly "live," if the film worlds seem brimming with an almost uncontainable amount of sound, this is due in large measure to the presence of extensive high frequency sound. When coupled with slow motion, a particular high frequency sound isolated in the mix can produce the impression of a sort of uncanny hyperacute hearing. In *The Matrix* (1999), for instance, we hear precisely synchronized tinkling of bullet casings hitting the ground in the midst of a hail of gunfire (for another example, see Figure 15-5).

Figure 15-5. *The Fellowship of the Ring* (2001). Contemporary sound design often "sweetens" effects in almost musical fashion for dramatic effect. Both of these frames come from the prologue, and each illustrates a different facet of the sweetened sound effect. In the first case (left), the sweep of Sauron's scepter is given an artificial, synthetic sound, whereas in the second case (right), the crash of the helmet is rendered with a very loud metallic clank. In each case, the effect is far larger than life, endowing it with the aura of the supernatural.

SCORING PRACTICES

The symphony orchestra has continued to enjoy a strong presence in block-busters. Howard Shore's score for *The Lord of the Rings* trilogy (2001–2003), for instance, deployed an exceptionally large orchestra supplemented by voices (both individual and choral) and exotic instruments (such as the Hardanger fiddle used for the Rohan theme). Increasingly after 1990, rock rhythm tracks have been combined with orchestral music to give action sequences increased drive. This technique has been especially associated with Hans Zimmer and some of his collaborators; and it is sometimes called the "Media Venture" sound, after the studio Zimmer ran until it was dissolved in a legal dispute with his partner. (Composers associated with Zimmer's studio include Klaus Badelt, Harry Gregson-Williams, and Jeff Rona.) A good example of this tech-nique can be found in Zimmer's score to *Blackhawk Down* (2001).

Orchestral music has continued to serve as the foundation for scoring blockbusters, but the decreasing costs and increasing quality of synthesiz-ers meant that, for most other films, composers drew more and more on the resources of the synthesizer, both as an independent instrument and as a substitute for orchestral instruments. Synthesizers and electronic mu-sic emerged in the film music medium beginning in the 1940s, where they were generally deployed to indicate psychologically deviant states of mind, dreams, the presence of aliens, or scientific super-rationality. Such connota-tions continued to be employed in Vangelis' synthesized score to *Blade Run-ner* (1982), where the synthesized quality of the music is thematically related to the synthetic status of the replicants; but those connotations seem largely irrelevant to his similarly synthesized score to *Chariots of Fire* (1981). In the latter score, the synthesizer is used simply as an instrument that generates an unusual sound.

With the development of high quality samplers in the 1980s, it became possible to make reasonable counterfeits of live acoustic music. Among the im-portant consequences of this change was a composer's ability to produce fairly accurate mock-ups of cues that allowed the director and producer to preview the music before it was recorded. In this way the composer was able to get bet-ter feedback before the music was brought to the scoring stage. In addition, by substituting synthesizers for some live players—especially strings—composers found they could cut music costs while still retaining an orchestral founda-tion. This was an especially important development for smaller, independent films, which in earlier years would have had to settle for at best an orchestra with just a handful of players. Today, such films are routinely scored with elec-tronics as the foundation of the sound track: live instruments are brought in to color the electronic score. This practice is even more prevalent in television, where it would be very difficult today to find a show that used only acoustic instrumentation.

In general, the convergence of advanced digital technology with the enormous increase of independent filmmaking over the past thirty years has both allowed and forced composers to create a score in innovative ways, including performing and improvising the score themselves, creating an score entirely with electronic synthesizers or samplers, and using personal computers and home recording technology to record a score in the privacy of the composer's own home. Examples of film scores that have utilized various techniques include those created and recorded on synthesizers (the scores by Vangelis mentioned above and *Witness* by Maurice Jarre (1985)), composed and improvised to picture (*Dead Man* by Neil Young (1995)), and even created, recorded and digitally manipulated in the composer's bedroom studio (*A Scanner Darkly* by Graham Reynolds (2006)). Robert Rodriguez is a contemporary director known for creating his own music (see him at work in Figure 15-6).

THE RISE OF RAP

With the rise of rap as a commercial genre in the 1980s, film studios worked to find a way to exploit this music's popularity, and already by the late 1980s it was not unusual to find rap being used on the sound track like any other popular music genre. Diegetically, rap could serve to establish time, place, and character, as in the case of Run-DMC's "Christmas in Hollis" in *Die Hard* (1988). Here, near the beginning of the film, Argyle (De'voreaux White) plays the song on the radio of the limo as he drives McClane (Bruce Willis) to the Christmas

Figure 15-6. Robert Rodriguez in his home studio.

party. This song is explicitly contrasted to Bach's Third Brandenburg Concerto heard at the party itself, a piece used to characterize the executive class milieu of McClane's wife, Holly (Bonnie Bedelia). Not surprisingly, one of the primary narrative tensions of the film turns out to concern class, which threatens the relationship between McClane and Holly.

Film makers have tried to exploit popular music performers as actors since at least Rudy Vallee in the earliest years of the sound film. The same has been true with rap, and the most successful film maker in this regard has been Will Smith. His films generally feature some of his own music, at least a title track, which can then be used for cross promotional videos and as part of a sound track album. *Men in Black* (1997) is a good example of this; the title song appears only over the credits.

Other films have been constructed more consistently around rap and a hip-hop ethos where the sound track is dominated by the music. Predictably, these films are generally set in a contemporary, urban environment. They are often divided into two categories: "hip hop" and "hood" films. Spike Lee's *Bamboozled* (2000) is an example of a hip hop film. *Boyz n the Hood* (1991) and *Menace II Society* (1993) are the two best known examples of "hood" films. Generally, these subgenres can be differentiated by whether the presentation of the urban environment is positive (hip hop, the city life) or negative (the "hood," gangsta rap). The hood films draw on the dystopic iconography of gangsta rap video, and they have so far proven the more commercially viable, but the valorization of crime in these films has also brought with it critical condemnation similar to what gangsta rap itself suffered, and many of the films remain controversial for this reason.

Production

PRODUCTION PHASES

Digital technologies have transformed film production. Sound has been recorded digitally since the 1980s, and increasingly films are being shot digitally as well. Special effects are done almost entirely through computer generated imagery (CGI) as is most editing—for both picture and sound. Digital editing offers speed and flexibility over traditional editing practices. The nonlinear editing of digital systems has allowed sound editors in particular to change how they approach a film. Digital editing is also nondestructive, meaning editors have more freedom to experiment because they know they can always go back to a previous version. On the other hand, the ease and flexibility of digital editing has made it more difficult to "lock" a picture (picture lock is the point in postproduction when picture editing is completed), meaning that components such as music dependent on a locked picture often face extremely tight postproduction deadlines.

During the postproduction phase, filmmakers have remarkable control over the factors that go into the sound track, including directionality (surround sound), the music's clarity many generations after the original recording (digital sound systems), and theater sound that is as close to what the filmmakers heard in the final dubbing sessions as possible (Tomlinson Holman's THX system for certifying theater sound). The rise of nonlinear editing systems such as AVID, of relatively cheap, but powerful film editing software such as Apple's Final Cut Pro, and of digital audio software such as DigiDesign's Pro Tools or Apple's Logic Studio has given editors enormously increased flexibility in manipulating sound and picture, and on-board computer recording technology is quickly relegating mixing boards and tape decks to extinction. Composers are now using this digital technology to modify their recorded scores with effects processors, time distortion and mixing techniques.

All these factors have transformed the overall effect films have on audiences. The clean, polished look and sound of films today are in stark contrast to films from years past. In fact, the shift from analogue to digital systems is seen by many to be as monumental a change as the invention of sound film itself.

In the two sections that follow, we outline the typical work of the music and sound departments in film production today, using the model of the commercial film industry in the United States.

MUSIC DEPARTMENT

Music Production

The basic division of labor for decisions about music are between the music supervisor, who is responsible for uses of existing music, and the composer, who creates the underscore. Because use of existing music tracks involves licensing and therefore can significantly affect the finances of a film, music supervisors are usually brought in during the planning stages. Even for films that use many popular music tracks, however, composers will usually remain the primary creative agent—if there is also a score. As postproduction schedules have grown ever shorter, most composers also lean heavily on the skills and time of orchestrators and music editors, especially as the deadline nears and in the environment of recording sessions. Steve Bartek, one of Danny Elfman's chief orchestrators, explains his role thus (also see Figure 15-7):

> [Elfman] sits with the director and the director is telling him, This works, this doesn't work, and Danny then deals with me, How can we change this while the orchestra is still rehearsing? I take his notes and we come up with some sort of solution and I call it through the headphones to the conductor to tell the players what to do, to help change it more to what the director wants. So there's a weird chain of command from Danny to me to the conductor to the orchestra.[2]

Figure 15-7. Music copyist Ron Vermillion, orchestrators Edgardo Simone and Steve Bartek, and *Meet the Robinsons* (2007) composer Danny Elfman (photo: Dan Goldwasser).

Once a score is close to completion but before it is passed on to the orchestrator, the composer will preview a mock-up score for the director's (and producer's) approval. On the basis of the mock-up, the director will decide whether the score is acceptable, needs to be rewritten or perhaps even abandoned (in which case a new composer might be brought in). Because the stakes of the mock-up session are so high, composers often have to spend as much time preparing the mock-up musical files as they do writing the score itself. (Figure 15-8 shows a prominent composer at work.)

Similar to the orchestrator is the synthesizer programmer, who is hired when a composer decides that the film score needs electronic instruments such as synthesizers and samplers but lacks either the time or the technical knowledge to produce the needed sounds on his or her own. Generally, a composer writes sketches, but in certain cues or for certain accompaniment parts, instead of indicating specific notes for a particular instrument, he or she may write only general descriptive phrases, such as "pinging choral bells" or "violent winds." The programmer then creates the appropriate sounds.

Mundane music production tasks such as making orchestra parts have been profoundly affected by digitalization. *Music preparation* refers to the various activities that entail the creation, organization, and adjustment of the notated music performed during a recording session. For many years, music

Figure 15-8. Composer Hans Zimmer working in his studio. Zimmer is widely recognized for delivering mock-up scores that are exceptionally accurate (photo: Dan Goldwasser)

preparation was the bailiwick of professional "copyists." Parts were created by hand using fountain pens and even although the copyists were spacing everything out by "eye"—without rulers—the resultant work were extremely legible; these craftsmen prided themselves on being artisans of the highest caliber. Beginning in the late 1980s, music notation software applications such as Finale and Sibelius were introduced into the marketplace and by the mid-1990s, the age of hand-written parts in film scores had passed. These software applications allow copyists not only to create engraver-quality scores and parts in a fraction of the time it would take to create them by hand but also to make changes and quickly reprint parts on site as required during a recording session (see Figure 15-9). The shift from hand-written manuscript to digital notation has necessitated a separate sub-group within the music production team that focuses specifically on the various tasks involved in music preparation. Music production teams can number anywhere from a handful to twenty or more people, but the tasks they perform can be broken down into four categories. Many times the same person may spend time doing more than one of these jobs during the production process. The music preparation supervisor coordinates the entire group and will usually be the point of contact with the composer and orchestrator. Several copyists, working under the supervisor, input the handwritten full score into the notation software and create score files for

Figure 15-9. Global Music Service copyists Jill Streater and Vic Frasier inspect a part engraved with Sibelius notation software during a recording session for *Harry Potter and the Goblet of Fire* (2005) at the Hall at Air Lyndhurst Studios in London, England.

each cue. Part extractors, using the same software, separate each individual part into separate files and format them for performance. These part files are finally sent to the librarians, who print out the paper parts, bind them, and organize them into folders destined for the musicians' stands. Several copies of the scores are also printed out for use by the composer, conductor, orchestrator, and score supervisor. The librarians may also be called upon to edit and reprint parts during the recording session as changes are made.

The scene of a large orchestra playing under the baton of a composer as the film plays behind it (as in Figure 15.10) may be the quintessential image that comes to mind when a film score recording session is mentioned, but it is by no means the only method found in the film music industry. Lower-budget film scores can be recorded using just a few individuals in a small recording booth. Using this more intimate method of recording, performers can record each part individually without a conductor and often times are asked to rerecord the same part several times to give the impression that a large number of instruments are playing the part at once (as mentioned earlier, this technique was used in the studio era to reduce the number of string players needed in a studio orchestra). Current technology gives composers the ability to record musicians who reside in other cities or countries; by linking studios through

Figure 15-10. James Horner conducts *Flightplan* (2005) (photo: Dan Goldwasser).

digital technology, a composer can sit in a recording studio in Los Angeles and record instrumentalists in New York, hearing them as if they were in the next room. This allows the composer greater freedom to choose individual musicians while also allowing professional musicians the flexibility to live and work outside of Hollywood. Figure 15-11 shows several photos of highly specialized musicians at work.

The recording session is the most exciting but also most dangerous point in the music production process for all involved. It is the moment when the score "comes to life" but is also affected by substantial time and financial constraints. Both the musicians and the recording studio are paid by the hour, which can create a conflict between composer (who wants the score to sound perfect), director (who wants the score to work perfectly with the film) and producer (who wants to complete the recording session without spending more than he or she feels is necessary).

Preparations for the recording sessions can begin as early as the preproduction stage. Once the composer has a music budget and a good idea of the appropriate instrumental forces for the project, he or she will contact recording studios to see about access to their services, copyists who will create the parts, and a contractor who will hire the musicians. In addition to the music prepara-

Figure 15-11. Because a film orchestra is not a fixed ensemble like a symphony, orchestrations often make use of exotic instruments.: (a) percussionist Emil Richards; (b) Duduk player Arman Gasparian; (c) Pedro Eustache performing custom-created pipes on John Debney's score for *The Ant Bully* (2006) (photos: Dan Goldwasser).

a | b | c

tion personnel already mentioned, the music editor also has a task in advance of the recording session. Few scores are recorded without some form of *pre-dubbing*: this means that the composer has already laid down several audio tracks with digital sampling synthesizers; the live musicians are then recorded along with the pre-dubs. The music editor, often assisted by a click-track operator (Figure 15-12), creates click tracks for each cue; these are played into the headphones of the musicians during the session.

As has been true since the studio days, composers often prefer to conduct their own scores, not only because they know the music better than anyone else but also because they will be in the best position to make changes on the spot (Figure 15-13). Adjustments to the score can run the gamut from simple changes in instrumental colors to substantial re-composing. An experienced director will recognize when a particular sound, musical gesture, or entire cue is not working in the interest of the picture, and he or she must be able to articulate the changes needed in a clear and concise way, almost as if he speaking to an actor. The composer in turn must be able to interpret what the director means and quickly translate that into a form that he or she can convey to the orchestra members. These moments can be trying for all involved, but they also give a unique look into a composer's creative process; usually a composer creates in the solitude of the private studio, but on the podium he or she is forced to act quickly and decisively.

If the composer is conducting, the orchestrator will normally be in the booth with the recording engineer and the director to act as the composer's "ears," alerting the engineer to specific events in the score (a score supervisor performs much the same role). The orchestrator or score supervisor also acts as a communication bridge between the director and composer, an important role because of the director's position in the hierarchy: he or she is the final arbiter of the score despite being the person with the least amount of musical knowledge and

Figure 15-12. Auricle click-track operator (and creator) Richard Grant. In 1984, Ron and Richard Grant invented the Auricle Time Processor, a software application that allowed for the creation and manipulation of a click track that could give the conductor immense control over the tempo of a cue, as well as for the digital imprinting of streamers and punches at the conductor's request onto the displayed film (photo: Dan Goldwasser).

experience. This is not a comfortable position for the director to be in, and the orchestrator or score supervisor can help to ensure that the director understands what is happening and that the communication lines between composer and director are open. The orchestrator can also see to it that the session runs at a good pace, because it is very easy for the director (and sometimes the composer) to view the orchestra as a giant (albeit expensive) plaything and experiment with requests for many different instrumental combinations. Because the composer is on the podium and cannot always keep track of the time, the orchestrator, score supervisor, and recording engineer can judiciously suggest that the session move forward if they see that the session is beginning to lag.

Music Postproduction

If the recording session is one of the most dramatic events in music production, then the postproduction process has to be one of the least. Once the music has been recorded, the composer and scoring mixer meticulously lis-

Figure 15-13. Composer Shirley Walker conducts during a recording session (photo: Dan Goldwasser).

ten to the different versions or "takes" of each music cue and decide which one to use in the film. After these choices are made, many details still require adjustment within each cue: balance changes, frequency adjustments, and sometimes even new material from the composer's personal samplers and synthesizers (Figure 15-14).

The final dubbing session (sometimes referred to as the Rerecording Mix Session) combines dialogue, sound effect, and music tracks as three rerecord-ing engineers mix them onto the final sound track (although having three mix-ers is commonplace in Hollywood, scoring sessions in New York and else-where will usually have only one or two). Many times this dubbing session will occur in a special dubbing theater that is equipped with an enormous mixing console placed in a central location within the room; this gives the engineers the most accurate idea of what the balances will be in a theater. The composer will attend these sessions along with the director, producers, and the various sound designers and editors who constructed the sound effects and dialogue tracks. Not surprisingly, these sessions can often involve intense discussions among the various parties about the balance of sound track elements, even if it is generally agreed that dialogue should have priority.

Figure 15-14. Screen Shot of Apple's *Logic Studio*, an integrated editing and mixing application often used in music production and postproduction.

SOUND DEPARTMENT

Sound Production

Although we used the term "music production" in the previous section, strictly speaking film music is mostly associated with postproduction, and in fact with the later phases of that process, after the film is "locked." Work on the other aspects of the sound track, however, is spread across both production and postproduction. The members of the sound team as a whole, especially the composer and the supervising sound mixer (who is responsible for conceiving the sound of the film much as the cinematographer is for its look) are often—although not always—hired and consulted during the preproduction phase, but the bulk of their work takes place during the time of postproduction.

Production sound consists of everything that is recorded while the filming is taking place. The production sound mixer is the person in charge of recording while on the set or location. The duties include choosing and placing microphones as well as recording and mixing the sounds from the various microphones. Although the primary concern of production sound is capturing dialogue, the production unit also records ambience, room tone, and some sound effects in order to facilitate both sound and picture editing. All things being equal, the mixer aims to capture as much direct sound and as little reverberation as possible (see the comment in the sidebar). Reverberation can be easily added in postproduction but it is nearly impossible to reduce or remove.

The limiting factor in miking direct sound is the need to keep the microphone out of the picture, which generally requires some distance between mike and subject.

Besides the production dialogue, the mixer also records "wild" lines. When there is a problem in production sound, particularly if some loud ambient sound on the set or location obscures the dialogue in the original shot, the production mixer will ask the actor or actors to repeat the relevant dialogue, matching the original shot as closely as possible.

The production sound mixer also directs the boom operator, who is the person responsible for following the actors with a boom microphone to ensure a consistent recording of dialogue while keeping the microphone out of the line of sight of the camera. After each day of shooting, the production sound mixer delivers a "mix track," which is used for the daily rushes as well as film editing in postproduction. Although the various mikes are generally recorded to different tracks, the mix track, as the name implies, mixes down those different tracks to a single track that can then be used by the film editor to cut against. The unmixed tracks are retained for the dialogue editors in making the final cut.

The objective I have as a production sound mixer is to achieve the cleanest dialogue tracks possible with the least amount of background sound.

—Les Larawitz (production sound mixer)[3]

Postproduction

Postproduction work on the sound track begins in earnest with a spotting session. Here the supervising sound editor (or sound designer) gives the composer a general notion of the effects in the various sequences. This allows the composer to write music with a sense of what other sounds will be present. The basic duty of a sound editor is to choose and place sounds on the sound track, that is, to gather or create sounds and produce instructions (a precise cue sheet) for mixing. Mixers then realize these instructions, creating a series of pre-mixes under the supervision of the appropriate sound editor. (In this sense editors place sound *on* the sound track whereas mixers place sound *in* it.)

Editors are especially concerned with the principle of continuity. According to the Motion Picture Sound Editors (MPSE), an advocacy group for sound editors, dialogue editors "painstakingly smooth out the production sound recorded on location," whereas "ADR [automated dialogue replacement] editors help to seamlessly weave the re-recorded dialogue that replaces problematic tracks."[4] The effects department similarly avoids abrupt cuts in room tone and ambient sound in order to maintain a stable definition of space and place within a sequence. They work to create a consistent background that helps maintain the illusion of unity in space and place.

Achieving such continuity is more difficult than it might seem. We need to remember that editors *build* the sound track out of various bits of audio. These bits consist of production dialogue and other production sound, ADR, library effects, foley and effects generated specifically for a film, as well as different types of music tracks. That is, the sounds of which the sound track consists are anything but continuous. Even production dialogue, which might seem like it should be continuous, is in fact recorded in a series of takes. These include not only those of the master shot but the various close ups and other cut-ins. So the task of the editors is not only choosing and placing these bits, but also combining them in a way that disguises their inherent discontinuity.

The music department has its own tasks in postproduction, of course, but in the sound department the work is typically divided into three units—dialogue, foley effects, and sound effects (sfx). Each unit will produce its own track—generally called a "pre-dub" or "stem"—and all of these will be dubbed down into a final mix during the dubbing session (or Rerecording Mix Session) that was described under the "Music Department" heading above. As the name "final mix" implies, this session occurs very late in postproduction. In fact, a series of final mixes is required because each of the various formats requires its own print master.

Dialogue

Dialogue is the responsibility of the dialogue editor, whose general concern is to produce dialogue that can most easily be mixed with other sounds. This means going through the production sound mix, stripping the dialogue tracks of as much background noise as possible, and devising strategies for masking any noise that cannot be cleaned out. In addition, editors try to isolate the dialogue of each actor whenever they can, because this allows each voice to be controlled separately in rerecording the dialogue stem.

One of the first tasks of the dialogue editor is to go through the shots selected by the picture editor, marking any that need fixing. The sound edits are often minor, such as replacing a word or phrase that an actor tripped over or that was obscured by incidental noise on the set or location. Sometimes a longer segment will have an excessive number of these problems; or for some reason the right material is not available to fix the dialogue through simple sound editing; or, after seeing the rushes, an actor (or the director) may decide that his or her recorded voice did not quite capture the emotion in an otherwise acceptable take. In these cases, the dialogue editor will place the segment on list for ADR.

In ADR, an actor is called back to rerecord portions of dialogue. Carefully watching (and listening to) the segment of film that is to have its dialogue replaced, the actor repeats lines as closely synchronized to the picture as possible. This process is known as "looping." The amount of ADR required is dependent on the quality of sound captured on set and location, the filmmakers' aesthetic priorities, and of course budget. As we noted in chapter 13, location shooting can pose particular challenges to sound recording due to the presence of unpredictable incidental noises or loud, but otherwise appropriate, environmental noises such as traffic, high winds, rain, waves, waterfalls, and so forth. Production sound team are highly proficient at figuring out ways to capture a clean recording under the most trying circumstances, but occasionally a location will pose a problem that even the most seasoned pro cannot solve. Another exception is high-budget action films, where the intricate choreography of actors and the noise of special effects make it difficult to record audio clearly. In these cases, dialogue is almost invariably rerecorded in ADR.

Directors vary greatly in their attitude toward ADR, but it is a basic and essential tool in most commercial filmmaking today. A good example of extensive use of ADR is *Apocalypse Now* (1979), where all dialogue was rerecorded. (The same is true for *Once Upon a Time in America* (1984); see the comments in Figure 15-15.).

Some filmmakers also are indifferent to problems with production sound because they feel the actors can move with less inhibition if they do not have to concern themselves with clearly articulating their words or noting the position of the microphone. Besides fixing mistakes, ADR also allows actors the possibility of separating voice and bodily action. Although a particular movement may require a lot of exertion, for instance, an actor (or director) may nevertheless want the character to sound relaxed to make a difficult movement seem easy. ADR Supervisor Juno Ellis says, "60 percent of looping is

Figure 15-15. *Once Upon a Time in America* (1984). As is typical of Sergio Leone films, all of the dialogue on this film was rerecorded in ADR. It took Paul Zydel, the ADR mixer, ten weeks to do all the rerecording on the film. According to Zydel, the dialogue of an average feature film consists of about 30 percent ADR, although it varies considerably by genre and the amount of location shooting. Most films, however, require some ADR.

done for technical reasons, and the other 40 percent is done because the director wants to try to get a little different nuance in the scene by changing a reading."[5] Finally, because ADR produces a very dry recording, it gives mixers more flexibility in terms of the volume level of the dialogue with respect to the other elements of the sound track.

Foley Effects

The name "foley" comes from an early practitioner of the art, Jack Foley. These specialized effects originated in the need to separate the dialogue track from the sounds of the actors' bodies because dialogue needed to be dubbed for a film's foreign language distribution; but dubbing the voice also meant removing the sounds of the body unless the two were somehow separated. We do not usually distinguish foley from effects in general because both fall into the formal category of "noises." Foley is created much like ADR through a process of looping; that is, it is produced in real time by a foley artist who makes such appropriate noises as the ubiquitous footsteps in synchronization while a segment of film plays (see Figure 15-16 for an example). A foley artist is primarily responsible for non-speech sounds made by the human characters. The results are often mixed to a separate track from the other effects in order to facilitate trimming, slip edits, and other small changes that occur between the rough and final cut.

The production unit for foley effects consists of the artist, the foley mixer, and the foley editor. As mentioned earlier, the foley artist creates the sounds,

Figure 15-16. *The Soundscapes of Middle Earth: The Two Towers* (2002). Simon Hewit, a foley artist, works on *The Two Towers* (2002). Foley artists break a scene down, usually recording one character's movements in each pass. Here, Hewit records Aragorn's movements.

often exaggerating or "sweetening" an effect in order to give the impression of being "cinematic." All of the effects are not recorded at once, but in a number of passes, which are then layered. The foley mixer is responsible for recording (or, for those captured during production, rerecording) the effects. As with ADR, the quality of the recording must be sufficiently consistent with that of the rest of the sound, especially the production dialogue, that it can be seamlessly integrated into the sound track. The foley editor is the sound editor who is responsible for processing the sounds in the foley stem, adjusting volume, selecting among takes and fine tuning the synchronization.

Sound Effects

Aside from the usual consultations in preproduction, the work of the effects department takes place almost exclusively in postproduction. The supervising sound editor spots the film, making decisions about the sorts of sound effects that will be needed, noting in particular the places that will require so-called "hard" effects. Hard effects are those that require close synchronization, which filmmakers call "hard sync." Using this cue list, the assistant sound editor draws on the resource of an effects library to produce a temp track. The temp track is used by the picture editing department to make a rough cut of the film. Working with the supervising sound editor, the sound effects editor then works on fine tuning the effects, inventing or collecting any sound effects that will be needed, and cutting them into the film.

Sometimes effects departments go to extraordinary lengths to get just the right sound. They may bang on guide wires and use contact mikes to record a distinctive metallic "thwap." They may drop cement slabs from a crane to obtain a suitably impressive "thud." They may work with a synthesizer to produce a sharp laser blast or an ominous rumble. They may layer sounds together, combining the onset of a dog barking with a crow call and a lion roar, producing a cry that is new but characteristically animal-like (see Figure 15-17 for an example of an unusual method to produce a particular sound).

When a sound proves to be useful and distinctive, it will often be recycled. The sound of the bow releasing its arrow from *The Adventures of Robin Hood* (1938) has been called on frequently. Sound designer Ben Burtt was still using it as late as the *Star Wars* films in the 1970s and 1980s. Although the bulk of sounds come from effects libraries, editors must also be careful not to recycle the same effect too often, as the "looping" can become quite noticeable (and therefore sound artificial). (Indeed, avoiding such looping effects is one reason foley is preferred to effects libraries for common human-generated sounds.) If a particular sound occurs often in a film—especially in a scene—a new effect might be needed for almost every occurrence to avoid the perception of reuse.

The creation of the sound effects tracks—typically the track for ambient sound is kept separate from other effects—takes place on approximately the

Figure 15-17. *The Soundscapes of Middle Earth: Fellowship of the Ring* (2001). David Farmer, sound designer on *Fellowship of the Ring* (2001), uses a plunger in a stream to make some of the sounds for the Watcher. Wet rubber mats also contributed to mix. The cry of the Watcher was rendered by an altered recording of a walrus grunt.

same schedule as the music. Given the tight schedules during postproduction, there is seldom time for any sort of close coordination between the music and effects departments. Consequently, composers often have to write music in anticipation of the effects they imagine will be present, and the effects editors must anticipate decisions composers might make. Both have to be on guard against "frequency masking," which occurs when two sounds, close in frequency, occur at the same time. The louder sound will cover up the softer sound. Frequently, effects and music come into unexpected conflict, which must be worked out, often awkwardly, in the rerecording session for the final mix.

Summary

Technological, commercial, and cultural changes that began in the 1950s and have accelerated through the 1990s into the present highlight the increasing sophistication of sound thanks to digital formats for recording, postproduction, and exhibition. The commercial exploitation and broad consumer acceptance of videotape and, more recently, the DVD have not only significantly changed the exhibition characteristics of the feature film and its commercial status as a commodity; we might add that the ready availability of VHS tapes and, more recently, DVDs has also greatly improved the opportunity for serious and detailed study of films.

Afterword

Part I of this book was concerned with acquiring terminology and skills for basic analysis of films and film segments, with a special focus, of course, on the sound track. Part II positioned the analytic descriptions in the formal-functional context of film style—and of course concentrated especially on music. Part III broadened the context for analysis and style to a general history of sound technology and aesthetics—and, perhaps inevitably, highlighted the industry in the United States.

Throughout, we paid attention almost exclusively to a single classical genre, the feature film. We have done so not out of prejudice but because the full-length feature film has been the dominant genre since its rise in the mid-1910s: during the picture palace and early sound-film eras, the feature film was not only the centerpiece of a theater's daily program but generally was also regarded by studios as their prestige product (in its A-film form, at any rate). The wide-screen spectacles and blockbusters of the 1950s and later only added to that perception, on the part of studios and audiences alike. Surprisingly, perhaps, this was one respect in which television actually aided the cinema rather than undermined it: during the first half of the century cinema had struggled to be taken seriously as art—as being on a par with the novel, stage play, opera, and painting; but after 1950 the distinction between the "big screen" and the "little box" reinforced the idea that the feature film could be understood as "high art," whereas television was "low" or popular art. (We might add that this change in attitude was helped along by the rise of the first serious scholars of American film, the French "filmologues" associated with the journal *Cahiers du Cinéma*.)

The historical trajectory of the feature film is parallel in a few essential ways to that of the novel from the later 18th through the end of the 19th century. Originally an "entertainment" form considered inferior to verse plays and poetry, by the late 1800s the novel had achieved the status of serious art, thanks to an accumulation of authorial achievements and to a gradual change in the level of societal acceptance. The novel in 1900 had a cultural impact not unlike the feature film in 2000. One striking difference is that film earlier on was an activity, an event, and, as we outlined in chapter 14, it was only in the 1980s when this changed, when the feature film was commodified as a physical object in a sales economy, something that had been true of the novel from the start (if you think about it, the VHS tape or the DVD in its case even looks like a book).

Since that time, dramatic changes of a different order have occurred: the rise of trans-national cinemas (truly, throughout the world), advanced video games, and, even more recently, internet video (from film delivery to computers to YouTube to film-game crossovers) (see a convergence of traditional film music and YouTube video in Figure A-1). These changes have had an impact on music, especially. Given the enormity of these changes, it is reasonable to ask, Where does it go from here? Or, given the bias toward feature film that has necessarily been a part of our historical narrative, What does the future of film

Figure A-1. YouTube screen shot.

music and sound look like? There is, of course, no sure way to predict what kinds of changes may occur, but several indications of where film and its music could venture next are apparent enough.

In chapter 15, we discussed changes in music and sound production brought about by digitalization. The overarching cultural shift over the past twenty years represented by the personal computer has affected almost every aspect of modern life, and the position of filmmaking in society is no exception. Software applications that are easily accessible today allow anyone with a modicum of expertise to work with the same tools that professionals use everyday, and the result can sometimes be impressive. In other words, not only are audiences much more knowledgeable about how films are made or how songs are written, they can do it themselves—what was once fantastical is now commonplace. A particular challenge has thus been posed to those in the film and music fields, as it is now much more demanding to attract and keep the interest of a more technically knowledgeable audience. This, combined with the ever-increasing financial risks that filmmakers and studios take to make and distribute their films, has maneuvered the studio-based film music industry into the position of playing it safe and the film sound industry into playing it loud—but, then, one or the other of these has been a common complaint almost since the beginning of the cinema (recall the poem from 1911 about Lizzie the nickelodeon pianist [ch. 10] or worries about the intrusiveness of music in early sound film [ch. 11]). Today, however, technology has delivered an almost inconceivable potential for cinematic sound, and one hopes that creative imagination—and production financing—will soon catch up to that potential. On the other hand, perhaps the studio-based film industry has finally matured to the point where little more can be expected—whether (and how) a new direction will be taken, only time will tell.

Technology-driven changes affecting film music and sound in the commercial film industry were also described in chapter 15. There we noted that samplers and synthesizers, once rare oddities in film scores, are now ubiquitous, and film scores made entirely with acoustic instruments are few and far between. Digital notation has made copyists of handwritten scores obsolete. Music editors from just a few decades ago would be hard-pressed to recognize any of the current tools used today. Portable digital recorders and non-linear editing applications have affected the sound designer and sound editor's creative processes, and where the recording session used to be the end of the composer's work in past years, today it is often just the first step.

We will also point out that recent advances in filmmaking equipment have forced changes in film music and sound practices. With films being shot completely in a green-screen studio (examples being *Star Wars I-III* (1999, 2002, 2005), *300* (2006), *Sin City* (2005), *Beowulf* (2007), and *Sky Captain and the World of Tomorrow* (2004)) and non-linear editing equipment allowing unlimited capabilities to the filmmaker in a fraction of the time, studios are requiring production schedules to be compressed to the point where composers and sound editors have less time than ever to add their components into the film. This circumstance has forced many postproduction teams on large-budget films to break the work up into portions, with several composers and sound editors working on a single project, on the model of animation artists, who each focus on one part of a film. The result is a regressive step: with the work parceled out this way, it is much more challenging to create a cohesive sound track.

If changes over the past twenty years have caused some problems, they have also created new opportunities and shifts in aesthetic choices. As it became feasible for individuals to rent and own professional-grade equipment and software, the independent filmmaker became an important force in and out of Hollywood. With directors like Robert Rodriguez, Quentin Tarantino, Richard Linklater, Wes Anderson, Sophia Coppola, and Paul Thomas Anderson all bringing their own strong tastes to their work (and influencing multitudes of up-and-coming film students), the landscape is slowly but inexorably morphing into one of greater collaboration between director and composer, but, at the same time, is influenced by the director's ever increasing sense of creative ownership of the entire film. The latter trend has already had profound impacts on the sound tracks of films; as we saw in chapters 13 and 14, studios in the 1960s and 1970s pushed songs into films with increased revenues in mind, but many filmmakers today have completely incorporated the concept of song as score into their creative process. These directors have a decidedly different musical and sound vocabulary than those preceding them, and it will be an important task for composers and editors to adapt to that vocabulary. New generations of filmmakers who have grown up watching films and television as well as listening to popular music can be expected to change the ground rules, perhaps becoming so intimately involved in the process that the demarcations between director, composer, and music editor become blurred.

Composers themselves are changing. In the first fifty years of the sound film in the United States, composers tended to "end up" in the film industry; whether they started in Broadway, like Alfred Newman or Herbert Stothart, or in the concert world, like Erich Korngold and Bernard Herrmann, most composers did not begin their careers with the intention of working in films. Since the 1980s, however, there has been an increased interest among young composers in writing music for film (and other multimedia), and several academic institutions in the United States, notably USC, NYU, UCLA, Miami, and Berklee, have created programs dedicated to instruction in music for media (Figure A-2; the composer is a graduate of USC's Film Scoring Program, founded by the late Buddy Baker). (The situation is more complex in most of the rest of the world; in Europe, Russia, and the major east Asian countries, for example, the writ-

Figure A-2. *Deep Sea 3D* (2006) composer Deborah Lurie and scoring mixer Armin Steiner (photo: Dan Goldwasser) .

ing of film scores by conservatory-trained composers who also write concert music has been a longstanding tradition.) At the same time, the increased opportunities for study in film music have not kept new artists from entering the medium from other paths such as popular music. Several well-known musicians from the popular music industry have been brought in to write original music for films; David Byrne and Peter Gabriel have both written music for film and, more recently, Jonny Greenwood of the band Radiohead garnered much attention for his score to Paul Thomas Anderson's film *There Will Be Blood* (2007).

Multimedia, particularly in the form of video games, is now very widespread in the United States and in most other countries. The first video games were the electronic equivalent of pinball games, but in recent years the video game industry has created an entirely new entertainment medium with extensive, complex first-person narratives, film-like visual and audio environments, and the potential for interactivity, not only with multiple controllers but also through the Internet. In the same way that books, movies, and television were the media by which generations could learn, be entertained, and expand their imaginations, video games allow the user to do all those things but with the additional concept of personal choice—each individual can react to an environment and decide what their character does, in effect creating their own story. This interactive, non-repetitive environment is ripe for music and sound, and since the late 1980s the opportunities for composers and sound designers within the gaming industry have flourished. Some games already allow soundtrack choices, but as this medium evolves and matures, the breadth and depth of musical interactivity within the games will certainly increase.

Finally, in a very short amount of time it has become a commonplace to say that, thanks to the Internet, the mindset of society in general—and not only in the United States—has veered away from the idea that creative work like films and music can be made only by specialists and has substituted for it a more egalitarian concept where everyone can create their own movies and music in the privacy of their own homes. This shift in mindset has and will create new challenges and opportunities for the creators of film and music, and not only those who do the work as full-time professionals. Listeners and viewers, too, are being challenged by the sheer number of films being produced and distributed, by the variety of aesthetic and ideological grounding of films (especially as one ranges across trans-national cinemas), and even by the variety in media—the differences between the feature film in the theater and on television, a topic that arose at several points in chapters 13–15, pale in comparison to the difference between the feature film (whether in the theater, on one's television, or on a computer cinema display) and a YouTube video. (Like "Xerox" in the early days of photocopying, we are using "YouTube" here to refer to all "small-screen" Internet-posted video.)

In the afterword of her classic scholarly study of film music, *Unheard Melodies* (1987), Claudia Gorbman writes about the increasing use of popular music as underscore (a trend of the 1980s that she attributes in large part to the influence of the music video). She observes that "the changing position of music in films is also having an effect on the norms of narrative film viewing, on the way we watch and listen to a story film."[1] If the feature film products of transnational cinemas and the variety of independent filmmakers, video games, and amateur video posted online are all having an analogous effect today, it can also be said that the underlying descriptive and critical listening skills—of the kind we have explored in this book—remain a constant.

Glossary

100% talkie In the late 1920s, a film with a complete sound track, including dialogue; to be distinguished from the "synchronized" film and the "part-talkie."

2-Shot See Figure G.1 at the end of this glossary.

Accelerando Musical term for a smooth and usually gradual speeding up of tempo.

Accent Sharp or sudden loud sounds in any sound track component; these can range from sounds that stand out only slightly from their surroundings to loud, disruptive noises (such as gun shots); in music, accent is also used to refer to the regularly recurring slight emphases that establish and maintain musical meter. Also see Stinger.

Acousmêtre (acoustical being) A special kind of character who exists in the diegetic space but is placed consistently offscreen. Being heard but not seen, such a character is defined wholly in terms of diegetic sound. Michel Chion's term.

Act Several sequences gathered in a broad narrative grouping, using the same general criterion of unity of time and place as for a scene. Typically, a film would not have more than three or four acts. Alternatively, "chapter."

Added value The additional information or aesthetic shaping that the sound track brings to the image track (and vice versa). Michel Chion's term.

ADR (automated dialogue replacement) See Dialogue replacement.

Ambient sound (environmental sound; environmental noise); background sounds appropriate to the physical space being depicted, such as crickets, water, or birds.

A-melodic texture Similar to monophony in diminishing the foreground/background distinction, but monophony occupies only a foreground, where an a-melodic texture has only background. See also Monophony, Homophony, Polyphony, and Melody and Accompaniment.

Anempathetic Sounds or music that are emotionally distanced, or not in empathy with the image track. Also see Empathetic.

Audio dissolve By analogy to image dissolve, a transition to song and dance in which diegetic accompaniment becomes nondiegetic or is sweetened by nondiegetic elements. Rick Altman's term.

Audiovisual contract Film viewers intuitively accept the notion that image and sound mutually influence one another. Michel Chion's term.

Audiovisual phrasing The patterning of sync points in a sequence. Michel Chion's term.

Background See Foreground/Background.

Background music Term often used for nondiegetic music. See Underscore.

Cinemascope Widescreen system introduced by 20th Century Fox in the 1950s; initially required a special screen and magnetic stereo sound; used multitrack sound, with four channels arranged center, right, left and rear (surround). Also see VistaVision and Cinerama.

Cinerama Widescreen format that offered the most advanced sound system, with seven-channel (five front, two rear) magnetic sound tracks; required specially equipped theaters and highly trained projectionists. Also see VistaVision and Cinemascope.

Clarity Aesthetic priority favoring the film's construction of a world that makes sense to us rather one that is faithful as possible to the real world.

Close-Up (CU) See Figure G.1 at the end of this glossary.

Compilation scores In the silent-film era, most scores were compiled—that is, not original music written specifically for a film, but mostly pre-existing works gathered and ordered for a particular performance. In the 1960s and later, the term refers to underscoring made up from pre-existing recordings, especially of popular music or jazz.

Continuity editing Film editing for "continuity," that is, where cuts are motivated through matches on action, glances, offscreen sound, etc. and where maintaining narrative clarity is a top priority.

Counterpoint (not to be confused with the same word used for musical textures: we prefer to reserve "polyphonic" for references to a lively, complex texture) Sound that plays "against" a scene; the failure of temporal synchronizing of image track and sound track elements, and the distancing effect that creates. Also see Synchronization.

Crescendo Gradual increase in the volume of sound.

Cross-marketing Selling products ancillary to a film—and, especially since the 1960s, designing film sound tracks for the purpose of promoting recordings.

Cue sheet During the silent-film era, lists of compositions, with their placements, sent out by studios or their agents as suggestions for theater musicians. In the sound-film era, a legal document that lists all music that appears on the sound track of a film.

Dialogue replacement (looping) (automated dialogue replacement, or ADR) The rerecording of dialogue to an existing segment of film.

Dialogue underscoring Music that accompanies speech, playing "under" it.

Diegetic/nondiegetic sound Diegetic was borrowed from literary theory to refer to the world of the narrative, the screen world or world of the film. Nondiegetic, then, refers to the level of narration: voice-over narration is nondiegetic—and so is underscoring.

Diminuendo   (or decrescendo) Gradual decrease in the volume of sound.

Dissolve   (lap dissolve) A means of joining two shots, the one briefly overlapping the other so that we momentarily see both shots simultaneously, one fading as the other becomes visible. Commonly used as a transition between scenes. See also Audio dissolve.

Distortion   Manipulation of directly recorded sound through filters and other devices.

Dolby   In the 1970s, after releasing a noise reduction system for stereo magnetic tape, Dolby Labs developed a similar system for the optical sound track to increase the frequency and dynamic response of sound on the release print.

Dolby digital   The original 5.1 Dolby digital (from 1992) carried six channels—left, center, right, two surround channels, and a separate channel for low frequencies. Competing systems from the same period include DTS (Digital Theater System) and SDDS (Sony Dynamic Digital Sound).

Empathetic   Empathy or emotional engagement is the default for synchronization of sound and image; the sound track is coordinated with the image track, following and emphasizing the mood of onscreen characters and action—the effect is empathetic or engaged. Also see Anempathetic and Neutral.

Establishing shot   A general view of the physical space to begin a scene.

Establishing sound   Sound track equivalent of an establishing shot—sounds that characterize the physical space of a scene at its beginning. Rick Altman's term.

Extreme Long Shot   (ELS) See Figure G.1 at the end of this glossary.

Film form   The overall design of a film, or the temporal articulations of its running time in relation to the deployment of conventional units such as establishing sequences, scenes, chapters (or acts), and so forth.

Film style   The basis of film style is the collection of techniques, practices, aesthetic preferences, and cultural and cinematic expectations that constitute the distinctive way narrative is "delivered" in any individual film.

Foley   Sound effects created artificially and added to the sound track.

Foreground/Background   A distinction of visual staging carried over to film and affecting the sound track as well: in the classical model, dialogue occupies the sonic foreground and music and effects the background.

Gaumont Chronophone   Sound synchronization system introduced in 1902 and frequently exhibited as a novelty in vaudeville houses before it moved into the nickelodeons; its principal defect was not in synchronization but in amplification.

Generic sound   (generic noise) Partially grasped speech of people in groups, such as guests at a party or persons in a crowd. Also called "walla."

Hard cut   A simple, direct cut from one shot or scene to the next in which the change in the sound track is as abrupt as it is in the image track. Also see Sound Bridge.

Homophony   Texture consisting of more than one line, but each line moves with more or less the same rhythm. See also Polyphony, Monophony, Melody and accompaniment, and A-melodic texture.

Image track   The visual component of a film.

Insert   A shot (often a close-up and usually still) that interrupts the visual flow of a scene; in silent films, inserts, as intertitles, provided speech or narrative information.

Intertitle   An insert that consists of text displayed on the screen.

Kinetoscope   Apparatus for viewing moving pictures invented by Thomas Edison.

Leitmotif   Term derived from 19th-century opera and applied to film music; when a musical theme (usually short) is developed (varied, reorchestrated) within a film, the theme acquires some of the properties of a word or symbol, with independent meaning or associations that can be called up when the theme is repeated.

Link   (sound link) The use of sound to bridge a series of cuts, transforming what might otherwise seem to be unrelated shots.

Masking   Watching the image track without audio or listening to the sound track without images.

Medium Close-Up   (MCU) See Figure G.1 at the end of this glossary.

Medium Long Shot   (MLS) See Figure G.1 at the end of this glossary.

Medium Shot   (MS) See Figure G.1 at the end of this glossary.

Melody and accompaniment   Probably the most common texture in music. A tune is supported by its accompaniment, making for a strong functional separation of foreground and background. See also Monophony, Polyphony, Homophony, and A-melodic texture.

Meter   In music, a regular, recurring unit of time corresponding to groups of beats—in other words, meter is a higher level organization of beats.

Mickey-mousing   Close synchronization within a shot or short series of shots, where music closely mimics screen action, cartoon style, blurring the boundary between music and sound effects.

Mise-en-scène   The setting of a film, or the way in which physical space and environments are depicted in a film. A theatrical term commonly used in film studies.

Mixing   The combination (and usually manipulation) of directly recorded sounds.

Monophony   The simplest musical texture; strictly speaking it consists of a single melodic line; the "background" is absent, consisting only of silence. In film sound, the background is either absent or minimally defined. See also Polyphony, Homophony, Melody and accompaniment, and A-melodic Texture.

Motifs   In literature, recurring figures; in sound film, these can be either visual or aural; for the musical "motive." See also Theme and Leitmotif.

Movietone   Sound-on-film process invented by Theodore Case; its portability made it especially useful for recording newsworthy events and it became the aural foundation of the newsreel by the mid 1920s.

Multiplex   A type of theater that began rapidly appearing in the suburbs in the 1960s; the architecture was primarily utilitarian (the most prominent feature was generally the concession stand); it contained multiple auditoria and centralized projection booths.

Music   In silent-film performance, the principal sound element; in sound film, one of the three components of the sound track.

Neutral music Music indifferent to the scene, neither significant to its narrative nor emotionally engaged—in other words, music that functions much like ambient or environmental noise.

Nickelodeon Storefront theaters that began appearing in appreciable numbers around 1905 and dominated film exhibition until the later 1910s; typically held between two and three hundred spectators.

Onscreen/offscreen "Onscreen" refers to the part of the film world that is within the camera's frame at any particular moment. "Offscreen" is whatever part of that filmic world we cannot see in the frame but may already have seen or may imaginatively project from the part that we can see.

Orchestra Musicians performing in a group; normally used for the historical European ensemble in which string instruments (violins and their relatives) are the dominant group, along with sections of wind and percussion instruments. In the silent era, an orchetra is any group of more than two musicians.

Orchestral music See Orchestra.

Orchestration Term musicians use to designate the art of choosing and combining instruments to produce a particular sound.

Part-talkie In the late 1920s, a film with a synchronized recorded orchestral accompaniment interspersed with talking sequences; to be distinguished from the "synchronized" film and the "100% talkie."

Phrase (music) More or less aligned with short-term memory, phrases are typically 6- to 10-sec segments articu-lated by means of devices such as a cliched cadence, a slight slowing down, a drop downward or stop on a long note in the melodic line, or starting over with the same melodic figure in the immediately following bar. The musical phrase is more like a sentence in language than like a phrase, which usually refers to an incomplete grammatical unit.

Picture palace In the later 1920s, a large well-appointed theater with a large orchestra and "mighty Wurlitzer"; dominated film exhibition but only in major metropolitan areas.

Pitch Musical measure of frequency; pitches are individual musical notes.

"Playing the picture" After about 1910, nickelodeon musicians were encouraged to coordinate their musical selections more or less closely with the screen action.

Plot The order in which story events are presented to us in a film. Also see Story.

Point of view sound (POV sound) Sound rendered from the perspective of a character in the film. "Imagined sound" is a special case of POV sound: the sound track presents what a character is hearing in his or her head.

Polyphony In music, characterized by an independence of musical lines; exhibits a relatively shallow hierarchy between foreground and background. Polyphonic textures are quite common in sound design. See also Monophony, Homophony, Melody and accompaniment, and A-melodic Texture.

Rhythm Closely connected with the term meter, but it usually refers to distinctive groupings of notes rather than to the regular groups of meter.

Ritardando   A smooth and usually gradual slowing down of tempo.

Scene   A number of shots (or, rarely, a single very long shot, or "long take") gathered together in terms of unity of time and space. Scenes, like shots, can vary greatly in length; on average, however, scenes typically last from 1 to 5 min.

Sequence   A series of scenes related as a narrative unit. In common usage, "sequence" is short for "sequence of shots" and thus can refer to any series of shots that are related by some criteria that is important to the person doing the analysis.

Shot   A single strip of film, the basic unit of continuity editing; can vary greatly, from 1 to 100 sec (or more).

Shot/reverse-shot pair   (S/RS) See Figure G.1 at the end of this glossary.

Silence   Absence of effects and ambient sound; tends to break down foreground/background distinction.

Sound advance   A type of sound bridge where we hear a sound before we see its associated image.

Sound bridge   A smooth transition between shots (or scenes) by means of different kinds of overlaps. Also see Hard cut, Sound advance, Sound lag, and Sound match.

Sound design   Sound editing viewed artistically or aesthetically in terms of the shaping of the sound track in a film; most often associated with complex practices of blending and layering the sound track elements since the early 1970s.

Sound effects   (sfx, effects, fx, or noise) all sounds other than music or speech. Also see Ambient sound and Foley.

Sound lag   Sound from one scene lingers over as we see images from the next.

Sound match   Sound belonging to one scene followed by a similar or identical sound belonging to the next scene.

Sound track   (audio track) The audio component of a sound film. The sound track has taken different physical forms over the course of time. Also see Soundtrack album.

Sound-off   Short for "sound offscreen." Offscreen sound is localizable as an object that *could* be shown but is not—that is, the sound suggests an object that is more than simply background.

Sound-on-disk   Sound recorded onto a cylinder (Edison), phonograph record, or CD and played in mechanical synchronization with the image track. Also see Sound-on-film.

Sound-on-film   Sound imprinted on the film strip itself, in optical, magnetic, or digital form.

Soundtrack album   Music from a film released as a phonograph album or CD. In the 1960s, music from films were often crafted as albums, with themes extracted from the score and then arranged as songs appropriate for play on commercial radio.

Source   Term commonly used for diegetic sound.

Source Music   Term commonly used for diegetic music.

Special scores   In the silent-film era, music composed for specific films and distributed by studios along with the film.

Speech   One of the three components of the sound track; human speech in language (non-speech sounds such as grunts are usually considered to be more like noise); also called "dialogue."

Stem   Another name for a component of the sound track. The three most important are Dialogue, Music and Effects. Foley and ambient sound often have their own stems.

Stinger   A sudden and sharp accent; most often applied to music (a loud chord or cymbal crash) but equally appropriate to speech (a shout or loud cry) or effects (gun shot or door slamming). Also see Accent.

Story   A chronological series of events; "narrative" is a possible synonym. Also see Plot.

Style topics   Conventional musical figures that evoke, represent, or signify a particular mood, place, emotion, or some other character trait in the narrative.

Sweetening   Sound effect rendered so that it seems to violate the conditions of verisimilitude through increasing volume above expected levels, adding unmotivated distortion, and otherwise altering the expected timbre. Also the alteration of sound (or music) through the use of overdubbing.

Symphonic underscore   Nondiegetic music played by a traditional European orchestra. See Underscore.

Sync point   (also spelled "synch point"; point of synchronization) The temporal coordination of sound and image.

Synchronization (sync)   Appropriate temporal linking of sound to image; aids the impression that sound emanates from the world of the screen, an effect that is essential to orienting our relation to the screen. Also see Counterpoint.

Synchronized film   In the late 1920s, a film with recorded orchestral accompaniment and sound effects; to be distinguished from the "part-talkie" and the "100% talkie."

Tempo   Perceived rate (beat or pulse) of sound or musical events. (In non-musical contexts, tempo is often used interchangeably with pace.)

Tessitura   (Higher or lower) register of the voice.

Texture   The functional relation of musical lines to one another; the number of musical strands or layers occurring simultaneously In recording and editing, the creation of sound texture is often called "layering."

Theme   In music, clearly defined melodies that are "developed" (or altered and commented on) in a composition; for short musical themes, the terms theme and motive are essentially interchangeable; in literature, a concise general statement about a story or poem that says what it is about. In film, a musical theme functions like the literary motif, a significant recurring sound element. Also see Leitmotif and Motif.

Timbre   Distinct coloring of sound.

Underscore   Nondiegetic music. Synonym for "background music" (a term we prefer to avoid because it confuses the nondiegetic with background physical space in the image track), "underscoring," "accompaniment," "commentative music," "dramatic scoring," or just "scoring."

Up-and-downer   In the studio era, a device that automatically raised and lowered music levels inversely with the presence of dialogue.

Vaudeville Middle-class theaters of the later 19th and early 20th centuries; offered mixed programs of music and other acts.

VistaVision Widescreen format whose aspect ratio eventually became a standard (1.85:1); its sound was coded on an optical track. Also see Cinerama and Cinemascope.

Vitaphone Sound-on-disk system developed for Warners by Western Electric, a subsidiary of AT&T; the first commercially viable system for synchronized sound. The Vitaphone system consisted of a special phonograph mechanically coupled to a projector. Enjoyed superior amplification compared to sound-on-film methods at the time.

Voice-off A special case of "sound-off" (q.v.); offscreen sound that highlights the voice.

Voice-over narration (voice-over) A person not seen (and who may not belong to the physical world shown in the film) talks directly to the viewer.

Volume Physical strength of the sound we perceive, its loudness. Strictly speaking, volume is defined by amplitude, which is the power of sound (normally as measured in decibels).

<table>
<tr><td>a</td><td>b</td></tr>
<tr><td>c</td><td>d</td></tr>
<tr><td>e</td><td>f</td></tr>
<tr><td>g</td><td></td></tr>
</table>

Figure G-1. *De-Lovely* (2004). Illustration of shot types. (a) Extreme Long Shot (ELS). (b) Medium Long Shot (MLS). (c) Medium Shot (MS). (d) Medium Close-Up (MCU). (e, f) Shot/Reverse-Shot (S/RS) pair, in typical over-the-shoulder fashion. Note that Cole is presented Close-Up (CU), whereas Linda is shown in MCU. This places the emphasis on Cole. (g) 2-Shot. The 2-shot is often used in conjunction with S/RS pairs, especially at the beginning and ending of the sequence. When used at the end of a sequence, it can also serve as a sign of reconciliation or the pair coming to a point of resolution. This is the case here, the 2-shot emphasized by moving to a tighter shot. (In this case, it is done by dollying in; it can also be done by zooming.)

Credits

Figure 2-16: James Buhler, Caryl Flinn, and David Neumeyer, eds., excerpt from p. 354 (upper 1/3 of Figure 4) in *Music and Cinema* © 2000 by James Buhler. Reprinted by permission of Wesleyan University Press.

Figures 2-10 and 2-20, Table 2-1: From James Wierzbicki, "Shrieks, Flutters, and Vocal Curtains: Electronic Sound/Electronic Music in Hitchcock's *The Birds*" in Music and the Moving Image. Copyright 2008 by the Board of Trustees of the University of Illinois. Used with permission of the University of Illinois Press.

Figure 8-2: Courtesy of John Waxman.

Figure 10-9: Courtesy of Bruce Calvert (http://www.silentfilmstillarchive.com).

Figure 10-12: "Westward Ho! (The Covered Wagon March)." Music by HUGO RIESENFELD. Lyrics by R. A. BARNET. © 1923 (Renewed) WB MUSIC CORP. All Rights Reserved.

Figure 11-12: Ad*Access On-Line Project—Ad #R0206, John W. Hartman Center for Sales, Advertising & Marketing History, Duke University Rare Book, Manuscript, and Special Collections Library: http://library.duke.edu/digitalcollections/adaccess/.

Figure 13-2: From Wm. E. Garity and J. N. A. Hawkins, "Fantasound," published in the *Journal of the Society of Motion Picture and Television Engineers*, p. 142, August 1941. Used with permission of the SMPTE Journal.

Figure 13-4: Courtesy of the Decurion Corporation.

Figure 13-11: Courtesy of Volta Music Corp, Ms. Catherine Hinen, and Patti Washington Music (ASCAP).

Figure 13-12b: ©RCA.
Figure 13-15: Courtesy of John Waxman.
Figure 14-4: Courtesy of Universal Studios Licensing LLLP.
Figure 14-5: Courtesy of LucasFilm Ltd.
Figure 14-11: ©Michael Ochs Archive/Getty Images.

Notes

INTRODUCTION

1. Robynn Stilwell, "Sound and Empathy: Subjectivity, Gender and the Cinematic Soundscape," in *Film Music: Critical Approaches*, ed. K. J. Donnelly (Edinburgh: Edinburgh University Press, 2001) , 182.
2. http://www.thecityofabsurdity.com/losthighway/lhsound.html.
3. Vincent LoBrutto, *Sound on Film: Interviews with Creators of Film Sound* (Westport, Conn.: Praeger, 1994): xi.
4. Claudia Gorbman, "Film Music," in *Film Studies: Critical Approaches*, ed. John Hill and Pamela Church Gibson (Oxford and New York: Oxford University Press, 2000), 45.
5. Aaron Copland, *What to Listen for in Music,* 2d edition (New York: McGraw-Hill, 1957), 253.
6. Franz Waxman, cited in Tony Thomas, *Film Score: The Art and Craft of Movie Music* (Burbank: Riverwood Press, 1991), 39.

INTRODUCTION TO PART I

1. Michel Chion, *Audio-Vision: Sound on Screen*, tr. Claudia Gorbman (New York: Columbia University Press, 1994), 5.
2. Michel Chion, *Audio-Vision: Sound on Screen*, tr. Claudia Gorbman (New York: Columbia University Press, 1994), 1 (title of Part One).

CHAPTER I

1. Annabel Cohen, "Film Music: Perspectives from Cognitive Psychology," in *Music and Cinema*, ed. James Buhler, Caryl Flinn, and David Neumeyer (Hanover, NH: Wesleyan University Press, 2000), 360.
2. Michel Chion, *Audio-Vision: Sound on Screen*, tr. Claudia Gorbman (New York: Columbia University Press, 1994), 145.
3. Max Steiner Collection, Brigham Young University.

4. Aaron Copland, *What to Listen for in Music,* 2d edition (New York: McGraw-Hill, 1957), 258.
5. Aaron Copland, *What to Listen for in Music,* 2d edition (New York: McGraw-Hill, 1957), 255.
6. Franz Waxman, unpublished document. Used courtesy of John Waxman.
7. Claudia Gorbman, *Unheard Melodies: Narrative Film Music* (Bloomington: Indiana University Press, 1987), 73.
8. Gideon Bachmann, "The Carrots Are Cooked: A Conversation with Jean-Luc Godard," in *Jean-Luc Godard: Interviews*, ed. David Sterritt (Jackson: University Press of Mississippi, 1998), 133.
9. Michel Chion, *Audio-Vision: Sound on Screen*, tr. Claudia Gorbman (New York: Columbia University Press, 1994), 155.
10. Ralph Vaughan Williams, "Composing for the Films," in *National Music and Other Essays* (London, Oxford University Press, 1963), 161.
11. Michel Chion, *Audio-Vision: Sound on Screen*, tr. Claudia Gorbman (New York: Columbia University Press, 1994), 187.
12. Aaron Copland, *What to Listen for in Music,* 2d edition (New York: McGraw-Hill, 1957), 255.

CHAPTER 2

1. Quoted in Vincent LoBrutto, *Sound on Film: Interviews with Creators of Film Sound* (Westport, Conn.: Praeger, 1994), 278.
2. Quoted in Vincent LoBrutto, *Sound on Film: Interviews with Creators of Film Sound* (Westport, Conn.: Praeger, 1994), 253.
3. Stanley Cavell, *Must We Mean What We Say?* (New York: Cambridge University Press, 1977 [1969]), 185-6.
4. Quoted in Vincent LoBrutto, *Sound on Film: Interviews with Creators of Film Sound* (Westport, Conn.: Praeger, 1994), 30.
5. Helen Hanson: "Sound Affects: Post-production Sound, Soundscapes and Sound Design in Hollywood's Studio Era," *Music, Sound, and the Moving Image* 1.1 (2007): 41.
6. Quoted in Vincent LoBrutto, *Sound on Film: Interviews with Creators of Film Sound* (Westport, Conn.: Praeger, 1994), 229-30.
7. Michel Chion, *Audio-Vision: Sound on Screen*, tr. Claudia Gorbman (New York: Columbia University Press, 1994), 10-13.
8. Quoted in Vincent LoBrutto, *Sound on Film: Interviews with Creators of Film Sound* (Westport, Conn.: Praeger, 1994), 236.
9. Quoted in Vincent LoBrutto, *Sound on Film: Interviews with Creators of Film Sound* (Westport, Conn.: Praeger, 1994), 99.
10. Quoted in Vincent LoBrutto, *Sound on Film: Interviews with Creators of Film Sound* (Westport, Conn.: Praeger, 1994), 43.
11. Walter Murch, "A Conversation with Walter Murch," *Transom Review* 5.1 (April 2005):46, http://transom.org/guests/review/200504.review.murch3.html (accessed January 28, 2009).

12. Quoted in Vincent LoBrutto, *Sound on Film: Interviews with Creators of Film Sound* (Westport, Conn.: Praeger, 1994), 96.

13. Walter Murch, "Dense Clarity—Clear Density," *Transom Review* 5.1 (April 2005): 7, http://transom.org/guests/review/200504.review.murch2.html (accessed January 28, 2009).

14. Franz Waxman: unpublished radio interview with Lawrence Morton, April 1950. Used courtesy of John Waxman.

15. Quoted in Vincent LoBrutto, *Sound on Film: Interviews with Creators of Film Sound* (Westport, Conn.: Praeger, 1994), 268.

16. Quoted in Vincent LoBrutto, *Sound on Film: Interviews with Creators of Film Sound* (Westport, Conn.: Praeger, 1994), 237.

17. Rick Altman, with McGraw Jones and Sonia Tatroe, "Inventing the Cinema Sound Track: Hollywood's Multiplane Sound System," in *Music and Cinema*, ed. James Buhler, Caryl Flinn, and David Neumeyer (Hanover, NH: Wesleyan University Press, 2000), 339–359.

18. Rick Altman, with McGraw Jones and Sonia Tatroe, "Inventing the Cinema Sound Track: Hollywood's Multiplane Sound System," in *Music and Cinema*, ed. James Buhler, Caryl Flinn, and David Neumeyer (Hanover, NH: Wesleyan University Press, 2000), 354.

19. Rick Altman, with McGraw Jones and Sonia Tatroe, "Inventing the Cinema Sound Track: Hollywood's Multiplane Sound System," in *Music and Cinema*, ed. James Buhler, Caryl Flinn, and David Neumeyer (Hanover, NH: Wesleyan University Press, 2000), 343.

20. James Wierzbicki, "Shrieks, Flutters, and Vocal Curtains: Electronic Sound/Electronic Music in Hitchcock's *The Birds*," *Music and the Moving Image* 1.2 (2008), http://mmi .press.uiuc.edu/1.2/wierzbicki.html (accessed January 29, 2009).

CHAPTER 3

1. Rick Altman, *The American Film Musical* (Bloomington: Indiana University Press, 1987), 62–74.

2. Alfred Hitchcock, "Direction," in *Footnotes to the Film*, ed. by Charles Davy (London: Lovat Dickson and Thompson, 1937); reprinted in *Focus on Hitchcock*, ed. Albert J. LaValley (Englewood Cliffs, N.J.: Prentice-Hall, 1972), 36.

3. Rick Altman, *The American Film Musical* (Bloomington: Indiana University Press, 1987), 63.

4. Michel Chion, *Audio-Vision: Sound on Screen*, tr. Claudia Gorbman (New York: Columbia University Press, 1994), 129.

CHAPTER 4

1. Mary Ann Doane, "The Voice in the Cinema: The Articulation of Body and Space," *Yale French Studies* 60 (1980): 33–34.

2. Erno Rapee: *Encyclopedia of Music for Pictures* (*"As Essential as the Picture"*) (New York: Belwin, 1925), 16.

3. Quoted in the Introduction to *Music and Cinema*, ed. James Buhler, Caryl Flinn, and David Neumeyer (Hanover, NH: Wesleyan University Press, 2000), 15.

4. Hugo Friedhofer: Linda Danly, ed., *Hugo Friedhofer: The Best Years of His Life, A Hollywood Master of Music for the Movies*, (Lanham/London: Scarecrow Press, 1999), 123.

5. Claudia Gorbman, *Unheard Melodies: Narrative Film Music* (Bloomington: Indiana University Press, 1987), 16–18.

6. Michel Chion, *Audio-Vision: Sound on Screen*, tr. Claudia Gorbman (New York: Columbia University Press, 1994), 1 (title of Part One).

INTERLUDE 1

1. The Internet Movie Database (or IMDb)): http://www.imdb.com/.

2. Roger Ebert, "Catch Me If You Can," *Chicago Sun-Times*, December 25, 2002, http://rogerebert.suntimes.com/apps/pbcs.dll/article?AID=/20021225/REVIEWS/212250301/1023 (accessed January 28, 2009).

3. Martin Marks, "Music, Drama, Warner Brothers: The Cases of *Casablanca* and *The Maltese Falcon*," in *Music and Cinema*, ed. James Buhler, Caryl Flinn, and David Neumeyer (Hanover, NH: Wesleyan University Press, 2000), 161–186. The quotations are from page 162.

4. Martin Marks, "Music, Drama, Warner Brothers: the Cases of *Casablanca* and *The Maltese Falcon*, in *Music and Cinema*, ed. James Buhler, Caryl Flinn, and David Neumeyer (Hanover, NH: Wesleyan University Press, 2000), 181.

5. Michel Chion, *Audio-Vision: Sound on Screen*, tr. Claudia Gorbman (New York: Columbia University Press, 1994), 192–98.

CHAPTER 5

1. Lawrence Morton, "Film Music of the Quarter," *Hollywood Quarterly* 3.4 (1948): 401–02.

2. Michel Chion, *Audio-Vision: Sound on Screen*, tr. Claudia Gorbman (New York: Columbia University Press, 1994), 58.

3. Max Steiner Collection, Brigham Young University.

4. George Burt, *The Art of Film Music: Special Emphasis on Hugo Friedhofer, Alex North, David Raksin, Leonard Rosenman* (Boston: Northeastern University Press, 1994), 129.

5. Martin Marks, "About the Music," in More Treasures from American Film Archives, 1894–1931 (San Francisco: National Film Preservation Foundation, 2004). The quotations in this section are from the DVD's program book, 146–148.

6. Claudia Gorbman, *Unheard Melodies: Narrative Film Music* (Bloomington: Indiana University Press, 1987), 79–80.

7. Claudia Gorbman, *Unheard Melodies: Narrative Film Music* (Bloomington: Indiana University Press, 1987), 95.

8. Gorbman, *Unheard Melodies: Narrative Film Music* (Bloomington: Indiana University Press, 1987), 97.

9. See David Neumeyer, "Hayasaka's Music for Rashômon," in *The Force of Vision 6: Inter-Asian Comparative Literature*, ed. Kawamoto Koji, Heh-Hsiang Yuan, and Ohsawa Yoshihiro, *Proceedings of the XIIIth Congress of the International Comparative Literature Association* (Tokyo: n.p., 1996), 477–486.

10. Claudia Gorbman, *Unheard Melodies: Narrative Film Music* (Bloomington: Indiana University Press, 1987), 79.

11. Royal S. Brown, *Overtones and Undertones: Reading Film Music* (Berkeley and Los Angeles: University of California Press, 1994), 165.

12. Graham Bruce, *Bernard Herrmann: Film Music and Narrative* (Ann Arbor: UMI Research Press, 1985), 35.

13. Fred Steiner, "Herrmann's 'Black-and-White' Music for Hitchcock's *Psycho*," in *Film Music Notebook* 1.1 (1974): 28–36; 1.2 (1974–75): 26–46. The quotation is from 1.1:34.

14. *The Hours* (Paramount Home Entertainment, 2002), catalogue number 33990.

15. Liner notes to Philip Glass, *The Hours: Music from the Motion Picture* (New York: Nonesuch, 2002), catalogue number 79693–2.

CHAPTER 6

1. Erno Rapee: *Encyclopedia of Music for Pictures ("As Essential as the Picture")* (New York: Belwin, 1925), 11.

2. Liner notes to Varese Sarabande CD VSD 5754: Elmer Bernstein, *To Kill a Mockingbird* (1997).

CHAPTER 7

1. Claudia Gorbman, "Film Music," in *Film Studies: Critical Approaches*, ed. John Hill and Pamela Church Gibson (Oxford and New York: Oxford University Press, 2000), 45.

2. Nicholas Cook, *Analysing Musical Multimedia* (Oxford and New York: Oxford University Press, 1998), 159.

3. Claudia Gorbman, *Unheard Melodies: Narrative Film Music* (Bloomington: Indiana University Press, 1987), 26.

CHAPTER 8

1. Schoenberg uses the German term *Grundgestalt*. On basic idea, see William E. Caplin, *Classical Form: A Theory of Formal Functions for the Instrumental Music of Haydn, Mozart and Beethoven* (New York: Oxford University Press, 1998), 264n11.

2. Erno Rapee, *Encyclopedia of Music for Pictures ("As Essential as the Picture")* (New York: Belwin, 1925), 13.

3. Justin London, "Leitmotifs and Musical Reference in the Classic Film Score," in *Music and Cinema*, ed. James Buhler, Caryl Flinn, and David Neumeyer (Wesleyan University Press, 2000), 87.

4. Frederick Sternfeld, "Music and the Feature Films," *Musical Quarterly* 33.4 (1947): 521.

5. Erno Rapee: *Encyclopedia of Music for Pictures ("As Essential as the Picture")* (New York: Belwin, 1925), 14.

6. Robynn Stilwell, "I just put a drone under him..": "Collage and Subversion in the Score of 'Die Hard'," *Music & Letters* 78.4 (Nov 1997): 551, 563.

7. Jeff Smith, "That Money-Making 'Moon River' Sound: Thematic Organization and Orchestration in the Film Music of Henry Mancini," in *Music and Cinema*, ed. James

Buhler, Caryl Flinn, and David Neumeyer (Hanover, NH: Wesleyan University Press, 2000), 255.

8. Royal S. Brown, *Overtones and Undertones: Reading Film Music* (Berkeley and Los Angeles: University of California Press, 1994), 347.

9. Martin Marks, "About the Music," in *More Treasures from American Film Archives, 1894–1931* (San Francisco: National Film Preservation Foundation, 2004), 147.

10. Julius S. Seredy, compiler, *Carl Fischer Analytical Orchestra Guide* (New York: Carl Fischer, 1929).

11. Quoted in Vincent LoBrutto, *Sound on Film: Interviews with Creators of Film Sound* (Westport, Conn.: Praeger, 1994), 240–41.

12. Quoted in Vincent LoBrutto, *Sound on Film: Interviews with Creators of Film Sound* (Westport, Conn.: Praeger, 1994), 32.

13. Quoted in Vincent LoBrutto, *Sound on Film: Interviews with Creators of Film Sound* (Westport, Conn.: Praeger, 1994), 279.

CHAPTER 9

1. Quoted in the Introduction to *Music and Cinema*, ed. James Buhler, Caryl Flinn, and David Neumeyer (Hanover, NH: Wesleyan University Press, 2000), 15.

2. Rick Altman, with McGraw Jones and Sonia Tatroe, "Inventing the Cinema Sound Track: Hollywood's Multiplane Sound System," in *Music and Cinema*, ed. James Buhler, Caryl Flinn, and David Neumeyer (Hanover, NH: Wesleyan University Press, 2000), 353.

3. Claudia Gorbman, *Unheard Melodies: Narrative Film Music* (Bloomington: Indiana University Press, 1987), 79.

INTERLUDE

1. All but the second of these questions is quoted from David Bordwell, *The McGraw-Hill Film Viewer's Guide*, supplement to David Bordwell and Kristin Thompson, *Film Art: An Introduction*, sixth edition (2001), 17.

2. Claudia Gorbman, *Unheard Melodies: Narrative Film Music* (Bloomington: Indiana University Press, 1987), 91–98.

3. Claudia Gorbman, *Unheard Melodies: Narrative Film Music* (Bloomington: Indiana University Press, 1987), 93.

4. Claudia Gorbman, *Unheard Melodies: Narrative Film Music* (Bloomington: Indiana University Press, 1987), 98.

5. Robynn Stilwell, "Collage and Subversion in the Score of 'Die Hard'," *Music & Letters* 78.4 (Nov 1997): 551.

6. Miguel Mera, *Mychael Danna's The Ice Storm : A Film Score Guide* (Lanham, Md.: Scarecrow Press, 2007), 119.

7. Julie Brown, "Ally McBeal's Postmodern Soundtrack," *Journal of Royal Musical Association* 126 (2001): 275–303.

8. Rick Altman, *The American Film Musical* (Bloomington: Indiana University Press, 1987), 152.

9. William Darby and Jack du Bois, *American Film Music: Major Composers, Techniques, Trends, 1915–1990* (Jefferson, NC and London: MacFarland, 1990), 13.

CHAPTER 10

1. Quoted in Max Wilk, *The Wit and Wisdom of Hollywood; From the Squaw Man to the Hatchet Man* (New York: Warner Paperback Library, 1973), 3.
2. Richard Abel, "The Most American of Attractions, the Illustrated Song," in *The Sounds of Early Cinema*, ed. Richard Abel and Rick Altman (Bloomington: Indiana University Press, 2001), 143–55.
3. Wilbur D. Nesbit, "Lizzie Plays for the Pictures" *Moving Picture World*, September 2, 1911), 617.
4. Clyde Martin, "Playing the Pictures," *Film Index*, December 31, 1910, 12.
5. Cited in Charles Hofmann, *Sounds for Silents* (New York: DBS Publications, 1970), 7.
6. Clarence Sinn, "Music for the Picture," *Moving Picture World*, November 26, 1910, p. 1227.
7. A.W.W., letter to Sinn, "Music for the Picture," *Moving Picture World*, February 14, 1914, 796.
8. S. L. Rothapfel, "Dignity of the Exhibitors' Profession," *Moving Picture World*, February 26, 1910, 289.
9. Erno Rapee: *Encyclopedia of Music for Pictures* (*"As Essential as the Picture"*) (New York: Belwin, 1925), 13.
10. Quoted in Gillian B. Anderson, *Music for Silent Films 1894–1929: A Guide* (Washington, D. C.: Library of Congress, 1988), xxiii.
11. "How the Cinematographer Works," *Moving Picture World*, July 13, 1907, 300.

CHAPTER 11

1. James Clancy, "The Human Voice as a Factor in the Moving Picture Show," *Moving Picture World*, January 30, 1909, 115.
2. Donald Crafton, The Talkies: American Cinema's Transition to Sound, 1926–1931 (Berkeley: University of California Press, 1999), 240.
3. Rick Altman, with McGraw Jones and Sonia Tatroe, "Inventing the Cinema Sound Track: Hollywood's Multiplane Sound System," in *Music and Cinema*, ed. James Buhler, Caryl Flinn, and David Neumeyer (Hanover, NH: Wesleyan University Press, 2000), 356, 358.
4. Quoted in Donald Crafton, *The Talkies: American Cinema's Transition to Sound 1926–1931* (Berkeley: University of California Press, 1997), 504.
5. Quoted in Donald Crafton, *The Talkies: American Cinema's Transition to Sound 1926–1931* (Berkeley: University of California Press, 1997), 504.
6. Quoted in Donald Crafton, *The Talkies: American Cinema's Transition to Sound 1926–1931* (Berkeley: University of California Press, 1997), 504.

CHAPTER 12

1. Robynn Stilwell, "Sound and Empathy: Subjectivity, Gender and the Cinematic Soundscape," in *Film Music: Critical Approaches*, ed. K. J. Donnelly (Edinburgh: Edinburgh University Press, 2001), 182.
2. James Cameron, *Sound Motion Pictures*, 6th ed. (Coral Gables, FL: Cameron Pub. Co., 1947), 298–99.

3. David Bordwell, Janet Staiger and Kristin Thompson, *The Classic Hollywood Cinema: Film Style and Mode of Production to 1960* (New York: Columbia, 1985), 54.

4. Leon S. Baker, "Technology in the art of producing motion pictures," in *The Technique of Motion Picture Production*, ed. Society of Motion Picture Engineers (New York: Interscience, 1944), 5–6.

5. James Lastra, *Sound Technology and the American Cinema* (New York: Columbia Unviersity Press, 2000), 160.

6. Sergei Eisenstein, "The Synchronization of the Senses," in *The Film Sense* (New York: Harcourt Brace Jovanovich, 1975), 69–112.

7. Linda Danly, ed., *Hugo Friedhofer: The Best Years of His Life, A Hollywood Master of Music for the Movies*, (Lanham and London: Scarecrow Press, 1999), 42.

CHAPTER 13

1. Barbara Kennedy, *Deleuze and Cinema: The Aesthetics of Sensation* (Edinburgh: Edinburgh University Press, 2003).

2. Quoted in John Belton, *Widescreen Cinema* (Cambridge, Mass.: Harvard University Press, 1992), 205.

3. Quoted in John Belton, *Widescreen Cinema* (Cambridge, Mass.: Harvard University Press, 1992), 203.

4. Cited in Jeff Smith, *The Sounds of Commerce: Marketing Popular Film Music* (New York: Columbia University Press, 1998), 58

5. Jeff Smith, *The Sounds of Commerce: Marketing Popular Film Music* (New York: Columbia University Press, 1998), 60.

6. Neil Lerner, "'Look at that big hand move along': Clocks, Containment, and Music in High Noon," *South Atlantic Quarterly* 104.1 (2005), 163.

7. Fred Binkley, "Mancini's Movie Manifesto," *Down Beat*, March 5, 1970, 16.

8. Jeff Smith, *The Sounds of Commerce: Marketing Popular Film Music* (New York: Columbia University Press, 1998), 69–99.

9. Jeff Smith, *The Sounds of Commerce: Marketing Popular Film Music* (New York: Columbia University Press, 1998), 61.

10. Julie Hubbert, "'Whatever Happened to Great Movie Music?': Cinéma Vérité and Hollywood Film Music of the Early 1970s," *American Music* 21.2 (2003): 197.

CHAPTER 14

1. John Belton, "1950s Magnetic Sound: The Frozen Revolution," in *Sound Theory, Sound Practice*, ed. Rick Altman (New York: Routledge, 1992), 154–67.

2. See, for instance, Geoff King, *New Hollywood Cinema: An Introduction* (New York: Columbia University Press, 2002), 1–9.

3. Justin Wyatt, *High Concept: Movies and Marketing in Hollywood* (Austin: University of Texas Press, 1994).

4. Quoted in David A. Cook, *Lost Illusions: American Cinema in the Shadow of Watergate and Vietnam, 1970–1979* (Berkeley: The University of California Press, 2000), 386.

5. Douglas Gomery, *Shared Pleasures: A History of Movie Presentation in the United States* (Madison: University of Wisconsin Press, 1992), 100.

6. Quoted in David A. Cook, *Lost Illusions: American Cinema in the Shadow of Watergate and Vietnam, 1970–1979* (Berkeley: University of California Press, 2000), 404.

7. David A. Cook, *Lost Illusions: American Cinema in the Shadow of Watergate and Vietnam, 1970–1979* (Berkeley: University of California Press, 2000), 386.

8. Quoted in David A. Cook, *Lost Illusions: American Cinema in the Shadow of Watergate and Vietnam, 1970–1979* (Berkeley: University of California Press, 2000), 390.

9. Quoted in Vincent LoBrutto, *Sound on Film: Interviews with Creators of Film Sound* (Westport, Conn.: Praeger, 1994), 95–96.

10. Quoted in Vincent LoBrutto, *Sound on Film: Interviews with Creators of Film Sound* (Westport, Conn.: Praeger, 1994), 133–34.

11. Quoted in Vincent LoBrutto, *Sound on Film: Interviews with Creators of Film Sound* (Westport, Conn.: Praeger, 1994), 134

12. Inga Kiderra, "Scoring Points," *USC Trojan Family Magazine*, Winter 2000, http://www.usc.edu/dept/pubrel/trojan_family/winter00/FilmScoring/Music_pg2.html (accessed January 28, 2009).

13. Geoff King, *New Hollywood Cinema: An Introduction* (New York: Columbia University Press, 2002), 165.

14. R. Serge Denisoff and George Plasketes: "Synergy in 1980s Film and Music: Formula for Success or Industry Mythology?" *Film History* 4.3 (1990), 257.

15. Justin Wyatt, *High Concept: Movies and Marketing in Hollywood* (Austin: University of Texas Press, 1994), 144.

16. Edwin Black, "Film Music: Too Much and Not Enough," *Film Score Monthly*, April 16, 1998, under "*Film Score* Daily Articles," http://www.filmscoremonthly.com/daily/article.cfm?articleID=2480 (accessed January 28, 2009).

17. "James Horner's Melbourne Seminar," *Soundtrack!* 11.41 (1992): 7.

CHAPTER 15

1. Quoted in Vincent LoBrutto, *Sound on Film: Interviews with Creators of Film Sound* (Westport, Conn.: Praeger, 1994), 184.

2. Lukas Kendall, "Interview with Steve Bartek," *Film Score Monthly*, December 1995; reprinted at http://www.boingo.org/articles/FSMBartek.html (accessed January 28, 2009).

3. Quoted in Vincent LoBrutto, *Sound on Film: Interviews with Creators of Film Sound* (Westport, Conn.: Praeger, 1994), 118.

4. http://www.mpse.org/history/history.html.

5. Quoted in Vincent LoBrutto, *Sound on Film: Interviews with Creators of Film Sound* (Westport, Conn.: Praeger, 1994), 213.

AFTERWORD

1. Claudia Gorbman, *Unheard Melodies: Narrative Film Music* (Bloomington: Indiana University Press, 1987), 163.

Index